THE ONE YEAR®

HEAVEN ON EARTH

DEVOTIONAL

THE ONE YEAR®

HEAVEN ON EARTH

DEVOTIONAL

365 Daily Invitations
to Experience God's Kingdom Here and Now

CHRIS TIEGREEN

TYNDALE®
MOMENTUM

An Imprint of
Tyndale House Publishers, Inc.

Visit Tyndale online at www.tyndale.com.

Visit Tyndale Momentum online at www.tyndalemomentum.com.

Tyndale Momentum, the Tyndale Momentum logo, *The One Year*, and *One Year* are registered trademarks of Tyndale House Publishers, Inc. The One Year logo is a trademark of Tyndale House Publishers, Inc. Tyndale Momentum is an imprint of Tyndale House Publishers, Inc., Carol Stream, IL.

The One Year Heaven on Earth Devotional: 365 Daily Invitations to Experience God's Kingdom Here and Now

Designed by Beth Sparkman

Published in association with the literary agency of Mark Sweeney and Associates, 28540 Altessa Way, Suite 201, Bonita Springs, FL 34135.

ISBN 978-1-4143-7674-5

Printed in the United States of America

21	20	19	18	17	16	15
7	6	5	4	3	2	1

Introduction

WHAT WAS THE major theme of the teaching of Jesus? That question is likely to prompt a variety of answers, most of them centering around what we commonly know as the salvation message. Yet words about salvation occur relatively rarely in the Gospels compared to another term: "the Kingdom." If we had to pick one dominant message of Jesus' words and actions, this would be it.

The ministry of Jesus was filled with statements about the Kingdom of God. The phrases "the Kingdom of God," "the Kingdom of Heaven," or simply "the Kingdom" occur more than ninety times in the Gospels alone. When Jesus first began to preach, He said the Kingdom of God was at hand (Mark 1:15). As He spent time with the disciples after His resurrection, His primary subject was to teach them about the Kingdom of God (Acts 1:3). On numerous occasions in between, He began parables with "The Kingdom of Heaven is like . . ." or described the Kingdom ways. And His followers picked up the theme in Acts. All of them demonstrated the Kingdom, some specifically preached about it, and as the book closes, Luke is sure to tell us that the Kingdom message was going forth unhindered. The Gospels and Acts are Kingdom-saturated works.

The idea didn't begin in the New Testament, of course. Israel saw its existence as a manifestation of God's Kingdom. Hebrew Scriptures rarely used the word like the apostolic writers did, but the theme is certainly in them. From the very beginning of God's redemptive history, He has sought to be seen as King over the world that rebelled against Him.

With that in mind, it's extremely important to think about, meditate on, and pray about the Kingdom message—not only so we can understand it, but so we can also live it and spread it. That's why the daily readings in this book exist. They are reflections on Scripture through the lens of a Kingdom citizen. They don't answer all questions or develop a comprehensive theology of the subject; they simply invite us into

Kingdom thinking and a Kingdom lifestyle. As followers of the King who spoke often about His Kingdom, these are issues and questions and ideas worth exploring.

Enjoy these readings as an adventure into the Kingdom of God. Ask Him questions as you read, and listen for His answers. Take each lesson of each passage to heart as you read His Word each day. And may the Kingdom come increasingly and powerfully in every area of your heart, your life, and your world.

The Kingdom Came

"The time has come," he said. "The kingdom of God has come near."
Mark 1:15, *NIV*

IN WORD

In Mark's Gospel, these are the first words out of the mouth of Jesus. Anyone who expected the end of evil and the beginning of utopia would have gotten excited at first and then grown disappointed in the coming years—especially when evil seemed to win decisively on a cross in Jerusalem. Clearly the coming of the Kingdom of God wasn't a sudden shift in the ways of the world or an overhaul of government structures. So what exactly did Jesus mean when He said the time had come? In what ways had the Kingdom of God come near?

Theologians are still trying to unpack that statement, but one thing is clear. The Kingdom was near because the King was near. People were healed. Evil was cast out of hearts. Dead people got up and walked around again. And truth astounded seekers and aggravated the keepers of the status quo. These are signs of the Kingdom and evidence that it has indeed begun to flourish. It is not a theory or an unattainable ideal. It is a dramatic intervention on a fallen planet. It is the beginning of a radical restoration.

The Kingdom is still growing and miracles still happen. That's because the King is still among us. He didn't come for a while and then leave—what would be the point of that?—or give us a taste we would never be able to experience again. He came to stay. So if the time had come and the Kingdom came near two thousand years ago, and Jesus remained with us as He promised, then the time has still come and the Kingdom is still near. Those who bow to the King have already entered the Kingdom.

IN DEED

What does that mean in the reality of daily life? It means we can still experience the miraculous, still see hearts fundamentally changed, still overcome evil, and still receive wisdom and revelation from the King's mouth. It means we need to look at the world not as others do but as citizens of another realm. And it means we need to act as though the time has come. Things are changing. Everything is becoming new.

ADDITIONAL READING: Luke 2:29-32

Wherever God rules over the human heart as King,
there is the Kingdom of God established.
PAUL W. HARRISON

The Reversal

Repent and believe the good news! Mark 1:15, NIV

IN WORD

Repent. It's such a negative-sounding word, a religious term that seems to fit fire-and-brimstone, street-corner sermons better than it fits our image of Jesus. Many who use it freely today mean it in harsh and judgmental terms, and we don't like that. It doesn't sound very loving. It doesn't even sound very helpful.

So what does this word actually mean? It depends. In Hebraic thought—the culture of Jesus—it implies a turning around and a changing of actions. In Greek thought—the language of the Gospel writers—it implies a change of mind, a new way to think. We can probably assume that the inspirer of Scripture, the Spirit who knows all cultures and future applications of His Word, meant it comprehensively. To repent means to have a change of heart and mind that results in a new direction and different actions. It's a reversal of the course we were taking—mentally, emotionally, spiritually, relationally, behaviorally, and in all other ways.

That means that the depressed can be happy. That's repentance. The discouraged can be encouraged. That's repentance too. The apathetic can choose zeal, the angry can choose forgiveness, the judgmental can choose grace, the immoral can choose purity, the dead can choose life. None of that is possible in our own strength—repentance in that context is simply another standard we can't live up to. But now that the King is here with His Kingdom . . . well, that changes everything.

IN DEED

The Kingdom of God is a reversal from earth's status quo. If we want to walk in its fullness, we'll have to accept cross-cultural experiences. The Kingdom is so different from our old way of thinking, feeling, doing, and relating that we'll need new paradigms and perceptions. That's repentance—stepping out of the old and into the new. It's a necessary journey into Kingdom life. And a much more pleasant one than most people think.

ADDITIONAL READING: Romans 12:2

> Everyone thinks of changing the world, but
> no one thinks of changing himself.
> LEO TOLSTOY

Our Focus

Seek the Kingdom of God above all else, and live righteously, and he will give you everything you need. Matthew 6:33

IN WORD

No one needs to encourage us to focus on our needs or our desires. We do that naturally—and almost constantly. Whether consciously or not, we're relentless about getting our needs and desires met in people, positions, possessions, and more. So when Jesus says to seek first God's Kingdom—to focus on that above all else—He's making a major statement. This is a radical shift in our attention. He wants to turn us outward rather than inward. He wants us to be preoccupied with something much bigger than ourselves.

That means when we do look inward, our number one question should be not about whether we are getting our needs met but whether the Kingdom is being formed in us. When we look at our households, families, friends, and other spheres of influence, we should see ourselves as catalysts for the Kingdom. Are we instigators of the Kingdom culture? Carriers of Kingdom attitudes? Provokers of Kingdom ideas? Vessels of Kingdom solutions? Speakers of Kingdom words?

This doesn't mean we will always be spouting off religious verbiage and annoying those around us. It does mean, however, that we will be influencers of the environment around us simply because we carry the Kingdom nature within us. We are inhabited by the King, after all, if we have believed in Him and therefore been united with Him. Living out that union is a Kingdom expression that cannot be quenched.

IN DEED

If we seek our fulfillment in people, positions, and possessions, we get neither fulfillment nor the Kingdom. But if we seek the Kingdom, we get both. So we can let go of the things we cling to and the desires we desperately want to satisfy, and embrace the Kingdom of God. We are assured that if we do that, we will not be needy, stressed, and disappointed. For a world full of needy, stressed, and disappointed people, that's extremely good news.

ADDITIONAL READING: Matthew 11:28-30

Desire only God, and your heart will be satisfied.
AUGUSTINE OF HIPPO

What Kind of Kingdom?

[Jesus] said, "I must proclaim the good news of the kingdom of God to the other towns also, because that is why I was sent." Luke 4:43, NIV

IN WORD

This is why Jesus was sent—to proclaim the Kingdom of God. That certainly isn't the only reason; He did a lot more than proclaim. But in a moment when He revealed why He kept moving around, this was His reason. And His words were deeply tied to what had just happened.

How did Jesus proclaim the Kingdom of God? He had just healed the mother-in-law of one of His disciples from her high fever, healed numerous people of a variety of other illnesses, and cast out demons and forbade them from speaking. His words about the Kingdom did not mark a shift in His activities; they indicated a continuation of the same thing. Jesus' mission involved getting people well and free from evil. He offered life and wholeness in real situations and in real places.

Somehow we have come up with the idea that the Good News of the Kingdom is nothing more than a message about how to be saved and go to heaven one day. But Jesus' ministry and message were much more comprehensive than that. They were a declaration of the rule and reign of His goodness in every area of life—of the *shalom* that everyone longs for. The government of God was being enforced in a spiritually and materially contrary world. The Kingdom is more than a spiritual ticket to salvation. It's a here-and-now way of life.

IN DEED

Most biblical commentators make a distinction between the gospel of salvation and the gospel of the Kingdom. Salvation is included in the Kingdom, but the Kingdom message is bigger. Jesus didn't just come to get us saved. He came to offer us the fullness of life with God now and forever. Salvation is the entrance. But the Kingdom is the prize. When we realize the difference, our faith grows dramatically. We realize God's kindness toward us. And our expectations of His goodness soar.

ADDITIONAL READING: Luke 4:18-19

Cry the gospel with your whole life.
CHARLES DE FOUCAULD

The Present and Future Kingdom

Because he was nearing Jerusalem, he told them a story to correct the impression that the Kingdom of God would begin right away. Luke 19:11

IN WORD

Jesus made statements that indicated the Kingdom had already arrived. "The time . . . is at hand," He said (Mark 1:15, ESV). "The kingdom of God is in your midst," He insisted (Luke 17:21, NIV). After all, the King was present. Therefore, so was the Kingdom.

But He also spoke of the Kingdom as a thing of the future. Yes, it had come; but it was also coming. And not as soon as the people thought. In fact, He told them a parable about waiting. A nobleman would be going on a journey to be appointed king, and no one knew how long he would be gone. His people would have to manage his resources while he was away, and one day he would return to assume his role as king.

How do we reconcile these statements? Has the Kingdom come, or is it going to come in the future? It isn't hard to imagine both. Anything that's a process involves a beginning and a time of fulfillment. And the Kingdom is certainly a process. The King had come, but He wasn't widely recognized during His ministry. The fullness of His reign would become visible much later.

IN DEED

We live in the midst of the process, and we're tempted by two extremes. One is to think the Kingdom has already come and whenever we have a bad day, to be discouraged that it isn't a very good one. The other view, more prevalent in this era of history, is to think it's entirely future—out there for us to experience one day, but not something we can experience and enjoy now. The truth is that the Kingdom has come, is now coming, and will finally come. The government of the King is ever-increasing (Isaiah 9:7), and it will break into our age with greater frequency and visibility. The Kingdom is wherever the King is. And He is both with us now and waiting to come again.

ADDITIONAL READING: Luke 17:21

In the gospel, Jesus is *autobasileia*, the Kingdom Himself.
ORIGEN OF ALEXANDRIA

Kingdom Promotion

To those who use well what they are given, even more will be given. But from those who do nothing, even what little they have will be taken away. Luke 19:26

IN WORD

We like to think God's Kingdom is a perfectly comfortable realm—that it will match every impulse we've ever had about "this is how it should be done," that it will resolve every sense of injustice we observed in this life. But will it? Or will we be offended by God's way of doing things, just as we are by other people? When we see others getting farther ahead and ourselves stuck and stagnating—or even losing ground—will we still be able to rejoice over God's goodness?

In this Kingdom, there's no attempt to even things out. Those who are most trustworthy and fruitful get more, and those who are less trustworthy and fruitful suffer loss even of what they had. Seeing those who have plenty get more and those who have little lose what they have may violate our sense of fairness, but we should understand. It's exactly how we treat people in the workplace, how we invest our resources, and how we value impersonal forces in this world. We approve whomever and whatever proves effective and worthwhile, and we overlook whomever and whatever doesn't. That has nothing to do with our love. It simply fits our goals and purposes.

Likewise, God doesn't love fruitless people less than fruitful ones. But He doesn't promote them out of a sense of fairness. It may be an uncomfortable dynamic, but it's the way of the Kingdom. Trustworthy people are entrusted with more.

IN DEED

This dynamic is not a "one day" Kingdom principle. It's now, already in effect in this age. God loves every one of His people as much as He could possibly love us, and He isn't a utilitarian employer. He'll invest heavily in those who need help. But He doesn't position all of us the same way. Our fruitfulness and responsibilities are contingent on our faithfulness. Small responsibilities lead to greater responsibilities when we handle them well. That's how Kingdom purposes move forward—and how we move forward with them.

ADDITIONAL READING: Matthew 20:1-16

Faithfulness in a little thing is a big thing.
JOHN CHRYSOSTOM

Both Ages

I pray that . . . you may know . . . his incomparably great power . . . not only in the present age but also in the one to come. Ephesians 1:18-19, 21, NIV

IN WORD

Much of Christendom today thinks in terms of "this world" and "that world"—life on earth and life in heaven. Perhaps that's because we see around us so many contradictions to the Kingdom that we assume all things Kingdom must be somewhere else. Or maybe we've simply given up on the possibility of the Kingdom coming in any visible way. But the Bible doesn't defer the Kingdom to some out-of-sight universe. It isn't a heaven-only thing. It's a this-world possibility.

Writing of Jesus' authority, Paul uses a phrase often used by Jesus Himself: this age and the age to come. The difference between that and the this-world-that-world alternative may seem subtle, but it's significant. Neither Scripture as a whole nor Jesus' teaching specifically will allow us to defer every good promise of God to another time or place. The mind-set that sees His reign only as "there and then" will lose faith in the "here and now." That isn't God's desire. He wants us to believe in all of His goodness—and expect to see it—now.

That will require a shift in perspective. Our wistful "One day, Lord," needs to turn into a "Why not now, Lord?" We'll have to be content with missteps and unanswered questions as we learn to recognize His current work and align our faith with what He's doing. But if we persist, we will see breakthroughs we once thought were reserved for another world. We'll see Jesus' authority in this age and the age to come.

IN DEED

By faith, press in to God to see His Kingdom manifest in your life and the world around you. Certainly it does not come in its fullness until the "age to come," but plenty of it is available for this age too. And because the issue is ages rather than worlds, we don't have to look only to heaven. Earth is longing for a revelation of the Kingdom among God's children (Romans 8:19). God invites us to demonstrate it.

ADDITIONAL READING: Romans 8:19

> He who shall introduce into public affairs the principles of primitive Christianity will change the face of the world.
> BENJAMIN FRANKLIN

Head over Everything

God has put all things under the authority of Christ and has made him head over all things for the benefit of the church. Ephesians 1:22

IN WORD

Jesus has always been the rightful King, but His kingship hasn't always been practically enforced. God put all things under His feet, which means, of course, that all things weren't already under His feet. This kingship is eternally true but progressively applied. As we thoroughly know from our daily experience, not everything goes according to His will.

But that's changing. God put Jesus on the throne and all things under Him. The King is now seated at the right hand of the Father. Many of us have already submitted to His authority, and we are given the royal assignment of bringing others in our spheres of influence into His realm. He has given us the ability to help our homes, workplaces, and communities shift from being theoretically under His feet to being practically under His feet. We are participants in growing the Kingdom.

This is the direction of history and, for those who believe, the current reality. No opposition, no obstacle, no situation or circumstance or person is greater than the authority Jesus holds and shares with us. Plenty of voices in our lives, including our own natural senses, tell us otherwise. But they lie. If we could see the authority He has—and that we have in Him—we would never yield to any contradiction to His Kingdom. His headship over everything would embolden and empower us.

IN DEED

Everything in our lives should reflect the gentle-yet-unyielding authority of Jesus. We easily acquiesce to the obstacles and contradictions because they look unyielding and overpowering. But they are smaller, weaker, and illegitimate. And they are futile in the face of a believer who insists on the authority of Jesus over all. Sooner or later, all of His opposition will confess that He is Lord. And our royal privilege is to recognize, announce, and implement His authority now.

ADDITIONAL READING: 2 Corinthians 10:3-5

> The only significance in life consists in helping
> to establish the Kingdom of God.
> LEO TOLSTOY

Whose Kingdom?

Your kingdom come, your will be done, on earth as it is in heaven.
Matthew 6:10, *NIV*

IN WORD

We make assumptions when we read the Bible through our own preconceived beliefs, and several common assumptions distort this verse. Though Jesus taught His disciples to pray, "Your kingdom come," many people hear instead, "Your Kingdom come (one day)." And though Scripture indicates a fullness of the Kingdom at His second coming, it in no way limits His Kingdom to the distant future. Jesus' prayer says only what it says. It's a prayer for God's Kingdom to come.

Why is this important? Because as we've seen, in deferring everything good to "one day," we tend to weaken in faith now. God will do miracles, but not now. Every knee will bow to Jesus, but perhaps none today. We may see some momentary blessings—or at least glimpses of them—but we can't expect them or enjoy them for long. But are these statements true? Nothing in Scripture would say so. It tells us we will have tribulation in the world and in this age, but it does not say we will have *only* tribulation. No, the biblical expectation is for a more imminent Kingdom. Not immediate, but imminent, and currently in the process of coming.

We wouldn't think of applying the same assumption to the next phrase—"your will be done (one day)"—because God's will is for anywhere at any time. But isn't that the essence of the Kingdom? Don't these phrases have parallel meanings? Doesn't the Kingdom's coming reflect His will being done in every way? Yes, the prayer of Jesus is sweeping and urgent. And it applies to the details of our lives today.

IN DEED

Try praying this prayer with specifics. "Your Kingdom come in my heart." "Your Kingdom come in my family." "Your Kingdom come at the office." "May Your Kingdom invade my Monday." "Let Your Kingdom rearrange my assumptions, my relationships, my world." However you can think to apply it, pray it fervently. It's a prayer that is always according to God's will. And a prayer God is waiting to answer on behalf of those who persistently believe.

ADDITIONAL READING: Matthew 16:19

Prayer is a summit meeting in the throne room of the universe.
RALPH A. HERRING

Whose Will?

Your kingdom come, your will be done, on earth as it is in heaven.
Matthew 6:10, *NIV*

IN WORD

We read the lines of Scripture without realizing how often we read between the lines. Virtually everyone does; we have our notions of what Jesus meant from what we've been taught or from the worldview we grew up with. So to what Jesus trained His followers to pray, "Your will be done," we often add a qualifier: "Your will (as opposed to mine) be done." We assume this is an inherent denial of self.

It can be that, of course. After all, it foreshadows His own prayer in Gethsemane: "My Father! If it is possible, let this cup of suffering be taken away from me. Yet I want your will to be done, not mine" (Matthew 26:39). But Jesus' prayer has broader implications. We could justifiably read it with other qualifiers too: "Your will (as opposed to Satan's) be done," or "Your will (as opposed to ungodly people's) be done." In truth, this prayer is a contradiction to any will other than God's, and we encounter a wide range of such contradictions from a variety of sources. The world, the flesh, and the devil are opposed to God. But may their will never be done. All we are going for in this prayer is God's will.

IN DEED

This prayer is about more than submission to the Father's will. It's a battle cry against everything that is wrong in this world. It's an assertive enforcement of the divine will over and above everything that contradicts it. When we pray for God's will to be done, we are issuing a Kingdom proclamation against the evil one, against the ways of the fallen world, and against the rebellious spirit that plagues the human race. We are calling for the Kingdom in every situation in which the fullness of the Kingdom has not yet come. And we are praying according to God's will.

Pray persistently and aggressively. Insist that the will of the Father be revered, both in visible and spiritual realms. You have a list of what to pray *for*; now add some things to pray *against*. Pray for whatever doesn't look like God's Kingdom to go and for His will to be done.

ADDITIONAL READING: Ephesians 6:10-20

Prayer is the mightiest of all weapons that created natures can wield.
MARTIN LUTHER

Which Realm?

Your kingdom come, your will be done, on earth as it is in heaven.
Matthew 6:10, *NIV*

IN WORD

Not everyone adds an assumption to the third phrase of this verse, but many do: "On earth as (a faint reflection of what is) in heaven." But if we really think about Jesus' prayer, we realize it has staggering implications. He is teaching His followers to pray that God's Kingdom would come and His will would be done on earth—not in heaven, not in some spiritual but indiscernible realm, but right here on earth—*just as it is* in heaven. There is no qualifier at the end that implies "as much as possible, though it will never look anything like heaven." No, this is a blanket, unequivocal statement. Jesus' desire is for earth to look like heaven.

Is this possible? It must be; Jesus would never urge His followers to pray for an impossibility. In fact, He told them that with God, all things are possible (Mark 9:23; 10:27). Surely He must be presenting a real possibility to the disciples. But it seems so unlikely. The Kingdom on earth as it is in heaven? God's will being done here just as completely as it is in that realm? Has He seen the condition of this fallen world?

Perhaps that's why we water down the impact of the Lord's Prayer. It's too big for us to take literally. It seems so far-fetched. It can't mean what it looks like it means. There must be more between the lines.

IN DEED

Would world history look different if the church throughout the ages had taken Jesus' prayer more literally and refused to compromise it by putting it off to the distant future or forgetting that it applies "on earth"? Perhaps. But we who claim the truth of Scripture and of Jesus' words can't be content with a weakened prayer. It has to be true—and possible.

Let this prayer shape your world. Pray it vigorously and pray it often. Let its true implications sink in, and let it feed and fuel your faith. Jesus has high expectations for the prayers of His people. We must too.

ADDITIONAL READING: Colossians 1:19-20

Large asking and large expectation on our part honor God.
A. L. STONE

The Restoration Project

He must remain in heaven until the time for the final restoration of all things.
Acts 3:21

IN WORD

God is into restoration. In the Prophets, He restores His people to the land, and they restore broken walls (Isaiah 58:12). Through Jesus, He restores His own image in redeemed image-bearers. In the end, He restores Eden's qualities, but in a city rather than a garden (Revelation 22:1-5). Even now, Jesus is in heaven waiting for His enemies to be made His footstool (Hebrews 10:13) and anticipating the time "for the final restoration of all things." Clearly, God is not letting any part of His plan fall through the cracks.

In the meantime—between the two advents of the King, when the ever-increasing Kingdom is being cultivated—we are to be restorers too. If God is into restoration, and if His people are to live in practical union with Him, then we are meant to be active in this restoration. We live in a broken world, but we are never told to let it remain broken. There is nothing about His creation that we are called to write off as a loss.

It's easier to think otherwise. Some things look like lost causes. Some hearts seem to be so hardened that they could never be open to redemption. Some relationships are so difficult that they appear hopeless. Some aspects of human society look unredeemable. But we are never authorized to make any of those assessments. If God calls us to demonstrate faith, hope, and love, we can never call anything impossible, hopeless, or unlovable. We are investing ourselves in a Kingdom that cannot and will not ever pass away. That should make us irrepressibly optimistic and relentlessly persistent.

IN DEED

How do we become restorers? Think about the "broken walls" in your life. Envision what the Kingdom would look like in your relationships, in your home and community, or in your physical and emotional health or that of the people around you. Then pray, live, work, and relate to others toward that vision. Step into the Kingdom picture in every way you can, gently and winsomely drawing others into it too. When your focus is a restoration of all things, you align yourself with the heart of God.

ADDITIONAL READING: Acts 1:6-8

> Wherever the bounds of beauty, truth, and goodness
> are advanced, there the Kingdom comes.
> FREDERICK DONALD COGGAN

Until . . .

The Lord said to my Lord, "Sit in the place of honor at my right hand until I humble your enemies, making them a footstool under your feet." Psalm 110:1

IN WORD

Which Old Testament verse is quoted more than any other in the New Testament? Not a prophecy about the coming of the Messiah, not a prophecy about the Cross and Resurrection, and not even a recap of the greatest commandment to love God wholeheartedly. No, the most quoted verse is this one from a psalm of David about the Lord sitting at God's right hand until His enemies are His footstool. Jesus used it to prove a point about Himself, Peter quoted it on the Day of Pentecost, and Paul and the writer of Hebrews referred to it in their writings. That means that the position of Jesus, as well as the timing of His return, was a major emphasis in the early church and to the Spirit who inspired our Scripture.

It's easy to understand why this prophecy is significant. What it means is another matter, with each New Testament writer using it for a slightly different purpose. But one thing is clear: It strongly implies that Jesus isn't coming back until His enemies are overcome.

Jesus' enemies have already been defeated, of course, but they haven't been rendered inactive. They are still rather influential in the world around us, and we battle spiritual opposition daily. So why doesn't He come back and deal with them? Because as this verse says, He is waiting for another victory to come. Apparently His people have a role in putting His enemies down.

IN DEED

That would not be possible by our own devices. But God is the active agent in this passage; He is the one who puts the enemies under the feet of His Son, at which time the Son will no longer sit. But until then, we are to be busy opposing the kingdom of darkness. Filled with the light of God, we warriors of the footstool are to enforce the victories He has won.

ADDITIONAL READING: Acts 2:32-35

Fight the good fight with all thy might; Christ
is thy strength, and Christ thy right.
J. S. B. MONSELL

Images in the Temple

So God created human beings in his own image. In the image of God he created them; male and female he created them. Genesis 1:27

IN WORD

There are several cues in the Creation account—numbers, vocabulary, sentence structures, and the like—that link it to the Tabernacle and the Temple (or vice versa). Many Old Testament scholars have therefore come to the conclusion that the world was designed as a temple for God, the Garden of Eden as its "holy of holies," and human beings as the "images" or "icons" of God in the temple. In fact, in the Greek translation of the Hebrew text, the word our Bibles translate as "image" is *eikon*, from which we get the word "icon." We were designed as God's icons much as church artwork throughout history has often been designed to represent His actual presence.

What does this mean? It means that for better or worse, we are God's "brand" in this world, the artwork on the walls and ceiling of His chapel, the icon on His social media pages, the public face of His invisible nature. And that scares us because we know how short we've fallen of His glory. Nevertheless, He didn't scrap us as His representatives and come up with another plan. He sent the icon of His invisible nature into this world (Colossians 1:15), the exact representation of His nature (Hebrews 1:3), to restore the shattered image. He breathed His own life into His followers (John 20:22), just as the Father breathed into dust in Eden and created the first image (Genesis 2:7). What was vandalized in the Garden is now being restored. We are becoming the exact icons of His presence.

IN DEED

That is what it takes to represent the King. We have to live as image-bearers do. We wear His "face" and represent His likeness. Just as emperors of the ancient world placed statues of themselves in public places in conquered territories, we must live as walking, talking "statues" of our King in the territories of this world, reminding every living being of His goodness and love. After all, He created this world for Himself, and He holds it in His heart with love. So must we.

ADDITIONAL READING: Colossians 1:15

> The rule of life for a perfect person is to be in the image and likeness of God.
> CLEMENT OF ALEXANDRIA

The Assignment

Be fruitful and multiply. Fill the earth and govern it. Genesis 1:28

IN WORD

We had it all. A beautiful garden, a sweet assignment, innocent relationships, and a tangible connection with God Himself. Then we lost it all.

That's the story of the human race and, more specifically, of our first parents. We like to think we might have handled things differently, but we know it isn't true. Sooner or later, we would have made the same mistake and squandered the privilege we had been given.

Part of that privilege was ruling the earth in partnership with God. It was His, to be sure, but He gave humanity stewardship over it. We were responsible. In this original commission, not only were we placed at the top of the created order, but we were also given mastery over wildlife and agriculture. The implication is that we were to spread God's order and government in all the places that were still untamed. We were Kingdom representatives even when there was no anti-Kingdom on this planet in rebellion against Him. We were divinely appointed agents of His will.

Something terrible happened in the Fall. In some mysterious sense, we handed some aspect of our God-given authority over to His vicious enemy. The world was still His, and we were still His agents. But we partnered with the "unKingdom," the hostile uprising against Him. We recklessly pointed our responsibilities in the wrong direction.

IN DEED

Jesus won the keys of the Kingdom back and gave them to His followers. We haven't used them nearly as often as we could or should, but we still have them. By faith, we can implement the divine will in chaotic and forbidding surroundings. That's our Kingdom calling, whether we realize it or not. It isn't simply to hang on until He comes. It's to be agents of His government even now. We tell the good news of the coming King, we demonstrate His nature, and we become good news to a ravaged, alienated world.

ADDITIONAL READING: Matthew 16:19

God is able to recover this image through grace
as we are conformed to Christ.
ALISTER MCGRATH

The UnKingdom

Now God saw that the earth had become corrupt and was filled with violence.
Genesis 6:11

IN WORD

This isn't what the Kingdom was supposed to look like. Eden hadn't looked like it very much either, but that's only because the mission hadn't been carried out yet. At least Eden was a reflection of God's goodness. But after the Fall, centuries of human history went in exactly the opposite direction of the Kingdom because its stewards were negligent, unequipped, and downright rebellious. The result was tragic, even devastating. Corruption and violence are not at all a picture of God's nature.

This is still the general condition of our world today. We can see places where the Kingdom of God has created a haven from the fallenness of the world, and some places where Kingdom values have drastically upgraded a culture's well-being. But even the havens and the cultural improvements mingle in a society made up of imperfect human beings, and our imperfections taint everything. In this age, we see a unique mixture of influences in which the true colors of the Kingdom are muted by the unKingdom and the true colors of the unKingdom are brightened up by the Kingdom. Some people see a bland mixture with little distinction, but our eyes are more discerning. We know where this is headed.

IN DEED

The contrasts will grow clearer as time goes on, and the choice between kingdoms will become more obvious. But in the meantime, our job as restored stewards is to paint the colors of the Kingdom everywhere we can and heighten the contrasts for others to see. The mission that was lost in the Garden has been given back to us along with the authority we once had and then squandered. The "second Adam," as Scripture calls our King, has secured the keys of the Kingdom for us and recommissioned us as His agents. That means a world that is corrupt and full of violence has a viable alternative. The days of the unKingdom are numbered.

ADDITIONAL READING: Matthew 28:18-20

> The more seriously we take the future promise of God's kingdom, the more unbearable will be the contradictions of that promise in the present.
> JÜRGEN MOLTMANN

Futility

Come, let's build a great city for ourselves with a tower that reaches into the sky. This will make us famous and keep us from being scattered all over the world. Genesis 11:4

IN WORD

God had told the first human beings to fill the earth and subdue it. They were to spread out, to be the governors of God's realm under His kingship. The beauty and order of the Garden were to expand into the earth's surrounding chaos. His Kingdom plan was for His glory to cover the earth through those He had created in His own image.

That isn't what happened, of course. There was a massive and prolonged turn in the opposite direction. One example of the many contradictions to God's plan occurred on the plains of Shinar, where the Babylonian empire would one day rise up. The human community devised a plan not to spread out and subdue the earth, as God had long ago ordered, but to come together and reach toward heaven. They rejected the idea of scattering and filling the earth with God's image-bearers and instead chose to cluster and make a name for themselves. They acted contrary to God's design.

Scripture and history both tell us how futile humanity's attempts at self-exaltation have been. Romans 8:20-21 specifically tells us that God subjected the world to frustration in order to send it searching for freedom and glory ultimately in Him. At Babel, the frustration and futility are on full display. God scatters the people and gives them diverse languages that prevent them from clustering. Their attempts to exalt themselves fail miserably.

IN DEED

Ironically, God's promise to His humble, dependent, redeemed children is to fill them with glory (Romans 8:21), and His assignment for them is again to fill the earth with the good news of His Kingdom (Luke 9:2). We receive what the people of Babel wanted, but by an entirely different means. We have glory and access to heaven. And we need to remember: No matter how things look, nothing in our lives is futile.

ADDITIONAL READING: Romans 8:19-21

> The glory of God is a living man; and the life
> of man consists in beholding God.
> IRENAEUS

All Things New

[The Lord said,] "Look! I am creating new heavens and a new earth, and no one will even think about the old ones anymore." Isaiah 65:17

IN WORD

If God has gone to such trouble to restore the "icons" of His presence—transforming us to look like His image once again—doesn't it make sense that He would restore the cosmic Temple in which He placed those icons to begin with? If the world was designed as a temple for Him, the Garden was the Holy Place within the temple, and the image-bearers were placed in the Holy Place to reflect Him, wouldn't He restore the world and the Garden just as He is restoring the image-bearers?

Of course, and that's exactly what we see in Scripture. The prophets foretold a new heaven and a new earth, and at the end of Revelation we see a restoration of Eden. It's now more than a garden—it's also the City of God—but the river of life and the tree of life are there. Eden makes a return.

Even in the days of Noah, when God promised destruction of all He had made, it wasn't a complete destruction as we might expect. The earth remained, and a family was preserved as a remnant. God doesn't throw away first drafts like a writer does; He knows from the beginning how things will go, and He has a plan. His plan for this planet is not ultimately for destruction but for restoration. There will be times of cleansing, but not of annihilation. Our King is making His Kingdom new.

IN DEED

That's what God does. He makes things new. Whether it's an individual life, a dead and decaying dream, a broken relationship, or an entire rebellious planet, He has a plan for renewal and restoration. He transforms broken images back into their right design. He heals broken bodies and relationships. He restores the years the locusts have eaten. He makes beauty out of ashes, turns mourning to dancing, and gives double blessings in places where a curse has done its devastation. In every area of life, He has a solution. Hang on to that promise. It flows from His nature, and His nature never changes.

ADDITIONAL READING: Revelation 21:1-5; 22:1-5

Christianity is not a system of doctrine but a new creature.
JOHN NEWTON

Breaking Dawn

The people who walk in darkness will see a great light. Isaiah 9:2

IN WORD

Kingdoms come and go. So do kings. Some come with great fanfare, and some leave in great turmoil. Others rise and fall routinely, just another character in a long line of succession. But when the King of the true Kingdom came, it was a remarkable advent. Unnoticed by many, an earth-shattering event for others. The humblest yet worthiest King ever to grace His realm. Lord of an invisible realm more real than any other. Human yet divine. It was like the sun rising after creation's deepest, darkest night.

That's how the prophet portrays the coming King. It's the dawning of a new era. The world was shrouded, cursed, captive, and completely unable to reach beyond its own limitations. Human hearts were incapable of fulfilling human hopes. Our ambitions were always farther than our reach. Our ability to have dreams was ever greater than our ability to attain them. We were fallen, corrupt, and destined to stay that way . . . unless someone from another world rescued us.

That's the nature of our King. He comes from somewhere else to be one of us and to bring us back into His realm. It's a different realm, and light can be awfully traumatic to eyes that are used to the dark. But He means for us to get used to it. He has come to change things in ways we have scarcely even dreamed.

IN DEED

The King has come to shine light into every dark corner of your life, not to expose you but to transform you into something that looks like His glory. Every hopeless thought, every cause of fear, every source of bitterness, everything that doesn't look like a reflection of His Kingdom—all are subject to His authority. Let Him shine His light wherever He wants. Ask Him to sensitize your spirit to the newness of His touch. Open your heart to receive every impulse, every breath, every hint of His Spirit. Submit every area of your life to His reign and let Him decree His goodness into it. Open your eyes to see the great light.

ADDITIONAL READING: Isaiah 60:1-3

The Light is that which illumines every person coming into this world.
AUGUSTINE OF HIPPO

Head of Government

A child is born to us, a son is given to us. The government will rest on his shoulders. Isaiah 9:6

IN WORD

God's Kingdom is a government. Some people may not like the sound of that—*government* can have some pretty negative connotations—but it's true. Our King manages resources, sets policy, establishes justice, pursues goals and purposes, and cares for the people. That's what government does.

As in any realm, citizens have a choice about whether they comply with that government or not. That choice comes with consequences, and it seems senseless to defy this kind of King, but the choice is real nonetheless. Just as physical laws have consequences that apply to every human being—gravity, momentum, and energy don't favor certain people over others, for example—God's standards are universally applicable. If we defy them, we experience unfortunate results, just as the person who steps off a cliff experiences the results of gravity. But if we learn the way His realm functions and choose to live according to its conditions, the consequences are extremely encouraging. We receive the peace of His government. We grow in wisdom and stature in the eyes of the King. And we find that He begins to share the governing with us.

IN DEED

Though we easily use the words *King* and *Kingdom* with Jesus, few people think of His reign as a government. But when we do, we begin to think in terms of our citizenship. What does He promise as governor of this realm? What are our responsibilities? What can we reasonably expect of Him, and what does He reasonably expect of us? Is it possible that the pain of this world—and often of our lives—is the result of misunderstanding or misapplying His policies? And what would our lives look like if we fully aligned ourselves with this government's objectives? These are questions that citizens ask when they are involved and engaged. And the ruler can trust His authority to those who answer them well.

ADDITIONAL READING: Revelation 3:21-22

If you do not wish for His Kingdom, don't pray for it. But if you do, you must do more than pray; you must work for it.
JOHN RUSKIN

Shalom

He will be called: Wonderful Counselor, Mighty God, Everlasting Father, Prince of Peace. Isaiah 9:6

IN WORD

When Abraham went out to battle and came back victorious, recovering all that the invading kings had taken, he encountered a man named Melchizedek, "king of righteousness" (Hebrews 7:2, NIV), who is also identified as the king of Salem—literally, king of *shalom*. David's son Solomon, whose name comes from the same word *shalom*, was lauded for establishing "peace on every side" (1 Kings 5:4)—the golden age, and a brief one, in Israel's history. Now, many centuries later, Isaiah speaks of a future ruler—a son who is a Father, a wonderful counselor, and a mighty God, who will be called Prince of *Shalom*.

What is this *shalom* that seems so elusive yet so desired? It's the fullness of life, the abundance of God's blessings, that state of being in which all is well and life is as it should be. We all long for it but see only brief glimpses of it in our lives—those fleeting moments when everything on the to-do list is done, those vacations that seem so idyllic, those times of joy when everything seems to fall into place or our desires are fulfilled. This *shalom* is an aftertaste of the Garden of Eden and a foretaste of the City of God, and it stirs us deeply. This is what life is all about. Deep down inside, we just know it.

IN DEED

This is what Jesus came to offer. The King is all about *shalom*. When He promised a more abundant life (John 10:10), this is what He was talking about. When He told His disciples that His words would give them fullness of joy (John 15:11), this is the picture. He comes for our *shalom*, a characteristic of the Kingdom we will always be stepping into more deeply and fully. And we can begin now.

How? By completely releasing our concerns into the hands of this Prince of *Shalom*. Living in His Kingdom means fully trusting in the King, knowing that everything He has designed for our lives, every aspect of His government in heaven and on earth, is for our good and our ultimate fulfillment. His *shalom* is the overflow of His goodness to us. And He invites us to taste and see it even now.

ADDITIONAL READING: Genesis 14:14-20

When I met Christ, I felt that I had swallowed sunshine.
E. STANLEY JONES

Always Increasing

Of the increase of His government and peace there will be no end.
Isaiah 9:7, *NKJV*

IN WORD

What would it be like to enter a world in which everyone is fulfilled, no one ever suffers injustice, and all needs are met? How would you feel if you stepped into that world and, still overwhelmed by the peace and pleasure of it all, realized it would never, ever end? We can hardly conceive of such things; we've never experienced that sort of world. But sometimes when we let our minds wander, we dream. Something inside us longs for that kind of existence.

This is the promise of Scripture. Not only is God's government being established, and not only will it never end, it will actually continually expand forever. That's the literal sense of this verse; it's the *increase* of His Kingdom that goes on and on, not just the Kingdom itself.

That's encouraging. Nothing instills more hope in us than the idea that our hearts will finally be filled, at rest, and completely unconcerned about the future. There will be nothing to dread and everything to look forward to. One day.

But it doesn't have to be just "one day." God is always urging His people to draw the future into the present by faith. Whatever picture you have of the Kingdom can begin to manifest itself in concrete reality in the present time. That's what faith is all about—that "on earth as it is in heaven" vision. This vision drives us to pray, speak, live, and love as citizens and warriors of the Kingdom. We are present-day representatives of the future reality.

IN DEED

Envision the future Kingdom and then live by faith as though it's a present-day fact. In many ways it is, and you are called to be a picture of it and to shape it for those around you. Like builders for the master Architect or representatives of the ultimate Ruler, we live the future in the now. And this kind of living will always increase and never end.

ADDITIONAL READING: Revelation 21:9-17

There can be no Kingdom of God in the world
without the Kingdom of God in our hearts.
ALBERT SCHWEITZER

God's Enthusiasm

The passionate commitment of the LORD of Heaven's Armies will make this happen! Isaiah 9:7

IN WORD

How does God feel about an everlasting, ever-increasing government based on righteousness, truth, and justice? Apparently, He gets pretty excited about it. Perhaps that sentiment doesn't seem to fit a dignified theology of His nature, but Scripture isn't shy about describing His emotions. And in this case, He's enthusiastic. In His zeal, He will accomplish all that the prophet has spoken.

We long for such a response from God. When we pray according to His promises, we want Him to be zealous about fulfilling them. When we bring Him our desires, we want Him to be as enthusiastic about them as we are. We want to know that just as He told Jeremiah, He is watching over His word to perform it (Jeremiah 1:12). We know that when He wants something to happen, He can make it happen.

Think of that: The power of God plus the zeal of God over a matter makes that matter a sure thing. Nothing can stop Him if He doesn't want to be stopped. Yes, it can be hard to understand His will and why it isn't always accomplished in our world, but when He speaks, His people believe, and His zeal surrounds that word, it's a done deal. The energy of God is an unstoppable force.

IN DEED

Remember that truth when you pray and grab hold of one of God's promises. If He has spoken a promise, it's because He wanted to. And if He wanted to speak it, He intends to fulfill it if its necessary conditions are met. There may be some response of faith or action lacking on our part, but there is nothing lacking on His. His zeal plus His power makes an irresistible combination.

Let that fuel your prayers and your faith. Let it raise your confidence in Him and comfort you during the long delays and detours of the faith life. Know that the things that matter to you also matter to Him. And whenever He is able to merge them with the plans of His government, His own zeal will accomplish them.

ADDITIONAL READING: Jeremiah 1:11-12

Learn to plead the promises of God!
AMBROSE WHALEY

Decisive Victory

[Jesus said,] "If I am casting out demons by the Spirit of God, then the Kingdom of God has arrived among you." Matthew 12:28

IN WORD

Jesus had delivered a man from blindness and muteness, and the religious leaders didn't know what to do with that. Clearly this teacher had supernatural power, but He also violated certain religious traditions and thus could not be from God. Therefore, His supernatural power must be from Satan.

Jesus pointed out the obvious. Why would satanic power cast a satanic influence from a man? Even the kingdom of darkness has enough sense not to divide itself like that. No, His critics didn't understand, but this was the power of God. There would be no split loyalties, no backtracking, no compromise with the kingdom of darkness. God has no need to negotiate with terrorists. Jesus takes a hard-line stance against evil.

This is still true. Kingdom life is not one of compromise. It's a hostile overthrow of an illegitimate regime. The kingdom of darkness illegally occupies this world, and the sovereign God sent His conquering Son to raise up a conquering people. The dictator's days are numbered; the good King has come to assume His throne.

IN DEED

Stage one of the overthrow involves the King's own people. He has left us as His agents in the midst of the kingdom of darkness so we can undermine it and overcome it. He could take over in a moment and cast the evil one out of creation, but that's not His way. He is demonstrating His power through weak vessels who fully depend on Him.

Understand your position as a hostile force against the kingdom of darkness. Its forces fear your potential and hope you never recognize it. But as you do, and as you step further into your calling, your demonstration of Jesus' power grows stronger. And the world around you will know the Kingdom of God has come upon them.

ADDITIONAL READING: Acts 1:7-8

Anyone who witnesses to the grace of God revealed in Christ is undertaking a direct assault against Satan's dominion.
THOMAS COSMADES

Revolution

Don't copy the behavior and customs of this world, but let God transform you into a new person by changing the way you think.   Romans 12:2

IN WORD

It's a common theme in literature and film. A small band of rebels breaks away from a massive, monolithic, oppressive machine of a government and finds a way against impossible odds to undermine the system. The revolution-against-the-evil-empire theme is rarely successful in actual history, but it's somehow embedded in our deepest desires. We're drawn to any story in which the noble few overcome the brutal masses. Courage in the face of tyranny captivates our imagination.

There's a reason this theme fascinates us. It's the story of humble servants of God going up against a world dominated by evil. On the surface, it looks impossible. Can love really overcome an every-man-for-himself culture? Are the powerful systems of this world really vulnerable to values like humility and sacrifice? Does a revolution against the prevailing spirits of the age really have a chance?

Yes—to all of these questions. Jesus came to overthrow an enemy posing as the rightful ruler of this world, and He called His followers into this uprising. We have to engage the world, not by adopting its spirit but by countering it with the Spirit of truth. Our attitudes, words, and ways are decidedly different, and they are more powerful than all the world has to offer.

IN DEED

Romans 12 captures the character of our revolution. It's a path to Kingdom-building. We don't tear down the culture that's there; like leaven in a lump of dough, we infiltrate and transform our relationships and surroundings from within. In many ways, this is a silent uprising. But it's a potent one, and ultimately unstoppable. We can't afford to live with a mind-set that acquiesces to the world's ways, nor can we simply separate ourselves from them. If we determine to live contrary to the culture of the age and insist on living the Kingdom culture, we who have been transformed become transformers. And the uprising grows stronger every day.

ADDITIONAL READING: John 15:8

All that is best in the civilization of today is the
fruit of Christ's appearance among men.
DANIEL WEBSTER

Living Stones

We are many parts of one body, and we all belong to each other.
Romans 12:5

IN WORD

"To each his own." "You'll have to pull yourself up by your own bootstraps." "Whatever I do on my own time is none of your business." These are just some of the many mantras of an individualistic age. They have elements of truth; we are individually responsible for our own actions and rightfully free from the judgments of others. But in spite of all our individualism, Scripture calls us members of one body, all interdependent and functioning as a whole. While we seek independence, God has designed us to depend on Him, often through His work in others. He is building a temple for His presence, and it has many stones.

Paul expressed that thought in Ephesians, where the body of Christ is actually a temple for God, and we are each vital members. And it's true: Unless a person has every spiritual gift and every experience anyone could ever have with God, he or she needs what God is imparting through other believers. If we want to know Him as thoroughly as possible, and He is an infinite God, we will have to be joined with multitudes through whom He is doing something different than what He has done in us. That's the only way to begin to see the fullness of His work on earth.

IN DEED

In this Kingdom revolution, we cannot function as isolated individuals, each with our own private Holy Spirit. Yes, we have a personal relationship with Him at a deeply intimate level, but we also can't get everything He offers on our own. We need the gifts of others, and they need ours. Their strength fuels our strength, and vice versa. No human being experiences God comprehensively. And no revolution succeeds if every participant is doing his or her own thing apart from the others. We need each other to experience God; and we need each other to grow His Kingdom. Only in unity is a fragmented world truly changed.

ADDITIONAL READING: Ephesians 2:19-22; 4:1-6

No man is an island, entire of itself; every man is
a piece of the continent, a part of the main.
JOHN DONNE

Simple Distinctions

Hate what is wrong. Hold tightly to what is good.   Romans 12:9

IN WORD

There have been times when Christians have rejected good words, deeds, or policies because they come from someone who isn't "in the faith." Conversely, there have been times when we accept what is wrong simply because it came from someone we accept as "one of us." For example, what does it say about us when we reject justice for the oppressed because it might be part of some deceptive "social gospel," or loathe rainbows because they have come to represent political movements and social agendas—all while God says He blessed us with the rainbow and repeatedly stresses the need for justice in His Word? What does it say about us when we embrace the Golden Rule coming out of a Christian's mouth and attack it coming out of a non-Christian's? Truth is truth, isn't it? It's true that the source and purpose of a word or action matter. But it's also true that good is good and evil is evil. And we get them confused often. The result is a serious loss of credibility among the watching world.

Paul gives us really simple instructions: Hate what is wrong; hold on to what is good. Our job is to do what God has told us in Scripture, regardless of whether other movements and agendas take up or let go of the same things. We don't measure ourselves by what others do or think. We don't need to compete for moral positions in some fabricated arena of Kingdom politics. We simply need to love good and hate evil.

IN DEED

Don't let the agendas of others twist you into positions you wouldn't take simply by loving God and embracing His values and purposes. Keep it simple. Honor what is good indiscriminately, whether it comes from a believer or not. And reject what is evil, whether it comes out of an unbeliever or not. Our spiritual uprising needs to have a clear vision of what the Kingdom looks like. We need to bless others without reservation. We need to be known for everything that is good and for nothing that is wrong.

ADDITIONAL READING: Psalm 34:11-16

We cannot love good if we do not hate evil.
JEROME

The Honor Code

Take delight in honoring each other. Romans 12:10

IN WORD

Honor comes naturally when we greatly esteem someone. We show signs of respect easily, sometimes even creating ceremonies and awards to demonstrate it to the deserving. Other times, we have to be told. And when it's difficult to honor a person, we may find it necessary to honor the position that person holds. At some level, we consider the need to give and receive honor as a significant part of the human experience.

Something happens when we express honor to other people, even if they don't think and talk exactly like we do. A blessing is released, and the one who is blessed often becomes open to the things of God. That happens with hardened hearts within the church, to be sure, but it also happens with hardened hearts outside of it. Giving honor, even to those who aren't "on our side," seems to open the flow of the Spirit into lives on both sides of the relationship.

That's a profound Kingdom value, and it's one of the most powerful ways to influence the world for God. Daniel honored the pagan kings he served, not preaching against them but blessing them, and God greatly impacted their hearts. Some churches today have chosen to honor the contributions of distinct ethnic or religious groups, not as an endorsement but as a sign of respect, and God greatly impacts their hearts too. Something about honor stirs receptivity to the one giving it in the mind of the one receiving it. It's a profound way to break down barriers.

IN DEED

Think about that. Both within the church and beyond it are walls of division that hinder the flow of the gospel of grace. Expressing honor brings them down. Why wouldn't we want that? It may be our instinct to withhold honor from those who oppose us—or even just rub us the wrong way a little—but that does nothing for the Kingdom. We will have to take delight in expressing honor liberally—to enjoy it and enthusiastically spread it around—if our spiritual revolution is ever to be successful. Only then can people see the real Kingdom culture and thrive in it.

ADDITIONAL READING: Philippians 2:3-4

> Goodness is something so simple: always live for
> others, never to seek one's own advantage.
> DAG HAMMARSKJÖLD

A Deeper Blessing

Bless those who persecute you. Don't curse them; pray that God will bless them. Romans 12:14

IN WORD

Few revolutions bless enemies or even attempt to honor them. Ours does. That's because we are revolting not against the world itself but against the captivity in which it is bound. There are spiritual enemies, to be sure, and we will be glad to evict and exile them. But our human opposition? We want the best for all of them—to preserve their lives, to bring them into a healthy and whole environment, and to introduce them to the King Himself. So we have nothing to gain by cursing anyone. Even the hands that oppress us are great candidates for grace.

That goes against our instincts, of course. Much of the Kingdom culture does. That's why this instruction—along with belonging to one another and radically honoring one another—comes after a command to change the way we think. If we continue to think as the world has taught us, we will never be able to express the Kingdom culture in any distinctive way. But if we reorient our minds to envision the Kingdom and its counterintuitive ways, we represent a decided difference in how to live. We demonstrate something altogether greater than the ways of the world. We prove ourselves to be rooted in something that goes much deeper than petty offenses or even brutal ones. We reveal that we are children of God.

IN DEED

God has already demonstrated that this is His modus operandi. While we were still in rebellion against Him, He sent His Son to die for us (Romans 5:8). He has shown us His mercy and called us to be like Him. Just as Jesus forgave those who executed Him, we are to forgive those who offend us or attack us. And not only do we forgive; we bless. We wish heaven's best on them. We offer them the life of the Kingdom because clearly they haven't yet experienced it. If they had, they would not be persecuting children of God. Their only hope is for someone to show them what real life is like—by offering a blessing from another realm.

ADDITIONAL READING: Matthew 5:43-48

> He that returns a good for evil obtains the victory.
> THOMAS FULLER

Seeds of Peace

Do all that you can to live in peace with everyone. Romans 12:18

IN WORD

Most revolutions aim for eventual peace but sow discord in order to get it. Not so with ours. We sow seeds of peace in order to overthrow a culture of discord and grow in its place an entirely different community. And by peace, we don't simply mean the absence of conflict. We mean unity, wholeness, and a genuine, heartfelt bond—deep, authentic peace. And we are instructed to do everything we can to get it.

Is that realistic? After all, peace isn't always up to us. There are times when we have done everything we can to reconcile with an adversary, forgive an offender, or seek forgiveness for our own offenses, and still we find the other party resistant. We can't force peace on anyone; that wouldn't be peace at all. But having done our part, we can live with a clear conscience and continue to hold open the possibility of reconciliation and restoration. We can choose to be "unoffendable," letting slights and affronts roll away without sticking to us. We can let disagreements lie dormant, refusing to pick up the case and try it again and again. We can be authentically ourselves while letting others be authentically themselves, praying not for them to see things our way but to draw close to the God of grace. These are the things that make for peace.

IN DEED

Living in peace with everyone is harder than it seems for those of us who actually have opinions and plans. The Word never tells us to compromise and let others run all over us; neither does it tell us to make sure we get our way. Where's the balance? We can only find it moment by moment, case by case, and always in fellowship with the Spirit who leads us. Peace is His plan, not ours. He will help us accomplish it. And He sends us into a world that is fragmented, highly offendable, and ready to rumble, with this mission high on His list of priorities. Let's do everything we can to fulfill it.

ADDITIONAL READING: Mark 9:50

> All men desire peace, but very few desire
> those things that make for peace.
> THOMAS À KEMPIS

By Doing Good

Conquer evil by doing good. Romans 12:21

IN WORD

It may sound like a line from idealistic literature or a kids' movie, but it's nevertheless a radical, countercultural agenda. We don't just attempt to conquer evil. We conquer it—*by doing good.* That means that whatever the prevailing culture of the world throws at us, the way to overcome it is not by lowering ourselves to the same set of standards. We enter into combat with entirely different weapons. Like a gladiator who brings a handshake rather than a sword into the arena, we appear to be headed for disaster. But God has a twist woven throughout this story. He defines "winning" entirely differently than most of the combatants think. The goal isn't to achieve your goal. It's to live with His character.

So all of those people who attempt to get love, wealth, happiness, accomplishments, status, positions, and pleasure in ways that do not reflect God's character may appear to be winning the battle, but they are actually losing it miserably. And those who seem to fall short of success but maintain the character of God are really more successful than everyone else. That's why Scripture can tell us to conquer evil by doing good. Reflecting the character of God is a victory in itself; and it further fuels a cultural revolution that will draw others into His goodness. Many will never come, keeping their eyes focused on a prize that isn't really a prize. But some will, realizing that it's better to walk with integrity in another realm than to dominate this one. Either way, God is honored. His goodness is displayed for others to see.

IN DEED

Keep doing good, no matter how difficult or unrewarding it seems. God has promised that those who persist in goodness will reap its rewards. We always bear fruit according to the kind of seeds we plant—eventually. Suffering from evil is no defeat. Returning evil for evil is. Overcoming it . . . well, that's a radical agenda. And we're promised that it will be a successful one.

ADDITIONAL READING: Galatians 6:7-10

The greatest pleasure I know is to do a good action by
stealth and to have it found out by accident.
CHARLES LAMB

The God Who Laughs

The one who rules in heaven laughs. The Lord scoffs at them. Psalm 2:4

IN WORD

History has been filled with terrifying forces—from ancient empires like Assyria and Babylon to modern-day terrorists and nuclear-armed superpowers, and many in between. There have been times when lesser rulers cowered in fear at the news of invading armies. But no matter how many powers rise up against their enemies, and no matter how many conquerors virtually deify themselves through their conquests, all are subject to God's overarching purposes. In fact, according to His Word, He laughs at their impotence. His enemies are never a match for Him.

We have enemies too, and we would love to be able to laugh at them the way God laughs at His. The problem is that we're small and our opposition is huge. Our obstacles seem insurmountable, our circumstances seem intractable, and the people who stand in our way seem immovable. If we could have God on our side, we could laugh with Him at the smallness of our problems. But when we face adversity, we get intimidated easily. It's bigger than we are. Like the wilderness wanderers who wondered if they could take the Promised Land, or the soldiers in Saul's army, who were paralyzed by Goliath's taunts, we watch our obstacles grow larger and our God seems to become smaller.

IN DEED

This is the opposite of faith. Whatever we focus on usually grows larger in our own minds, and that's a problem when we gaze at our problems. It only produces fear. Instead, we need to gaze at God and allow our faith to grow. Even more than that, we need to realize that He actually *is* on our side, just as we had hoped. Not only is He infinitely larger than any adversity we face, He is faithfully with us and working on our behalf. He is as invested in our journey as we are.

What does that mean for us? It means when we see an obstacle or enemy, it is minuscule compared to God. And it is opposed to Him because it is opposed to one of His children. Therefore, we can laugh. Just like He does.

ADDITIONAL READING: Numbers 14:1-9

There is never a fear that has not a corresponding "fear not."
AMY CARMICHAEL

His Inheritance—and Ours

[The Lord says,] "Only ask, and I will give you the nations as your inheritance, the whole earth as your possession." Psalm 2:8

IN WORD

It's an astounding promise. God, speaking to His Son, doesn't just foretell that the nations will belong to the one true King. He urges the Son to ask for them, as though the giving is contingent on the request. But it's a prayer that is sure to be answered. When the beloved Son, fully in line with the Father's will, prays a prayer that the Father has promised to answer, it's a sure thing. The nations will belong to the Son.

That's a wonderful truth, but what does it have to do with us? Well, before the Son ascended to the throne at the right hand of God, He gave His followers an assignment to make disciples of all nations—not just people among the nations, but entire "nations," or collective groupings of people as a whole. There is a social side of the mission that encompasses much more than each individual. And even though the Son could simply ask the Father, as the messianic promise assures Him, the mission is to include the followers of the Son. That transforms His prayer from "Lord, give Me the nations" to "Lord, give *us* the nations." That's different. And much more encouraging.

IN DEED

Have you ever prayed with that kind of unity with the Son? Perhaps you've prayed for people of all nations to come to Christ, but have you prayed with Him that people of all nations—and whole nations themselves—would be given to "us"? He in us, we in Him, all in the mission together. That unity in prayer with the King Himself adds faith and power to our requests. We aren't praying that we would win nations ourselves, or that God would give the Son the nations. We are praying along with Jesus that we, together with Him, would be inheritors of a Kingdom full of vast nations.

Let that truth shape your vision of where history is leading and fuel your prayers. In the Spirit, we are partners with God in taking territory for Jesus that, according to the prophecy, we will reign over with Him. There is no greater destiny than that.

ADDITIONAL READING: Romans 8:17

The impulse to prayer, within our hearts, is evidence
that Christ is urging our claims in heaven.
AUGUSTUS HOPKINS STRONG

Power in Praise

I will exalt you, my God and King, and praise your name forever and ever.
Psalm 145:1

IN WORD

How do you want to experience God? Your answer may vary depending on your need of the moment. When you need to be rescued, you want to experience Him as the Rescuer. When you need provision, you want to experience Him as Provider. And when you need God's government in your direction, your circumstances, or your relationships, you want to experience Him as King.

How do you do that? One way is to worship the attribute of God you need to experience. When you need provision, for example, the best approach to Him is not to beg for provision but to worship Him as the Provider. So when you need His government in some area of your life, it helps to worship Him as your King. That may sound manipulative, and human nature assures us that manipulation is a genuine temptation. But that's not how God sees it. He shows up in our lives in whatever ways we magnify Him. (We can't make Him larger, of course, but we make Him larger in our own vision. That's what Scripture means when it says to "magnify" or glorify His name, as in Psalm 34:3, ESV.) Praise is often much more powerful than prayer, simply because praise is filled with faith, and prayer very often isn't. When we exalt the King, the King shows His splendor and majesty.

IN DEED

Exalt the Lord, magnify Him, praise and worship Him for all He is and does. But when you have a specific need, build your faith by gazing at His goodness in that area of need. That can be difficult—we tend to focus on our lack rather than on His goodness when we're in trouble—but do it anyway. Your attitude will soon change and your faith will swell, and God responds to faith. He fills our worship with His presence. And the presence of the King is exactly what we need.

ADDITIONAL READING: Psalm 34:1-7

If worship does not change us, it has not been worship.
RICHARD FOSTER

Enduring Goodness

Your kingdom is an everlasting kingdom. You rule throughout all generations.
Psalm 145:13

IN WORD

Every few years in a democracy, the citizenry goes through a transition. Sometimes it's a traumatic transition, and sometimes it goes relatively smoothly. But it always involves debate, an analysis of issues, a search for truth and values, and a good bit of fear. We live in the unknown, never certain about our future and reluctant to leave it in the hands of flawed leaders—the only kind we have. We don't see far enough into the future to feel completely safe.

We don't have much experience with confidence in a government. So even when we're told of the certainty of God's Kingdom and the permanence of its foundation, we have a hard time resting. Am I really secure in this realm? Will I have all I need? Am I going to face overwhelming difficulty? Is this King going to let me down?

If we're honest, we'll admit how freely these questions fill our minds at times. All human beings struggle with trust. The root of every temptation is doubt about God's goodness—wondering whether He is holding out on us or whether He will really come through when we need Him. If we think His goodness might not apply to us personally in an area in which we desperately crave satisfaction, we will be tempted to fulfill our own needs. We have to be able to fully rely on His heart if we want to be safe and secure in His realm.

IN DEED

The good news is that we can. His Kingdom is unshakable. It won't be moved. It doesn't transition every few years to a new leader, nor does anyone need to debate His policies. His Kingdom lasts forever, and its overriding characteristic is the goodness of the King. The answer to our nagging question of whether He will come through for us is yes. He will. In love and power, He establishes not only His realm but the people who inhabit it. We can rest, trust, and believe.

ADDITIONAL READING: Revelation 11:15-19

Trust involves letting go and knowing God will catch you.
JAMES DOBSON

The Family Inheritance

Since we are his children, we are his heirs. In fact, together with Christ we are heirs of God's glory. Romans 8:17

IN WORD

Wealthy people who are generous share a lot of their wealth with their friends. They freely offer their cabins or condos, invite guests to extravagant parties, and help those in particular need. They let their resources overflow to the people around them.

But the children in the family get an entirely different benefit. Children don't get the spillover effects of wealth; they inherit the bulk of it. They don't get the leaves of the tree of resources; they get the roots of it. All that the family owns belongs to the family. The kids don't have to get close to the parents to enjoy the wealth. They are already as close as anyone can get.

That's how God views us in His Kingdom. We may pray for some spillover effects of His wealth—a few blessings and answers to prayer here and there—but His intent is to give us the entire inheritance. Jesus is the Son of the Father, and because of that relationship He inherits everything. All of heaven and earth is His. The kingdoms of the world become the Kingdom of the Christ. He is worthy of every inch of the universe, its material realms as well as its spiritual realms. And because we are related to Him—because we have been adopted into the family through union with Jesus—we are heirs with Him.

IN DEED

It's almost too much to absorb. There is nothing the Son is not worthy to inherit, and while we are not worthy in ourselves, we have been made worthy in Him. Whatever He gets, we get. Whatever He enjoys, we enjoy. Whatever He inherits is also ours. We can hardly imagine such a position, but it's true. God bestows His blessings on His children not as rare gifts but as Kingdom insiders. We are the royal family.

We can access some of those resources now through prayer and faith. And we will experience much more in the fullness of the Kingdom. Let that encourage you. Let it sink in. You are not just a friend. You are in the household. It's all yours.

ADDITIONAL READING: Galatians 4:6-7

> Christ is a jewel worth more than a thousand worlds.
> . . . Get him and get all; miss him and miss all.
> THOMAS BROOKS

Pain and Promise

But if we are to share his glory, we must also share his suffering. Romans 8:17

IN WORD

In some areas of the world, people are flocking into the Kingdom. In many, however, people tend to explore the Christian faith, grab hold of salvation, develop some degree of a personal relationship with God (especially for purposes of prayer and receiving from Him), and carry on with their daily activities as usual. In other words, they major on salvation but not on the Kingdom community. That's a start, but it isn't a Kingdom lifestyle.

Why are many reluctant to immerse themselves in a Kingdom lifestyle? Because that lifestyle involves sacrifice and usually a fair amount of pain. Christianity places no value in suffering for the sake of suffering, but suffering is usually a by-product of our faith. When we enter a new Kingdom, we unavoidably leave one behind. That can be traumatic for us and the people around us. It creates friction between us and the world. We embrace Kingdom ways only at the expense of the ways of the world. That can involve tension or even rejection.

Scripture makes it clear that there is enmity between God and the world—not the created world, but the world systems that run counter to His character. Why wouldn't there be suffering in the Kingdom? In this interim period when the Kingdom is growing in a hostile environment, pain happens. It's part of life in this age.

IN DEED

But pain isn't a permanent part of life. In the age to come, there will be no pain for those with royal blood. Kingdom citizenship will be nothing but blessing, far removed from the vestiges of the curse. But for now, we live in the friction. It isn't easy. We have to be prepared.

Take heart. The foretastes of glory come with a promise of greater glory. God doesn't share His glory with rivals (Isaiah 42:8), but He freely gives it to His own (John 17:22). Our inheritance includes His own radiance within us. And this promise is far greater than any pain in the process.

ADDITIONAL READING: Acts 14:22

Calvary is God's great proof that suffering in
the will of God always leads to glory.
WARREN WIERSBE

Designed for Glory

All creation is waiting eagerly for that future day when God will reveal who his children really are. Romans 8:19

IN WORD

The world is hungry for glory. That's why talent contests are popular on TV, why young kids dream of growing up to be elite athletes, and why we have a fascination with the "stars" in our culture. We use "idol" terminology around this phenomenon, and it's true that much of it is self-serving. But there's also an element of our true identity in it. Deep down, we know we were designed to shine. We were created to be demonstrations of glory.

Every human being was created in the image of God. How could an image-bearer not be shaped for glory? It's embedded in our identity. We have His attributes, or at least the potential for them, and we were made as vessels for His presence. When we are redeemed, born of His Spirit, and re-conformed to His image, we are truly in a position to reflect greatness. The divine seed is planted within us.

This is what all creation is longing to see. The world doesn't consciously have this desire, but millennia of false philosophies and disappointing saviors have sent us practically begging for someone to step into the spotlight with solutions and a connection with the supernatural. That's what God has in mind for us. Even now, and especially as the Kingdom grows into its fullness, the children of God are being revealed. The world will see a kind of human being far different from what it assumed possible.

IN DEED

There's no reason to wait. Why not go ahead and live in a way that confounds observers? We want people to look at us and notice a difference. We want them to think, *Hmmm, that's not normal*—not in a disparaging way but in admiration that God is doing something unusual in us. We want to shine with His glory.

How can we do that? Adopt His attributes. God has given us great and precious promises that allow us to share in His divine nature. Not one day, but now. Never downplay that potential. It isn't necessary. Glory is a now and future inheritance.

ADDITIONAL READING: 2 Peter 1:3-4

The glory of God is man alive, supremely in Christ.
LEON JOSEPH SUENENS

Freedom and Glory

Against its will, all creation was subjected to God's curse. But with eager hope, the creation looks forward to the day when it will join God's children in glorious freedom from death and decay. Romans 8:20-21

IN WORD

Freedom and glory. Few people know either, at least in any deep and meaningful way. Even for those who have political freedom and the glory of stardom, inner issues continue to enslave and degrade. Futility has been an inherent part of the human condition since the Fall. We crave both freedom and glory with every inch of our being, but both are frustratingly elusive.

Life in the Kingdom is an answer to the futility of the ages, an escape from what we thought was the human condition. That frustrating finiteness, those limitations we accepted as "normal," those flaws we embraced as "only human"—all are temporary exceptions to our created design. We were made for so much more.

We won't find much of that promise in common religious teaching. Most religious principles don't liberate us; they confine and enslave us. Most practices and disciplines do more to highlight our futility than they do to empower us for glory. The only way we experience either freedom or glory is by being so thoroughly filled with and saturated with the Spirit of the King that we step into an entirely new state of being. It's a new dimension of living. And it's no longer frustrating and futile.

IN DEED

If you aren't experiencing the state of freedom and glory that is part of your inheritance, ask God for it. Look past religious assumptions and preconceived ideas of what it ought to look like. Go ahead and step into what creation is waiting for. You don't have to wait like the rest of the world does.

That doesn't mean you won't have trials or pain, or that life will immediately become full of joy and absent of sorrow. It does mean, however, that you won't be enslaved by the fallen nature, limited to visible and material dimensions, or shaped by finite restrictions. And you'll know the kind of life the rest of the world is longing for.

ADDITIONAL READING: 2 Corinthians 3:17-18

My chains fell off, my heart was free. I rose,
went forth, and followed Thee.
CHARLES WESLEY

The Rightful King

The kingdom of the world has become the kingdom of our Lord and of his Messiah, and he will reign for ever and ever. Revelation 11:15, *NIV*

IN WORD

According to common Christian belief, the kingdoms of the world will disintegrate in defeat, and the Kingdom of the Lord will rise up and take their place. That's how the end of days is pictured. But that isn't what Scripture tells us. No, the kingdoms of the world—the earthly domains now governed by fallen human beings—will be redeemed and restored to their rightful King. The nations won't lose their identity at the second coming of Christ; they will find their fulfillment in it.

We see a hint of this in the temptation Jesus endured in the wilderness. The adversary gave Him a very real option: He showed Jesus the kingdoms of the world with all their splendor and glory and then offered to give them to Jesus—for a price. Jesus would have to bow down and worship His enemy (Luke 4:5-7). The temptation was real because Jesus came for that purpose—to win the kingdoms of the world. But this devilish shortcut was certainly the wrong means. Nevertheless, the kingdoms were on the heart of the King.

During the temptation, Jesus never denied the glory of the kingdoms. Their glory was real. Like human beings made in the image of God, earthly communities have the potential to reflect divine fellowship. Though they have fallen far short of that goal, they are not irredeemable. If we look, we can see the glory and the potential. We can find something in them desired by God.

IN DEED

Look for the redeemable qualities of your culture. They are there for discerning eyes to see. When you find them, covet them for the Kingdom. Pray, speak, live, and love in ways that bring them into their true identity. Whether you work in education, media, government, business, family, church, or any other sphere of society, you have opportunities to influence your world with Kingdom values and solutions. Let the King come to them *through* you long before He comes *for* you.

ADDITIONAL READING: Luke 4:5-7

Redeeming the culture is the never-ending mission of the church.
CHARLES COLSON

Kingdom Manifesto

. . . to loose the chains of injustice . . . to set the oppressed free . . .
Isaiah 58:6, *NIV*

IN WORD

The best way to find out what a kingdom is like is to look at the heart of the king. What is his vision? What are his values? What does he want to accomplish? What kind of people does he surround himself with? When it comes to the Kingdom of God, we get a glimpse of the answers in numerous sections of Scripture—the inspired book is, after all, the revelation of who God is—and one of the clearest is Isaiah 58.

In this passage, the prophet voices God's manifesto for His people. It's a snapshot of the Kingdom culture, a summary of values that are important to Him. His people have fallen short of the vision, specifically in how they treat the disadvantaged in society. How can God's Kingdom have disadvantaged people? Doesn't His goodness overflow to everyone? Aren't those assigned to represent Him actually supposed to reflect His true nature? Somehow the leaders in His Kingdom forgot. Somehow we do too.

There is no injustice in heaven. There are no oppressed people. If God's Kingdom is to come on earth as it is in heaven—if earth is to reflect His unfallen realm—then someone needs to address the injustices. Someone needs to look out for the oppressed. Someone needs to right the wrongs. Wherever they exist, it isn't His Kingdom.

IN DEED

The prophets voiced this Kingdom culture often. Clearly, justice is important to God. It is not an insignificant theme represented by a few passing comments. No, this is a reflection of God's heart. It is not His will for people to suffer, and especially not for some of His people to oppress others. Injustice is a violation of His nature and His heart. It is a contradiction of the divine character.

Synchronize your heart with God's on this issue. Speak up for those who are unjustly treated. Live with compassion and understanding, even toward those who have put themselves in an unfortunate position. Remember God's mercy toward you and demonstrate it as extravagantly as you can.

ADDITIONAL READING: Luke 18:1-8

> If the Christian tries to spread the good news of salvation through Jesus Christ, he should also join in the fight against social injustice.
> JOHN R. W. STOTT

Kingdom Generosity

. . . to share your food with the hungry and . . . when you see the naked, to clothe them . . . Isaiah 58:7, *NIV*

IN WORD

Imagine visiting a children's home funded and directed by a wealthy benefactor. Most of the children are well clothed, well fed, and well supplied with toys and games. But a few are barefoot, dirty, wearing tattered shirts, bony, and excluded from recreational activities. They are left to fend for themselves, perhaps because they don't quite fit in, or maybe because they haven't behaved as well as the others. Regardless of the reason, the discrepancy is disturbing. It raises all kinds of questions about the benefactor and his staff. And when you find out this was not his intention—that he has provided plenty of resources for everyone—your anger turns toward whomever is squandering the funds. Someone has clearly discriminated against the poor children and violated all sense of goodness. It seems so wrong.

It *is* wrong. That's a picture of how hungry children might appear to an objective observer of God's Kingdom. Surely no one would expect exact equity among every child, but none should be hungry. That doesn't fit the culture of His Kingdom by any-one's definition—except perhaps the privileged children's. To everyone else, it makes no sense.

IN DEED

This is not a political issue best addressed by government policy. It's a spiritual issue that tests the hearts of God's people. As John points out centuries later, the love of God within a person will compel that person to care for the hungry and hurting (1 John 3:17). The absence of that care reflects an absence of the love of God. That's a problem. A big one.

Make it a practice to ask God what's on His heart. He will highlight a variety of expressions of His love, and this will often be one of them. He doesn't want anyone in His Kingdom to be poor, and He wants His Kingdom to extend everywhere. That has huge implications for us. And it compels us to express His love very practically and tangibly.

ADDITIONAL READING: 1 John 3:17

When we turn our backs on the poor, we turn them on Jesus Christ.
MOTHER TERESA

Behind Breakthrough

Then your light will break forth like the dawn. Isaiah 58:8, *NIV*

IN WORD

There's a connection between our willingness to fulfill the desires of God's heart and His willingness to fulfill ours. We may not know how to explain that theologically; it sounds a lot like earning His favor or being rewarded for good behavior. But it's a solidly biblical principle. When mercy and resources stop flowing out from our lives, God's blessings tend to stop flowing in. When we return to the generosity that reflects His nature, He returns to the generosity He demonstrated to us to begin with. He lets our willingness to bless others affect His willingness to bless us.

The truth is that God always wants to break forth like the dawn in our lives. He wants to overflow with His goodness. That's His default attitude toward His people. He doesn't reward us for occasional obedience; He withholds for occasional disobedience. His normal posture is to extend an open hand.

That means that when we experience lack in our lives, it should affect our perception of ourselves rather than affecting our perceptions of Him. He isn't the problem. He may be waiting for us to take on more of His nature, to meet the needs of people in a way that reflects Kingdom values. While we're focused on our believing and receiving, He may be focused on our unwillingness to give. After all, He gave us a promise through Jesus: We will receive according to the measure we use (Luke 6:38). A heart open enough for blessings to flow out is a heart open enough for blessings to flow in.

IN DEED

If you need a breakthrough in your life, this is one place to look. The promise applies not just to ministries of help for the hurting but for every expression of God's compassion and mercy. He wants His Kingdom to be reflected in this world among His people. When we withhold Kingdom benefits from those who need them, He shows us what it's like by withholding some from us. But when we learn to invest in His desires, He's much more inclined to invest in ours.

ADDITIONAL READING: Luke 6:37-38

> Many a man becomes empty-handed because he does not know the fine art of distribution.
> CHARLES SPURGEON

Open Communication

Then you will call, and the LORD will answer; you will cry for help, and he will say: Here am I. Isaiah 58:9, NIV

IN WORD

Every relationship has moments when communication is difficult and other moments when it flows easily. Our relationship with God is no exception. At times, He seems distant. But the Kingdom ideal is for us to experience deep communion, hearing His voice and knowing He hears ours. The Kingdom culture is one of open communication. We were designed to hear and be heard and to draw close to the heart of the King.

Why isn't that always the case? Partly because the Kingdom is still in the process of coming. In that process, we hear the voices of other kingdoms, we get distracted by the busyness of our lives and by other relationships, and if we're completely honest, we sometimes walk out of step with the true Kingdom. The open communication we desire depends on our focus, our attention span, and our willingness to align with Kingdom values and purposes. According to Isaiah, God's responses to our calls often hinge on our return to a Kingdom lifestyle.

That should highly motivate us to eat, drink, and breathe the environment that flows from God's being. He is surrounded by praise, His throne sits on righteousness and justice (Psalm 89:14), and He embodies love, compassion, and mercy. Those are our cues; we can't go wrong by embracing the nature and the desires of God.

IN DEED

Learn to read Scripture, particularly passages like today's verse, in which God expresses His desires for us, not as a collection of dos and don'ts but as a template of Kingdom culture. God is not interested in developing a race of robotic servants. He wants a realm full of people who have adapted to the lifestyle, who have cultivated the mannerisms, the expressions, the values, and the attitudes of the King Himself. His instructions are not directed at our behavior; they are directed at our hearts. When we embrace them as expressions of His heart, His answers flow more freely.

ADDITIONAL READING: Psalm 89:14-18

> Heaven is not a space overhead to which we lift our eyes; it is the background of our existence, the all-encompassing lordship of God within which we stand.
> HELMUT THIELICKE

Satisfied

The LORD will guide you always; he will satisfy your needs in a sun-scorched land and will strengthen your frame. You will be like a well-watered garden, like a spring whose waters never fail. Isaiah 58:11, *NIV*

IN WORD

Most people spend their lives on a relentless search for fulfillment. Many people never find it. There's a wide range of reasons for that, like being self-centered, pursuing empty dreams, developing unworthy attachments, and neglecting or rejecting God's will. The bottom line beneath all dissatisfaction is investing our hearts in something that doesn't matter as much as we thought it did—or in other words, in something less than God. He uses people, places, possessions, and positions to satisfy us, but He never places them above Himself as our ultimate fulfillment. When we are empty and unfulfilled, it's because our hearts have been misdirected.

Here in Isaiah, this misdirection—this seeking after fulfillment in ways we weren't designed for—has caused God's people to neglect others and serve themselves. God would love to satisfy them, but they haven't positioned themselves for it. They have turned their attention away from Him and His ways, pursuing instead their own plans. They have given in to the temptation every human being faces.

IN DEED

God's promise to guide us always, satisfy our needs, strengthen us, and make us like a well-watered garden and an unceasing spring is a description of the *shalom* we all crave. It's the peace and fullness of His Kingdom, but it's offered only to those who accept the Kingdom culture as their own. It's the fulfillment we've all sought—often futilely— and it's an open invitation to His people. This search does not end in disappointment, no matter how many other disappointments we've suffered. It's a promise to every heart that hopes in Him.

ADDITIONAL READING: Isaiah 40:29-31

If a man is not made for God, why is he happy only in God?
If man is made for God, why is he opposed to God?
BLAISE PASCAL

Better than Before

Your people will rebuild the ancient ruins and will raise up the age-old foundations; you will be called Repairer of Broken Walls, Restorer of Streets with Dwellings. Isaiah 58:12, *NIV*

IN WORD

A careful reading of Scripture will show us that God not only longs to redeem us, He wants to restore us too. The church in general has not expressed that message clearly over the centuries, but it's true. God is a repairer at heart.

That means it's okay to pray for missed opportunities to come around again, even if they come around in another form. It's okay to ask for the restoration of things lost. It's vital to seek not only forgiveness but reconciliation, not only healing but health, not only survival but thriving. Just as God promised ancient Israelites that they would return from captivity and prosper—and that the glory of the new Temple would be greater than the glory of the old one (Haggai 2:9)—He wants us to express His best to the world around us. He can make up for years the locusts have eaten (Joel 2:25) and place His people in higher, better places than ever before. He fills us with hope.

Many Christians don't know that. Some think the goal of redemption and restoration is to return us to our pre-fallen state—innocent like Adam and Eve. But God isn't turning back the clock. In His economy, every loss can be followed by a gain that catapults us further than before. Adam was without sin, but he wasn't God. We can have God's own Spirit living within us. Where redeemed human beings end up is far better than where we began. And the new heaven and new earth will far exceed the old ones.

IN DEED

Know the heart of God well enough to hope beyond measure. Place no restraint on your expectations for what He is doing with you and those around you. Participate in the process; seek His restoration everywhere and in everyone. Yes, the process may be hard, but the outcome is more beautiful than you can imagine. Why? Because you and this world are a restoration project, and God is a master craftsman. And you are designed to be like Him.

ADDITIONAL READING: Haggai 2:6-9

When I say "hallowed be thy name; thy kingdom come," I should be adding in my mind the words "in and through me."
J. I. PACKER

Power, Not Posturing

The Kingdom of God is not just a lot of talk; it is living by God's power.
1 Corinthians 4:20

IN WORD

Paul had already reminded his readers in Corinth of his attitude when he came. He preached words not of human wisdom but of demonstrable power (1 Corinthians 2:4). Why? Because the message of the Kingdom is not a matter of talk. It's a matter of experience, of change, of the Spirit actually at work in people's lives. So as he confronts the "all talk" people in this letter, he states this truth again: At its core, the Kingdom life is a powerful one. It is not simply a different lens for looking at the world, a message of encouragement for the discouraged, or theological explanation of atonement. It *is* all those things, but it's more. It's a life fueled by the infinite Spirit flourishing within us.

If the gospel of the Kingdom isn't practical—something we can experience moment by moment—then it isn't the good news we were looking for. That's the conclusion many have come to, usually subconsciously. Plenty of Christians have given up on the gospel's power, accepting it as a belief system but then looking elsewhere for practical help with daily life. But the Spirit of the Kingdom is available for insights, wisdom, miracles, breakthroughs, comfort, direction, and more. We can't systematize His work or explain exactly when, where, and how He works, but we can emphatically decide that He does. And when we do—when we believe and ask and pursue—He leads us into a quality of life that surpasses whatever we have experienced before.

IN DEED

Does that mean constant success and the end of hardships? Of course not. But it does mean we can truly overcome and receive real solutions to the obstacles and problems of life. We can never be content with a faith that consists of nothing more than words; we must relentlessly go after the Spirit's power wherever and however He offers it. He did not come into this world so we could have great conversations; He came so we could have real life in all its fullness.

ADDITIONAL READING: 1 Corinthians 2:1-5

The same power that brought Christ back from the dead is operative within those who are Christ's. The resurrection is an ongoing thing.
LEON MORRIS

One Direction

Anyone who puts a hand to the plow and then looks back is not fit for the Kingdom of God. Luke 9:62

IN WORD

Few invitations lead with warnings of the difficulties involved, but Jesus was always realistic with potential followers. The Kingdom is not for people who want a comfortable, easy life. It's for people who want a meaningful life anchored in truth. And to pursue that kind of life necessarily involves coming up against all its contradictions, both internal and external, many of them hostile. So the follower of this King should be prepared for some hardships, free from distracting obligations, and clearly focused on the goal. Looking back is not an option.

Jesus presented a picture to make His point. A farmer doesn't pull the plow; the ox handles that. The farmer guides the plow, and the only way to guide something in a straight line is to look forward while doing it. If the farmer turns around and looks behind, the furrow will be crooked. That's not the best way to work a field. The farmer won't cease to be a farmer; he just won't be a very good one. He'll need to learn his craft a little better to really be fit for the job.

Jesus isn't telling potential followers, "Suffer hardship or don't bother coming at all." But to experience Kingdom life the way we are designed to experience it, we'll have to be single-minded about it. The Kingdom isn't about what already happened; it's about what is to come. And we'll need to keep our eyes looking ahead if we want to see it well.

IN DEED

Too many Christians are weighed down by the things in their past—or by the peripherals and distractions going on around them. Focus forward, diligently looking to see what God is doing and how you can be a part of it. Know that it requires constant attention and may involve hardship. Those who are looking for a comfortable life will find the Kingdom uncomfortable for now. But when you gaze into God's plan, everything else fades into the background. Focus brings clarity. And it brings the Kingdom into view.

ADDITIONAL READING: Philippians 3:12-14

> Give me a person who says, "This one thing I do,"
> and not "These fifty things I dabble in."
> D. L. MOODY

Worth the Price

We pleaded with you, encouraged you, and urged you to live your lives in a way that God would consider worthy. For he called you to share in his Kingdom and glory. 1 Thessalonians 2:12

IN WORD
Nothing in the gospel tells us to be worthy of the Kingdom. In fact, it tells us just the opposite—that none are righteous, none deserve grace and mercy (which by definition can't be earned), and only Jesus can accomplish what we need. But that isn't what Paul is talking about in this passage. He isn't telling his readers to be worthy of their inheritance in the Kingdom. He is urging them, since they have already received Kingdom citizenship, to actually live like Kingdom citizens.

This isn't a surprising statement, is it? People hired at a company are told to live in a way that reflects the company's interests. Athletes who play for a team are to embrace the standards of the team. Immigrants who become citizens are urged to uphold the laws of the land and learn its language and culture. Adopted children are to take on the name and the ethos of their new family. Why would Kingdom citizens be any different? Having been taken into the Kingdom of light, we are to live as enlightened people. If we are to share in God's Kingdom and glory, we need to live the role of heirs of such enormous privileges. We become what we have been called.

IN DEED
Never strain to become worthy of God's favor as though you could earn it. But always grow into the privilege bestowed on you. Live not as one who earns but as one who embraces what has been given. You've been given new clothes, so wear them. You've been given a new name, so use it well and represent it honorably. You've been given the keys of a Kingdom, so carry them with the intentions of the King in mind. Whatever gifts are included in the gospel, refuse to squander them. Instead, embody them. Prove that it was worth it to God to give them to you.

ADDITIONAL READING: Titus 2:11-14

The destined end of man is not happiness, nor health, but holiness. God's one aim is the production of saints.
OSWALD CHAMBERS

The Substance of Heaven

The people believed Philip's message of Good News concerning the Kingdom of God and the name of Jesus Christ. Acts 8:12

IN WORD

It was essentially a spiritual showdown, though neither participant would have categorized it that way. On one side was Simon, a magician who had amazed people for years with his unexplainable phenomena. On the other was Philip, a believer in the Jewish Messiah who preached a powerful message accompanied by miracles. Philip's combination of message-plus-miracles was apparently more impressive than Simon's feats, even though Simon had a reputation for being "the Power of God." The crowds were drawn to Philip, and even Simon was impressed enough to believe. In this spiritual showdown, the Holy Spirit won.

Clearly, the Kingdom message Philip preached was not just a philosophy or a worldview. Philosophies and worldviews don't match up well against paranormal signs. People are always drawn to evidence over ideas. They believed Philip's message about the Kingdom because it was accompanied by evidence of power over the world and over other spirits. It was a taste of heaven on earth.

That's what the Kingdom message is all about, isn't it? The prayer Jesus gave His followers was toward that specific end—that God's will and His Kingdom would come on earth as they were already being experienced in heaven. When Philip preached, people encountered the environment of heaven, and they were drawn to it.

IN DEED

The Kingdom message cannot be preached as an idea; it has to carry some substance of heaven with it. If people do not experience freedom, newness, hope, meaning, deliverance, healing, and wholeness along with the message, then they haven't heard Kingdom truth. In whatever we say about the Kingdom, people need to encounter the power of God in it. That's what brings them into it.

Make that your goal—to speak words that are so filled with Kingdom life that people encounter God when they hear them. Let your words be filled with hope, truth, freedom, healing, and more. Wherever you go on earth, give them a taste of heaven.

ADDITIONAL READING: Acts 5:12-16

I would not be Christian but for the miracles.
AUGUSTINE OF HIPPO

Random Acts of Blessing

[God said,] "Whenever Aaron and his sons bless the people of Israel in my name, I myself will bless them." Numbers 6:27

IN WORD

"May the LORD . . ." Three phrases begin this way in the blessing God gave Aaron to say over Israel. The blessing invokes God's protection, pleasure, grace, favor, and peace. It is an expression of His goodness on the people in general and on whomever the priest might specifically choose. The priest could speak it "whenever"—no limits, no specific events, no regulations. It was a benedictory free-for-all. And God promised to honor these words.

We might see such a blessing as a nice thought or best wishes, a pleasantry in conversation that may or may not carry any weight. But in God's economy, words of blessing are concrete, the currency of actual experience. They are the powerful answer to a world that lies under a curse, drawing God's favor both to the blesser and the blessed. They bring heaven to earth. According to God, they are profoundly effective.

How often do we take advantage of this powerful Kingdom privilege? Human nature prompts us to withhold blessing from those we disagree with, those who offend us, or those we simply don't know very well. We want to bless those we love. But freely and indiscriminately? We're much more reserved with our goodwill. We want to know who we're dealing with. We can be very discriminating in our blessings.

IN DEED

God uses the blessings of His priests—all who love and serve Him in the power of His Spirit—to step into lives. For whatever reason, He generally intervenes in this world to the degree we ask Him to. Blessings are an open invitation for Him to step in and target the people who need Him most. Why would we withhold that from anyone?

Make it a point to bless people—as they pass by you on the street, pull in front of you in traffic, carry out their business all around you, wherever. Whether they hear it or not isn't the point; God does. He will honor your words, build His Kingdom, and change lives. Including yours.

ADDITIONAL READING: Numbers 23:20

Words that do not give the light of Christ increase the darkness.
MOTHER TERESA

The Re-Genesis

Just as everyone dies because we all belong to Adam, everyone who belongs
to Christ will be given new life. But there is an order to this resurrection:
Christ was raised as the first of the harvest; then all who belong to Christ will
be raised when he comes back. 1 Corinthians 15:22-23

IN WORD

When the first humans relinquished their divine privilege of governing the world with God, they invited a host of side effects into this world. The worst of these is death, a horrific, unnatural characteristic of the unKingdom. The image-bearers, the icons of God, cut themselves off from life through their treason in Eden. Only a miracle, some kind of re-genesis, could restore true, lasting life to the walking dead.

That's exactly why Jesus came—to effect a re-genesis, a new creation. He promised abundant life to those who come to Him in faith, and He breathed His Spirit into His disciples before He left them, just as the Father had breathed life into dust in Eden and brought a man to life. The exact icon of God came to fulfill our original assignment, and then He died our death in order for us to be filled with His life. It was an unforeseeable restoration, though prophets had hinted at it and forecast its coming. The one died and was raised for many so that the many might live in Him.

We dare not reduce this life to a spirit-only disembodied existence. The resurrection of Jesus, the second Adam, was thoroughly physical. Our resurrection could not possibly be "less than." The firstfruits are not different fruits. They are simply first. We will be raised just as He was raised.

IN DEED

Imagine that. This Kingdom will be filled with bodies that long ago walked this earth and then died. The God who created every atom in the universe certainly knows how to reconstruct a physical body, and He will do it according to our original glory, adding the glory of Jesus' resurrected body to the design. The aches and pains will be gone. The inconvenience of physical setbacks and needs will become irrelevant. And death will be no more. Live in that hope, fully expecting the comprehensive restoration of the genesis to come.

ADDITIONAL READING: 1 Thessalonians 4:13-18

The seed dies into a new life, and so does man.
GEORGE MACDONALD

We Win

After that the end will come, when he will turn the Kingdom over to
God the Father, having destroyed every ruler and authority and power.
1 Corinthians 15:24

IN WORD

Paul pictures Jesus ruling His Kingdom, destroying all opposition, and then handing the Kingdom over to the Father. We may not understand all the implications of that—Revelation 11:15 is pretty clear that Jesus will reign forever, and Revelation 22:3-6 is just as clear that His saints will reign with Him forever. But in this Kingdom, power struggles are never an issue. He reigns, we reign, the reign is handed over to the Father . . . however it works, we win. The good side is victorious. The Kingdom ends up completely in the right hands and shared among all interested parties.

Knowing the end of the story may not seem all that significant when we're having a hard day, but it is. Looking forward to that end means we never completely lose hope, never have a reason to say things just aren't going to get better. Knowing the future outcome sustains us in present trials.

A lot of Christians need to keep that perspective. Many fret and worry about the direction of the world, lamenting how things are getting worse and worse, certain that believers are going to end up losing the battle until Jesus comes to rescue us from it. But that's not how this story plays out. In light of His promises to be with us and empower us, suggesting that the people of God lose the battle is tantamount to saying God Himself loses the battle. It's an absurd thought. Jesus comes back to greet His victorious bride, not His defeated servants.

IN DEED

Live from that sense of victory today. Embrace a hopeful view of the end times. Yes, there will be trials, but they will not overcome us. We overcome them. Evil is undone by the power of Jesus in the people who are filled with His Spirit. We have no reason to lament this story or even the daily grind. The Kingdom ends up in the right hands. And we'll have forever to celebrate it.

ADDITIONAL READING: Revelation 11:15

You can fight with confidence where you are sure of victory. With Christ and for Christ, victory is certain.
BERNARD OF CLAIRVAUX

Forever Reign

Christ must reign until he humbles all his enemies beneath his feet.
1 Corinthians 15:25

IN WORD

Paul is referring to Psalm 110:1, a verse often quoted in the New Testament. But wherever the psalm tells us that Jesus will sit at God's right hand until God puts His enemies under Jesus' feet, Paul says that Jesus must reign until He puts His enemies under His feet. And the verse prior to this one says the end will come after Jesus has destroyed all dominion, authority, and power—the time when many of us think His reign begins.

How do we make sense of these verses? One common view of the end times has Jesus coming back (not sitting at the Father's right hand) in order to put His enemies under His feet. And those who hold this view often see Christians losing the battle in this world until Jesus comes back to rescue them. From what we can discern from the cues in Scripture, it seems that Jesus is reigning with the Father now. He will come back after His enemies have been put under His feet, *and* He is coming in order to put His enemies under His feet—perhaps with more finality and visibility. Though Paul says He will reign "until," we know from Revelation that He will reign forever and ever. There will be no end.

IN DEED

Figuring out the end times can be confusing. So it's a good thing Scripture never tells us to figure it all out. It tells us essentials—that Jesus is King, that He reigns not only *for* His people but *through* His people, and that even though He already reigns, He is coming to reign forever. We're part of His reign now; we have authority over His enemies even now and can participate in putting them under His feet (Luke 10:19). And we will be part of it then, as we will reign with Him as kings and priests (Revelation 1:5; 5:10). Whether or not we fully understand the order of things, we know His reign is in heaven and on earth, both now and forever, and we are active in it in both realms and for all time. It's worth getting up in the morning for that. And it can influence the attitudes and actions we carry into each day.

ADDITIONAL READING: Luke 10:17-19

Until that time, we are under orders from the
King of kings to proclaim His message.
BILLY GRAHAM

Hang On to Hope

We want you to know what will happen . . . so you will not grieve like people who have no hope. 1 Thessalonians 4:13

IN WORD

Death is indeed a fact of life in this world, and it's certainly worth grieving. Death doesn't belong in the Kingdom picture. We instinctively know it's not right, it's not our original design, and it must be overcome. It's enemy number one.

So we grieve whenever we come face to face with death, but we don't grieve like others do. Much of the world either dreads the end or refuses to spend much time seriously thinking about it. And when it comes, they grieve the loss of life rather than celebrating the life that was lived. Why? Because apart from the promise of eternal life, the world is left with nothing better than wishful thinking about a vague afterlife. That isn't a solid hope. We have something much better.

We have hope. Real, concrete hope. In English, "hope" has a range of meanings, and we use it casually—as in "I hope it doesn't rain today" or "I hope things get better soon." That kind of hope is the wishful thinking the world has about death. They hope it isn't final. But biblical hope is different. It's present enjoyment of a future reality, an active looking forward to what we know to be true. It isn't hypothetical or vague. It's the truth of the future in our hearts today.

IN DEED

Whatever it takes, cultivate hope. In any trial, setback, adversity, opposition, or anything else that comes against you or brings you down, find something positive about it or envision what good might come from it. That doesn't mean you should deny real feelings or deny the hardships, but neither should you honor evil with your words and expectations. God is bigger and better than any circumstance. He always has a redemptive plan for every situation we find ourselves in. There is no problem for which He does not already have a solution—including the problem of death. Find His promise and purpose in *everything*. And hang on to hope against everything that tries to steal it from you.

ADDITIONAL READING: Romans 4:18-21

If you do not hope, you do not find out what is beyond your hopes.
CLEMENT OF ALEXANDRIA

Reunion in the Air

Together with them, we who are still alive and remain on the earth will be caught up in the clouds to meet the Lord in the air. Then we will be with the Lord forever. 1 Thessalonians 4:17

IN WORD

In the ancient Near East, as well as many other cultures throughout history, victorious kings would return to their home cities after a battle, bringing captives with them. The citizens would come out of the city to greet the returning army and the conquering king. And the entire entourage would return with the king into the city for him to continue his reign.

That may be the picture Paul gives us in 1 Thessalonians 4:17. Many assume that we meet the returning King in the air and then go off with Him into heaven, but in light of other passages that show Him reigning on earth, the more accurate picture may be of our meeting Him in the air and returning with Him into the "city" where He will continue His reign. Regardless, we know He will reign and we will be with Him forever. The location isn't the big issue, since He will reign over everything everywhere. Our union "with Him" is infinitely more important. We who are alive—those in whom He now lives but whose eyes cannot see clearly—will see Him clearly. Everything that was evil in this world will be undone, even death.

IN DEED

That basic truth of Christianity may not impress those of us who are looking for deeper truths in Scripture today, but when someone close to us dies, there's nothing deeper we need to hear. This is it, the ultimate comfort, the hope that keeps us going in a death-filled world. That's why Paul's next sentence urges us to encourage one another with these words. At any given moment, we can face existential questions of life, death, and meaning that overwhelm all our other questions. When we do, we need to know: Not only is He coming, He is coming to reign. And we will be with Him forever.

ADDITIONAL READING: Ephesians 4:7-8

Our Lord has written the promise of resurrection not in books alone but in every leaf in springtime.
MARTIN LUTHER

Kingdom Style

In this world the kings and great men lord it over their people. . . . But among you it will be different. Luke 22:25-26

IN WORD

Imagine being in a classroom and hearing your teacher explain what presidential authority is like—as though the information was vital for you to know. Would you wonder why he felt it necessary to prepare you for a position few people ever hold? Would you think he was out of his mind? Why would you need to know the demands of the presidency unless you were actually going to be president?

On the night before He was crucified, Jesus had a last meal with His followers and gave them some final instructions. One of the more surprising instructions—and quite a bit of what He said was surprising—began with this statement. "This is what authority is like in the Gentile world," He essentially told them, "but that isn't how authority works in My Kingdom." The words may seem familiar to readers of the Bible, but have you considered the implications? Why is Jesus telling former fishermen and other assorted commoners what kingship is like?

Because they are going to have authority in His Kingdom. Some of them already suspect so; they have asked to sit at His right and His left. But they don't know what kind of Kingdom this will be, and they certainly don't understand their role in it. They still have no real sense of the Kingdom culture. Even so, they are being prepared to rule—at least by the King's definition of ruling.

IN DEED

How does a king or a ruler in the Kingdom of God act? Not with unyielding, overbearing authority. Not with unreasonable or self-serving demands. Not like the rulers of the world do. No, that's not the King's style, and it can't be the style of the agents who govern under Him. He rules for the sake of others, serving and meeting needs. His greatness is seen in His willingness to not act great.

ADDITIONAL READING: Psalm 89:14-19

Unless a life is lived for others, it is not worthwhile.
MOTHER TERESA

Line of Succession

[Jesus said,] "You are those who have stood by me in my trials. And I confer on you a kingdom, just as my Father conferred one on me." Luke 22:28-29, NIV

IN WORD

Most Christians are humbly reluctant to see their role in the Kingdom as significant. "It's all Him," we say. And there's truth to that. As He told His followers, they can do nothing without Him (John 15:5). But He didn't say they have no importance, that they have no role in His Kingdom, or that they have no authority in that role. He did not call them meek and lowly servants who should never assume anything more than that they were sinners saved by grace. No, He elevated them to the status of friends and conferred on them a Kingdom. Like a prince going away on a journey, He gathered His closest loyal partners around Him and gave them royal responsibilities.

The fascinating line in this verse is about *how* this Kingdom is being conferred: "just as my Father conferred one on me." Not something less than the Father's gift to the Son, not a responsibility more suited to a mere employee, but "in the same way as" His Father handed the Kingdom over to Him. We can hardly believe Jesus would entrust such a treasure to this group of followers, but He did anyway. And that begs a startling question: Did He also hand it over to us?

He must have. The first group of disciples is no longer around to manage Kingdom affairs. It's true that they have a special role in sitting on thrones and judging the twelve tribes of Israel, as verse 30 tells us, but the Kingdom is handed down to every successive generation of royal stewards. That's us. We have a huge role to play.

IN DEED

Don't take that role lightly. Let it shape your priorities, your goals in life, your relationships now and forever, and even your moment-by-moment interactions and activities. Your words matter. Your decisions matter. Your attitudes matter. Everything in your life is now Kingdom business. The Prince has said so. The Kingdom given to Him by the Father is, in very significant ways, in your hands.

ADDITIONAL READING: 1 Peter 2:9-10

The price of greatness is responsibility.
WINSTON CHURCHILL

Goodness Manifested

Suppose . . . you say, "Good-bye and have a good day; stay warm and eat well"—but then you don't give that person any food or clothing. What good does that do? James 2:15-16

IN WORD

Countless Christian teachers have made the mistake of limiting the gospel of the Kingdom to "spiritual" matters. It's true that the spiritual realm is the source of all else, and therefore that's where salvation begins. But it certainly doesn't end there. If it did, Scripture would not promise us a bodily resurrection; Jesus would not have demonstrated the Kingdom with physical healing and miraculous multiplication of food; the prophets would never have addressed issues like injustice, loneliness, brokenheartedness, poverty, and disease; and the city of God in Revelation wouldn't have physical dimensions. But as we know, the resurrection is physical, Jesus' miracles were tangible, the prophets focused on daily concerns that were visible, and the city of God has streets of gold and light and all sorts of visual manifestations. The Kingdom is not about disembodied spirits floating around in heaven. It's about life that's more real, more concrete, and more practical than we've ever known it to be.

That's why James, for one example among many, emphasizes the actions of faith. Good theology is not a picture of the Kingdom. Practical kindness and provision are. Wisdom and understanding are certainly part of the Kingdom, but they have to be applied in order to mean something. The spiritual realm has enormous practical implications.

IN DEED

Don't get caught up in "spirit only" thinking. The Kingdom isn't an ethereal idea, it's a manifestation of the King's goodness. Telling someone to be warm and filled may be a Kingdom desire, but it isn't a Kingdom expression. Warming and feeding someone . . . well, that's what the Kingdom looks like. The realm of God is comprehensive. And we have every right—and even the obligation—to apply it to every area of life.

ADDITIONAL READING: 1 John 3:18

God's goodness is the root of all goodness; and our goodness, if we have any, springs out of His goodness.
WILLIAM TYNDALE

Kingdom Works

Faith by itself isn't enough. Unless it produces good deeds, it is dead and useless. James 2:17

IN WORD

Jesus was—and still is—a man of action. He certainly knew His way around a theological discussion, but His teaching was more than theory. He did things. Lots of them. Out in the open. He broke through in this world not with a new philosophy or religion but with a way of life. Divine works flowed through Him.

That's our model. We have been given a Kingdom of action, not a Kingdom of ideas, theories, and good theology. There's nothing wrong with seeking understanding, but understanding isn't enough. Neither is "faith" in the sense of simply believing the right things intellectually. If we are to be royal stewards of the divine will, we will be very active people. That's the Kingdom culture.

God often bears more fruit through zealous believers who have great faith and sloppy theology than He does through believers with precise doctrine and lots of reasons to be cautious. That's because the zealous believers with sloppy theology are more open to seeing God work in unconventional ways—His specialty—while the fastidious theologians are intent on defining how God might do things. Adventurers in faith have no desire to limit Him and deep desires to see His works in action.

IN DEED

There is no shortage of people in this world who talk the talk. In the age of social media, when everyone has a platform and plenty of words to fill it with, opinions are flying around everywhere. But God hasn't conferred on us a Kingdom of opinions. He has given us a Kingdom of power and works. Yes, there are words, but they are not empty ones. They carry weight and accomplish things. Everything about His Kingdom is meaningful and substantial. And those who live in His ways will always be intent on accomplishing His works.

ADDITIONAL READING: Matthew 5:14-16

> Do all the good you can by all the means you can, in all the ways you can, to all the people you can, in all the places you can, as long as ever you can.
> JOHN WESLEY

From the Heart

The Kingdom of God is not a matter of what we eat or drink, but of living a life of goodness and peace and joy in the Holy Spirit. Romans 14:17

IN WORD

Nearly all religions, including Christianity, tend to develop rules to guide behavior and practices. We forget that if we are living from a truly transformed heart, rules are unnecessary; and if rules are necessary, the problem is with the heart, not the behavior. The Spirit in us yearns to change us to the degree that we can simply be ourselves—our true selves—without having to be conscious of "oughts" and "shoulds." When we are truly transformed, we can act naturally and be who we were designed to be.

The problem is that we are in a process of transformation. Sometimes the heart, not yet fully changed, needs to be told what to do. So we develop disciplines and structures and habits, not from within but from external commands and constraints. And slowly, imperceptibly, these external structures become permanent rather than temporary. They form the basis of our lives. We cease to live by the Spirit, by Christ in us, and rely on rules.

Paul reminds us that the Kingdom of God is not a matter of eating and drinking—or any other external, behavioral guideline. Sure, the Spirit in us will impact every area of our lives, but by transforming our nature rather than disciplining our behavior. The Kingdom of God produces deeply internal righteousness, peace, and joy that work their way outward into other aspects of our lives. But it all begins within.

IN DEED

If following Jesus is a constant effort of training yourself in the right behavior, shift your focus instead to your heart—or rather to the Spirit, asking Him to transform your heart. Jesus didn't come to make us better people; He came to make us new people. If He is genuinely in our hearts, we can live from our hearts. We can be filled up with truth, peace, and joy—the attributes of the Kingdom—and let them overflow.

ADDITIONAL READING: Galatians 5:22-23

Those in whom the Spirit comes to live are God's new Temple.
They are . . . places where heaven and earth meet.
N. T. WRIGHT

Justice and Favor

Give your love of justice to the king, O God, and righteousness to the king's son. Psalm 72:1

IN WORD

Psalm 72 is more than a prayer for a king. It's a picture of Israel's hopes. It speaks of justice and righteousness, prosperity and blessing, honor and glory. It's the *shalom*—the wholeness and fullness and peace—that every human heart longs for. The people's expectations for their king, and therefore their kingdom, looked a lot like this.

It begins with justice. When we speak of God's judgment, we often have in mind His eternal decrees against sin, a spiritual and cosmic settling of accounts. But there's another kind of justice in Scripture that is purely focused on society and its problems. It involves human governments and social dynamics. It isn't about the last day; it's about today. The Bible's common calls for justice—whether exercised by governing authorities or by God—are about establishing justice *for* the oppressed, not about establishing justice *against* the oppressor. It's a call for mercy.

Any Christian who doesn't take this call seriously doesn't understand the Kingdom of God. We can't ignore justice issues in this age and simply long for the day when God will make everything right. If He wants things to be right, He wants us to help make them so now. We won't get it done perfectly; Jesus said the poor will always be with us. But He never said that's an excuse not to meet the needs of the poor. God expresses profound concern for those who are at the bottom of society.

IN DEED

If we are to be Kingdom people, we need the King's heart. And if we want to see a picture of the King's heart, Psalm 72 is a powerful one. It echoes the prophecy from Isaiah 66:1-2 that Jesus quoted in Luke 4:18—God anointed Him to preach good news to the poor, release captives, give sight to the blind, and declare the Lord's favor. Kingdom people are advocates of favor for all who need to see the kind heart of God. Before we ever even think of His judgments, we are to declare His justice—His support for those in need. We demonstrate the Kingdom by demonstrating the heart of the King.

ADDITIONAL READING: Luke 4:16-21

Justice is the foundation of kingdoms.
LATIN PROVERB

Fruit of Righteousness

May the mountains yield prosperity for all, and may the hills be fruitful.
Psalm 72:3

IN WORD

God loves righteousness and justice for their own sakes. They represent His nature and are a comfort to His people. But they go further than that. They have ripple effects. When righteousness and justice are expressed in the land, the land bears fruit in greater measure.

That's what this psalm—and many Scriptures—tell us emphatically. We don't like to think of a cause-and-effect relationship between our sin and the land's fruitlessness, but there seems to be a solid connection in God's Word. The rest of this psalm spells it out—the righteous flourish, prosperity abounds, grain grows, and crops thrive (verses 7 and 16). God promises blessing to groups of people who line up with His nature.

Does this mean trials, tribulations, and suffering are always the result of some sin on our part? Of course not. The righteous often suffer in this world simply because they live in a fallen world. It does mean, however, that eventually and increasingly, aligning with God's nature has benefits for communities and cities and countries. We don't earn His favor, but we can certainly position ourselves to receive it. He loves to support those who seek His Kingdom.

IN DEED

This is no license for legalism. It's entirely possible to conform outwardly to the letter of the law and have a heart that's far from God. No, this is about seeking His Kingdom above all else, internally and externally. When the King's heart beats within us, especially at a corporate level, blessings follow. Why? Because those who become *like* Him also become a vessel *for* Him. He rides into our world on the roads we establish in our hearts. He responds to faith. He calls His royal children to welcome the ways of their Father.

Be a Kingdom person in your community. Bless. Serve. Demonstrate righteousness—not judgmental moralism but the merciful heart of the King. See what God does. Sooner or later, there will be fruit.

ADDITIONAL READING: Isaiah 55:12

> When Christians stand up for righteousness and justice,
> they evidence the power of the living God.
> CHARLES COLSON

The God Who Crushes

Help him to defend the poor, to rescue the children of the needy, and to crush their oppressors. Psalm 72:4

IN WORD

Some passages of Scripture disturb us. They call for judgment against enemies—something Jesus emphatically did not do even while He was being condemned and crucified. Old Testament prophets write of vengeance, and psalmists pray for the punishment of those who hurt them. These aren't dominant themes in Scripture, of course, but they are there. And they don't seem very merciful.

God is merciful, to be sure. But in His mercy, He opposes evil. We would do the same, reacting harshly to anyone who threatened our spouses or children. When people we love are being harmed, we do whatever it takes to stop the one who harms—not because we are aggressive but because we defend. Likewise, God doesn't crush enemies because He is full of hate; He crushes them because He is full of love.

Later verses in the psalm make this clear. This picture of a good king and a fulfilled kingdom takes a hard line against injustice. Neither the king's purpose nor God's is to crush; it's to deliver the needy, take pity on the weak, and rescue the oppressed and afflicted (verses 12-14). When the time is right, He takes decisive action against evil forces. That's what His Kingdom is like.

IN DEED

Kingdom people should be filled with a fiery attitude against evil—not a preachy "thou shalt not" at every hint of misbehavior, but active defense of the defenseless. It isn't our job to crush the oppressor—God tells us to leave vengeance to Him (Deuteronomy 32:35; Romans 12:19). We are to be merciful. But in our mercy toward those who suffer injustice, we can't afford to be passive toward those who inflict it. Being quiet in the face of evil is tantamount to aiding and abetting the enemy. In most kingdoms, that's treason. In God's, it's a forgivable offense that needs to be corrected. We need to remember who we are: representatives of the King in a hostile environment. Seek to make things right.

ADDITIONAL READING: Luke 18:6-8

> Silence in the face of evil is itself evil. . . . Not to speak is to speak; not to act is to act.
> DIETRICH BONHOEFFER

The God Who Refreshes

May the king's rule be refreshing like spring rain on freshly cut grass, like the showers that water the earth. Psalm 72:6

IN WORD

We long for seasons of refreshing. Life has a way of taking us into dry deserts, dark forests, and dangerous mountain paths. Those parts of the journey sometimes give us a sense of adventure, but when they drag on, we need relief. The good news of the Kingdom is that God promises it. The picture of God's realm in Psalm 72 includes a gentle rain that refreshes us and leads to a harvest.

Sometimes those dry deserts and dangerous places are our own fault. We wander into them either by passive negligence of God's purposes or active rebellion against them. Our own guilt tells us we have to put up with the consequences; we've made our bed, so now we have to lie in it. But while there are consequences to sin, we belong to a God who is truly merciful. The seasons of refreshing aren't only for those who have innocently endured a hard time; they are for *everyone* who has endured a hard time. He doesn't leave us in the desert, even if we walked away from Him to get there. He listens to our cries for relief.

God's Kingdom is in some sense a restoration of Eden, or at least of Eden's satisfying, fulfilling blessings. One day we will fully experience these blessings, but even now we get to taste many of them. Weary souls can have their strength renewed; we can "mount up with wings like eagles" (Isaiah 40:31, ESV). We can know that the hard seasons of life are temporary.

IN DEED

In your longings for the Kingdom, don't be afraid to ask God for seasons of refreshing—for the dews and gentle rains of His love to fall on you and bring new growth. Not all of life is a problem to endure; much of it is a blessing to enjoy. If the blessings ever begin to seem few and far between, ask Him for relief. Open your heart to receive His touch and His promise. Let His rains refresh you.

ADDITIONAL READING: Acts 3:19-20

Encouragement is the oxygen of the soul.
ANONYMOUS

The God Who Wins

All kings will bow before him, and all nations will serve him. Psalm 72:11

IN WORD

In this psalm, the desire for all nations to honor the king is in the form of a blessing. In Psalm 2, it's in the form of a prophetic prayer request (2:8). But in Philippians, it's a certain fact (2:9-11); and in Revelation, it's a completed picture (5:13). What begins with human implications for a human king takes on divine overtones for the King of kings. The Son will receive the worship of the nations because He is the guaranteed victor over humanity's rebellion.

His victory is no brutal beat-down. Unlike the rulers of our age who win their battles with decisive force, our King has quashed earth's rebellion with kindness and love. His victory over all the forces of evil in both visible and invisible realms is complete and final. When history ends, He will be the undisputed champion. And the whole earth will be filled with His glory.

That's important to know when you feel defeated. No matter how overwhelmed you feel by evil, opposition, oppression, discouragement, or futility, you are a member of the winning team as a child of the King. You may wonder why His victory isn't manifesting in your life at the moment. There are plenty of reasons for that, not the least of which is that He is teaching you to overcome in His strength. But regardless of your questions, victory is certain.

IN DEED

If you're struggling today, remind yourself that you're on God's winning team. You serve a victorious God who gives you access to His weapons for victory. Learning to wield them may be a painful process that requires patient endurance and faith, but those enduring, trusting investments of your heart will not go unrewarded. Faith and patience always lead to some kind of blessing, and overcomers in the Kingdom grow stronger in each battle. The end result isn't just a victory *for* the King; it's a victory *with* the King. Through His grace and generosity, His throne, His reign, and His spoils of war are yours.

ADDITIONAL READING: Revelation 2:26; 3:21

> God is never defeated. Though He may be opposed, attacked,
> and resisted, the ultimate outcome can never be in doubt.
> BROTHER ANDREW

The Good Harvest

The harvest is great, but the workers are few. So pray to the Lord who is in charge of the harvest; ask him to send more workers into his fields. Luke 10:2

IN WORD
In this world, expansionist kingdoms are frowned upon. That's because they usually expand by coercion against the will of the people. They conquer and control. They intimidate. They take what doesn't rightfully belong to them.

Not so with God's Kingdom. He sent His Son into this world to reclaim what was lost, to restore what was broken, to release what was held captive, to re-create what was destroyed. He conquers with kindness and pursues with winsome affection. He chooses influence over control, invitation over intimidation, and cooperation over forced compliance. And He takes only what rightfully belongs to Him, which happens to be everything.

So Jesus didn't tell His followers to go out and coerce other followers. He sent them as workers into a harvest and urged them to pray for many more workers to join the fruitful labor. The job of this conquering force was not to kill and capture but to heal and declare the Kingdom of God. That's it. They were bearers of exceedingly good news.

Perhaps that's why our harvests are sometimes so meager; we've declared news that doesn't sound very good to many people. We've proclaimed messages other than the Kingdom of God. We haven't always conquered with love.

IN DEED
We have to recapture the spirit of the harvest. We need the right prayer focus (on harvesters, not on fruit), the right message (the good news of the Kingdom, not just the Good News of salvation), and the right attitude (mercy over judgment and kindness over contentiousness). People flocked to Jesus because His goodness was obvious. His Kingdom grows when we make it obvious too.

ADDITIONAL READING: Isaiah 9:7

> "Gospel" signifies good tidings that . . . make a man's heart glad, and make him sing, dance, and leap for joy.
> WILLIAM TYNDALE

The First Word

Whenever you enter someone's home, first say, "May God's peace be on this house." If those who live there are peaceful, the blessing will stand; if they are not, the blessing will return to you. Luke 10:5-6

IN WORD

Many throughout history have gotten this wrong. Some on their mission from the King have entered a house, literally or figuratively, by first saying, "Repent." Others have entered houses with the word *obey*. Still others have entered the discussion with a message of judgment or righteousness or ideology. And while all of these messages may become part of the conversation, they aren't the beginning. When Jesus sent His friends into the harvest, He sent them with a message of peace.

Yes, Jesus came preaching repentance (Mark 1:15), but the emphasis wasn't on the sin, it was on the Good News. And He backed it up with healing and deliverance and blessing. He came with a message of wholeness, joy, fullness, restoration . . . *shalom*. Above all, He came to bring peace between God and those alienated from Him.

Jesus made it clear that He came to save, not to condemn (John 3:17). That's His purpose. Yet the primary message many people hear from the Christian community is a message of condemnation. We may want to bless those around us, but those around us don't always trust our motives. They see an agenda beyond blessing. They think we will love them only if they become like us.

IN DEED

As Kingdom citizens on a Kingdom mission, we need to remember that all topics of conversation—sin, repentance, obedience, and everything else—take place in the context of peace. This is a Kingdom of *shalom*. Its workers are *shalom*-minded people looking for *shalom*-hungry people whose hearts will align with a *shalom*-focused God. If that's the lead message, many will receive it.

ADDITIONAL READING: John 3:17

The way from God to a human heart is through a human heart.
S. D. GORDON

A Disease-Free Zone

Heal the sick, and tell them, "The Kingdom of God is near you now." Luke 10:9

IN WORD

In Luke 4:40-44, Jesus healed and delivered many people and then declared that He must go and "proclaim the good news of the kingdom" elsewhere too (NIV). In Luke 9:2, He sent His followers to heal the sick and preach the Kingdom. Here in Luke 10, He tells a larger group of followers to heal the sick and tell them the Kingdom has come near. Again and again, healing and the Kingdom of God are linked. One is a characteristic of the other. Where God reigns, things get better.

Most of us have seen a similar phenomenon. We know God still heals. At some times and some places He seems to do it more readily than at other times and places. The prayers of faith of some believers seem to be gifted with healing power in unusual degrees. We may not understand all the nuances and variables of this Kingdom phenomenon, but we know enough to consider it a Kingdom attribute. In a showdown between Jesus and disease, Jesus wins.

That's actually true of any obstacle in life. In the showdowns between Jesus and sin, Jesus and circumstances, Jesus and lack, Jesus and the dark forces of this world, and even Jesus and death, Jesus wins. Overcoming is an integral part of the Kingdom. It isn't just something He does; it's something that becomes a part of everyone who belongs to Him and whom He sends out in His name. No situation, no relationship, no opposition is too big for Him—and those who live in Him by His Spirit.

IN DEED

Is there any situation in your life today that doesn't look like the Kingdom? Know that it will bow to Him and to you, if not soon then at least eventually. Speak to the intractable problems of life and tell them that the Kingdom has come near. Create Kingdom outposts wherever you are—areas of life that are free from any non-Kingdom influence. No obstacle in life is a match for the King who lives within you.

ADDITIONAL READING: Mark 9:23

> The temperature of the spiritual life of the church
> is the index of her power to heal.
> EVELYN FROST

The King's Backing

[Jesus said,] "Anyone who accepts your message is also accepting me. And anyone who rejects you is rejecting me. And anyone who rejects me is rejecting God, who sent me." Luke 10:16

IN WORD

As Kingdom citizens, we honor our King. We follow Him, obey Him, and worship Him. We forsake our own interests in order to live for His. In our commitment to Christ, our lives become all about Him.

But there's more. We aren't just loyal subjects. We're also His representatives in this world. He doesn't want mere servants; He wants partners. As we grow into His likeness, we have the opportunity to become His mouthpieces. We voice His words and demonstrate His character. We increasingly reflect His glory.

That's a high privilege many Christians are reluctant to embrace. Perhaps it seems too presumptuous, or maybe even too demanding. We don't think we're worthy (which isn't the point) or capable (which isn't the problem). In this calling to be His representatives, we forget two important facts: (1) This was His idea, not ours; and (2) He empowers us for the task.

We need to remember the identity God gave us as His reflectors and representatives. We become like Him, and we express His will in this world. But we also need to remember the relationship that makes it all possible. Good parents have no trouble saying, "If you hurt my child, you have to deal with me." And God is certainly a good parent. Our relationship with Him means that when we go into a potentially hostile world, we do so with the backing of the King Himself. If anyone rejects the child who bears His name, they are rejecting Him. He takes the welfare of His children personally.

IN DEED

The calling to represent God in this world can be intimidating because we know how imperfect we are. That humility is good. But our weakness is backed by His strength— and His commitment, His zeal, and His love. We do not serve Him as independent contractors; we represent Him as one of the family. And He always watches over His own.

ADDITIONAL READING: 1 Peter 4:11

The crowning wonder of God's scheme is that He entrusted it to men.
HENRY DRUMMOND

Fallen Foes

[Jesus said,] "I saw Satan fall from heaven like lightning!" Luke 10:18

IN WORD

Jesus taught His followers to pray for God's Kingdom to come. In Luke 10, as well as other places in the Gospels, He sends them out as representatives of the Kingdom to enforce His authority. In both cases, His people have to understand the implied result: If His Kingdom comes, another kingdom has to go.

That puts Kingdom citizens on the battle lines of a spiritual conflict and on the cutting edge of a cultural transformation from one Kingdom to another. The middle of a conflict is an exciting place to be, but it's also a sobering one. The stakes are high. The usurper himself, the rebel against heaven, is losing his grip on his illegitimate domain. There is opposition, and it's often intense; desperate dictators are usually at their worst when they are losing their grip. But there is no doubt about the demise of this one. He's going down. Jesus witnessed it on the spot.

Our mission in the world is to see this fall repeated frequently. We want Satan to fall in every area of our lives and in every corner of our society. We want him out of families, schools, businesses, government agencies, entertainment and media, and more. We want his lies, his tactics, and his mean-spirited attacks to stop. We want to purge our lives of his influence in every way. We want his fall to be complete.

IN DEED

We can be exceedingly thankful that Jesus won that victory—He cast out the "ruler of this world" (John 12:31). He initiated the final offensive and determined its outcome, but He left us to enforce the terms. Though Satan has fallen from heaven, he is still far too active. We've seen his handiwork. Like the early followers of Jesus, we have been sent into the world to exercise Kingdom authority over evil.

What does that look like? It may vary from person to person, but we know it doesn't involve submission to the enemy's plans. We don't acquiesce to his demands. We pray for God's Kingdom to come, declare His victory, insist on His purposes, and never rest until the impostor's kingdom is gone.

ADDITIONAL READING: John 12:31

The first step on the way to victory is to recognize the enemy.
CORRIE TEN BOOM

The Right to Trample

[Jesus said,] "Look, I have given you authority over all the power of the enemy, and you can walk among snakes and scorpions and crush them. Nothing will injure you." Luke 10:19

IN WORD

Life isn't easy. In some seasons, perhaps, everything falls into place naturally, but we have enough experience to know that's not the norm. Few things in life come easily. Decisions are difficult, relationships take effort, plans don't always work out, health is fragile, and pain is inevitable. And if we're spiritually sensitive, we recognize that evil is hunting us down. Sometimes we give in to temptations, sometimes we're attacked by words or circumstances, and sometimes we just lose heart. Brokenness is part of the human condition. In a fallen world, we feel defeated.

This is not the promise God gave His people. In Deuteronomy 28:13, He told them they would be the head and not the tail—*if* they followed Him wholeheartedly. If they didn't, then they would be the tail and not the head. As we know from history, human nature doesn't fully obey God, and we have to deal with the consequences. Left on our own, we're trapped in a cycle of futility.

Jesus changed that. His promise of authority over the enemy is a gift to all who believe in Him. We can now claim the promise of Deuteronomy 28. We can be the head and not the tail. All those things the world once held over us are now under us. In the spiritual pecking order of the universe, we're at the top, not the bottom. As children of the King, we are subject to no one but the King.

IN DEED

This doesn't mean all our problems are solved. Sometimes they may even intensify. But they don't weigh on us as though we are helpless and under their domain. With spiritual authority and resolve, we can overcome them, handle them, even turn them around for good. Instead of being victims, we become victors. We overcome. That's the promise of the gospel. We may have to learn how to wield His authority, but we never need doubt that we have it. All the power of the enemy is infinitely weaker than the power of the One within us.

ADDITIONAL READING: Deuteronomy 28:12-14

Men ablaze are invincible. Hell trembles when men kindle.
SAMUEL CHADWICK

With the Humility of a Child

[Jesus said,] "I praise you, Father, Lord of heaven and earth, because you have hidden these things from the wise and learned, and revealed them to little children." Luke 10:21, NIV

IN WORD

Granted the authority of the Kingdom and being placed at top levels of the spiritual pecking order of the universe, we could develop a superiority complex. And we would, except for one thing: That isn't the nature of the King. Wielding all authority, Jesus came to serve. In spite of all His accomplishments and glory, He's humble. He's worthy of everything, but He doesn't demand our hearts. He invites us into His blessings. We share in His authority because He generously allows us to do so.

Not only is humility the nature of the King, it's also the appropriate attitude for beings with our background. We remember where we came from. We know we didn't earn this. We were worthy of a far worse fate, but the mercy of the King rescued us from it. We became the ultimate rags-to-riches story.

So our response to the authority of the Kingdom is never pride; it's gratitude. We don't exercise that authority for self-promotion but for love of God and others. We overcome evil by liberating others from its destruction. That's why we have been given the keys of the Kingdom. It isn't a power trip. It's a confrontation against everything that contradicts the truth, beauty, and love of the Kingdom.

IN DEED

Make that your mission in life—to stand for God's Kingdom by claiming spiritual authority over all that opposes it. With the humility of a child, learn how to exercise that authority wisely. Don't use it in arguments or selfish agendas. Don't put it on business cards or T-shirts as though it's a credential to boast about. Use it in faith. It's your spiritual trump card against all the enemy's purposes, your veto of his agenda. You don't have it by being wise and learned. You have it because the King revealed it to you as His child. Learn to wield it exactly as Jesus showed you.

ADDITIONAL READING: Matthew 16:19

It is a contradiction to be a true Christian and not to be humble.
RICHARD BAXTER

God of Justice

The LORD reigns forever, executing judgment from his throne. Psalm 9:7

IN WORD

If you're like most people, something in you hates injustice. It bothers you when arrogant people get their way and continue to think they are better than everyone else. It rubs you the wrong way when honest, hardworking people are trampled on because of someone else's selfish agenda. And it angers you when children are abused, hearts are wounded, and the powerful casually disregard the needs of the weak. You were wired with a sense of right and wrong.

Why is this embedded in your nature? Because you were made in God's image, He feels the same way you do about injustice, only more passionately. He is drawn to the humble and resists the proud. Selfish agendas violate His nature. It angers Him when people are abused, disregarded, and overcome by evil. He hates corruption and cruelty.

The skeptic will ask, "Then why doesn't He do something about it?" But the skeptic doesn't see the whole picture. When all the layers of reality are exposed, we will see how God allowed the world to continue in its fallen condition—only for a time—in order to separate those who trust Him from those who don't, to try the hearts of those who love Him, to give rebellious hearts every chance to change and pursue the right course. God may have ample reasons beyond our understanding to allow what He has allowed, but we know He will not allow it forever. He *has* done something about it. In the big picture, evil is on a leash. And it is a very temporary condition.

God establishes justice. He makes decisions. He sorts out what's right. The declaration that He is on His throne is not a threat of condemnation; it's a promise of restoration. He will make everything right.

IN DEED

We can take comfort in knowing that God will put the world back in order, but will He do that in our individual lives? Clearly the promise encompasses the personal interests of those who call Him King and trust His purposes. He is a repairer by nature, and His love for you is intense. Rest in that fact. He reigns over every detail of your life.

ADDITIONAL READING: Psalm 115:1-3

> God's justice guarantees that ultimately all
> that is unfair will be dealt with.
> JOSEPH STOWELL

Vindication

For you have judged in my favor; from your throne you have judged with fairness. Psalm 9:4

IN WORD

A raw deal, the short straw, the wrong end of the stick—whatever the idiom, it's painful and embarrassing to feel slighted, betrayed, or usurped. It's one thing to lose a game, but another to lose in life's circumstances. Defeat eats at us and, if we aren't careful, sows seeds of bitterness in our hearts. When we've been wronged, we just want things to be made right.

That's an implicit promise of Scripture for those who cling to the God of justice. It makes no sense for His Word to declare how just and righteous He is while His people continue to get the consolation prize rather than His full blessings. Yes, we understand the fallen condition of this world and the fact of persecution. We're humble enough to realize not everything is going to go our way. But we are also in a living relationship with a victorious God who calls us overcomers and promises that all things will work together for our good. Sometimes we just want—and need—Him to vindicate us.

He will. His justice is personal. You can appeal to this God. The Word of God calls Jesus the Advocate. When injustice threatens, when court systems seem callous or nonsensical, when ungodly people inflict suffering, you can appeal to a higher authority. It doesn't mean He will work everything out as you expect Him to immediately, but it does mean He will work everything out. History will not end with lingering injustices. You will be vindicated everywhere you need to be.

IN DEED

Call to the God of justice. Call to Him persistently, brashly, even relentlessly—just like the widow Jesus commended for pestering an unjust judge. If an unrighteous judge is bothered enough to grant justice, will not a good God quickly establish justice for His chosen ones who cry to Him day and night (Luke 18:7)? Of course He will. He is a God of vindication. He establishes truth and righteousness in His world. And He responds to those who cry out to Him.

ADDITIONAL READING: 1 Peter 4:1-6

Storm the throne of grace and persevere therein, and mercy will come down.
JOHN WESLEY

Never Forsaken

Those who know your name trust in you, for you, O LORD, do not abandon those who search for you. Psalm 9:10

IN WORD

God has never forsaken those who seek Him. He is trustworthy. Faithful. Relentlessly good. We can invest our hearts in Him. Right?

That's the big question hanging over our hearts throughout our lives. We know the right answer if we've accepted His Word as truth. And oh, how we want it to be true. But virtually every human being has gone through experiences of hardship and pain—some of them while knowing God could have intervened if He wanted to. Somewhere deep inside us are lingering questions that were first introduced in a garden long ago: *Is this King good? Is He good to me personally? Will He let me down, or can I trust Him with whatever is dear to my heart? Not just to do what's best for Him and His purposes, but also what's best for me? Even when I've failed?*

This is perhaps the biggest internal battle we will ever fight. Much in our lives will cast Him in a negative light, and we have some unholy help putting on the wrong lenses for viewing these things. Will we choose to trust God's goodness regardless of what we see? He strongly supports those who do, though that support may be hard to see in the moment. Some people have already bought into the bitter lie that they have been forsaken. Eventually, however, those who hold on to trust will shine brightly in a world of shadows.

IN DEED

Much of life is a discovery process about truth and reality. But there are a few truths we can anchor ourselves in. This is one of them. God is good. Relentlessly good. No matter what we see. No matter how it feels in a moment of crisis. No matter what we think He could have/should have done to help us out of the crisis or deliver us from pain. Regardless of the evidence of experience—which, by the way, we see from an extremely limited perspective—He has never forsaken those who seek Him. Hold on to that. Forever.

ADDITIONAL READING: Psalm 145

> Though men are false, God is faithful.
> MATTHEW HENRY

The Really Good News

He told them, "Go into all the world and preach the Good News to everyone."
Mark 16:15

IN WORD

The word *gospel* is part of the basic vocabulary of most Christians. We use it to describe the message of Jesus, one of the first four books of the New Testament about Jesus' ministry, or a genre of music. Many are aware of its common translation as "Good News." We take it for granted that the gospel equals Jesus equals goodness.

But there's a difference between our intellectual understanding of "gospel" and how we apply it to our lives and the lives of others. In the experience of many, the gospel hasn't been very good news at all. Some believers, misunderstanding the freedom it gives or the depths to which it can take them, feel burdened by its high standards or unrealized fulfillment. And those outside the faith tend to equate it with the condemnation they sense from Christians, the political views of vocal Christians, or a holier-than-thou facade Christians often present. None of that seems good.

What is the truly good news Jesus sent His followers to preach? That the Kingdom is coming, and the King is very kind, generous, and welcoming—even to those who do not accept Him. This King will put everything right, heal all wounds, wipe away every tear, and establish true freedom in this world. Life on earth will be "as it is in heaven," and heaven is better than human stereotypes have portrayed it. This Kingdom is the desire of all nations and the longing of every human heart.

IN DEED

Much of what we preach to all creation is not the Good News. Many Christians preach the Good News to some of creation—usually those who agree with them—while those who preach to all creation often present news that isn't very good. The true gospel is always appealing, always winsome, always a blessing to those who need it. Not every hearer will recognize its goodness or its value, but they should at least hear of it. Our assignment as Kingdom citizens is to make sure they do.

ADDITIONAL READING: Isaiah 52:7

Christ's riches are unsearchable, and this doctrine of
the gospel is the field this treasure is hidden in.
THOMAS GOODWIN

Those Who Believe

Anyone who believes and is baptized will be saved. But anyone who refuses to believe will be condemned. Mark 16:16

IN WORD

The best part of the Good News is that everyone who believes can become citizens of the Kingdom. There is no lengthy application process, no citizenship exam, no temporary green-card status. You are either in the Kingdom or you aren't. And the requirement for entry is really simple.

That doesn't mean it's easy. Mark 16:9-14 is all about belief in something that seems hardly credible—a man raised from the dead after a brutal execution. Those who saw Him believed, but those who had to rely on the testimony of eyewitnesses didn't. They were rebuked for their "stubborn unbelief" (verse 14). It isn't any easier today to believe in a resurrection than it was then; skepticism is rampant in our age just as it was in the first century. And in our age, we haven't seen Lazarus come out of the tomb or witnessed Jesus' miracles of healing. Belief—a key characteristic of Kingdom people—is hard for some hearts to grasp.

Nevertheless, it's a necessary dividing line between those who love the King and those who don't recognize Him. And though we haven't seen the miracles of Jesus in the flesh, we have numerous testimonies of miracles that point us to Him today. Whether or not we have seen something like the Resurrection ourselves, we will be rebuked if we don't believe the eyewitness accounts of His works. Faith hears of His goodness and knows it's true.

IN DEED

Skepticism is not a Kingdom attribute. That may be our natural inclination, and we may look down on those who believe the supernatural too easily. But the Kingdom is given to those who can see beyond the visible and accept the ways of the King. Those who believe have chosen to see into His unseen realm and have planted their feet firmly in it.

ADDITIONAL READING: John 20:29

The gospel was not good advice but good news.
WILLIAM RALPH INGE

Signs of Belief

These miraculous signs will accompany those who believe. Mark 16:17

IN WORD

Like it or not, the Kingdom is a realm of signs. It's not quite as invisible as we've made it out to be. Yes, sometimes it's hidden. But it's never completely absent. Instead of developing theology that apologizes for signs, we need to embrace them. The Kingdom is accompanied by evidence of the Kingdom. That's what Jesus said.

That doesn't necessarily mean that if a sick person doesn't get well, then we're living in unbelief. Or that if someone dies by snakebite, then Jesus' promise isn't true. Or that any ongoing presence of the demonic means we're powerless to cast it out because of our sin. The Kingdom is much more textured than that. We don't claim that He always heals or delivers, just that He often does. We have to be comfortable with some degree of mystery.

But we do need to choose our perspective. Some people assume an absence of signs and then have to explain miracles as exceptions. Faith assumes a presence of signs and treats an absence of miracles as the exception. If we don't see Scripture fulfilled in our lives, it's better to press in to God for wisdom and revelation than to come up with theological caveats about why that verse no longer applies. A discrepancy between Scripture and experience is an invitation to draw closer to God, not a theological problem to explain. Whenever the Word presents a deeper, fuller experience, we are welcome to seek it.

IN DEED

If any promises of Scripture are unfulfilled in your life, don't explain them away. Go after them with all your heart. Ask God to show you more of Himself in your search. Let Him be your teacher. He loves the kind of faith that cannot rest until all the treasures of His Word become practical reality. Whatever He promised remains an open invitation.

ADDITIONAL READING: John 14:12

We must reach the point of preferring to die rather than
to have a ministry without fruit and without power.
FERNANDO VANGIONI

From the Throne

When the Lord Jesus had finished talking with them, he was taken up into heaven and sat down in the place of honor at God's right hand. Mark 16:19

IN WORD

On the surface, it looks like Jesus left His disciples. We know He sent His Spirit to them, and He had told them it would be better this way (John 16:7). But He was no longer physically with them. He was in heaven, and they were on earth.

But we in the Kingdom of God know not to look at the surface. The truer picture is that while Jesus is on His throne and His followers are on earth, His Spirit is in His followers on earth and His followers are seated with Him in heaven. We are not confined to this realm, and He has not left it. Both He and we operate in both realms simultaneously.

The beauty of this plan is that as priests and kings in His Kingdom, we can present the needs of humanity to God and the power of God to humanity. He is seated on His throne, not as an absent deity but as distributor of Kingdom authority. Through those who believe, He offers His strength to all who need Him. He may be sitting on His throne, but He is actively walking and talking through His people.

IN DEED

Never forget your connection with heaven. You are an intersection between two realms—a living, breathing gateway for Kingdom power. Your prayers come not from a place of desperation but from a place of victory. Your message is spoken not from tentative speculation but from divine revelation. If you are relying on Him, your strength is not your own but the evidence of divine power. You are in a much better position than you think.

Learn to live from that position. It's always true, but it only manifests practically when you learn to see it. Don't let anyone from any realm convince you that your human flaws and frailties disqualify you from extraordinary work. You are a representative and reflection of the King to everyone around you.

ADDITIONAL READING: Ephesians 2:6

> We are the wire, God is the current. Our only power is to let the current pass through us.
> CARLO CARRETTO

In Partnership

The disciples went everywhere and preached, and the Lord worked through them, confirming what they said by many miraculous signs. Mark 16:20

IN WORD

"The Lord worked through them." He didn't have to. In fact, much teaching in modern Christianity minimizes our role in the mission and emphasizes His. After all, He is sovereign and can do whatever He wants whenever He wants. But God seems always to work in partnership with His people. He urges us to pray for His will to be done, as though human agency is necessary; He calls us to work and serve, as though human effort is vital; and He gives us His authority and His name, as though He fully trusts us to manage His affairs on earth. He is a partnership kind of God.

This is evident even in creation. "Let us make human beings in our image," He proposed in the beginning (Genesis 1:26). The Trinity is a fellowship of mutual desire and fulfillment, each member serving another selflessly. Clearly the nature of this fellowship is meant to transfer to Kingdom people, who reflect God's heart. If He is a partnership kind of God, we are to be a partnership kind of people.

This partnership can change our perspective of everything in God's Kingdom. In light of His Spirit's work within us, we pray *with* Him instead of praying *to* Him (Romans 8:26-27). We labor together *with* Him as His ambassadors (2 Corinthians 5:20). We speak His words and serve in His strength (1 Peter 4:11).

IN DEED

In the council room of this universe, don't see yourself as sitting across the table from God. You and He are on the same side, talking and working together to accomplish His purposes. Because of His sovereign power, it doesn't have to be that way; but His sovereign will has chosen this. He is thoroughly relational, and the partnership of the Trinity overflows into the fellowship of His people. We have to learn to work with Him rather than for Him. We are partners with heaven. It's the only way for His mission to fit His nature.

ADDITIONAL READING: 2 Corinthians 5:18-20

Nearness to Christ, intimacy with Him, assimilation to His character—these are the elements of a ministry of power.
HORATIUS BONAR

The Usurper

You said to yourself, "I will ascend to heaven and set my throne above God's stars. I will preside on the mountain of the gods." Isaiah 14:13

IN WORD

Something went wrong in the King's domain. It happened before any of us were born, and Scripture doesn't explain the details, so we don't know the full picture. All we know, from piecing together the story, is that one of God's highest creatures rebelled against Him, taking plenty of angels and eventually the heart of humanity with him.

At the core of this rebellion was a spirit of pride, a desire to be ruler rather than a subject in God's realm. In his heart, the usurper wanted to raise his throne above all others. He didn't want to be part of God's story; he wanted to write his own.

That's a common theme running throughout the history of humanity. We see it in this passage about the king of Babylon, though the words seem to point to the original usurper from another realm. We see it in the first act of human disobedience in a garden long ago. And unfortunately, we see it in our own lives. At many points, every one of us has decided to create our own path, write our own story, dictate our own agenda either in direct contradiction to God's purposes or in careless negligence of them. Any time we say, "Not His will but mine," whether overtly or subtly, we conform to the ways of the usurper. That original act of pride has spread like a deadly contagion into every corner of our world.

IN DEED

There's only one way to turn back to the ways of the King, and that's through deep humility. Humility is reflected in our worship, in what Scripture calls repentance, and in the way of the cross that Jesus walked and called His disciples to follow. There's more at stake in this walk than simply doing the King's will; it's a matter of forsaking the spirit of the usurper and stopping the spread of the deadly contagion. And it's fully embracing the culture of the Kingdom—and the heart of the King.

ADDITIONAL READING: James 4:5-7

Nothing sets a person so much out of the devil's reach as humility.
JONATHAN EDWARDS

From Heaven

He raised us from the dead along with Christ and seated us with him in the heavenly realms because we are united with Christ Jesus. Ephesians 2:6

IN WORD

We are in a privileged position. That would be true regardless of where we came from, but Scripture makes it clear that we came from a state of death into new life. We were in darkness, captivity, and wrath, inherently rebellious against God and influenced by evil forces. But as characters in the ultimate rags-to-riches story, we have been raised to new life, transferred to the Kingdom of light, and seated with the King in heaven. All because of His unfathomable love and grace.

Though this is true and most Scripture-savvy believers know it, few of us live this way. We live as though we are still trapped in a world of darkness and looking forward to heaven. We live very earthly lives while holding on to the hope that we might experience a bit of heaven. But that isn't an accurate perspective. If we really believe passages like these—the great declarations of apostolic writings that we are already in Christ where He lives—then we are living heavenly lives while walking the earth. Our citizenship is in the Kingdom, and we are seated in its place of power. We aren't earthly beings trying to get to heaven. We are heavenly beings charged with bringing heaven to earth.

IN DEED

How can we do that? First, we need to know the atmosphere we truly live in. We need to see it, feel it, count on it, know that it's true. We are to live and breathe in the atmosphere of heaven and exude it here. We may live among the darkness, but we don't draw our energy from that place. We draw our energy, our hopes, our motivation, our very lives from another realm. And if we take the opportunity, we can bring our life in that realm to bear on the realm we once came from. Our attitudes, actions, prayers, power, and purposes can—and must—influence earth with the blessings of heaven.

ADDITIONAL READING: Philippians 1:27

Sanctify yourself and you will sanctify society.
FRANCIS OF ASSISI

Trophies of Grace

God can point to us in all future ages as examples of the incredible wealth of his grace and kindness toward us, as shown in all he has done for us who are united with Christ Jesus. Ephesians 2:7

IN WORD

We may think we live private lives, and in many respects we do. We are hidden in Christ (Colossians 3:3). But God has a plan for His own glory. No artist wants to create masterpieces that remain unseen by the world, and God is the ultimate artist. He has every intention of putting His greatest works on display, and according to His Word, we are some of His greatest works. At times in this age and emphatically in ages to come, He plans to point to us as examples of His lavish grace. As former citizens of darkness and current citizens of the Kingdom of glory, we are destined to be in His showcase.

Some of us may be embarrassed by that kind of attention, but we'll have to get over the embarrassment. This demonstration of grace is primarily about God, not us. We certainly benefit, and for grace to be meaningful, it has to have an object. In that sense, it *is* about us. But the bigger story is about the Giver, not the recipients. His best works are for the display of His glory. We are Exhibit A in the case that God is full of love, mercy, compassion, grace, and comfort.

IN DEED

Think about that. Many attributes of the King would never have been seen in a perfect environment like heaven, where mercy, forgiveness, healing, deliverance, and comfort are not needed. But these characteristics come into stark relief against the backdrop of our fallen world. Your pain? It's there as an occasion for God to show His deliverance and comfort. Your need? It's there to show His provision. Your sin? It's the stage on which His mercy becomes visible. It's a privilege and honor to play the role of His trophies, and the demonstration will be visible for countless ages to come. Our lives are the perfect landscape for His most beautiful works.

ADDITIONAL READING: Revelation 5:9-10

I have a great need for Christ; I have a great Christ for my need.
CHARLES SPURGEON

MAR
26

Planned Beforehand

We are God's masterpiece. He has created us anew in Christ Jesus, so we can do the good things he planned for us long ago. Ephesians 2:10

IN WORD

Imagine finding a map to buried treasure. You don't quite know how to interpret it, but you know someone who does. You call that person, ask some questions about the symbols and directions on the map, follow every instruction as you discover what each one means, and eventually arrive at the place where the treasure is buried. You dig it up and celebrate the rewarding experience.

What are the key facts about this process? (1) The treasure is already there; (2) a map and a guide will help you find it; and (3) it's up to you to do the legwork. If you think about it, those are exactly the same key facts about doing the works God has given us. He has already planned for us to do good works and has laid them out in front of us. He has given us His Word and His Spirit, both available to answer our questions and guide us in the process. And we have to actually get up and step into the things He has prepared for us. Like treasures in a field, the works of the Kingdom are waiting for us to discover and bring to the surface.

IN DEED

God has called each Kingdom citizen to be a treasure hunter. We rarely just stumble into the works of the Kingdom. We have to go searching for them. There are plenty of clues, and we need to ask lots of questions. That's one of the ways we build our relationship with the Spirit; we ask and listen for answers. Over time, He guides us, unveils secrets, and shows us where and how to do His works. But the works are already there. He planted them and leaves them for us to discover.

That's how the Kingdom adventure works. If we understand the process, move in the directions He leads, and exercise faith at the time it is needed, we will participate in the works of God. And the world will be blessed with treasures it never knew existed.

ADDITIONAL READING: John 14:12

We have a call to do good, as often as we
have the power and the occasion.
WILLIAM PENN

In the Spirit

Instantly I was in the Spirit, and I saw a throne in heaven and someone sitting on it. Revelation 4:2

IN WORD

"In the Spirit," John saw the throne in heaven—and "someone" seated on it. You don't see such things in the flesh. Natural eyes don't have the capacity for spiritual realities. Our senses feed our brains with information, and our brains fit the information into categories. But there are no categories for heavenly visions. Throughout this vision of the throne room, John uses phrases like "had the appearance of" and "looked like" because human languages have no words for what he saw. The colors were too dazzling, the shapes and sounds too indescribable, the dimensions too unfamiliar. Human assumptions can't take in such a scene; only the Spirit can provide the means to take it in.

Scripture tells us we have access to the throne room of God (Hebrews 4:16), but most of us access it blindly. Must it be that way? Not necessarily. The more we depend on our natural senses, the more we "see through a glass, darkly," as Paul put it (1 Corinthians 13:12, KJV). But the more we are "in the Spirit"—not just as our position in Christ, as is always true, but in practical experience—the more we will get glimpses of throne-room realities. The door in heaven is open to our spiritual senses if we learn how to tune in to them in the Spirit.

IN DEED

People who believe heavenly glimpses are impossible will never have them unless God sovereignly imposes them. But those who hunger for the presence of the one on the throne as though seeing His dwelling is a viable possibility will find Him coming into focus frequently. If our goal is to intellectually process the Word without relying on spiritual revelation, we'll end up with rationales. But if we are saturated in the Spirit's presence, our minds will grasp what normal reason could never discover on its own. All of heaven will open up to us. And the one seated on the throne will pour His deep, transforming truth into our hearts.

ADDITIONAL READING: Ephesians 6:18

No one can understand spiritual mysteries by carnal reason.
THOMAS BENTON BROOKS

The King's Delegation

Twenty-four thrones surrounded him, and twenty-four elders sat on them.
They were all clothed in white and had gold crowns on their heads.
Revelation 4:4

IN WORD

God is the sovereign King of the universe—unequaled, unrivaled, unquestionably.
So it's no surprise that most people emphasize His authority without considering the
possibility of sharing it. Humans—or any beings other than God—are too imperfect
and too limited to qualify for a crown.

Surprisingly, then, the elders around the throne are dressed in white garments—
symbols of purity—and wearing golden crowns. They have regal authority given by
God Himself. They submit to the throne, but they also represent it. They are less than
God, but they are empowered to act in His place. Yes, they will cast down these crowns
and worship God—that's what godly leaders do—but that doesn't mean the crowns are
illegitimate. They couldn't have them in the throne room unless the crowns had been
given by the One who sits on the throne. These elders are reigning with Him.

How can this be? God is always relational, so He doesn't rule in isolation. He surrounds Himself with trustworthy stewards who will rule with Him. From the earliest
pages of Scripture, He chose created beings to share dominion with Him over the
earth, and He has a long history of bringing prophets and kings and simple disciples
into His courts. As a thoroughly relational God, He is a delegator at heart.

IN DEED

We don't know exactly who the twenty-four elders are. Some say they are the leaders of
the twelve tribes plus the twelve disciples, and some say they aren't human at all. But
we do know that God gives Kingdom roles to those who worship Him wholeheartedly.
Next to His throne or not, His children are royals. We are entrusted with His wisdom
and charged with implementing His will. Those who worship Him, consider themselves unworthy of a crown, and willingly offer any crown to Him are the ones who
receive a crown in the first place. We can enjoy the presence of the King.

ADDITIONAL READING: Mark 10:35-40

> We may think God wants actions of a certain
> kind, but God wants people of a certain kind.
> C. S. LEWIS

Indescribable

From the throne came flashes of lightning and the rumble of thunder. And in front of the throne were seven torches with burning flames. This is the sevenfold Spirit of God. Revelation 4:5

IN WORD

This throne room is no ordinary place. The One seated on the throne has the appearance of jasper and ruby, and a rainbow encircles Him. This place—or realm or dimension—is pulsing with electric energy and beating with the sound of thunder. And if that weren't overwhelming enough, there are seven blazing torches in front of the throne and odd, all-seeing creatures around it. And the torches are the seven spirits of God.

Seven spirits? We describe God as a Trinity—three beings who are distinct persons yet the same essence—and Scripture repeatedly calls the Holy Spirit *the* Spirit, not *a* Spirit. Yet the visions of Revelation also tell us there are seven spirits. What are we to make of that?

Do the seven spirits correlate with the seven churches of Revelation? If so, why not more? There were far more churches in that era than the seven to which John addressed his letters. Do the seven spirits represent distinct characteristics or functions of God? If so, why aren't those characteristics or functions explained to us? We don't know the answers to these questions. All we can say is that the revealed God is still surrounded with mystery, He's more than our finite minds can comprehend.

IN DEED

That's what we learn from this vision—not that God is revealed as more definable but that He is revealed as more overwhelming. If we have tried to make a systematic theology out of Scripture and turn truth into a formula or a clear, schematic design, we have all our categories undone when we get a glimpse of God. This King will not be defined or even understood. He can only be experienced—and only by those who are willing to relate to someone as bold as thunder, as unpredictable as lightning, as creative as creatures and colors can tell us, and as purposeful as seven spirits on a mission.

ADDITIONAL READING: Ezekiel 1

> The radiance of the divine beauty is wholly inexpressible;
> words cannot describe it, nor the ear grasp it.
> FATHER PHILIMON

True Meaning

Whenever the living beings give glory and honor and thanks to the one sitting on the throne (the one who lives forever and ever), the twenty-four elders fall down and worship the one sitting on the throne (the one who lives forever and ever). Revelation 4:9-10

IN WORD

Why are we here? What is the purpose of life? What does it all mean? These are the existential questions the philosopher in every human heart has asked throughout history. A glimpse into the throne room shows us an answer, or at least part of one. The ultimate value in creation, apparently, is worship of the King. All kinds of creatures bow before Him, unable to utter words that don't reflect His honor and glory. This rainbow-encircled, thunderous, blazing presence is the highest value in all of existence. We were created not as independent beings but in relation to Him. He is the reference point for everything.

That means that if we pursue other things with greater zeal, we are out of sorts with this throne-room reality. If we dishonor Him or even neglect Him, we stand in contradiction to the epicenter of all visible and invisible universes. If we think, speak, or act in any way that does not reflect that we and all things were made by Him and for Him, we are falling short of our true design. If the heart of existence is the throne room of God, worship is the heartbeat.

IN DEED

That doesn't mean all of life is a never-ending hymn or praise chorus, or that heaven is an eternal church service, or that we become devoid of personality and pleasure for the sake of reverence and awe. No, it means we become fully alive, pulsating with the adventure of knowing Him and being overwhelmed by Him, throbbing with the desire to dive deeper into His presence and experience the unexplainable. The world needs people who are blazing with the excitement of His presence—and who will burn with the mystery of His presence for all to see. Only then is the world drawn to its true purpose. And only then do hearts with big questions find their rest.

ADDITIONAL READING: Isaiah 6:1-4

The worship of God is not a rule of safety; it is an adventure of the spirit.
ALFRED NORTH WHITEHEAD

The Key to Life

I saw a Lamb that looked as if it had been slaughtered, but it was now standing between the throne and the four living beings and among the twenty-four elders. Revelation 5:6

IN WORD

Imagine being in John's position. In the Spirit, you've entered a portal into heaven and witness firsthand the epic vista of God on His throne and creatures covering Him in worship. It's sensory overload, with all the power of a galactic storm and all the beauty of an otherworldly dream. Your heart is pounding, captivated by the wonder of it all. Excitement, fear, awe . . . it's more than you can process. Then suddenly you see a figure that's both familiar and like nothing you've ever seen before.

Slain but standing. That's the jarring vision John sees of the One he leaned comfortably against at a supper years before. Two millennia of Christian history may have taken all the surprise out of this picture for us, but let the full impact sink in. At the center of the throne—which is at the center of the universe in a realm usually unseen, in this pulsating place from which all life and energy flow—stands the majestic figure with mortal wounds still visible. With all power at His disposal, the King's own Son was executed by twisted, finite human beings. Yet having been dead, He stands surrounded by glorious beings who worship Him. It's a stunningly incongruent picture. And it sums up God's plan perfectly.

IN DEED

The Lamb is at the center of everything. Never forget that. Not only is He preeminent in the nerve center of the universe, He's central to our existence. If He had remained dead, life as we know it would have been snuffed out. If all things exist through Him (Colossians 1:16), His death without resurrection would have been like pulling the plug on the universe. But nothing could take life from the source of life. And nothing can remove Him from the center of His own creation. Only when we see Him there—and think, speak, and live accordingly—do our lives make sense. Cultivating that vision every moment of every day fills us with energy, purpose, and power.

ADDITIONAL READING: Daniel 7:13-14

> The ascension of Christ does not represent His removal from the earth, but His constant presence everywhere on earth.
> WILLIAM TEMPLE

Handled with Care

Each one had a harp, and they held gold bowls filled with incense, which are the prayers of God's people. Revelation 5:8

IN WORD

Virtually every believer has had the sensation at times that his or her prayers are going no farther than the ceiling. There are times when we feel little connection with God and wonder if He's listening. But when God pulled back the veil for John to see, the apostle got a glimpse of the "prayer processing center" for the universe. And what he saw is remarkable.

It should be profoundly encouraging that our prayers are handled in a place of exceeding power. It should also be encouraging that these prayers are considered incense worthy of golden bowls. The care and materials with which our requests are held confirm that we are known and loved. We are regarded highly enough in heaven to have our desires and petitions considered in such an important, holy place. Our prayers made it past the ceiling after all. They made it all the way to golden bowls in the place of power in another realm.

This is how Kingdom business is done. We don't serve God blindly. He is not a dictator who issues orders without regard for the hearts of His people. He invites us to enter into partnership with Him, and He receives our requests with a strong desire to answer them. Like sweet-smelling incense, our petitions rise to His throne room where they are handled with great care by those with authority. The Kingdom advances not by force but by human desire mixed with the divine will.

IN DEED

Let that vision fuel your prayers today. There is no reason to be discouraged, regardless of what you see. Even if you've been offering the same petition for decades, it hasn't fallen on deaf ears. It's filling a golden bowl like incense, and the aroma pleases the heart of your Father the King. Don't lose heart; keep praying; zealously deposit your desires in this epicenter of power. They move the hand of the Father, and His hand moves the world.

ADDITIONAL READING: Revelation 8:3-5

The world may doubt the power of prayer, but the saints know better.
GILBERT SHAW

Divine Royalty

You have caused them to become a Kingdom of priests for our God. And they will reign on the earth. Revelation 5:10

IN WORD

Peter calls it "a royal priesthood" (1 Peter 2:9, NIV). John, in Revelation 1:6 and 5:10, refers to "kings and priests." Both writers point to God's promise to Moses that God's chosen people would be a kingdom of priests and a holy, set-apart nation (Exodus 19:6). Regardless of the exact wording, we can be confident of this: that we have a priestly function and a royal function. We reign with Jesus (Revelation 20:6).

Priests have a distinct role: They represent human beings to God (through prayers, petitions, confession); and they represent God to humanity (declaring His words, will, and forgiveness). It's a specific place in the vertical relationship between God and people. Kings, on the other hand, have another role: to cultivate, implement, protect, and govern relationships between human beings. It's a specific place in the horizontal, human-to-human connection with each other. Together, the vertical and horizontal relationships form a cross, with the kings/priests and the intersection of the lines. We are uniquely positioned to serve the Kingdom and the King.

We have a great role model for that. Jesus is the archetypical king/priest. We can fulfill this dual role because He fulfilled it and then called us to be like Him. What He is, we become. He is the example of what it means to be fully human, and He puts His Spirit within us to empower us for that deep and satisfying expression of life. We are His likeness in this world (1 John 4:17).

IN DEED

Focus on your roles as a king/queen and as a priest. You are both. As a priest, you stand at the intersection between heaven and earth, presenting the needs of those around you to God and the supply of God to those around you. And as a member of the royal family, you have the backing of the king, the authority of the family name, the DNA of the divine heritage to implement His will in this world. Learning these roles may take a lifetime, but applying them even now will powerfully influence your domain.

ADDITIONAL READING: 1 John 4:17

> The most high and infinitely good God has not granted to angels the power with which He has invested priests.
> JOHN CHRYSOSTOM

Fellow Citizens

Then I looked again, and I heard the voices of thousands and millions of angels around the throne and of the living beings and the elders.
Revelation 5:11

IN WORD

We are not alone in this Kingdom. We see a range of living creatures on earth, none with the capabilities of human beings. But realms unseen to us are full of ministering spirits (Hebrews 1:14), living creatures around the throne (Ezekiel 1:5-14; Revelation 4:6) and likely many other places, and worshiping angels who constantly shout God's praises (Isaiah 6:3). There are also fallen spirits that torment human beings and are tormented themselves (Mark 1:23-27). There are realms we don't see, and the universe is filled with beings we don't see. According to Scripture, we are clearly not alone.

Though we typically can't see into angelic realms—although many have gotten glimpses at times—the spirits who serve God are extremely relevant to us. We benefit from their work; they express the hand of God and carry out His will in our lives (Psalm 103:20-21). In some yet-unknown way, we will have a role in judging spirits (1 Corinthians 6:3). And we will join the multitudes around the throne to worship with them. There are many fellow citizens of the Kingdom who play a vital role in our journey.

IN DEED

Though the angelic realm is largely a mystery to us, it is more relevant than most Christians think. We don't pray to angels or worship them, of course, but they implement answers to our prayers and worship with us. That means that if you feel lonely or isolated in your prayers, worship, or work, the feeling is an illusion. If you think you are powerless in your words or actions, your thoughts are deceiving you. You are not a one-dimensional creature, and you were never intended to live that way. Your feet are planted both in heaven and on earth, in this realm and the spiritual realm, and you are much more effective when you live with that perspective. You are accompanied by a multitude of fellow worshipers.

ADDITIONAL READING: Hebrews 1:14

Millions of spiritual creatures walk the earth unseen,
both when we wake and when we sleep.
JOHN MILTON

Blessing God

Blessing and honor and glory and power belong to the one sitting on the throne and to the Lamb forever and ever. Revelation 5:13

IN WORD

Why do created beings worship God? Not because He is so needy for affirmation that He surrounded Himself with sycophants. Not because His ego requires constant stroking. Not because it's commanded and we therefore must comply. No, God receives worship because He is exceedingly worthy of it. He is beautiful and generous and a greater marvel than we've ever seen. Praise is the natural, spontaneous response to seeing who He really is. And around the throne, seeing is inescapable.

We don't have that sort of vision every day. We need to remind ourselves of who God is and steep ourselves in His goodness. Like David, we sometimes need to command our own souls to bless God and remember His gifts and mercies (Psalm 103:1-5). Our worship isn't nearly as spontaneous as that of the throngs surrounding the throne. We need to worship from a place of seeing dimly.

Believe it or not, that kind of worship is an enormous blessing to God. He values the praises of those who "see" Him without seeing, who offer up a sacrifice of praise from dark places and seemingly hopeless circumstances. A self-prompted, whispered word of worship from the darkness speaks as loudly to Him as shouts of glory in the light. He knows how effortlessly worship flows in His throne room. But those who sit in prisons, who press through deep wounds, and who rise above their suffering to honor His name are precious to His heart.

IN DEED

Vibrant worship is happening in the throne room right now. Even when we don't have a clear vision of that scene, we can join the multitudes in praise. This is part of our created purpose. Expressions of gratitude and glory have a powerfully transforming effect on our own hearts, our outward circumstances, and our relationships. And they bless the God who created us to be—anywhere and at any time—worshipers at heart.

ADDITIONAL READING: Psalm 103:1-5

We must never rest until everything inside us worships God.
A. W. TOZER

The Present King

*[The Lord said,] "I have always moved from one place to another with a tent
and a Tabernacle as my dwelling."* 2 Samuel 7:6

IN WORD

David brought the Ark of God and a reconstructed tabernacle to Jerusalem. God blessed him and gave him rest from his enemies. Yet David was uncomfortable that he was living in a king's palace and the Ark of God's presence was still housed in a tent. It didn't seem right. So he told Nathan the prophet of his desire to build a temple for God—a permanent place for His presence. And Nathan assured him it was a good idea.

But Nathan got another word from God that night. God loved the heart behind the temple idea, and even agreed to have one built. But not by David. The king's desire would be fulfilled in the next generation. Even with His "yes," God made it clear that a temple wasn't necessary. He had always dwelled with His people. He had been with Abraham and the patriarchal family, from altar to altar and even in surprising encounters like Jacob's dream at Bethel. He had given instructions for the Tabernacle in the wilderness and guided His people daily through forty years of wandering. He had spoken through Samuel and called David to be king before David even thought of himself as a king. God had not been absent. A temple, as admirable as David's desire was, still was not essential for these people to worship their God.

IN DEED

That's the kind of King we serve. It's His nature to be present. Most kings expect their subjects to come to them. Citizens can journey to the palace and request a hearing in the throne room, which might or might not be granted. The king is passive and must be actively sought. But our King is different. He goes to His subjects. He approaches His citizens and asks for a hearing with them. He leads us through wildernesses of all kinds, and even when we aren't aware of His presence, He's there. Yes, He invites us to come to Him just as He comes to us, but He doesn't require a specific location other than the one we always carry with us: our hearts. Is the Lord in His temple? If you're inhabited by His Spirit, yes. And He moves with you, answers you when you call, and blesses you with His ever-present goodness.

ADDITIONAL READING: 1 Corinthians 6:19-20

God is above, presiding; beneath, sustaining; within, filling.
HILDEBERT OF LAVARDIN

The King's Choices

*This is what the LORD of Heaven's Armies has declared: I took you from
tending sheep in the pasture and selected you to be the leader of my people
Israel.* 2 Samuel 7:8

IN WORD

When God told Samuel to anoint David as king, David was out in the fields tending
flocks. Even his own father and brothers seemed to consider him a marginal member
of the family. The older brothers fit the image of a king: rugged, manly, strong in their
opinions, and skilled as warriors. David was into music and sheep. Sure, he had killed
a lion and a bear in defense of his flock, but nobody else had witnessed those events.
Other than that, he spent most of his time passively, with no one to talk to but God.

But that was the key. The insignificant brother was conversant with the King of
the universe. He had cultivated the heart and the art of worship. He was strong in an
entirely different arena than his brothers—a skilled warrior in the making, to be sure,
but even more skilled at a greater endeavor. He was learning the heart of God.

Those are the kinds of people our King chooses to represent Him—people who are
responsive to Him, humble yet strong, seekers of His heartbeat. Our origins neither
qualify us nor disqualify us. Our past scars and missteps do nothing to dissuade Him
from choosing us. He has His own sort of preparation that doesn't match the world's
standards. He chooses us like He chose David: He looks for the heart of a worshiper
and a warrior of faith.

IN DEED

Many of us look at our own potential for success with the same eyes the other sons
of Jesse did. We forget that God is not bound by the images our world has created. It
makes no difference whether we fit the stereotype of a good businessperson, artist,
minister, father, mother, or whatever else. Our heavenward attributes are far more
important than the impression we make. Sure, we need skills and excellence and
strengths. But most of all, we need the heart of a worshiper. That's who our King
looks for. His people are called to be *His* people in every way.

ADDITIONAL READING: 1 Samuel 16:1-13

God wants the heart.
THE TALMUD

Honored by God

[God said to David,] "Now I will make your name as famous as anyone who has ever lived on the earth!" 2 Samuel 7:9

IN WORD

God honored David's request because He knew David's heart. But He didn't just stop at honoring David's request. He honored David. Personally.

Why? God had chosen David out of obscurity for his humility and sincere heart. God loves those characteristics. So it may seem odd that God took David out of a humble position and put him in one that engenders pride and corruption. But who else could He trust in such a position? David was prepared for the responsibility and authority of kingship precisely because he was unlike typical kings. As a human being, David was corruptible like everyone else; but he was less corruptible than the proud and unstable. God was not reluctant to bestow honor on someone whose heart belonged to Him.

It isn't God's intention for His people to live in perpetual obscurity. He loves humility, but He also exalts the humble. He has no problem giving generous gifts. We should have no problem receiving them. He has destined us for greatness, even in the eyes of the world. Though we tend to add a caveat—greatness only in the Kingdom, never in the world—God often offers both. There is no fine print at the end of His promises. He has destined His people, especially the humble ones, for good things.

IN DEED

If your humility has kept you from desiring success or prominence, take heart. God is more than willing to establish you, not only in the eyes of Kingdom citizens but also in the eyes of the world. That doesn't mean you will be loved by everyone or make the cover of magazines. You may never win awards or receive applause, and you may even have detractors. David certainly did. But you will be raised up and firmly planted in secure places with honor. Over time, your reputation will be vindicated by the God who loves your worshipful heart. If you have made it your desire to honor Him, He has destined you for honor in His Kingdom.

ADDITIONAL READING: 1 Peter 5:6-7

To the humble He reveals His secrets, and sweetly
draws nigh and invites him unto Himself.
THOMAS À KEMPIS

Rest in the Battle

I will give you rest from all your enemies. 2 Samuel 7:11

IN WORD

Our King is well acquainted with warfare. So are His people. No matter how zealously we follow God, it seems that everything in life is contested. We don't love Him, worship Him, or serve Him in a vacuum. The world is full of critics, skeptics, and the agenda of an evil-hearted enemy. Neither God nor His people have any illusion that there is peace on every side.

Notice, however, that God never told David He would remove his enemies. He simply promised to give him rest from them. There's a difference. And David certainly had enemies, his kingdom erupting in conflict in the years after his sin against Uriah the Hittite. Yet eventually David would emerge undefeated, his kingdom would endure, and it would be eternally established as the Kingdom of the Messiah. The "rest" didn't come immediately, and it didn't come easily. But it came. Just as God promised.

That's how His promise works out for all who honor Him with their deepest desires. We may encounter adversity, but it will not get the better of us. We may have detractors, but their opinions won't be confirmed. We may face the hostile opposition of the evil one's agenda, but it won't last. There will be rest, not just from some of our enemies, but from all of them. That's our King's desire for His subjects.

IN DEED

It's easy to become battle-weary. It's also easy to develop a defeatist attitude in the midst of the fray. But we need to understand the desire of our King to establish His people. He calls us overcomers, more-than-conquerors, corulers forever with Him. He sees the end of the battle far more clearly than we do. And from that big-picture perspective, He offers us small-picture hope. There is an end to the conflict, in this age and in the age to come. He will give us needed respite. And victory is absolutely certain.

ADDITIONAL READING: Romans 8:35-37

We sleep in peace in the arms of God when we
yield ourselves up to His providence.
FRANÇOIS FÉNELON

Eternal Extravagance

Your house and your kingdom will continue before me for all time, and your throne will be secure forever. 2 Samuel 7:16

IN WORD

God lavished promises of honor on David because David's desires honored God. His promises to us won't look exactly like David's—kingship over Israel's tribes doesn't really match the calling we've been given today—but they will look something like that. How do we know? Because these promises are more about the heart of God than about David. They aren't indiscriminate; they belong to those who worship God wholeheartedly and serve Him humbly. But they do reflect God's desires for His people forever.

Think about it: David's throne became eternal because a Son of David has established it forever. And that Son invites us to sit on the throne with Him. We are seated with Him in heavenly places (Ephesians 2:6), and we have been told we will reign with Him (Revelation 2:26-27; 3:21; 5:10; 20:6). Throughout Scripture, God has promised us His presence, His defense, and His honor, just as He did with David. All He is looking for is hearts that are completely His.

IN DEED

David responded to God's promises with gratitude, acceptance, and even deeper humility (2 Samuel 7:18-29). Surely he was disappointed that he would not be able to build the Temple himself, but he was astonished at the blessing of God beyond the Temple. As God focused on blessing David, David focused on blessing God. It was a mutual relationship of honor.

Many Christians pray to God with the expectation of His blessing but without a commitment to bless Him. But the fullness of His promises are for those who honor Him before seeking to be honored—who long to do great things for Him rather than simply expecting Him to do great things for them. Hearts fully devoted to Him will see His full devotion in all its extravagance. And God's devotion to His people will never end.

ADDITIONAL READING: Jeremiah 31:3

God's gifts put man's best dreams to shame.
ELIZABETH BARRETT BROWNING

Beyond Our Imagination

I tell you the truth, of all who have ever lived, none is greater than John the Baptist. Yet even the least person in the Kingdom of Heaven is greater than he is! Matthew 11:11

IN WORD

Jesus thought highly of John the Baptist, the prophet who prepared the way for His message in this world. John had been set apart by God from the moment of his conception and had fulfilled his role exactly as God had planned. He endured hardships, isolation, and rejection for the sake of the Kingdom, and even lost his life at the hands of another king. If anyone other than Jesus could lay claim to completing his Kingdom mission, John could.

So, we might think, John ranks really high in God's esteem, right? Yet in spite of his faithfulness, zeal, perseverance, and obedience, he was a mere human being living under the Fall. None was greater, Jesus said, but He quickly followed with an astonishing statement. The position of Kingdom citizen is greater than the greatest human before the Kingdom era. The inauguration of the Kingdom brought a quality of life and a privilege of royalty that the human race had never known. Yes, Abraham, Moses, David, the prophets, and John were all amazing human beings. But they were not expressions of the fullness of the Kingdom. And we can be.

Jesus' statement has little to do with rankings in heaven. We will surely see the great heroes of faith in the age of Kingdom fullness, and we will honor them. No, His statement is concerned more with the nature of the Kingdom itself. We have been given greatness by the King, and regardless of what anyone has accomplished in this realm, His realm offers a higher life. It's greater than we can imagine.

IN DEED

Never underestimate the privilege of being a Kingdom citizen. Never see yourself as a run-of-the-mill human being who merely has a different worldview than others. You are sheer greatness because God says so. The new covenant is infinitely greater than the old. And citizens of the Kingdom are infinitely greater than citizens of the world.

ADDITIONAL READING: 1 Peter 2:9-10

God looks at you as if you were a little Christ. Christ stands beside you to turn you into one.
C. S. LEWIS

Clash of Kingdoms

From the time John the Baptist began preaching until now, the Kingdom of Heaven has been forcefully advancing, and violent people are attacking it.
Matthew 11:12

IN WORD

Jesus offered two descriptions of the clash of kingdoms. In Matthew 11:12, the Kingdom of Heaven has come with force and violent people have attacked it. In the other account, the Kingdom message has been preached, and people are "forcing their way into it" (Luke 16:16, NIV). In either case, we get the impression that the Kingdom comes with considerable trauma and friction, and it isn't a smooth experience. There's a confrontation going on, a clash of kingdoms that puts Jesus and us on the front lines in a power shift for the ages.

That's no surprise to any of us. Perhaps some have had a relatively smooth experience in leaving the kingdom of darkness and entering the Kingdom of light, but not many do. The Kingdom of God doesn't just tiptoe around quietly in this age, even if many of our citizens are tentative. Whether visibly or behind the scenes, it breaks into the world with considerable impact. Every inch of this realm is contested, and so is every inch of our lives. Just as it took ten plagues and a lot of conflict for the Israelites to break free from Egypt, it takes considerable faith, resolve, and persistence for us to shift our loyalties from one kingdom to the other. Some end up somewhere in the middle, and they are deeply conflicted. But ideally we break into the Kingdom that has broken into this world with zeal. And it usually isn't a seamless transition.

IN DEED

Go for everything the Kingdom offers with everything in you. Be bold. God welcomes followers who seize the opportunity He gives. And when there's backlash, shaking circumstances, opposition, and trials, don't back down. This was never going to be a clean and simple event. It's the cosmic version of a seismic shift, and there are rumbles in heaven and earth. Kingdoms don't clash quietly. But only one will last, and it's worth the trauma of entering.

ADDITIONAL READING: Luke 16:16

> The soul that is united with God is feared by the
> devil as though it were God Himself.
> JOHN OF THE CROSS

The Power

The LORD your God is with you, he is mighty to save. Zephaniah 3:17, *NIV*

IN WORD

The most common malady of the human spirit—and the strongest enemy of our faith—is fear. That's why the most common biblical command is "fear not," "do not be afraid," or something similar. "Be strong and courageous," people of faith are told repeatedly in the Word. The dynamic is clear: Fear and faith are at opposite ends of a spectrum, and when we move toward one, we move away from the other.

But a command to "fear not" doesn't mean very much unless we're given a good reason. The human mind usually does not dispense with its fears without an explanation. Instead, we need to know why fear is illegitimate and why we should be courageous and full of faith. So God, through Zephaniah, gives us our reason. Soon after He assures the remnant that they will be able to lie down at night without fear, He tells them why. Fear is illegitimate because "the LORD your God is with you, he is mighty to save." God's people do not need to fear, because He is powerfully sovereign over everything that can make us afraid.

We know that intellectually. Our minds are familiar with this truth. And maybe that's the problem; familiarity breeds complacency. Truths that remain only in the mind are taken for granted and neglected, and they never sink into the heart, where they can actually impact us where we hurt. We can remind ourselves repeatedly that God is mighty to save, but until we feel that truth in the depths of our heart, we will remain afraid.

IN DEED

What do you fear today? How do those fears constrain you and limit what you are able to do? What task has God called you to do that would require a scary step of faith? Spend some time meditating on the God who is mighty to save—the God who delights in and rejoices over you—and ask yourself, "Why am I afraid?" Let the truth of God's power sink in, and you will be well equipped to take a huge step of faith—and to lie down at night unafraid.

ADDITIONAL READING: Deuteronomy 31:6

God incarnate is the end of fear; and the heart that realizes that
He is in the midst . . . will be quiet in the midst of alarm.
F. B. MEYER

Honor and Praise

"I will give you honor and praise among all the peoples of the earth when I restore your fortunes before your very eyes," says the LORD.
Zephaniah 3:20, *NIV*

IN WORD

God is the object of our worship, worthy of all praise and honor and glory forever and ever. But in a remarkable turn of events, when God restores and gathers His people and makes them plainly visible in the eyes of the world, He will give us praise and honor. The harsh opinions of the world that have kept people of faith in low esteem will suddenly be turned into favor. The social systems that made human power, ingenuity, economics, and achievement the ultimate goal of life will be exposed as always superficial and now obsolete. And those who believed in a humble Messiah who won people into His Kingdom through a humiliating execution will be revealed as the wisest and most powerful of all. Our lowly submission to our God will result in exaltation in His Kingdom.

Isn't that amazing? The first will be last and the last will be first. Those who served the most, who offered themselves as living sacrifices, and who maintained their love in the face of hatred will be lifted up and honored. Meanwhile, all those who invested their lives in the passing values of an ego-driven world will have to look up to the ones they once discounted. In the end—whether of a captivity, in Zephaniah's time, or of time itself—God's people are revealed as sons and daughters of glory.

IN DEED

Remember God's promise when you feel drawn to the values of the world and the idols of the age. Do not give any piece of your soul to the things that will one day be made low. They sap the life out of those who cling to them. Instead, invest your heart in an invisible Kingdom that will eventually be the last—and best—Kingdom standing.

ADDITIONAL READING: Revelation 3:11-13

The glory of God is a living man; and the life
of man consists in beholding God.
IRENAEUS

For His Pleasure

Our God is in the heavens, and he does as he wishes. Psalm 115:3

IN WORD

Some religions teach fatalism. "Whatever is going to happen is going to happen." "If it's meant to be, it will be." "Everything happens for a reason." The assumption is that human beings have little or no impact on the divine will—that whatever God wants to do, He is going to do. And He isn't going to ask us about it.

Christians believe God is sovereign—that He is ultimately in control and will certainly accomplish His purposes. But Scripture also affirms that we can influence Him with our prayers and impact the way His purposes are accomplished. He incorporates us into His plans, and He uses those who are willing more integrally than He uses those who aren't. Despite the voice of our inner fatalist—and most of us have one— we can partner with Him in His Kingdom work.

There are times, however, when we feel too much responsibility in that Kingdom partnership. We act as if everything depends on us, as if God will quickly move on to someone else if we don't play our cards right, as if our capacity to blow it is greater than His capacity to make sure His will is done or our prayer is answered. We obsess over whether we qualify for the partnership and fear being left out of His plans if we don't measure up. Instead of a God who does whatever He pleases, we end up with a God who does only what we earn, deserve, or arrange by pulling the right spiritual strings. And we live very stressful lives.

IN DEED

Relax. God is on His throne, and He does whatever He pleases. Yes, some aspects of His will for your life are dependent on your response, but He is patient and merciful and will keep setting you up for breakthroughs and blessings. He is not capricious in His generosity, dangling gifts in front of you and then pulling them away when you fail a test. He does not tease His children. His will for you is relentlessly good. It pleases Him to bless you. And as His own Word says, He does whatever He pleases.

ADDITIONAL READING: Psalm 103:19

> The goodness of God knows how to use our disordered wishes
> and actions, lovingly turning them to our advantage.
> BERNARD OF CLAIRVAUX

Our Domain

The heavens belong to the LORD, but he has given the earth to all humanity.
Psalm 115:16

IN WORD

Long ago in Eden, God gave human beings authority over the earth (Genesis 1:28).
It wasn't full autonomy; we were meant to implement His will as stewards of His
authority—a partnership between the Creator and the created, blending our desires
and decisions with His overall purposes. God entrusted us with a lot.

When God brought us into partnership with Him, He didn't give us authority over
everything. We aren't masters of the universe. He gave us dominion over this planet.
When Revelation tells us we will reign with Him forever, the domain is the new earth.
Even now, we have authority in this realm and a sacred responsibility to learn how to
exercise that authority. The well-being of the planet—and the people around us—
depends on our fulfillment of the role He assigned.

That doesn't mean we can't influence the invisible world. Scripture speaks of "spiritual forces of evil in the heavenly realms" (Ephesians 6:12, NIV). Our prayers and
our actions impact this unseen battlefield because this battlefield influences earthly
activities. God is above the fray in the highest heaven—what Paul referred to as the
"third heaven" (2 Corinthians 12:2)—where no battle rages. But wherever spirits of
darkness dwell in places that affect our earthly existence, we have authority. God has
given it to us in order to implement His victory.

IN DEED

Many people confuse these distinctions, either claiming spiritual authority in realms
where they don't have it, or disowning human authority in all earthly matters because
it's all God's domain. Today's verse affirms the distinctions clearly. All authority in
every realm belongs to God, and the highest heavens are exclusively His domain. But
He has given earth to mankind. We are to actively, assertively seek to establish His
Kingdom on this planet, praying for His will to be done and His Kingdom to come,
and living out the answers to our own prayers. The King is filling His Kingdom with
people who understand the Kingdom ways.

ADDITIONAL READING: Genesis 1:28

Already we have within us the life of heaven.
GEORGE ELDON LADD

God's Joy in Giving

He made known to us the mystery of his will according to his good pleasure.
Ephesians 1:9, *NIV*

IN WORD

God feels pleasure. That may come as a surprise to people who think He is angry most of the time, always focused on sin, watching us from a distance, or without feelings at all. But according to His Word, God feels a range of emotions (we, who are made in His image, should easily recognize that in Him), and one of those emotions is pleasure.

What causes God to feel pleasure? Probably a lot of things—He is not a discontent, frustrated being. One of the things He enjoys most is clearly stated in the Gospels. He thoroughly enjoys giving His children the Kingdom (Luke 12:32). In the context of Jesus' statement to His followers, the Kingdom involves freedom from worry about food, clothes, and the substance of life. All is freely given to those who rest in Him. The King is good to His citizens.

Part of the gift of God's Kingdom is expressed in today's verse. He enjoys making known to us the mystery of His will. That pleases Him. He doesn't want His will to be a secret. The purposes and plans from before the foundation of the world, the grand designing of fulfilling everything in Christ and bringing all things under His headship, are there for us to see. He has revealed them. Like an artist unveiling a masterpiece carefully and precisely crafted for years, God has unveiled the mysteries of the Kingdom for His people. And He takes pleasure in our discovery of its wonders.

IN DEED

Ask God to show you the mystery of His will. Invest yourself in His masterpiece by marveling over it, exploring it, learning about it, and implementing it. His Kingdom is not simply a work to admire; it's for audience participation. So ask Him for Kingdom insights that you can put into practice and use to impact the world around you. Pray for divine solutions to earthly problems. Ask for His Kingdom to come on earth as it is in heaven, and volunteer to be a vehicle for the answer. And feel His pleasure over your request.

ADDITIONAL READING: Luke 12:32

> You must live with people to know their problems,
> and live with God in order to solve them.
> PETER TAYLOR FORSYTH

God of Purpose

Everything I plan will come to pass, for I do whatever I wish. Isaiah 46:10

IN WORD

God leaves a lot up to human will. Again and again in His Word, He gives us conditions. "If you fully obey the LORD . . . you will experience all these blessings" (Deuteronomy 28:1-2). "If my people . . . will humble themselves and pray . . . I will hear from heaven and will forgive their sins and restore their land" (2 Chronicles 7:14). "If you forgive those who sin against you, your heavenly Father will forgive you" (Matthew 6:14). The list could go on and on. He freely offers His goodness and grace, but a lot of things depend on how we receive them.

But God doesn't leave everything in the hands of fickle human beings. He knows ahead of time how to accomplish His plans, and He will do it. Sure, He brings willing human beings into the process—He knows us, calls us, chooses us, and more—but there's no risk of His overall plans and promises being left undone. We might miss out on something He offers, but He doesn't miss out on anything He purposes. As we have seen, He does all that He pleases.

That's why Christians panicking over the headlines makes no sense. Neither does anxiety over threats to our well-being. Those headlines and threats serve us well as a call to action—God never tells us to rest to the point of being passively uninvolved in His purposes—but they are not cause for alarm. We can be fully confident in His ability to direct the course of history and our own lives.

IN DEED

We are to work faithfully as though God's instructions are our full responsibility, and rest completely as though the results are fully up to Him. That's a hard balance for many of us—we tend to push too actively or relax too passively—but it's a thoroughly biblical balance. Are we called to action? Yes. Are we called to restful trust? Yes. The former is what we do with our mouths, hands, and feet. The latter is what we do in our hearts—where we can be profoundly confident that God will do what He pleases.

ADDITIONAL READING: Exodus 14:14

Work as though everything depends on you; pray
as though everything depends on God.
ANONYMOUS

God of Promise

I have said what I would do, and I will do it. Isaiah 46:11

IN WORD

We serve a God of promise. He says what He means, and does what He says He will do. That isn't true in every Kingdom; we're well familiar with campaign exaggerations, broken promises, and spinmasters specializing in damage control. We've swallowed lies as truths and accepted failures as successes, simply because we believed what we were told. But we never need to fear deception in the Kingdom of our King. He doesn't spin His truth to make it palatable or add fine print to His promises. His Word is His bond.

It's possible to be mistaken about what He has said, of course, but only when we choose to apply His promises more broadly than He meant them. Even so, He means them pretty broadly. Despite the explanations of those who feel the need to clarify His Word for Him, He really does mean what He says. Those who believe Him—who insist against all odds and against all outward evidence that what He says is true—will find Him faithful. History will vindicate every word of God that was resolutely and persistently accepted and believed by one of His people.

That means that if we call ourselves believers, we need to actually believe! Our job is to cultivate faith in what He says. His big-picture purposes will be accomplished—there's no question about that—but He prefers to implement His will in cooperation with human beings. Our prayers and faith are an indispensable part of His plan. He will do what He says for anyone who actually hears what He says and grabs on to it.

IN DEED

Invest your life in grabbing hold of the things of God. Listen for His Kingdom agenda and let your heart latch on to it. Hear His promises and tell your mind to grip them tightly, whether you understand them fully or not. Determine to be known as someone who trusts God implicitly, just like a child who knows no guile. Know the heart of your King, and depend on Him to do exactly what He has said He will do.

ADDITIONAL READING: 2 Corinthians 1:20

Faith expects from God what is beyond all expectation.
ANDREW MURRAY

Recovering All

Abram recovered all the goods that had been taken, and he brought back his nephew Lot with his possessions and all the women and other captives.
Genesis 14:16

IN WORD

The church has done a pretty good job of teaching a gospel of redemption. We've been bought back and cleansed of sin, set free from captivity. That's our message. But it isn't the whole message. Restoration is an essential part of the gospel. God doesn't just redeem us from the past; He restores what has been lost. History is headed toward a full restoration of everything that has been lost and broken, and we can participate in the process even now. The Kingdom of God is one of repair and restoration.

Abram's recovery mission is a great picture of the Kingdom spirit. Kings from around the Dead Sea had decided to declare their freedom from foreign powers, and war broke out when the kings of those foreign powers came to reclaim their servant-nations. The invading kings sacked Sodom, Gomorrah, and their allies, taking everything and everyone—including Lot and his family. Abram, who to this point had been very tentative around the rules of Egypt and Canaan, suddenly amassed an army and went after them. And victory wasn't enough. He pursued the enemy all the way past Damascus and recovered all that had been taken.

IN DEED

That's the attitude we should have as members of God's Kingdom. We should never compromise on anything the enemy has taken. No illness, injustice, or deception should slide by uncontested. God has given us the keys of the Kingdom, and everything the enemy steals, kills, or destroys is stolen, killed, or destroyed illegally. Jesus has won, yet His people often continue to act defeated.

Go after the spoils of war. Pray aggressively. Address injustices. Seek the *shalom* God intended for this world. Bless everyone—including those outside the Kingdom. Remember that the enemy was stripped of power at the Cross. Do everything in your power—and God's within you—to recover all.

ADDITIONAL READING: 1 Samuel 30

> By a Carpenter mankind was made, and only by
> that Carpenter can mankind be remade.
> DESIDERIUS ERASMUS

Faith Takes Action

Melchizedek, the king of Salem and a priest of God Most High, brought Abram some bread and wine. Genesis 14:18

IN WORD

We don't know where he came from or where he went. Scripture is silent on the background of Melchizedek. All we know is he is both a king and a priest; his name means "king of righteousness"; he is the king of Salem, or literally *shalom*, which sounds virtually identical to "prince of peace"; and he comes with bread and wine and a blessing.

It's hard not to pick up on the messianic symbolism of this character. Some even believe he is the preincarnate Christ, an ancient appearance of Jesus Himself. Regardless, this encounter is a divine endorsement of Abram's endeavor. His pursuit of the invading kings far beyond his own region was the right thing to do. His aggressive approach was commended, even though it seems a little uncharacteristic for the usually docile patriarch. God sent someone to bless Abram because, in this case, faith wasn't the final word.

Think about that. This father of faith who would wait decades for a promised son didn't just sit in his tent and believe God would resolve everything for him in this situation. He didn't wait when the situation was urgent. He trusted God not to recover everything *for* him but to recover everything *through* him. His faith led to action.

IN DEED

We need to understand this. Faith is the currency of God's Kingdom, but faith isn't always passive. Sometimes faith waits for decades, and sometimes it prompts us to get up and do something now. When the enemy is on a rampage, passivity is not an option. It isn't the Kingdom way. We may receive from God through faith and patience, but we confront the enemy with faith and urgency. Some things simply have to be addressed right away.

Learn to discern the difference. Never be passive toward evil. When you ask for the Kingdom of God to come, you are asking for rival kingdoms to go. And in God's strength, you play a part in the transition.

ADDITIONAL READING: James 2:14-26

Expect great things from God. Attempt great things for God.
WILLIAM CAREY

God's Victory

Melchizedek blessed Abram with this blessing: "Blessed be Abram by God Most High, Creator of heaven and earth. And blessed be God Most High, who has defeated your enemies for you." Genesis 14:19-20

IN WORD

The king of righteousness, the king of *shalom*, blessed Abram in the name of God Most High, the Creator of heaven and earth. This is no ordinary blessing in a time when Abram's family members are the only human beings known to follow the one true God. The mysterious priest speaks for this God and validates Abram's exploits. He rejoices with Abram in his victory.

But is it really Abram's victory? Not according to the blessing. Yes, Abram saw the injustice and gathered more than three hundred men. Yes, Abram pursued the invading kings all the way to the far north of the land and beyond. Yes, Abram rescued the people and brought back the spoils. But Abram didn't win this victory; God did. Abram's faith was inspired and supported by someone with much greater power. Abram was the agent, but God was the instigator and the provider.

That should give us extreme confidence in our battles. We may feel as if we're going against the enemy all alone, feeling the weight of circumstances and facing an uphill climb, but the reality of the situation is different. In truth, our warfare against evil and injustice is fully ours and fully God's—our hearts and His in unity, our actions prompted by His inspiration, our efforts and His strength. When the dust has settled, we can claim the blessing of Melchizedek: God has defeated our enemies for us.

IN DEED

We all long to claim this same victory, and we can. God looks at our faithfulness and trust, accepts our worship, invites even our weakest efforts, and then fights our battles for us. We don't have to worry about being left on the battlefield alone. We don't have to dread the encounter. We simply go as He leads and trust Him to be there. And He is. The Most High wins victories for His people.

ADDITIONAL READING: Psalm 144:1-2

> All God's giants have been weak men who did great things for God because they reckoned on His being with them.
> HUDSON TAYLOR

The Cycle of Blessing

I will make you into a great nation. I will bless you and make you famous, and you will be a blessing to others. Genesis 12:2

IN WORD

God promised to make Abraham into a great nation. We can trace the historical fulfill-ment of that promise as God grew Abraham's family into the people of Israel, which eventually became the vehicle for the Messiah, who then sent His followers to the ends of the earth to draw people into God's Kingdom. Truly the blessing covenant that began with one man became a worldwide phenomenon that continues to bear fruit.

While biblical scholars discuss the meaning of the covenant and its implications for believers today, many miss the Kingdom dynamic embedded in God's promise. It begins with a blessing given to Abraham, and ends with Abraham blessing others. Abraham receives the benefits of the covenant, but he also spreads them around. He receives and then gives. The blessed becomes a blesser.

That's God's intention for all His people, though many of us miss it. We can be so focused on receiving from God that we forget about giving. We are zealous about the gifts without being zealous about sharing them. We want to be blessed but often miss the joy of being a blessing. We need to remember that God pours life and joy and provision into us not only for our sake but also for the sake of others. Or as Jesus put it, "Freely you have received; freely give" (Matthew 10:8, NIV). In Luke, Jesus even reverses the order: "Give, and you will receive. . . . The amount you give will determine the amount you get back" (Luke 6:38). In other words, "Demonstrate that you under-stand the Kingdom dynamic, and you will be increasingly allowed to participate in it."

IN DEED

This is the cycle of the Kingdom: God gives, we receive. We give, others receive. Others receive, and all of us give glory to God. Then God gives even more. We dis-rupt that cycle by neglecting any single element of it, but we can step back into it at any time. We are blessed in order to bless.

ADDITIONAL READING: Luke 6:37-38

God has given us two hands: one for receiving and the other for giving.
BILLY GRAHAM

Kingdom Growth

All the families on earth will be blessed through you. Genesis 12:3

IN WORD

God's greatest works often start very small. A nation from a childless couple, a Kingdom from a mustard seed, a global rescue mission from a baby in a manger—all are case studies in His tendency to obscure His works from all eyes except those of faith. Fully capable of making a scene and dazzling all observers, He prefers to begin almost imperceptibly. Mighty oaks grow from small acorns because that's how God has designed His world.

So it should be no surprise when a covenant given to one man results in a worldwide blessing that extends to all peoples—every single ethnic/linguistic/social group on the planet. It has taken a long time to get to them; the mission is still in progress. But while missionaries and sending agencies and supporters are eagerly strategizing for the evangelization of the world, the covenant continues to bless those of us who have been impacted by Abraham's seed and the Messiah who came from it. The far-reaching blessing never ends.

This big-things-from-small-beginnings dynamic also applies to you personally. It should be no surprise if your calling begins with a whisper and a seemingly minor act of faith, or if your God-given dreams are fulfilled after simmering for years, unnoticed by anyone else. With God, you can't measure the greatness of the end by the size of the beginning. "Little" very often ends up "huge."

IN DEED

Expect great things from God, even when your opportunities seem small or insignificant. In fact, expect them *especially* when your opportunities seem small and insignificant because this is His modus operandi. Participate in His worldwide mission to whatever extent you can, knowing that the same dynamics of fulfillment apply to your life at an individual level. Never despise the Kingdom of "small things." It is leading to enormous impact.

ADDITIONAL READING: Luke 13:18-21

Be assured, if you walk with Him and look to Him, and expect help from Him, He will never fail you.
GEORGE MÜLLER

Carefree Kingdom

Can all your worries add a single moment to your life? Luke 12:25

IN WORD

Jesus went to great lengths to get worry and fear out of the hearts of His followers. In Luke 12, He assures them that they are more precious than the birds of the air and the flowers of the field. Though the rest of the world lives in stress over food and clothes, God wants the citizens of His Kingdom to be carefree about such matters. He tells us not to worry because He is fully capable of caring for us.

Notice that Jesus did not tell us not to worry because nothing bad will ever happen. He promised provision, but only after declaring a larger principle: Our lives are about things much greater than food and clothes. "Life is more than food, and your body more than clothing"(Luke 12:23). Yes, He is God the provider, but He is also God the bigger picture. Above and beyond everything we face in this tangible world, our lives are rooted in a larger story than the day-to-day narrative most people see us living in.

That's why worry doesn't fit the Kingdom culture. It's an intensive focus on the smaller story. Like a reader who gets the facts of the plot but misses the overarching themes, worriers miss the truth between the lines of their lives. God sees the bigger picture and invites us into it. He gives us a greater perspective.

IN DEED

Worry isn't in the heart of the King—not even a trace of it. Therefore, it shouldn't be in the hearts of Kingdom citizens. We can live with full confidence that God doesn't neglect His people. Those who are faithful to Him are never forsaken by Him (Psalm 37:25). That frees us up to focus entirely on the larger themes of life. God doesn't want His people distracted by peripheral details; He wants our hearts to be fully engaged with what He's doing in the world. Instead of being preoccupied with survival, we invest ourselves in Kingdom issues and trust our needs to the One who promised to meet them. We can live carefree.

ADDITIONAL READING: Psalm 37:25-26

Worry is an intrusion into God's providence.
JOHN HAGGAI

Crowned with Glory

Look at the lilies and how they grow. . . . Solomon in all his glory was not dressed as beautifully as they are. And if God cares so wonderfully for flowers that are here today and thrown into the fire tomorrow, he will certainly care for you. Why do you have so little faith? Luke 12:27-28

IN WORD

Maybe this is just a promise about provision. Maybe Jesus simply wanted to assure His followers of God's ability to clothe and feed them. But the heart of God shows up in even greater depth between the lines of this passage. One of His goals in creation is to clothe His world with His own glory. He doesn't just want to clothe us; He wants to make us shine.

It would be easy to feel helpless and hopeless about that. After all, if not even Solomon was clothed as beautifully as the flowers of the field, how can we measure up? But Jesus isn't telling us to measure up. He's telling us to relax. God has put glory into everything He has made, including us. Above all His creatures, we are made in His image for many reasons, one of which is to carry His splendor. We don't have to do anything to qualify for that privilege other than allow Him to fill us and then simply be ourselves. No striving or straining is required; in fact, that only gets in the way. We were created "a little lower than God" and the angels, specifically to be vessels of glory and honor (Psalm 8:5; Hebrews 2:6-7). The King wants the members of His Kingdom to look a lot like Him.

IN DEED

If we ever had the impression that God is interested only in obedience—in the compliant behavior of human servants—this passage corrects us. God loves beauty. He crowns His creation with glory not because He has a big ego but because He delights in extravagant generosity. Like an artist whose creativity and sensitivity show up in the finer details of His masterpiece, God's artistry is devoted even to the throw-away foliage of the fields. How much more is He interested in making us beautiful in His eyes? We can relax—and fully entrust ourselves to the zeal of the Artist.

ADDITIONAL READING: Psalm 8

> God passes through the thicket to the world, and wherever his glance falls he turns all things to beauty.
> JOHN OF THE CROSS

The Kingdom Adventure

Seek the Kingdom of God above all else, and he will give you everything you need. Luke 12:31

IN WORD

Imagine being the Creator. Imagine crafting humanity in your own likeness, endowing them with glory, positioning them to reflect the very best of your Kingdom or, even more importantly, your own heart as King. Would you then saddle them with so many responsibilities for basic survival and well-being that they didn't have time for the treasures of your Kingdom? Of course not.

Neither would God. It is never His intention for us to be so fully occupied with sustaining ourselves that we don't have time for a relationship with Him or each other. Granted, much Kingdom business and many Kingdom issues come up in the context of daily life and interaction, but many of us are so absorbed in keeping our heads above water that we wouldn't think of taking time to enjoy the swim. God didn't create us for busyness. He created us for Himself.

That means we have every right to end our preoccupation with survival and to-do lists and focus instead on the King and His Kingdom. To some people, that brings to mind full-time evangelism and discipleship, but the Kingdom is much bigger than that. Seeking His Kingdom means seeking His way of doing life, of exploring the truth and beauty of His creation, of gazing into His face and being transformed by the view. That's what we were created for. And the promise of Jesus is that God will take care of the peripherals if we invest ourselves in that.

IN DEED

Seek first the Kingdom of God, not because it's a requirement of a demanding God but because it's an invitation into an adventure with Him. You can't take a lot of baggage on this adventure, and you wouldn't want to anyway. Being weighed down with schedules and concerns doesn't enhance the experience, so our Guide on this adventure relieves us of that pressure. He promises to take care of all the details if we will focus all our energy on the adventure with Him. It's not only a good deal—it's a liberating one.

ADDITIONAL READING: Psalm 84:11

Faith in the Kingdom of God is what makes us light
of heart and what Christian joy is all about.
JOHN MAIN

The King's Pleasure

Don't be afraid, little flock. For it gives your Father great happiness to give you the Kingdom. Luke 12:32

IN WORD

A lot of Christian instruction tells us how we have to measure up in order to get God's greatest blessings. Our teachers don't state things exactly that way, but that's the implication of their words. Holiness and righteousness are prerequisites for many of the Kingdom's benefits. "He answers our prayers only when our will aligns with His" (which never really fully happens until we're extremely mature, of course). "He provides for our needs but rarely our wants, unless our wants are thoroughly selfless and sanctified." And on and on. Or so we seem to think.

It's not that way, of course. Our religious instincts make God a begrudging giver, and then only to those who are spiritually worthy. But the tone of the Gospels and the message of Scripture in general is that God is an extravagant giver who loves blessing even the least worthy in this world. He is radically generous to sinners and saints alike, delighting in surprising us with gifts of grace and glory. And He especially delights in giving His gifts to those who look forward to them rather than those who worry about whether they are going to happen. He rewards fearless hopers with the fruit of their hopes.

IN DEED

Kingdom privileges cannot be earned. Sometimes we have to position ourselves for them—you don't give a teenager the car keys unless he has done a little preparation work. The keys of the Kingdom are a powerful tool for those with wisdom to use them. But they are still given by grace. It isn't our worthiness that allows us to enjoy the glory of the Kingdom. It's the Father's pleasure that invites us into it.

Life can be a struggle, but never let that struggle convince you that the Father is reluctant to bestow Kingdom blessings. He isn't. He looks forward to the gifts He gives, loves His own generosity, and delights in seeing smiles on the faces of His children. Enter into everything He offers without reluctance. Boldly ask for more insights, answers to prayer, and miraculous intervention. He is pleased to provide all we need and more.

ADDITIONAL READING: Matthew 16:19

God is all that is good . . . and the goodness that everything has is His.
JULIAN OF NORWICH

Forever Increasing

The purses of heaven never get old or develop holes. Your treasure will be safe; no thief can steal it and no moth can destroy it. Wherever your treasure is, there the desires of your heart will also be. Luke 12:33-34

IN WORD

We live in a physical world. We have material bodies that we feed with material nourishment in order to sustain ourselves to do material work, from which we earn material money and buy material possessions. There's nothing wrong with that. It's unavoidable; this is the dimension God has placed us in. But we were designed to function in other dimensions too, and when we come into His Kingdom, we regain that capacity. We think thoughts by the Spirit, influence both material and spiritual realms, and begin to see life not as "sacred" and "secular" but as all-encompassing under our King. And we have the ability to invest in eternity.

How is that possible? When we become Kingdom citizens, our abilities and possessions become Kingdom property. We can leverage the very visible things of this world for spiritual purposes. We can transform temporary blessings into lasting investments. We can take the substance of one realm and leverage it for the benefit of the other. We can sow seeds that will never stop bearing fruit.

IN DEED

Think about that. In this age, we marvel at how early investments in our twenties can multiply into substantial benefits in our seventies and eighties. But our investments in God's Kingdom never cease to multiply throughout eternity. They bear fruit upon fruit upon fruit, in this age and the age to come. That's why Jesus tries to shift our priorities. The investments we make in the material world are subject to damage, theft, and a wavering market. The investments we make in the Kingdom are safe, secure, and forever increasing. Wherever we invest our hearts, our treasures will follow. And if our hearts are rooted in eternal realities, our treasures never end.

ADDITIONAL READING: 1 Timothy 6:17-19

The world says, "The more you take, the more you have."
Christ says, "The more you give, the more you are."
FREDERICK BUECHNER

First Things First

At that time every one of your people whose name is written in the book will be rescued. Daniel 12:1

IN WORD

When Daniel wrote the words given to him by God, "your people" meant Judah's captives in Babylon. But the prophecies of Daniel have cosmic implications that go far beyond the chosen nation of Israel at a particular time in its history. His book speaks of the time of the end, of national powers that did not exist when he wrote, and of cataclysmic conflict in the heavens and on earth. Daniel wrote of ultimate events.

Though many people sift through the apocalyptic nature of Daniel to discover when, where, and how these things will take place, there's a deeper message to be gleaned. God rather plainly gives us the "what" and the "why." The very fact that God is cultivating a people for Himself, purifying them and preserving them for the end, is worth more of our focus than all the secrets we want to know. The point is that God has a book, names are written in it, and He will, without any shadow of doubt, deliver those who are listed there. God's Kingdom is unalterably secure.

We need to know that in uncertain times. The truth is that every era has been an "uncertain time," and the knowledge that God is in the business of restoration and preservation is vital. Daniel's prophetic times may apply to a specific generation, but his prophetic principles certainly do not. They are everyone's. The prophecies of the delivering God are never irrelevant.

IN DEED

When you read of the end of time and the coming Kingdom in books like Daniel and Revelation, make first things first. Before deciphering seasons and events, decipher this: God has a book, and knowing that you're in it is monumentally important. Not only do you need to know the security of your destination, you also need to know the nature of the God who gets you there. If you don't, discerning the end of days will terrify you. If you do, discerning the end of days won't really matter.

ADDITIONAL READING: Mark 13:29-32

In God's faithfulness lies eternal security.
CORRIE TEN BOOM

Last Things Later

What I have said is kept secret and sealed until the time of the end. Daniel 12:9

IN WORD

When the truth is told, mysteries are solved. At least that's the way it is with human beings, and that's what we expect from Scripture. But the dynamic doesn't usually apply to God; His revelation often deepens the mysteries surrounding it. When God speaks, His people learn something. And when we learn from Him, more questions are raised.

The Lord's word to Daniel is typical of His word to any of us: He reveals Himself and hides Himself. He spells out truth for us, and He seals it up in secrecy. The entire Bible is a revelation of ultimate truth, and yet it leads to more ultimate questions that we cannot have answered until the end of time. The more we know about God, the more we want to know.

Haven't you seen this principle at work? We are given a clear picture of how sin entered this world, but why God let the serpent roam the Garden remains a mystery to us. We marvel at Israel's exodus from Egypt, but God gives us no answers about why His chosen people were enslaved for four hundred years to begin with. We have seen the glory of the Son in the Cross that redeems us, but we still haven't plumbed the depths of its mysteries. Every time God reveals a "what," we feel compelled to ask a "why." And the absence of answers drives us deeper into Him.

IN DEED

That's how God designed His Word. He told Daniel deep mysteries of the Kingdom, but He only whetted the prophet's appetite. The ultimate end remained sealed; full disclosure would not come for ages.

Why does God operate this way? That itself is a mystery, but we can guess at why: His people seek Him only when their appetites have been whetted. Not before, and not after being satisfied. And God wants to be sought. So He reveals truth and waits. He waits for us to come further in, to dive into the mysteries, to seek the knowledge only He has—until the day the mysteries are revealed.

ADDITIONAL READING: Colossians 2:2-3

We taste Thee, O Thou living bread, and long to feast upon Thee still.
BERNARD OF CLAIRVAUX

Living in the Now

As for you, go your way until the end.   Daniel 12:13

IN WORD

The messenger who spoke to Daniel laid out provocative, tantalizing predictions for the prophet to write. He revealed deep mysteries that generation after generation for millennia to come would explore. Then, as if speaking to someone with restricted access to eternal secrets, the angel told Daniel to go his way.

Yes, these marvelous truths were not for Daniel and his generation. They had an immediate application in the deliverance of God's people, of course, but they would not be ultimately fulfilled in Daniel's presence. Like Moses the great prophet, who dealt in divine mysteries on a daily basis, Daniel found that the fulfillment of the promise would come outside of his own lifetime. He was to know and to write, not to live through it.

That's often the way it is with those who read God's Word. We see in Scripture the scope of world history—and even glimpses of cosmic history—yet we experience only what we learn of God's character and His ways. Some of us were there during this or that great move of His Spirit, and some of us may be there when Jesus comes again. But God's revelation is not primarily about those who experience the key events of time; it's about those who experience the Person of eternity. Most of life isn't epoch-altering; it's going our way—God's way—day in and day out. And we're to keep going that way until we've finished our days.

IN DEED

Many Christians focus their spirituality around major events, whether those events are personal milestones or history-making headlines. We set our hearts on the big-ticket items of experience rather than on the day-to-day constancy of spiritual maturity. Like Daniel, our eyes and ears may be full of astounding, monumental truths. But also like Daniel, we're called to live well in the little things.

Try not to live your spiritual experience as a series of mountaintops, but rather as a continuous journey in the valleys and the plains. See the mountaintops, but walk where you are. As you look toward the coming of Jesus, live in the presence of Jesus.

ADDITIONAL READING: 1 John 2:28

> There is only one time that is important—now. It is the most important time because it is the only time we have any power over.
> LEO TOLSTOY

Living for the End

At the end of the days, you will rise again to receive the inheritance set aside for you. Daniel 12:13

IN WORD

Most of us live our lives with a conscious focus. We have a vision of what we would like to be, or how we would like to live, and we pursue it. That vision can be shaped primarily by work, relationships, lifestyle, family, location, leisure, or any combination thereof. But few people live with a focus on the end of days. Few are single-minded about the inheritance to come.

That's true not only of those unaware of the gospel, but also of those who have believed in it for a long time. We're very conscious of the principle of Matthew 6:33— "Seek first his kingdom and his righteousness, and all these things will be given to you as well" (NIV)—but we easily become absorbed in the "all these things." Our focus on eternal fruitfulness fades into the more urgent awareness of this month's bills, or that opportunity that's slipping away, or that home we want to buy, or . . . well, you know your list, and it probably goes on for a while. The point is that priorities are subtle in the ways they shift, and we can mistakenly think we're focused on an eternal inheritance while we're really driven by an immediate agenda. Unlike Daniel, we don't have a visible angel reminding us to set our hopes on the end of days.

We do, however, have testimonies just as valid, even more so. We have God's written Word, we have the encouragement of His Spirit within us and in the believers around us, and we have visible evidence that our bodies don't last forever. Together, they point us to ultimate goals, the final day when God settles everything, the rewards of the Kingdom that are promised us in many, many passages. We have no reason not to lay up treasures in heaven rather than anxieties on earth.

IN DEED

Remind yourself constantly today of your true focus. Realize that your decisions are not a matter of the next few decades but of the age to come, and base your decisions on that realization. Remember that at the end of days, you'll rise up and receive an inheritance.

ADDITIONAL READING: Matthew 6:33

Faith in God will always be crowned.
WILLIAM S. PLUMER

The Kingdom Culture

God blesses . . . Matthew 5:3-11

IN WORD

We live in a Kingdom of blessing. Not every citizen knows that. Many people think God's Kingdom is a culture of demands and expectations, of impossible purity, of feigned lifestyles, or simply of crushing burdens that are somehow meant to develop our character. But the Son of the King says differently. When He began to teach, He first described the Kingdom culture and the attitudes of the citizens who are most highly favored and blessed. He decreed the happiness of His people.

That's what "blessed" means: happy, content, thriving in your sweet spot. When people move to another country, they want to know how to fit into the culture and avoid unnecessary clashes with its people. The Beatitudes are Jesus' explanation of how to minimize culture shock in His Kingdom. Those who maintain these attitudes are those who are most likely to fit in and enjoy the experience.

The Beatitudes are filled with important insights about the Kingdom of God, but near the top of the list are these two: (1) This is what the Kingdom culture is like, and (2) the King wants His citizens to be happy. In spite of sermons we might have heard contrary to these two points—that the Sermon on the Mount is only for a specific era or dispensation, and that God wants us to be holy, not happy (as if the two were unrelated)—the words of Jesus are very clear. The Kingdom is home to people who hold these attitudes, and the Kingdom is a happy place.

IN DEED

There are plenty of paradoxes in the Beatitudes—like how it's possible for a mourner to be happy—but this Kingdom has no shortage of paradoxes anyway. Jesus doesn't ask us to fully understand eternal truth; He asks us to embrace it. Those who do will discover a kind of contentment and peace that the world—our culture of origin—can never offer. Our spirits are truly at home when immersed in the attitudes of the Kingdom.

ADDITIONAL READING: Deuteronomy 28:1-6

> The character we find in the Beatitudes is nothing less than our Lord's own character put into words.
> BILLY GRAHAM

A Culture of Humility

God blesses those who are poor and realize their need for him, for the Kingdom of Heaven is theirs. Matthew 5:3

IN WORD

It's a common biblical theme: God loves and blesses humility. "These are the ones I look on with favor: those who are humble and contrite in spirit, and who tremble at my word" (Isaiah 66:2, NIV). "And what does the LORD require of you? To act justly and to love mercy and to walk humbly with your God" (Micah 6:8, NIV). "Though the LORD is great, he cares for the humble" (Psalm 138:6). The quotes could go on and on. Jesus didn't open up a new theme; He emphasized an old one.

That's because the Kingdom is eternal. The character of the Kingdom doesn't change over time because it reflects the unchanging character of the King. If He has ever honored humility, He always will. It's His nature to do so.

When Jesus blesses the poor in spirit, that's essentially what He is blessing. It's a true humility—not self-deprecating behavior but a deep sense of need and an understanding of where the human heart stands in relation to God. If we are poor in spirit, we will realize how desperately we need divine help for everything. We may approach His throne boldly, but we won't approach Him arrogantly. We will always be in awe of the privilege we've been given, aware of the grace and mercy that sustain us, and willing to comply with whatever He asks of us. A spiritually poor heart is not presumptuous, complaining, or entitled. It's forever grateful.

IN DEED

Jesus offers happiness to such hearts. The King "opposes the proud but gives grace to the humble" (1 Peter 5:5). If you take Him for granted, feel entitled to His benefits, or condescend to others, you won't fit the culture of His Kingdom very well. But if you are selfless, deferential, and servant-hearted, you will experience the support of God Himself. That may take time—it's a test of character to watch others push you down while you're waiting for God to lift you up—but His promise is certain. Those who know their deepest needs will find Him meeting them.

ADDITIONAL READING: Isaiah 61:1-3

> For those who would learn God's ways, humility is the first thing, humility is the second, humility is the third.
> AUGUSTINE OF HIPPO

A Culture of Broken Hearts

God blesses those who mourn, for they will be comforted. Matthew 5:4

IN WORD

We want to add words to the blessing. We want an explanation of why the mourners mourn. Are they grieving death? Their own sin? The condition of the world? The suffering they must endure? It could be any of these. It could even be all of them. All we know is that Jesus promises comfort to the brokenhearted.

That, too, is an ancient theme in Scripture. Psalm 34:17-19 declares it clearly, specifically with regard to those who suffer because of or in spite of their righteousness. The world is a place of many trials and troubles, and things don't always work out well for those who believe. Only redemption promises glory and makes our lives ultimately worthwhile. As Paul would say, if our hope is only in this life, we should be pitied above all others (1 Corinthians 15:19). But current suffering is never worth comparing to future glory (Romans 8:18). Broken hearts, crushed spirits, and days of mourning come to an end.

This is the promise of Jesus. He came to destroy the works of the evil one (1 John 3:8). He undoes all kinds of evil and its consequences, offering beauty for ashes and joy instead of mourning (Isaiah 61:3). His ministry wipes away every tear (Revelation 21:4). The mourning of the heart is temporary; the comfort of God lasts forever.

Even so, the culture of the Kingdom does not demand that we get rid of a broken heart as quickly as possible. There's no need to cover it up, no need to fake a smile, no need to pretend to be happy when our hearts are crushed. We should be relentless optimists; in the Kingdom of God, the best is always yet to come. But mourning is an appropriate response to the brokenness of this world and of our own lives.

IN DEED

Don't embrace mourning as a friend, but don't see it as an enemy either. It opens your heart to the promises of God and the joys of His Kingdom. It turns your face toward glory, now and forever. And it comes with a promise of joy.

ADDITIONAL READING: Psalm 34:18

Faith lives in a broken heart. . . . True faith is
always in a heart bruised for sin.
THOMAS WATSON

A Culture of Brokenness

Blessed are the meek, for they will inherit the earth. Matthew 5:5, *NIV*

IN WORD

Jesus was well familiar with Hebrew Scripture. He quoted it often and expanded on its truths. The blessing for the meek is one of those quotes; Psalm 37:11 says the same thing. The meek will inherit the land and enjoy peace and prosperity. The gentle people of Israel—the ones who have power without abusing it, who could promote themselves but don't, who submit themselves to God without rebelling against Him— are the ones who will actually inherit the nation.

Jesus reiterates this—the word translated "the earth" is also the word for "the land," as in the country—and possibly expands on it. On a much grander scale, those who are last will be first, not just in Israel but in the new earth. On a cosmic stage, these people will be exalted and rule with Christ in His Kingdom.

Who are the meek? They are lowly in heart, unassuming, unpretentious, and gentle. Meekness can imply brokenness, as in the case of a horse that no longer resists his master's bridle. The word can refer to humility—an attitude Jesus has already included in the blessing of the poor in spirit—and it is especially seen in those who have other options. Whether it's referring to people with earthly status and power or children of the King with spiritual privilege and the keys of the Kingdom, the meek don't oppress, push, control, manipulate, berate, complain, or wield a heavy hand. They understand the kindness and gentleness of God, and they demonstrate it.

IN DEED

Kingdom people are not self-promoting. We may be bold, persistent, and even brash in spiritual pursuits, but we don't buy into the "every man for himself" philosophy of the world. It doesn't fit the Kingdom culture, and we don't have any need for it anyway. A person with a meek heart can trust God for promotion and position rather than forcing him- or herself into it. Meekness is an attitude of confidence in Him. And it leads to blessing.

ADDITIONAL READING: Psalm 37:11

Perspective of the meek: "In himself, nothing; in God, everything."
A. W. TOZER

A Culture of Hungers

God blesses those who hunger and thirst for justice, for they will be satisfied.
Matthew 5:6

IN WORD

The Olympic athlete stood on the medal stand listening to his national anthem. Years of hard work and dedication were now being rewarded with gold and honor. Analysts could point to various reasons he won—his technique, his physical attributes, his perseverance—but there was one larger reason underlying them all. He won a medal because he had spent his life hungering for it.

To a very large degree, we will be defined and directed by our hungers in life. We are pointed in the direction of our desires. They motivate us, determine our focus, and keep us going when we're tempted to lose heart. They turn our face toward a goal, and we generally grow in the direction we're facing.

That's why Jesus blesses us if we hunger and thirst for righteousness—or "rightness," justice, and truth for ourselves and for the world. That's the direction we will grow in. Unlike an Olympic athlete—or anyone else who desires something strongly and expends a lot of effort for it—we don't get it by hard work. We must seek it and be persistent in our desire, and we must cooperate with God in His work in us and through us. But in a very real sense, this attribute can only be given. We hunger and thirst; He fills.

IN DEED

We're different from an Olympic athlete in another regard too: We don't have to worry about whether we will achieve the goal. That's the promise of this Beatitude. Jesus doesn't say those who hunger and thirst for justice, rightness, and truth *might* be filled, or may find success, or *could possibly* be rewarded. He says we *will* be filled. It's definite. This goal is not beyond our reach because it's up to Him, and everything is within His reach. For those of us who hunger for the right things, that's extremely good news. The end of our search is not futility and frustration. The reward is fulfillment, and it's inevitable. Our hungers drive us to exactly the right place.

ADDITIONAL READING: Psalm 107:9

It is a sure mark of grace to desire more.
ROBERT MURRAY M'CHEYNE

A Culture of Mercy

God blesses those who are merciful, for they will be shown mercy.
Matthew 5:7

IN WORD

When the Bible talks about mercy, it doesn't simply mean "forgiveness." Years of focus on our own sins may paint the word in that color for us, but it's much more comprehensive. It certainly includes forgiveness, but it also implies having compassion on those who are in need and taking pity on the miserable by helping them in practical ways. That applies to our fallen condition, to be sure, but it also applies to specific times of distress. Those who are able to treat others compassionately—forgiving, providing, comforting, and more—are those who will receive the same treatment from God.

That brings into focus several proverbs about the poor and oppressed, as well as verses like Luke 6:38. With whatever measure we use, it will be measured back to us. We don't like to think of God's treatment of us being dependent on our treatment of others, but to some degree it is. Our experience of Him will reflect how well we've represented Him to those in need.

With that in mind, demonstrate mercy. Don't take pleasure in anyone's hardship, even an enemy's. Bless those who curse you. Forgive with the greatness of the grace God has shown you. Take pity on those in desperate situations, praying for them and meeting their needs practically. In other words and in all other ways, have a heart.

IN DEED

God's Kingdom is a realm in which hearts are soft and the vulnerable are safe. Just as Jesus was moved with compassion to heal, deliver, and forgive, so are the citizens of His Kingdom moved with compassion toward human suffering in all its forms. This goes beyond politics and economics; it's a matter of the spirit. And those whose spirits are sensitive enough to show the compassion of God will experience His compassion in increasing measure.

ADDITIONAL READING: Psalm 41:1-3

The more godly any man is, the more merciful that man will be.
THOMAS BENTON BROOKS

A Culture of One Thing

God blesses those whose hearts are pure, for they will see God. Matthew 5:8

IN WORD

Our hearts aren't completely pure. We know that. We've been told by a prophet that they are desperately wicked (Jeremiah 17:9), and though we've also been told by a prophet that we can have a new one (Ezekiel 36:26), we know some old things that still take place there. So when Jesus blesses the pure in heart, we aren't very encouraged. We're pretty sure we don't qualify. We jump back to the first Beatitude and take comfort in our poverty of spirit. But for this Beatitude, we lose heart at the prospect of having a pure one.

The good news is that Jesus isn't talking about spotlessness, at least not in practical terms. Perhaps He is referring to the cleansing that comes from His blood and the renewal that comes from His Spirit, but there's even more to it than that. Having a pure heart means being singularly focused. The pure in heart are concerned with one thing: They are wholehearted in their desire for God. Their hearts are not distracted or filled with clutter. They are pure in their pursuit of Him and His Kingdom.

That's encouraging. We can do that. It isn't easy—we get distracted by lots of details in life—but we know what it's like to be single-minded about something. A man in pursuit of his beloved, an athlete in pursuit of his prize, a researcher in pursuit of his great discovery—these are common human experiences. If that's what it means to have a pure heart, we understand.

IN DEED

Some have called it a "magnificent obsession" or more biblically, a "pearl of great price," or some other picture that captures the surpassing worth and beauty of the prize. Paul cast aside everything for it (Philippians 3:8), and we should too. That's what Jesus urges His listeners to do. The pure in heart live in all-out pursuit of the things of the Kingdom, and of the King Himself. And they hang on to a promise: that their wholehearted devotion will result in the reward of seeing God.

ADDITIONAL READING: Psalm 24:3-6

Spiritual truth is discernible only to a pure heart, not to a keen intellect.
OSWALD CHAMBERS

A Culture of *Shalom*

God blesses those who work for peace, for they will be called the children of God. Matthew 5:9

IN WORD

You long for it. We all do. It's that state of peace, wholeness, contentment, and completion—a sense that everything is right in your world. We spend much of our lives trying to arrange it, plan for it, pay for it, and pursue it however else we can. Why? Because this Hebrew concept of *shalom*—a word we often translate as "peace"—is what we were made for. We were created for fullness of life.

That's essentially what Jesus was talking about when He promised abundant life, and it's at the heart of what He's talking about here. Yes, peacemakers help reduce conflict and bring people together, but the bigger concept of *shalom* is surely behind this Beatitude. Blessed are those who make *shalom*, who seek restoration and wholeness in their lives, the lives of others, and the world at large. *Shalom* is a Kingdom pursuit because it's in the heart of the King. He wants us all to be well.

Most of us understand that instinctively. We know the world is not as it should be, and neither are our own lives. We desperately long for the satisfaction and fullness of a restored, abundant life. And we're pretty good about seeking it for ourselves. But Jesus' blessing goes beyond ourselves. The true seekers of *shalom*, the peacemakers who will be happy, are those who have a global focus. They pray for God's Kingdom of *shalom* to come here on earth, just as it is in heaven. They seek the Kingdom culture everywhere.

IN DEED

Shalom is the prevailing climate in God's Kingdom. People who thrive on conflict, contentiousness, criticism, cynicism, angst, and all other anti-*shalom* attitudes can't experience it. But if we are among those who seek it—if we are true peacemakers of this world who cultivate wholeness, harmony, and abundance—we will be blessed, entirely happy, and called the children of God. *Shalom*-makers partner with God to transform lives and advance the Kingdom culture. We reflect the heart of our Father so thoroughly that we become vessels of His *shalom* everywhere.

ADDITIONAL READING: Numbers 6:24-26

If the basis of peace is God, the secret of peace is trust.
J. NEVILLE FIGGIS

A Culture of Easy Targets

God blesses those who are persecuted for doing right, for the Kingdom of Heaven is theirs. Matthew 5:10

IN WORD

Imagine playing golf your entire life under the mistaken belief that the object of the game is to have the highest score. Instead of going straight for the hole, you simply have fun hitting the ball anywhere. You wonder why some people think the game is so difficult; you must be exceptionally good at it, as hitting the ball away from the hole comes so naturally to you. Then one day you discover that the object of the game was opposite of what you'd always thought. Confused, embarrassed, and with an overwhelming sense of having wasted so much of your time, you gaze back at the futility of your life. You can't go back and start over. It's too late to redeem the experience.

That's what it will be like when those who pursued temporary wealth, status, and pleasure at the expense of lasting treasures see the true picture. They will realize that the goal of life wasn't to get as much out of it as possible but to put as much into it as possible. They will be confronted with the fact that they spent their entire lives going after the wrong goals.

In that context, it makes sense that those who endured persecution while hanging on to the goal of righteousness—rightness, justice, goodness, and truth—will inherit the Kingdom. They saw the true picture and hung on to it, even when it cost them dearly. They dismissed their pain and humiliation in order to cling to lasting treasures. They played the game right.

IN DEED

Standards in the Kingdom culture aren't the same as the standards of a fallen world. Everything is measured differently. The goal isn't to reject as much temporary pain as possible in order to experience as much temporary pleasure as possible. It's to reach out for the true prize, whatever it costs. Yes, Kingdom people become easy targets in that scenario. But we are blessed. We fit the Kingdom culture perfectly.

ADDITIONAL READING: 1 Peter 3:13-14

If you were not strangers here, the dogs of
the world would not bark at you.
SAMUEL RUTHERFORD

A Culture of Rewards

Be happy about it! Be very glad! For a great reward awaits you in heaven.
Matthew 5:12

IN WORD

Many Christians aren't comfortable with the idea of rewards. We're saved by grace, not by works. Grace doesn't earn rewards; it receives blessings. And even if God gave rewards, it would be self-serving of us to seek them, right? No, surely rewards aren't part of this Kingdom of selflessness and grace.

But they are. Jesus talked about them often. It's true that there's nothing we can do to earn salvation—it's a free gift of grace—but God loves to honor people who have responded to Him well. He knows we don't deserve rewards—not in the sense of earning a proper payment—but He gives them anyway. Those who insist on living in the Kingdom culture even when another kingdom makes it painful and difficult please Him with their choices. He longs to bless hearts that are completely His. So in this Kingdom, rewards are given generously.

We don't know exactly what those rewards are like, only that they will be great. We probably couldn't comprehend them even if we were told. What we do know is that a Kingdom lifestyle—humility, sensitivity, deference, zeal for justice and truth, compassion, wholeheartedness, restoration, endurance—is well worth whatever it costs us. God never lets our sacrifices be greater than our blessings. He gives rewards because He's generous toward those who love Him.

IN DEED

Enjoy the generosity of the Father. The Beatitudes aren't impossible standards to live up to. They are invitations to participate in the Kingdom culture and reap its unfathomable benefits. When hearts and minds conform to this spiritual environment, the result is blessedness, happiness, and whatever rewards the King wants to give. They don't make life easy in this age, but they make it very worthwhile. And the rewards only get better in the age to come.

ADDITIONAL READING: 1 Timothy 6:17-19

> God is more anxious to bestow His blessings
> than we are to receive them.
> AUGUSTINE OF HIPPO

Suddenly

The Lord you are seeking will suddenly come to his Temple. Malachi 3:1

IN WORD

When God comes to His Temple, it will happen suddenly. We should be well aware of that fact. When Jesus came, it seemed sudden to Jews who weren't expecting Him. When His Spirit came upon us, it seemed like a sudden event. When Jesus returns, it will happen in the twinkling of an eye (1 Corinthians 15:52). When God's presence comes upon this world, it always feels like a surprise.

To God, however, there's nothing sudden about it. He has planned His movements from before the foundation of the world. He spent centuries cultivating a people from whom the Messiah would come forth. He has taken years with most of us to prepare us for His work in our lives. God has a plan for each of us that He has known from before the foundation of the world. What seems like divine spontaneity to us is not spontaneous at all to Him.

What does that mean for us? It means that the wisdom of God is perfectly suited to each of us individually and to the world as a whole. He knows the road into each person's heart, and He knows the times and eras of opportunity in each culture. We don't always understand His timing and His ways, but we can count on the fact that they make sense. He is a very rational God with a very well-crafted plan. When we don't understand what's going on in life, we can know that He does.

IN DEED

Be ready for God's opportune times. When He moves in your life, it may seem sudden. To Him it isn't sudden, of course, and He has timed His work well. Even so, we sometimes miss what we're seeking because we aren't prepared to receive it.

Pray today for readiness. Ask God to open your eyes to whatever He wants to do, whenever He wants to do it. Ask Him to prepare you, to tune your antennas to His wavelength, to help you understand what He's doing in your life. Let His "suddenly" find you ready and waiting.

ADDITIONAL READING: Mark 1:14-15

We block Christ's advance in our lives by failure of expectation.
WILLIAM TEMPLE

Purified

He will be like a blazing fire that refines metal, or like a strong soap that bleaches clothes. Malachi 3:2

IN WORD

A refiner's fire burns out impurities and makes a metal pure. A launderer's soap washes out dirt and stains, and bleaches garments white. And when Jesus comes, He will have those effects on the human race.

Jesus has already cleaned and purified, of course. He did that in many ways in His first coming by forgiving sins, cleansing leprosy, healing infirmities, offending the prideful, and, ultimately, by shedding His blood on a heavenly altar and opening the way for us to enter the Holy of Holies. As He taught, as He healed, and as He died, He had the effects of a refiner's fire or a launderer's soap on us. And as we follow Him in discipleship, He still does.

Even so, the Second Coming will be different. The separation of tares from wheat, of dross from silver, and of stains from white garments will not be a process but a sudden event. Jesus will dramatically separate sheep from goats, or the saved from the unsaved. Though He has been refining and cleaning our hearts for the last two thousand years, He will refine and clean the earth in a moment. And blessed are those whose lives are ready for the division.

IN DEED

Is your life ready for the division? When Jesus comes, will His refining and cleaning be a statement of the obvious in your life? Or is your life the sort that is an inextricable blending of the holy and profane, of the pure and the impure? In other words, are you trying to follow Him and other loyalties at the same time? Are you double-minded?

Whatever it takes, be purified. Be refined. Let all dross be burned out, all stains removed. Your salvation was a one-time cleansing, but your experience of His presence in your life is not. And if sin has made you unfamiliar with that presence, His coming will be a severe shock indeed. Let the Refiner and Launderer have His way with you—in every area of your life.

ADDITIONAL READING: 2 Peter 1:8-11

God desires the smallest degree of purity of conscience
in you more than all the works you can perform.
JOHN OF THE CROSS

The Agenda

Then the LORD *will have men who will bring offerings in righteousness.*
Malachi 3:3, *NIV*

IN WORD

God has an agenda. It isn't a selfish or manipulative agenda, like many of ours are. It is, however, relentless and unfailing. God will not be denied fulfilling the purpose of His creation. He will have fellowship with and be worshiped by those made in His image, and He will not stop until His mission is accomplished. Contrary to the opinions of the hosts of hell, His plan cannot be thwarted.

Every creature ought to be aware of that. It's literally a crying shame that many people around this world are oblivious to the necessary direction of history. God gave us a perfect object lesson in His Word when He purified the Levitical priests through captivity and judgment. But that was not a comprehensive, permanent cleansing, and it certainly wasn't the end of God's purifying work for Israel or for this world. All of history is hurtling toward the ultimate cleansing and a totally pure eternal Kingdom. When Jesus comes again, there will be no going back.

In Christ, we are a royal priesthood in this world—a purified royal priesthood (1 Peter 2:9)—and it's our responsibility to inform our world of its destiny. Those who are on board with God's agenda in God's way will enjoy the perfect Kingdom forever, and those who are opposed to God's agenda will not. And for those who are opposed, there will be weeping and gnashing of teeth. They will see the staggering difference between the Kingdom of light and the kingdom of darkness, and they will realize that the small choices of today have determined on which side of that difference they'll stand. Truly, the mission of the royal priesthood is a sobering mission.

IN DEED

Are you sobered by the thought of your mission? Is your agenda the same as God's—to see people bring offerings in righteousness to the King of all creation? To rescue those outside of God's Kingdom and to celebrate with those inside of it? If not, line up with destiny. There's no better place to be.

ADDITIONAL READING: Revelation 22:10-15

Christian mission is the only reason for our being on earth.
ANDREW MURRAY

Kingdom of Light

This is the message we heard from Jesus and now declare to you: God is light, and there is no darkness in him at all. 1 John 1:5

IN WORD

Dark kingdoms make for good stories. From ancient mythology to modern fiction, the presence of evil is almost always at the center of the plot. But it's never the goal; it's an obstacle to overcome, an agenda to thwart, a threat to endure. It's the part of the story that needs to go away before the story ends.

We live in just such a story, where a dark kingdom intrudes on a beautiful creation and obscures the Kingdom of light. Many in our world are so blinded by the darkness that they don't even believe light actually exists. They see not truth and lies but opinions; not good or evil but relatively better or worse; not black and white but gray. But the message of the gospel is that the Kingdom of God is a Kingdom of light because God Himself is light—so thoroughly light that no hint of darkness is in Him at all. He is relentlessly good, beautiful, and true. And His Kingdom belongs to those who recognize that and enter into the goodness, beauty, and truth.

It's easy to get disoriented in our world, where darkness has distorted all that is good. In this realm, lies can seem advantageous, commitments can seem much too restrictive, love can turn selfish, greed can come in handy, and even evil can be attractive. Like a dirty mirror or a rain-drenched window, the kingdom of darkness can play tricks on our eyes. What we think we see isn't always real.

IN DEED

Whenever you find yourself in a morally, ethically, or relationally confusing situation, look for light. Don't be swayed by gray areas, relativistic arguments, or hypothetical suggestions that muddy the picture. Anchor yourself in truth, beauty, and love in its purest sense. Like a moth to a flame, gravitate toward the light God has given you. The Kingdom culture is bright and clear.

ADDITIONAL READING: John 1:1-5

In darkness there is no choice. It is light that enables us to see the differences between things; and it is Christ who gives us light.
AUGUSTUS W. HARE

The Model Citizen

Those who say they live in God should live their lives as Jesus did. 1 John 2:6

IN WORD

It isn't easy to learn a new culture. Immigrants to a new country often stick out for the clothes they wear, the mannerisms they express, and the values they hold. The acculturation process goes relatively quickly for some, but others never quite blend in. The multitude of unwritten social cues and expectations can be overwhelming.

We can be thankful that God is patient with us as we learn the Kingdom culture. Sometimes we get lost in the details too, just as a foreigner does when adjusting to a strange land. But fitting into the Kingdom of God isn't primarily a matter of analyzing the culture like a social scientist would. God has made it much simpler for us. If we want to know the culture of our Kingdom, all we need to do is look at the attitudes and actions of the King.

John put it another way to his readers: If we say His life is in us and we live in His Kingdom, we must live as Jesus lived and walk as He walked. Looking around at Kingdom citizens today, we might conclude that not many people know this. The twenty-first-century church hardly looks like first-century Galilee, so the visible Kingdom will naturally vary from the King's original environment. But do we speak as He spoke? Are we driven by the same purpose that drove Him? Do we have the same compassion and commitment? Do we love, heal, and forgive, as He loved, healed, and forgave? Are we visible manifestations of the character of God?

These are penetrating questions, even for those who claim to have followed Him for years. We easily call ourselves Christians, but can we easily call ourselves Christlike? We must if we want to thrive in His Kingdom.

IN DEED

Learn the Kingdom culture well by looking at the King. Don't embrace any models of Christianity that don't look a lot like Christ. Measure yourself by no other standard. In everything you do, be like Him.

ADDITIONAL READING: Ephesians 5:1-2

It is time that Christians were judged more by their likeness to Christ than their notions of Christ.
LUCRETIA MOTT

True Love

Do not love this world nor the things it offers you, for when you love the world, you do not have the love of the Father in you. 1 John 2:15

IN WORD

God loves the world. One of the New Testament's most famous verses says so; He loves the world so much that He sent His Son to die on our behalf. But when John tells us not to love the world or anything in the world, he's referring to an entirely different concept. God loves the world to redeem it; we human beings often love the world—including its corrupt ways and human-devised systems—in order to feed our own idols with its offerings. He loves it sacrificially; we tend to love it selfishly. In other words, we have cravings we think the world can fulfill, so we exploit it as much as we can. And that isn't really love at all.

The Kingdom culture is filled with love for human beings and God's creation—a beautiful world full of precious souls. It's others-centered. But competing cultures, still capable of reflecting beauty, truth, and love at times, are nevertheless fundamentally self-centered. Political systems and economic systems tend to gravitate toward the pitfalls of power and greed. Religious systems tend to gravitate toward attempts to achieve salvation by discipline and effort rather than receiving it by grace. Relational dynamics are often infected with self-love rather than sacrificial love. Over time, the world looks very different from the Kingdom of God.

Therefore, the love of one excludes the love of the other. We can't embrace both the ways of the world and the ways of the Kingdom. They conflict with each other. We can love the world as God loves it, but we can't pursue its offerings as others do. We have to choose where to root our hearts.

IN DEED

Root your heart in eternity. We can experience plenty of blessings in this age as we engage in the world, but we can't set our hearts on them. We look exclusively to the hand of God for all we need, knowing the difference between what lasts and what doesn't. Our love for the Father eclipses all rival loves.

ADDITIONAL READING: James 4:4-6

A man's spiritual health is exactly proportional to his love for God.
C. S. LEWIS

Shaped by Hope

All who have this eager expectation will keep themselves pure, just as he is pure. 1 John 3:3

IN WORD

The world is full of false religious impulses—disciplines that change behavior without changing the heart, self-inflicted punishments as signs of penance, superficially imposed attitudes that only mask deeper flaws, and many more. At the root of many of these impulses is a desire to be pure. That's a good desire that reflects the truth of our impure condition, but human beings seem to be woefully ignorant of how to fulfill that desire. Most attempts are full of self-effort, and a corrupt self can never make itself pure. That would be like a fire trying to put itself out with fire, or a mud puddle trying to cleanse itself with more mud. It won't happen. When the source is the same as the subject, nothing is going to change.

So how can this God-given desire for purity be fulfilled? By looking to the source. John introduces this thought by directing our attention to the Father's love (1 John 3:1), and emphasizes that we will be changed simply by seeing Jesus (3:2). Or as is often said, we become what we behold.

We always grow in the direction of our loves, don't we? It's natural. Whatever we love, whatever we gaze at affectionately, whatever we truly long for tends to shape us. Boys don't try to act like their favorite athlete; they just do. Young musicians don't work at emulating their favorite star; they just do. Lovers don't impose painful disciplines in order to draw close to each other; they just do. So if we see divine love and gaze at the One who embodies it, we are filled with reciprocating love and become like Him. We are transformed by our hearts' affections.

IN DEED

That's how change happens in the Kingdom culture. It isn't a set of rules no one wants to obey. It's an environment that captivates our hearts, draws us to the King, and shapes us to be like Him. We are filled with hope in His coming, and like a bride or groom anticipating the wedding, our longings do the work of preparing us. In the process, we become pure just as He is pure.

ADDITIONAL READING: 2 Corinthians 3:18

We cannot help conforming ourselves to what we love.
FRANCIS DE SALES

From Death to Life

If we love our brothers and sisters who are believers, it proves that we have passed from death to life. But a person who has no love is still dead.
1 John 3:14

IN WORD

This world is broken. You know that; you see evidence of it every day. You also know the explanation given in the early chapters of Genesis. One act of rebellion invited the rebellious spirit into the core of our souls, resulting in catastrophic consequences for the human race. And that rebellious spirit is self-centered by nature. It reverses the flow of the most powerful force in the universe to feed ourselves rather than others. It turns love inward.

That's a deadly direction. Our own love was never meant to be spent on ourselves. It was meant to flow outward, to be fully received from God and fully spent on Him and each other. When we enter the Kingdom of life, that tragic reversal is reversed again; love is turned back to its proper direction. The King bathes us in His love, we receive it in gratitude, and then we are free to offer it back to Him and to everyone else. That's how we experience life instead of death.

If that isn't our experience, we are still living in the culture of another kingdom, no matter how many times we've prayed to receive Christ or declared our Kingdom loyalties. Love is evidence that we are truly living in a Kingdom environment, drinking in life rather than death. Without it, we are still walking in darkness and experiencing the fruit of rebellion. We are missing the benefits of the Kingdom.

IN DEED

Always check the direction of your love. Is it flowing outward? Is it truly turned toward God and others? It's okay to admit that it isn't; every human being has had to deal with vestiges of the Fall, even after coming into the Kingdom. But if your life feels more like death, then the direction of your love may be the reason. The Kingdom culture is overflowing with the love of the Father. Fully drink it in. Bask in it. Saturate yourself in it. Then let it spill over lavishly into the lives of others. You and they will begin to experience the fullness of life.

ADDITIONAL READING: John 5:24

Pour into our hearts the attitude of Your love.
HANS URS VON BALTHASAR

A Place of Presence

This is how we know that we live in him and he in us: He has given us of his Spirit. 1 John 4:13, *NIV*

IN WORD

"This is how we know." Phrases like this show up often in John's first letter because one of his purposes in writing is to distinguish between true Christ-followers and false ones. Conscientious people ask themselves if they are believing the right things, understanding the truth, and living the way God intends. John answers those questions. And one of his answers points to the presence of the Spirit.

God's Kingdom is a place of presence. It isn't simply a belief system competing with other ideas and ideologies, nor is it a code of conduct competing with other lifestyles. Beliefs and behaviors certainly belong in the Kingdom, but they alone don't define it. Above all, the Kingdom is a realm in which the King is manifestly present. He shows up. He may be here or there at this time or another, always on the move and hard to get a handle on, but He doesn't remain absent or only silently and theoretically present. He is *actively* present. *Manifestly* present. His work can be witnessed clearly.

Other religions can't claim that. They seek to know by arguments and proofs and historical evidence—the same things Christians often point to in apologetics discussions. We have those things, to be sure, but we have more. We have testimony. We have experience. We have an undeniable Spirit who has given us evidence of His work within us and around us. We have gifts and power and attitudes that can only have come from Him. We have divinely changed lives.

IN DEED

Many believers go through seasons of searching. Is He really there? Is He active in my life? Is He any different from other belief systems? The answer of Scripture is yes, but it's even more than that. The answer is that being "in Christ" and having Christ in us are not just theology or theory, they are experiences. He has come to us. His Kingdom is where He dwells.

ADDITIONAL READING: John 15:1-8

Seek this power, expect this power, yearn for this power.
And when this power comes, yield to Him.
MARTYN LLOYD-JONES

A "No Fear" Zone

Such love has no fear, because perfect love expels all fear. If we are afraid, it is for fear of punishment, and this shows that we have not fully experienced his perfect love. 1 John 4:18

IN WORD

Human beings are full of fears. They nag us during the day and sometimes keep us up at night. They almost always seem reasonable even when they are completely irrational. They come from a multitude of directions and get energy from a multitude of past experiences. We have an almost endless capacity for asking "what if?" and thinking of negative answers to the question.

But how about these "what ifs"? What if we were completely, thoroughly loved by a being who was full of extravagant love and capable of doing whatever He wants? What if this being was constantly watching out for our best interests whether we perceived Him doing so or not? What if He was always by our side whether we sensed Him or not? What if He loved those of us who believe in Him so much that we could not possibly fail beyond repair even if we tried? What if we were so secure in Him that all our fears were unfounded?

The promise of Scripture is that all these things are true. These aren't hypothetical possibilities; they are reality. All of God's promises are "yes" and "amen" in Christ (2 Corinthians 1:20). The Kingdom culture is a place of no fear because the King's presence eliminates all dangers. Sure, we can rebel and run away, and then we have plenty to fear. And sure, we have a fear of God that overwhelms us with His majesty. But fear of anything ultimately doing damage to our well-being while we're in His presence? That's totally unreasonable. The perfection of His love precludes any fear we might have.

IN DEED

Live in freedom from fear. Jesus came not only to deliver us from sin but also to deliver us from the fear that so often lies behind our sins. Our insecurities do not serve us well, and the love of the Father makes them unnecessary. We are completely, forever safe in Him.

ADDITIONAL READING: 2 Corinthians 1:20

The chains of love are stronger than the chains of fear.
WILLIAM GURNALL

Invincible

Every child of God defeats this evil world, and we achieve this victory through our faith. 1 John 5:4

IN WORD

It's a beautiful promise—everyone born of God overcomes the world. But what exactly does that mean? Do we eventually become sinless, even after falling to the same sins again and again? Do we find success, even after running into the same obstacles repeatedly? Do we become immune to trials and tribulations or perhaps even no longer have to deal with them? Are we ever able to insulate ourselves from the pride and corruption of the world? What does "overcoming" look like?

You may answer those questions in a variety of ways, depending on your particular weaknesses and run-ins with the world's ways. Whatever your situation, overcoming the world can imply a lot of things: It no longer defines you; it's no longer your judge; it's no longer your dominant influence; it no longer kicks you around; you no longer listen when it tells you how meaningless or fruitless or wasted your life has been; and you no longer live by its demands. "Overcoming" means you live above the world's ways. You have a higher purpose and an otherworldly source of life. You win victories over the world's systems and aren't victimized by its trends and whims and criticisms. You are rooted in a Kingdom that overlaps with the presence of a false value system but is never subject to it. You will endure longer and live deeper than anything the world can offer you. You are born of God.

IN DEED

Refuse the world's mind-sets. Reject its false identities. By faith, you live in the Kingdom culture as one of its permanent citizens. By faith, you are not a victim, a mistake, or a temporary phenomenon. By faith, you are a child of the King who will win battles, tear down walls, remove obstacles, and plunder the rival kingdom. And because He is in you—because you are not left to your own resources—you cannot be defeated. Eventually, somehow, you will overcome.

ADDITIONAL READING: Romans 8:31-39

A person who wholly follows the Lord is one who believes that the promises of God are trustworthy, that He is with His people, and that they are well able to overcome.
WATCHMAN NEE

Conversations with the King

This is the confidence we have in approaching God: that if we ask anything according to his will, he hears us. And if we know that he hears us—whatever we ask—we know that we have what we asked of him. 1 John 5:14-15, *NIV*

IN WORD

We have a very conversational King. He doesn't offer His provision anonymously, though some receive it that way. He doesn't fulfill orders as though He were a vending machine. He doesn't mail out catalogs or ship from a warehouse. He likes to be asked. In conversation. It's the Kingdom way.

He also promises that we can ask specifically and be answered specifically. Many people offer up scattershot prayers, hoping they hit anything that's available. Many of us add "if it's Your will" to the end of every request because we don't have any confidence that we might know what His will is—even though He has revealed quite a bit of it. We're tentative in our prayers and reluctant to assume an answer. But the God of the Bible promises to give us what we ask for.

John includes a caveat with this promise: that we ask "according to his will." Some take that to mean we may or may not get what we ask for because the odds of our understanding His will are pretty slim. That may result in a theology that makes prayer unnecessary at all. If it's His will, He's going to do it anyway, whether we ask or not; and if it isn't, no amount of asking is going to make it so. But God's intent is for us to know His will, ask for it to be done (and it might not be if we don't ask), and then see the answer. That's the dynamic of the Kingdom, and it's a promise.

IN DEED

Ask boldly. First saturate yourself in the King's wisdom and ways, then ask to be filled with His desires. Let His will become yours, then pray your heart out. This is how the Kingdom comes on earth as it is in heaven, how the business of the Kingdom advances against the agenda of the enemy. He does His work on earth through His people, and He almost always does it in the context of genuine conversation.

ADDITIONAL READING: John 15:7-8

> Whether we like it or not, asking is the rule of the Kingdom.
> CHARLES SPURGEON

The Gift of Understanding

We know that the Son of God has come, and he has given us understanding so that we can know the true God. 1 John 5:20

IN WORD

The world is full of agnostics—literally non-knowers, people who claim (about God or any other subject) that they just don't know. Acknowledging darkness in the midst of a dark kingdom is certainly understandable, but we aren't left in the darkness. When we come into God's Kingdom, we come into a culture of understanding. The King wants us to know things. He wants us to be able to see clearly.

That doesn't mean we'll see everything, or that we won't go through some disorienting times, or that we'll have answers to every question. We are never promised omniscience, and sometimes true faith means clinging to God in spite of unexplained mysteries of problems and pain. But there are some things we can know regardless of what we see—that's what faith is. We are promised wisdom and understanding when we ask for it. And that understanding comes in the form of Jesus.

That may seem shallow at first glance, but it really isn't. The world is in search of wisdom; we seek a deeper connection with the wise one. Scholars seek to know facts; we seek to know a Person. Most people want to understand life; we want to understand God.

These are significant distinctions. Our understanding is based in a relationship of trust. Our limited mental capabilities are not enough to unravel the mysteries of the universe, but our relational connection with the Son of God is enough to put the mysteries on the shelf until we see more clearly. In the Kingdom culture, we have to embrace a foundational concept that truth is a knowable Person, not a set of facts. And in our knowledge of Him, we have life.

IN DEED

Cling to that at all times, especially during hard times. Security comes not in knowing the path ahead but in knowing the one who walks it with you. Facts will not comfort you. He will. And over time, He will give you understanding.

ADDITIONAL READING: Psalm 32:8-9

> It has pleased God that divine truths should not enter the heart through understanding, but understanding through the heart.
> BLAISE PASCAL

A Kingdom of Promise

The LORD now said to Moses, "Send out men to explore the land of Canaan, the land I am giving to the Israelites." Numbers 13:12

IN WORD

God made a promise long ago to Abraham, Jacob, and Joseph that He would bring His people out of Egypt and back into the land of their inheritance. He kept His promise by sending Moses back into Egypt on a mission of deliverance. Now, after bringing them through the waters and teaching them His will, the time had come for fulfillment. The people were now ready to enter the Promised Land.

Or were they? God instructs Moses to send twelve men into the land on a reconnaissance mission. Their assignment was not to determine whether the promise was valid; it was to strategize the conquest and settlement. After all, quite a few Canaanites already lived there. It might be good to have a plan when taking the land back from them.

Somehow the spies misinterpreted their mission. They let their fears and their very human logic get the best of them. They forgot that the Promised Land was actually *promised* land. Even so, God would get His people there eventually. He does not neglect His own words, even when His people forget them or rebel against them. Yes, the generation of rebels missed the fulfillment, but the fulfillment still came. That's because God's Kingdom is based on the reliability of His own plans.

IN DEED

That's good to know. We can miss many of the blessings of the Kingdom ourselves, but we can't mess up the Kingdom agenda. God is building it, fulfilling it, and blessing it, regardless of how we respond. When we pray for His Kingdom to come and His will to be done on earth as it is in heaven, the outcome is certain. We don't have to wonder if it's going to happen. God's promises never fail.

Mine God's Word for His promises. Don't let fear rob you of their fulfillment; let faith fill you with expectancy. The Kingdom is given to those bold enough to believe it, those who take God at His word and don't let go. Cling to the vision He has placed within you; it was put there for a reason.

ADDITIONAL READING: Romans 4:18-21

On these [promises] we are to build all our expectations from God; and in all temptations and trials, we have them to rest our souls upon.
MATTHEW HENRY

A Kingdom of Faith

Caleb tried to quiet the people as they stood before Moses. "Let's go at once to take the land," he said. "We can certainly conquer it!" Numbers 13:30

IN WORD

God puts His promises out there, but they usually apply only to those who accept them. That's because faith is the currency of His Kingdom—like dollars in the United States or euros across the Atlantic. You can't get much of anything in God's Kingdom without believing what He has said. Salvation, a transformed heart, an answer to prayer—all are given to those who believe. Those who don't may receive many common blessings in spite of themselves, but they don't receive the Kingdom. Faith is the key to fulfillment.

Joshua and Caleb were the only two spies whose lives were extended long enough to receive what God had pledged to give. Why? Because they believed when everyone else thought they were being foolish. Being perceived as arrogant, naive, presumptuous, and out of touch with reality didn't faze them. They anchored themselves in what God had promised, knowing that the God of promise doesn't lie.

We see this dynamic in the ministry of Jesus often. "Your faith has healed you" and "if you have faith" are commonly repeated phrases in His encounters with those who needed His touch. The clear implication is that without faith, the outcome would have been different. That doesn't mean that every time a prayer goes unanswered, the asker didn't have enough faith. Kingdom life is more complex than that. But it does mean faith is very often the difference between receiving and not receiving.

IN DEED

Kingdom citizens are, above all, people of faith. We understand that the King responds to those who trust Him, who hang on His every word, who reject the opinions of others for the sake of His faithfulness. We apply our faith not only to what He has promised but also to what He has instructed and what He has done. We accept it all because it comes from Him. That kind of faith is transforming, fulfilling, and entirely pleasing to Him. And it's always eventually rewarded.

ADDITIONAL READING: Hebrews 3:12-19

I do not want merely to possess faith; I want a faith that possesses me.
CHARLES KINGSLEY

A Kingdom of Perseverance

If the LORD is pleased with us, he will bring us safely into that land and give it to us. It is a rich land flowing with milk and honey. Do not rebel against the LORD, and don't be afraid of the people of the land. Numbers 14:8-9

IN WORD

"If the LORD is pleased with us . . ." That sounds awfully performance-oriented for a God of grace, but Caleb's words turn out to be accurate. God was not pleased with the fear and complaining of the multitudes, so He waited to give the Promised Land to their children. The majority view neglected an essential fact about God's processes: They aren't instant.

We forget that too. When we become convinced of God's plans for us, we expect to see them coming to pass immediately. They rarely do. The path from Egypt to Canaan was traumatic to begin with—it took ten plagues and a miraculous exodus to get free—and there were hardships immediately after freedom came. We forget that there might be dry seasons, obstacles, enemies, and severe temptations to complain about along the way. We easily lose heart, see the need for perseverance as a sign that something has gone wrong, and weaken in faith. All the while, God's promise lies before us, waiting for those who have both faith and patience. Only this tandem of attitudes makes the inheritance possible (Hebrews 6:12). One or the other is not enough.

IN DEED

Perseverance is a necessary Kingdom attribute. The writer of Hebrews urged his readers not to shrink back in fear or unbelief, citing the spies' report in the wilderness and the people's response to it as the prime example of what *not* to do. The Kingdom is not a place of fear, complaining, or weak wills. It's a place of encountering obstacles and opposition and overcoming them, of enduring to the end, of setting our sights on the inheritance and never swerving from it. Remember that in whatever you face today. Nothing can undo God's plans for you if you anchor yourself in what you know to be true and refuse to be moved.

ADDITIONAL READING: Hebrews 6:12

He who perseveres makes every difficulty an advancement and every contest a victory.
CHARLES CALEB COLTON

A Kingdom of Interceding

In keeping with your magnificent, unfailing love, please pardon the sins of this people, just as you have forgiven them ever since they left Egypt.
Numbers 14:19

IN WORD

This wasn't the first time Moses interceded for the people. They angered God with a golden calf at the foot of Mount Sinai, even as God was issuing commandments against idolatry. God offered to wipe Israel out and begin afresh with Moses, but Moses pleaded with God for the sake of His reputation. God relented and forgave His people. The prayers of a human being turned the divine will back in their favor.

Now in the wilderness, even in the face of outright rejection of the promise, the same dynamic is repeated. God offers to destroy the people and make a great nation out of Moses, but Moses pleads for the people again. Again, God relents. He hears the prayer and accepts it. A punishment remains, but so does the promise.

Why does this dynamic repeat itself? Is God really so shortsighted that He gets distracted from His long-range plans and has to be redirected back to them by the vision of a human being? No, for some reason left unexplained in Scripture, God intervenes in the affairs of people to the extent that a person asks Him to. He put the affairs of this world under the domain of the first humans, and He never removed the responsibility from us. The partnership between God and humanity to tend the Garden and govern the affairs of earth remains. It's still a partnership. So He often indicates what would happen if He acted unilaterally, practically inviting a human agent to plead for another course. Then He responds the way He intended—in partnership with those who ask Him.

IN DEED

Make intercession for this world—for those in your domain, your family, your friends, your coworkers, your church, your community, and more—a high priority. It's how Kingdom business gets done. The partnership between God and human beings is the way the Kingdom works on earth. Ask, seek, and knock. Intercede and invite God to accomplish His greatest purposes.

ADDITIONAL READING: Isaiah 59:16

> Do not let us fail one another in interest, care, and practical help; but supremely we must not fail one another in prayer.
> MICHAEL BAUGHEN

A Kingdom of Receiving

I am as strong now as I was when Moses sent me on that journey, and I can still travel and fight as well as I could then. So give me the hill country that the LORD promised me. Joshua 14:11-12

IN WORD

What must Caleb have thought all those years he wandered with his people in the wilderness? It wasn't his fault Israel rebelled in fear and unbelief. He had believed. Yet his piece of the promise was delayed just as much as the Promised Land was delayed for the rest of the nation. God had pledged to preserve his life, but forty years is a long time to wish things had been different. Every step of the way, he could easily have regretted the hard-heartedness of his peers.

Most of us live with some sense of regret. Some of us are almost eaten up with it, lamenting the lost years, wondering "what if" about misplayed moments in our lives, and wishing we could get some of those decisions back. Caleb certainly felt regret, even though he hadn't deserved the consequences of Israel's rebellion. But even when our mistakes have cost us dearly, God is able to preserve us for the promise, to restore the years the locusts have eaten (Joel 2:25).

When Caleb finally entered the Promised Land—he and Joshua were allowed to experience it after the rest of their generation died away—he insisted on receiving the fulfillment of the promise that had been made to him. It wasn't arrogance; he wasn't being pushy. He was simply claiming what God had spoken to him, and he had every right to do so. He had waited long enough.

IN DEED

Life is filled with waiting. That's part of living in relationship with a very patient and thorough God. But we don't wait without purpose; we're waiting *for* something. And when the time comes, God suddenly fulfills what He said He would do. We may have wondered if that day would ever come, but the Kingdom is not a place of empty promises. God means for us to receive them and rejoice in the fulfillment. And when we do, it's as if the years didn't matter. It's never too late to enjoy what He has done.

ADDITIONAL READING: Joel 2:25-27

Faith in God will always be crowned.
WILLIAM S. PLUMER

A Kingdom of Denial

[Jesus said,] "If any of you wants to be my follower, you must turn from your selfish ways, take up your cross daily, and follow me." Luke 9:23

IN WORD

"Turn from your selfish ways"—that is, deny yourself. Jesus called this a "must," and those who take His words seriously have tried to do just that for centuries. We've seen flagellants trying to beat themselves into submission, disciplinarians trying to train themselves to be godly, and the privileged taking vows of austerity to divest themselves of attachments. We've also seen people with genuine, God-given desires deny that any human desire is worthy of fulfillment. What we haven't seen—or at least haven't seen very often—is people who so enjoy investing in others that they neglect their own efforts and interests.

That's a problem. Every effort to defeat the self is self-defeating, and not in the way intended. When self focuses its efforts on self, the self is only going to get stronger. Flagellants, disciplinarians, vow-takers, and desire-deniers have one thing in common: They are extremely self-focused. And that isn't self-denial at all.

No, true self-denial is simply a matter of turning your attention toward God and others so often that you hardly notice your own issues. The question of whether your desires are fulfilled or not doesn't need to be settled; you simply choose not to notice it. Whether you've disciplined sin out of your system isn't an issue you obsess about; it just doesn't apply because you're looking elsewhere, not inward. For true followers of Jesus to deny themselves, they need only to look at Him and love His people. That *is* self-denial. It's an entirely outward focus.

IN DEED

Don't spend much energy trying to deny yourself. It won't work. While denying yourself and taking up your cross is a necessary value of the Kingdom culture, it isn't one you fulfill by trying. You don't empty yourself of selfishness by looking at yourself; you empty yourself of selfishness by filling yourself with something else. Let yourself be filled with Jesus, and self will never be a problem.

ADDITIONAL READING: Galatians 5:16

If you take little account of yourself, you will
have peace, wherever you live.
ABBA POEMEN

Losing and Saving

[Jesus said,] "If you try to hang on to your life, you will lose it. But if you give up your life for my sake, you will save it." Luke 9:24

IN WORD

A vacuum cleaner is always pulling, sucking, drawing in whatever it can. Its direction is inward. Other objects, like a fan or a leaf blower, may blow outward, giving off rather than pulling in, but there's nothing outward about the vacuum. It's constantly trying to fill an empty space.

By nature—our fallen nature, that is—human beings are like vacuum cleaners. We're always trying to get what's outside of us and bring it into our own territory. We're always trying to fill an empty space by attracting things to ourselves—relationships, possessions, positions, achievements, interesting experiences, and more. We're accumulators trying to fill our lives up, trying to grab life wherever we can get it.

Jesus told His followers that's not the way to life. In fact, it leads to death, or at least a sense of deadness that keeps us feeling empty. The way to life is altogether different; it's to stop trying to grab life and instead become a giver of it. We forget about ourselves and invest in others. We become God-focused rather than self-focused. We are more intent on giving than receiving. That's the Kingdom culture. That's life.

Martyrdom is one example of a sacrificial life that gives for the sake of others, and specifically for the sake of God, but Jesus was referring to more than martyrdom. He was referring to our direction. Are we pulling in or flowing out? Are we our own center of gravity, or do we revolve around Him and others? Are we desperately trying to save our own lives—to grab life-giving things and experiences—or willingly offering life-giving support to those around us? One way leads to death, the other to life as it was meant to be.

IN DEED

Learn to flow outward. Forget about grabbing everything you can. Don't pursue your own fulfillment, whether in people, places, possessions, positions, or anything else. Flip the switch that changes the direction of your flow, and experience life coming into you from above.

ADDITIONAL READING: Acts 20:32-35

The more a man denies himself, the more he shall obtain from God.
HORACE BUSHNELL

Seeing the Kingdom

I tell you the truth, some standing here right now will not die before they see the Kingdom of God. Luke 9:27

IN WORD

Jesus was speaking to a crowd as His disciples stood around Him and listened. "Some standing here" would see the Kingdom of God before their death—implying that others would not, and also implying that we see the Kingdom in fullness only in another realm. But Jesus also told a crowd that the Kingdom of God was among them (or even within them), and that the Kingdom of God was at hand. So if He was demonstrating the Kingdom, yet not all would see it before death, what does it really mean to see the Kingdom?

Perhaps He meant that even though the Kingdom and the King were readily present, only some of them would recognize the reality of this Kingdom. Or maybe He was pointing to the advent of the Spirit on Pentecost and beyond. After all, the Kingdom manifests in a variety of ways at various times—in signs and wonders of prophets and apostles, in healing and deliverance, and in love, peace, and joy. But it is really seen in its glory when we see the King in His glory. And that happened to three who were standing there only a few days later.

Peter, James, and John witnessed the transfiguration of Jesus on the mountain, and He was dazzling. The Kingdom is an altogether different reality from what our eyes normally see. Those who have gotten a glimpse of the risen Jesus have gotten a glimpse of the Kingdom, but the full vision comes when we tangibly enter another realm. The brilliance of the King illuminates everything.

IN DEED

Keep your eyes open for evidence of the Kingdom. If you choose, you can see it all around you. But know that whatever you see, there's more, and your ability to see centers on your willingness to see Jesus exclusively. All the glory of the Kingdom is wrapped up in Him. The closer to Him you are, the more of the Kingdom you experience.

ADDITIONAL READING: Luke 9:28-36

Once you have tasted flight, you will walk the
earth with your eyes turned skyward.
LEONARDO DA VINCI

Beautiful

God has made everything beautiful for its own time. Ecclesiastes 3:11

IN WORD

God is writing a story. But like all great stories, it's full of ups and downs, twists and turns, and impossible situations that seem to have no possible solution. No one is moved by a story with perfect characters and a few bumps in the road, but grand epics with plenty of humor and drama and happy endings are inspiring. That's the kind of story God is writing. And each one of us is in the middle of it.

Many people have chosen to judge God in the middle of the story. That's easy to do; if any fictional character could talk to his author, he would likely have plenty of complaints about the brutality of the plot. That plot often seems to go in the wrong direction, but the character doesn't yet see the end. If he could, he would be encouraged. But when everything looks bleak, as all good plots do at times, we tend to judge the author for letting us down.

God makes everything beautiful in its time. The Kingdom story doesn't end in the middle, when everything looks bleak. It doesn't leave us hanging in impossible situations, wondering how we might possibly survive and lamenting that the enemy seems to get away with *everything*. No, this plot is the kind that intrigues audiences with its twists, amazes us with its resolution, and provokes thunderous applause at the end. We might be sitting on the edge of our seats and biting our nails all the way through, but when it's over, we exhale and talk about it being the best story ever. It's beautiful—in its time.

IN DEED

Trust God in the middle of the story. Don't draw any conclusions until you see what His conclusions look like. Know that the plot ends well, and whatever obstacle you're facing today is a normal twist for a great storyteller like God. We are not living in the midst of a tragedy; the Kingdom story is both stunning and satisfying. And it's beautiful in its time.

ADDITIONAL READING: 1 Corinthians 2:8-9

> The hilltop hour would not be half so wonderful
> if there were no dark valleys to traverse.
> HELEN KELLER

Eternity in the Heart

He has planted eternity in the human heart, but even so, people cannot see the whole scope of God's work from beginning to end. Ecclesiastes 3:11

IN WORD

God has put eternity in the human heart—not just the thought of the everlasting, but the things of eternity. Our truest desires are deep and lasting. Our purpose is centered in the eternal King. Our future is integrally tied into the story He is writing. And our hearts are constantly looking for connections with that story.

That's why we so desperately try to fill our lives with meaning. We were made for it. When we begin to see the big-picture story, we begin to live with a sense of adventure. Life is no longer a series of mundane tasks. Every interaction, every responsibility is not only significant for what it accomplishes; it's significant for the *way* we accomplish it. We see His story going on inside of us, and everything we do and say takes the plot a step further. And we see His story going on inside of others, and everything we do has the potential to impact the way they experience it. The transformation at the center of this story—the one going on inside of us and others—does not come without challenges and obstacles. You might be fighting a raging battle inside while facing circumstances that look normal to everyone else. Hardly anyone knows the major role you're playing, but you do. It's enormously significant. When you see the big picture, suddenly the stakes are high.

IN DEED

You have choices. You can see the items on today's to-do list as a series of insignificant tasks, or you can see them—particularly your approach to them—as a vital scene in the eternal story. You may have never noticed how your attitudes and outlook affect those around you, but they do. You may have never realized the ripple effects of the battles you win, but they extend much farther than you think. Eternity is in your heart because God wanted you to live with that perspective. Step into His story in every area of your life, and live as though everything has meaning. Because it does.

ADDITIONAL READING: Colossians 3:15-17

> The Kingdom of God is where our best dreams
> come from and our truest prayers.
> FREDERICK BUECHNER

Kingdom of Light

The light shines in the darkness, and the darkness can never extinguish it.
John 1:5

IN WORD

We were born into a kingdom of darkness. Sure, we've gotten glimpses of light, and most of us have managed not to sink as deeply into darkness as others. But the systems of this world are not set up selflessly or efficiently, and those with power rarely wield it exclusively for the benefit of others. We know that because millennia of human governments, economies, and other social systems have not solved poverty, crime, greed, or corruption. Like a civilization that can't see beyond its own borders, we've never grasped pure and holy alternatives. Our world can be a very dark place.

On the other hand, this world is not a kingdom of total darkness. Though unbridled sin and corruption would make it so, God has sent light into the world to shine into dark places. Some of us have seen the light without becoming light ourselves, while others of us have seen it and begun to reflect it clearly. Meanwhile, many can hardly tell the difference. Maladjusted eyes don't distinguish light from dark but perceive everything as some shade of gray. They benefit from the light but don't recognize its source. The kingdom of darkness has blinded them to the light of the world.

Even so, the light has come, and we can't afford to live in the gray. Our job is to make distinctions, to choose daily which kingdom to dwell in—not which kingdom to belong to, for our faith has already settled that, but which one to experience moment by moment. Human beings make hundreds of choices a day, and Kingdom citizens must always choose light. Darkness does us no favors.

IN DEED

If you want to overcome, learn to live in the light. That's what Jesus meant when He said to seek His Kingdom above all else (Matthew 6:33) and what John later wrote to Christians who were confusing the source of their life (1 John 1:5-7). Many claim fellowship with God and then choose darkness. It won't work. Daily decisions, even small ones, make a difference. Real life happens only in the light.

ADDITIONAL READING: 1 John 1:5-7

> Every time you make a choice, you are turning the central part of you . . . into something a little different from what it was before.
> C. S. LEWIS

Children of the King

To all who believed him and accepted him, he gave the right to become children of God. John 1:12

IN WORD

"We're all children of God." That statement is foundational in popular spirituality, that mixed collection of beliefs embraced by those who are nonspecifically religious. And in a sense, it's true. We're all made in God's image and created by Him. He is in some ways a Father to all.

But the New Testament is more specific about the fatherhood of God, applying it not to all who have been born naturally but only to those of us who have been born of His Spirit, who have been given the divine nature by virtue of faith in Him. We are children of an entirely different realm who have God's own DNA planted within us. We were once only part of His creation, but now we are adopted into the royal family.

That means the Kingdom of God is not an impersonal government, a spiritual movement, or a world religion. It's a family business. There's work to be done, but it's done in the context of personal and intimate relationships. We may be corrected at times, but there's no possibility of being fired. We don't have to worry about being exploited or abused, nor do we have to settle for mediocre pay or unfavorable policies. All decisions from the top are made with our best interests in mind. This family comprises the Kingdom of light because our King has no interest in darkness. We are royalty in a bright and shining realm.

IN DEED

Think of what it means to carry the divine nature within you. It means there is a light in you that can't be extinguished, a purity in you that can't be corrupted, a source in you that will never run out of energy, and a drive in you that never gives up. You are shaped for relentless love, hope, peace, grace, and joy. You have access to divine wisdom and power. In a world of darkness you are made to shine—just like your Father.

ADDITIONAL READING: 2 Peter 1:3-4

Adoption gives us the *privilege* of sons, regeneration the *nature* of sons.
STEPHEN CHARNOCK

The King's Battle

Who is this in royal robes, marching in his great strength? Isaiah 63:1

IN WORD

When the world thinks of Jesus, it pictures the Jesus of a made-for-TV miniseries: misty-eyed, peace-preaching, disillusioned with the religious establishment, and an advocate of a better way. He's portrayed as a good teacher who was brutally, unjustly crucified—and as an epilogue to the main story, was raised from the dead. He's an enigmatic prophet and mystic from whom we can learn a lot.

But that's not a full picture of the Jesus of Scripture. The portrayal is true as far as it goes, but it doesn't go far enough. It doesn't capture His role as the incarnate deity who came from heaven to ransom captives. It doesn't reflect the zeal of His mission or the intensity of His words. It doesn't depict the epic agenda of a God who decisively confronts a rogue creation and destroys the evil that ravages it. It gives us a lot of information about the Teacher and almost none about the Warrior King.

Scripture portrays the Messiah of God as a powerful, passionate defender of His beloved people. He strides forward in strength, wearing robes of royal authority. Behind the King who rode a donkey into Jerusalem is a Swordsman who rides a warhorse in Revelation. The humble nature of Jesus as He relates to people is backed by the militant nature of the Son of God as He relates to evil. The Savior is not passively sitting in heaven watching the tragedies of earth unfold. He is an active general who is coming against evil in awesome power and devastating precision.

IN DEED

When you get discouraged about life in this world, remember who is in charge. Learn to see behind the scenes. Though evil runs rampant in the circumstances you see, you and your Messiah are partners in power. You can join with Him in the battle and exercise heavenly vengeance on all that His enemies have sown in this world. Never forget that your Savior, meek and mild, is also a zealous warrior robed in splendor. Appeal to His righteous power whenever and wherever you need it.

ADDITIONAL READING: Revelation 19:11

He has sounded forth the trumpet that shall never sound retreat.
JULIA WARD HOWE

The Fighter's Zeal

*It is I, the L*ORD*, announcing your salvation! It is I, the L*ORD*, who has the power to save!* Isaiah 63:1

IN WORD

God is often perceived as emotionless. After all, if He created all things and is sovereign over them, He has no need to get angry or jealous, or to celebrate as though He's surprised about a good turn of events. He's always calm and dignified in our minds, never rousing Himself to battle. And while that perception is very religiously embraced, it isn't accurate. It isn't how God portrays Himself in Scripture.

No, God strides forward in strength, loudly proclaiming His righteous agenda, His royal robes stained in blood from the battles He fights. Isaiah's rhetorical question, "Who is this in royal robes, marching in his great strength?" (63:1), comes on the heels of God's emphatic, global announcement of the mission of the Savior (62:11), and it's answered decisively by the Lord Himself: It is He, the I Am, the One who gets mad at evil and counters it with truth and righteousness, the One whose overwhelming power is mighty to save. This is no dispassionate God.

If we really understand the passions of God, it changes the way we live. We aren't afraid to ask Him to confront the evil we see and to give us the courage and power to confront it with Him. We don't have to add "if it's Your will" to prayers that we know to be entirely consistent with His will. While the world wonders why God remains so distant and passive, we recognize Him as the last warrior standing, blood-stained from battle. We know the power of His sword and how precisely it cuts down lies and wickedness. We follow His lead and approach the kingdom of darkness with zeal and a holy agenda.

IN DEED

Most Christians walk through life feeling beat up. Get close to the heart of God, however, and that feeling has to vanish. Our God is a God of action. He does not remain silent when we invite Him to rouse Himself to intervene in our battles. He doesn't get pushed around by the adversary. Knowing that the mighty Warrior is on our side gives us the freedom to feel and act victorious. And it gives us the faith to see the victory come.

ADDITIONAL READING: Psalm 24:7-8

> Faith is a living, bold trust in God's grace, so certain of God's favor that it would risk death a thousand times trusting in it.
> MARTIN LUTHER

The Judge's Message

I have been treading the winepress alone; no one was there to help me.
Isaiah 63:3

IN WORD

According to Isaiah, God was appalled that no one was with Him to represent Him and intercede on behalf of this world (v. 5). No one supported Him in His wrath or His redemption, so He worked out salvation with His own arm. He clothed Himself in human flesh and accomplished His victory Himself—all by Himself. We didn't think the way He did about the condition of the world, and we didn't see the solution. None of us was with Him.

But now we know. We know what His vengeance will be like. We know that He hates evil so much that He poured out His wrath on His bloody, beaten Son. We know how mangled Jesus was on the cross, and we understand now that this mangled figure is a picture of God's attitude toward our sin. We know that when Jesus comes again to judge the living and the dead, it will not be a gentle, peaceful event. And we know what's in store for those who spurn His righteousness and His salvation.

Knowing all these things, what should our response be? How should we address the needs of our world? Should we preach mercy, or warn of impending judgment? Should we demonstrate the kindness of God that leads to repentance, or should we proclaim the severity of God that crushes sin? The answer is yes—all of it. Mercy and kindness, severity and judgment. The heart of God is big enough and passionate enough to contain both. Ours must be too.

IN DEED

What God really desires for us—He makes it clear when, through Isaiah, He looks around for partners—is to be honest with our world. We are to be honest about the extravagant mercy of our Savior, and we are to be honest about the terrifying nature of a God who hates all that violates His righteousness. We are to teach the way of salvation and the consequences of rejecting it. We are to lead with a clear demonstration of His kindness and follow with a clear statement of His wrath. We are to speak the truth in love.

ADDITIONAL READING: 2 Peter 3:3-9

> My grand point in preaching is to break the hard
> heart and to heal the broken one.
> JOHN NEWTON

The Believer's Agenda

The time has come for me to avenge my people, to ransom them from their oppressors. Isaiah 63:4

IN WORD

The Messiah has a dual agenda: vengeance and redemption. The first time He came, it was all about redemption. The second time, it will be all about righting wrongs and judging wrongdoers. We can be grateful that the redemptive work came first; otherwise, we'd all fall under His righteous sword. But God mercifully sent our Savior long before judgment, and He has given us at least a couple of millennia to reap a harvest of salvation. Though the day of vengeance and the year of redemption are both on His heart, the year of redemption came first and lasts longer. The day of vengeance is just a matter of cleaning up the rebels' mess.

According to Scripture, the ultimate goal for God's people is to be conformed to the image of the Son. If the King has vengeance and redemption on His heart, what does that say about us? The implications are clear: We are to be as fired up about evil and as zealous about redemption as He is. We are to have a dual agenda just like His.

That doesn't mean that we are to take up a lifestyle of violence in order to bring about God's agenda. Other religions make that mistake and wreak all sorts of havoc on this world. We, on the other hand, have a different sort of violence to embrace. Wherever we see hatred, we oppose it with relentless love. Wherever we see injustice, we make things right. Wherever we see poverty, we provide. Wherever we see pride, we counter it with humility. And wherever we see evil, we pray our hearts out and take an unwavering stand against it.

IN DEED

You may see Christian character as a passive approach to the world's problems, but it's far from that. It's an active, intrusive, even violent opposition to the kingdom of darkness. It shines light into corners that can't stand light. In your life as a believer, adopt the Messiah's agenda. Expose lies and injustice, and sow seeds of righteousness aggressively. Live with a heart of hostility toward evil and mercy toward its captives.

ADDITIONAL READING: Psalm 97:10-12

> You were rubbed with oil like an athlete, Christ's athlete
> . . . and you agreed to take on your opponent.
> AMBROSE OF MILAN

The Message

During the forty days after his crucifixion, he appeared to the apostles from time to time, and he proved to them in many ways that he was actually alive. And he talked to them about the Kingdom of God. Acts 1:3

IN WORD

Jesus came preaching the Kingdom. He urged a change of heart, mind, and direction because "the Kingdom of God is near" (Mark 1:15). He told parables of the Kingdom, told us to seek the Kingdom above all else, and instructed us to pray that it would come on earth just as it is in heaven. So, after His resurrection, during His last forty days on earth, what topic did He focus on with His followers? The Kingdom of God, of course.

The Kingdom wasn't simply part of Jesus' message; it *was* Jesus' message. This was the core of His teaching, the realm to which He called all who believe in Him, the lifestyle He demonstrated and proclaimed to those with ears to hear. He invited us into a supernatural lifestyle because that's how Kingdom citizens live. He intrigued us with Kingdom paradoxes because some things can't be easily explained. He showed us Kingdom fruit because it's available to all who make His presence in their lives a priority. He made it clear that history is hurtling toward a fulfillment of God's purposes on this planet. The King was focused on establishing His domain.

If your conversations with the King aren't filled with thoughts of the Kingdom—what it looks like, how it thrives in your life, how you can cultivate it and further it, how it's different from any Kingdom you've lived in before—then perhaps your conversations are off-topic from His main concern. That doesn't mean He doesn't care about your immediate needs and the details of your life; He certainly does. But He cares about integrating them into His Kingdom purposes. He wants you to see them with a Kingdom perspective. He talks about the Kingdom a lot.

IN DEED

Good conversationalists talk about what the other person is interested in. When you do that with Jesus, you'll find yourself in rewarding conversations that go deeper than you might have thought possible. Your understanding of the Kingdom will grow, and your desire for it will be stirred. And you may see it coming in ways you haven't expected.

ADDITIONAL READING: Mark 1:15

To want all that God wants . . . this is the Kingdom of God.
FRANÇOIS FÉNELON

A Rough Transition

They encouraged them to continue in the faith, reminding them that we must suffer many hardships to enter the Kingdom of God. Acts 14:22

IN WORD

Paul had been stoned, dragged out of Lystra, and left for dead. Perhaps he was—his executioners weren't likely to mistake unconsciousness for death. Either way—whether he was resurrected or simply revived—he had been brutally treated. His message of the Good News had resulted in some really bad consequences.

So when Paul and Barnabas told the believers in the next town that we go through many hardships to enter the Kingdom of God, they were speaking from experience. They weren't simply having a bad day; they were in frequent danger. And while their statement seems like a requirement—as if hardships can earn us the right to become Kingdom citizens—it's more of an observation. Entering the Kingdom of God is a wonderful experience, but it isn't always an easy one. There are challenges. The kingdom of darkness doesn't give up its denizens easily.

You've probably experienced that phenomenon. Like the Pharaoh who had to be convinced through ten plagues to let God's people go, the captor of our souls doesn't remain passive when we leave his domain. The fact that his domain is illegitimate and ultimately defeated doesn't deter him; he still fights for territory. And the most intense battlegrounds in this fight are the territory of your heart, your fellowship with other believers, and your perceptions of the King.

IN DEED

That's where many believers get tripped up. We suffer hardship and then accuse the King of allowing it. But God isn't the source of the hardships. We stand in the midst of a clash of kingdoms. Having seen the light, we're done with the kingdom of darkness, but the kingdom of darkness isn't done with us. We should therefore not be surprised when we run into obstacles or opposition. It's normal on kingdom pathways. And our response must be like that of Paul and Barnabas: Get up and keep going, persistently and relentlessly until the Kingdom comes in full.

ADDITIONAL READING: John 16:33

Endurance is not just the ability to bear a
hard thing but to turn it into glory.
WILLIAM BARCLAY

Unhindered

He welcomed all who visited him, boldly proclaiming the Kingdom of God.
Acts 28:30-31

IN WORD

The book of Acts begins with Jesus teaching about the Kingdom of God, and it ends with Paul teaching about it—unhindered. That's significant because we've seen hindrances in the middle of the story as early believers encountered opposition and obstacles, sometimes from within their own ranks. But the overriding message in Acts is that the Good News of the Kingdom is contagious and unstoppable. It's accompanied by the power and provision of God, and it will continue until its completion.

That's why the story of Acts ends without ending. It leaves us hanging in the middle of the plot, primarily because the plot is still being written. Even today, we are writing chapters of the Kingdom in the way we live, speak, and act in the name of Jesus. As a prophet once wrote, the greatness of God's Kingdom will never stop increasing (Isaiah 9:7). Every believer is a part of that story, and every believer's role is important. The reason the book of Acts doesn't have a firm ending is that the ending is up to us.

Live in the book of Acts. Don't try to duplicate the same stories of the early church as though the Kingdom hasn't grown or advanced since the first century; we live in a different time, and some of the issues we face are different. But the message is the same, the power available to us is the same, and the King who gave us the Kingdom mission is the same. Acts isn't just the story of Peter, John, Philip, Stephen, James, and Paul. It's the story of you.

IN DEED

If you really want Acts-like faith, take up the message that begins and ends the book—the Good News of the Kingdom. This message includes spiritual salvation, but it's bigger than that. It begins with faith in the King, but it leads to great exploits and adventures on His behalf. It addresses your individual life, but it draws you into a bigger story. Live in that story with all boldness and no hindrance.

ADDITIONAL READING: Mark 16:19-20

The crowning wonder of God's scheme is that He entrusted it to men.
HENRY DRUMMOND

The Same Spirit

The Spirit of the LORD will rest on him. Isaiah 11:2

IN WORD

The Spirit of the Lord rested on Jesus. He quoted another prophecy of Isaiah to make that point when He preached in His home synagogue: "The Spirit of the LORD is upon me, for he has anointed me to bring Good News to the poor" (Luke 4:18). When God sent His Son into this world in human flesh, stripped of all His divine, supernatural rights (Philippians 2:6-8), He invested in Him the Spirit of His own character. As God would later do in every person of faith in and obedience to the gospel, He gave the human Jesus His own divine nature. The Spirit and the flesh met in Christ.

God's desire in sending His Son was not just to save the world. Salvation is just the beginning. No, God's desire was to save people first in order to pour His Spirit on them and in them. We are to be like Jesus, not just in habits and outward performance, but in inward nature. God's plan was (and still is) to have a multitude of incarnations of Himself—human beings clothed in His Spirit—to be ambassadors and reconcilers in this rebellious world. We are the temple of God Himself. The presence of God in this world is His Holy Spirit in human hearts.

IN DEED

We tend to see so clearly the uniqueness of Jesus that we forget that He is also the prototype of all of redeemed humanity. That's why He told His disciples that He was sending them into the world the same way the Father sent Him (John 20:21). That's why He told them they would do even greater works than He did (John 14:12). That's why a ragged band of disciples was able to turn the world upside down in a few short decades.

Never forget that Jesus is your prototype. God's Spirit rested on Jesus. It's also His desire for His Spirit to rest on you. In faith and obedience, walk the path He ordains for you, and ask Him for the same Spirit He invested in His Son.

ADDITIONAL READING: Luke 4:18

As the body of Christ, we are to be like Jesus so
that we too reveal God to the world.
WILLIAM R. L. HALEY

Modest Missiles

They will destroy and overcome with slingstones. Zechariah 9:15, *NIV*

IN WORD

As we rest in the strength of God, He rearms us with His kind of weapons. These weapons are like slingshots; they're dwarfed by Goliath's sword and scorned by any self-respecting army. But they rely on the power and accuracy of God Himself, deflecting the glory of victory from man to God. As instruments of human warfare, they are completely impotent. In the hands of our Warrior, however, they are powerfully destructive.

Yes, our prayers can destroy the works of the enemy. They can thwart his evil purposes and expose his lies. They are weapons we can use from inside the fortress, where we're safe and God is on the battlefield. They have the power to cripple evil generals and take captive guerrilla fighters. To the world, they look like kids' toys, but empowered by God, they can slay giants. There are only two things that can render them impotent: neglect and unbelief.

It's true; God won't answer prayers we don't pray. If we don't sling the stones He has handed us, they won't have any effect on the battlefield. Likewise, if we sling them without any belief that they'll hit a target or that God will empower them, they fall to the ground harmlessly. God uses the warfare of those who can rest in His power and shoot slingshots from the fortress. If we don't do our part, He may not fight our battles.

IN DEED

How many stones have you flung at the enemy today? Are you using your humble weapon of warfare? Like a boy facing Goliath with five stones, or another boy offering Jesus a few loaves of bread—or even like the humble Messiah riding into town on a donkey—we can trust God to take what's mundane to us and use it to powerfully change lives. His Kingdom is built on such humility. We can wield our modest weapons with confidence that they are more effective than the high-tech arsenals of our adversary. Our prayers are in God's hands. No enemy can withstand such an assault.

ADDITIONAL READING: 2 Corinthians 10:3-4

> Prayer is a strong wall and fortress of the church; it is a good Christian weapon.
> MARTIN LUTHER

Heaven on Earth

The punishment that brought us peace was on him, and by his wounds we are healed. Isaiah 53:5, *NIV*

IN WORD

We celebrate the gift of salvation. Most of us celebrate because of the eternal life we know we'll have in heaven. Though we suffer pains and trials today, we know it won't be this way forever—that in heaven there will be no more sorrow and no more tears. We look across the Jordan and into the Promised Land, wondering when we'll cross over and leave this wilderness behind. We love the prospects of our future.

But our King's ministry is much more than a ticket to future glory. It has present applications that, by faith, allow us to taste glory right now. Many of God's promises are for "the land of the living" (Psalm 27:13). His benefits are more than a distant hope (Psalm 103:2-5). The punishment that Jesus suffered on our behalf brought us peace—notice the fullness of life experienced by His followers in Acts—and we are healed by His wounds. The blessings of salvation began the day Jesus left a tomb behind. If we place all of our hopes in the future, we're missing an enormous part of salvation.

IN DEED

Does your life revolve around a future hope or a present reality? The truth is that both should shape the decisions of each day. But when the life we live doesn't measure up to the life we're promised, we're often content to shrug our shoulders and assume the promises of God are all for our life beyond the grave.

God disagrees. He gave His disciples the gift of faith, in order to bring heaven into the now. Jesus even commanded His disciples to pray that God's will be done on earth as it is being done in heaven. The truth of salvation is not just that we will go to heaven, but that heaven will come to us in the here and now—if we believe. Live in that truth, praying and acting as though the Kingdom is invading your life. The punishment that brought us peace and healed our wounds means that it truly is.

ADDITIONAL READING: Psalm 103:2-5

It is certain that all that will go to heaven
hereafter begin their heaven now.
MATTHEW HENRY

World Changers

I will give him a portion among the great, and he will divide the spoils with the strong, because he poured out his life unto death. Isaiah 53:12, *NIV*

IN WORD

Imagine what the inheritance of the Son of God is. Psalm 2 says the whole earth and all the nations are included in His inheritance. Paul referred to heavenly riches, and Peter spoke of an inheritance that will not fade away. What's really incredible is what else the New Testament writers say about the inheritance of the Son: It is shared with us.

That's what Isaiah's prophecy is pointing to. God looks at the obedience of His Son with delight and turns all creation over to Him. Jesus is the heir of the King's estate, and with an infinite King, the estate is greater than any mind can imagine. The extravagant God is ridiculously wealthy with all kinds of riches, and He wills them all to His Son. His Son, in turn, shares His inheritance with His bride—all who believe in Him. It's the best deal we ever got.

Did you realize that? The Bible gives us two pictures of eternal inheritance: The Father gives everything to the Son, who shares with His brothers; and the Father endows everything to the Bridegroom, who allows His bride to marry into His wealth. That means that God bestows on us what Jesus deserves from His obedience. And if we think about what Jesus really deserves . . . well, that's a staggering thought. And the truth is that it's ours as well as His.

IN DEED

Too many Christians walk through this world convinced that God answers only our small prayers, that His arm has to be twisted to give us what we need, that He's reluctant to use us to change lives. But God and Scripture shout, "No!" When He promises His Son the nations, He promises us the nations. When He promises His Son the extravagantly life-giving, fruit-bearing Spirit, He promises us the extravagantly life-giving, fruit-bearing Spirit. Faith takes hold of those promises and won't let go. And those with that kind of faith become history-makers and world changers. To Him—and to us—are given the spoils of His victory.

ADDITIONAL READING: Ephesians 1:18-22

Faith is to believe what you do not yet see. The reward for this faith is to see what you believe.
AUGUSTINE OF HIPPO

Intentional Negligence

Let the Holy Spirit guide your lives. Then you won't be doing what your sinful nature craves. Galatians 5:16

IN WORD

The Kingdom life is a matter of walking in the Spirit. That's not a controversial state-ment; virtually every Christian would agree with it. But not all Christians remember it on a day-by-day or moment-by-moment basis. Instead, we turn our attention to the flesh and try to stamp it out, starve it, get rid of it, or any other such direct approach. Human logic tells us that if we want to stop gratifying the desires of the flesh, we should focus on denying those desires. But this logic leads us only to frustration.

Think of the absurdity. Are we really going to be able to stamp out the power of the flesh in the power of the flesh? Is self-discipline really our best option when the self is the problem to begin with? Does any problem really get better by our obsessing over it? Or is there perhaps a better way?

Paul says there's a much better way, and it doesn't involve addressing the flesh at all. Instead, we choose to walk by the Spirit without even paying attention to the flesh. If we're filled with the Spirit and living by His direction and desires, we won't exactly have room for the flesh to grow stronger. Ignoring our misplaced desires may seem negligent and irresponsible—doesn't somebody have to deal with them firmly?—but focusing on them only honors their power. Pay them no attention. Invest yourself fully in the Spirit. Let that life overcome the one you're leaving behind.

IN DEED

If what we focus on tends to grow larger, then the only way to become stronger in the Spirit is to focus on the Spirit. Or for another commonly used illustration, whatever you feed will strengthen, and whatever you starve will weaken. Just as God is not at all obsessed with His enemies, we don't have any reason to be obsessed with ours—even the ones within. Our only preoccupation is a holy connection with the Spirit Himself. In Him, we have everything we need to think, feel, desire, speak, and act in Kingdom ways.

ADDITIONAL READING: Romans 8:5-14

Work designed for eternity can only be done by the eternal Spirit.
A. W. TOZER

Freedom to Love

Don't use your freedom to satisfy your sinful nature. Instead, use your freedom to serve one another in love. For the whole law can be summed up in this one command: "Love your neighbor as yourself." Galatians 5:13-14

IN WORD

Paul assures his readers that we are free in Christ. Whatever else that means—freedom from law, freedom from sin, freedom from God's judgment—it doesn't mean freedom *to* sin. God does not release captives for them to go right back into the behaviors that held them captive. Freedom should never make unholy indulgence acceptable to us.

But then Paul turns his attention to love. Why? It doesn't seem like a natural direction for the conversation to turn. How are indulging the flesh and serving in love opposed to each other? After all, we live in a culture that is perfectly comfortable with immoral behavior "as long as it doesn't hurt anyone." Can't we do what we want and be loving toward others? Apparently not, according to Paul. There's something about the flesh that wars against love. Selfish desires and attitudes undermine relationships rather than strengthening them.

We know that love is at the center of the Kingdom culture. Therefore selfishness can't be. And ultimately, all sin is based in self-centeredness. Yes, we're free from the demands of the law and the penalty of sin, but freedom is a responsibility. We're to use it well. The Spirit of Jesus within us will fulfill His own purposes, and those purposes do not include self-centered attitudes and behaviors. If we don't have love, we aren't experiencing the Kingdom, whether we're citizens or not.

IN DEED

"Serve one another in love." This is normal behavior in the Kingdom of God, but it's far from normal in our society and even in many of our churches. We compete with each other far more often than we serve each other. But the Kingdom is not a place of competition, of striving, of getting ahead, or of selfish indulgence. It's a place of radical other-centeredness. We are fully free to love without fear of losing anything in the process.

ADDITIONAL READING: 1 Corinthians 13

> Love, like warmth, should beam forth on every side,
> and bend to every necessity of our brethren.
> MARTIN LUTHER

Consider the Source

The Holy Spirit produces this kind of fruit in our lives: love, joy, peace, patience, kindness, goodness, faithfulness, gentleness, and self-control.
Galatians 5:22-23

IN WORD

The gardener plants a seed and then cultivates the land around it. He doesn't produce the fruit, nor does he determine its exact shape and size. In most cases, he also doesn't determine how it will be prepared, what recipe it will contribute to, or who will eat it. He simply plants the seed and does everything he can to give it the right conditions to grow.

That's how it is with the fruit of the Spirit. We can't force these Kingdom attributes by focusing on their size and shape, by scheduling how they will be used and in what situations, or by trying to control them by any other artificial or arbitrary efforts. All we can do is tend to the seeds and the conditions. God does the rest.

But most of us don't approach them that way. We focus on developing patience, or we work on demonstrating love, or we discipline ourselves with self-control. The more biblical approach is to throw ourselves fully into a relationship with the Spirit without any attention to developing the fruit. If we are thoroughly in fellowship with Him, the fruit happens. We don't strive for it, script it out, or dictate its forms. We plant ourselves in Him and expect to grow.

IN DEED

When we say we need greater fruit of the Spirit, what we really mean is that we need a deeper experience with the Spirit. We don't need love, joy, peace, and so on; we need Jesus. He *is* all of those things, and He will produce them in us as we love Him and enjoy His fellowship. Our responsibility? Create the right conditions for His fruit to grow in us. That means spending more time with Him, asking Him to fill us continually, telling Him what we love about Him, and willingly yielding our hearts to Him. When we create those conditions, it's impossible for fruit *not* to grow. The Spirit thrives in conditions that honor and adore the King.

ADDITIONAL READING: Romans 15:13

O Holy Spirit, descend plentifully into my heart.
Enlighten the dark corners of this neglected dwelling
and scatter there Thy cheerful beams.
AUGUSTINE OF HIPPO

Beyond Formulas

Since we are living by the Spirit, let us follow the Spirit's leading in every part of our lives. Galatians 5:25

IN WORD

Long ago in the wilderness, the wandering Israelites followed the cloud by day and the fire by night. Whenever the cloud and fire remained in one place, the Israelites remained in that place. Whenever the cloud and fire lifted up and departed, the people packed up and followed. It was a very unpredictable lifestyle, but it weaned the former slaves of their limited expectations. Life under Egyptian masters was formulaic and systematic. Life with God was anything but.

It's still that way. While religious systems teach us how to live by formulas, God teaches us to live by His own movements. That may look random to us, and it can be very disorienting, but it isn't random to God at all. Our approach to life as Kingdom citizens is altogether different from our former approach and other people's approaches to life. Our fallen human nature longs for rules, principles, systems, and step-by-step instructions. We want to know what to expect. The Spirit says, "Follow Me."

To really experience the Kingdom life, we have to become comfortable with a Person rather than a plan. It may help to have plans sometimes, but never to hold them tightly. We may crave rules and principles, but God wants us to have a relationship with Him, not with a set of rules or principles. Whether we like it or not, responsiveness to Him is the norm of the Kingdom, no matter how many unpredictable paths He leads us down. The Spirit will take us places, in our hearts and in our circumstances, that we might never have foreseen.

IN DEED

Never turn your faith into a formula. Learn instead to relate to God personally and intimately. When you do, the fruit of the Spirit will spring up within you and accomplish what laws and principles never could. There will be less and less room for sin and selfishness, and more desire for life in abundance. And the Spirit Himself will fulfill that desire.

ADDITIONAL READING: Romans 8:1-4

Breathe on me, Breath of God, till I am wholly Thine; until this earthly part of me glows with Thy fire divine.
EDWIN HATCH

Real Freedom

You have been called to live in freedom. Galatians 5:13

IN WORD

Paul wrote often of being a bond servant to Christ. He also wrote of his freedom in Christ. So which is it? Is he free or a slave of Christ? The truth is that serving Christ is the only way to freedom because He is the only one whose yoke is easy and whose burden is light. Unfortunately, throughout Christian history and up through today, the church has often proclaimed a message of freedom while embodying a message of captivity—to rules and formulas, to specific doctrines and decrees, to an idealized spirituality that may look great on a willing volunteer but can crush someone with a different calling. Instead of teaching conformity to Christ—who is anything but a conformist—we've far too often taught conformity to a church culture. And that isn't freedom at all.

Whatever binds you to Christ as His willing bond servant is good. Whatever binds you unwillingly to laws, rules, and regulations may be very religious, but it isn't the Spirit. It's wonderful for us to feel compelled by our love for Him; it's brutal to feel compelled by other people's expectations. Yet the truth of the Kingdom is that we are free. We live in freedom, are filled with a very free Spirit, and are called to obey out of no other motive than love.

IN DEED

If you don't feel free in your relationship with God, consider the possibility that others are placing demands on you that He is not. You serve an out-of-the-box Creator who clothed Himself in flesh and lived an out-of-the-box life. Human beings generally insist on social conformity, but God urges spiritual conformity to His Son. There's a world of difference between the two. One stifles us; the other sets us free. One fears originality; the other makes it possible. One leads to slow and silent death, the other to life in abundance. As you receive the Spirit's love for you and cultivate your love for Him, you will find Him opening up worlds of possibilities for you—and setting you completely free.

ADDITIONAL READING: 2 Corinthians 3:17

> The Spirit of God . . . gives liberty; and that is about
> the last thing we have in many of our churches.
> D. L. MOODY

Shine

Arise, Jerusalem! Let your light shine for all to see. For the glory of the LORD rises to shine on you. Isaiah 60:1

IN WORD

In a prophetic passage about Zion, and ultimately about all of God's people, Isaiah sees the light coming into a dark earth. But he doesn't just picture the light of God piercing the darkness. He pictures the light of God *on His people* piercing the darkness of the world. The words of this prophecy are not an appeal to God to rise and shine. They are an appeal to the people of God to rise and shine. The day of oppression, of captivity, of living under the darkness rather than above it, are over.

That's a great message for people who feel powerless and who, according to their past experiences, might have every reason to feel that way. There's nothing in this passage that says, "Base your expectations of God on your past experiences." There's nothing here that points back to disappointments or futility. No, this is an ode to a new day, a signal that a new era is breaking into this world and that it's coming through the people of God. This is a declaration that times of disappointment and futility are passing away and new things have come.

Do you realize the implications? In God's redemptive story, a new day has come, is coming, and will come. It first applied to the captives of Babylon, but it was bigger than that, a plot twist in the epic of God's restoration of a broken world. Jesus initiated a new era, but this era hasn't yet reached its apex. The light is still overcoming darkness.

IN DEED

You have an invitation, a calling, a responsibility to shine. God wouldn't ask that of you if you weren't able to do it. All of creation is waiting for the revelation of those who are His children (Romans 8:19). We are reflections of His glory, now to some degree but always in increasing measure. As humble and unassuming as you may want to be, you were really designed to shine with the glory of God in such a way that people living in a dark world notice. You don't have to force it or fabricate it; you simply must live in close fellowship with Him. His light has risen, is rising, and will continue to rise upon you.

ADDITIONAL READING: Romans 8:18-21

To be a witness . . . means to live in such a way that one's
life would not make sense if God did not exist.
EMMANUEL SUHARD

Made for Glory

Darkness as black as night covers all the nations of the earth, but the glory of the LORD rises and appears over you. Isaiah 60:2

IN WORD

"God will not share His glory with another." This paraphrase of Isaiah 42:8 and 48:11 is often expressed in absolute terms, as if God never shares His glory with anyone at all. But these verses were stated in the context of idolatry. For a fuller picture, we need only to look at Moses, who shone with the glory of God (Exodus 34:29-30); at the prayer of Jesus to share His glory with His followers (John 17:22); at how God transforms His people into a glorious image (2 Corinthians 3:18); at how we will be glorified with Christ (Romans 8:17-18); and at Peter's insistence that we can participate in the divine nature (2 Peter 1:4). In fact, we were originally made in God's image and are being restored to that image in Christ. Is it possible to bear His image without also bearing His glory? Of course not. The idea is absurd, and the result would be less than glorifying to Him. No, we were created for glory.

According to Isaiah's prophecy, the Lord rises on His people and His glory is seen on us. We are participants in the divine drama, not just spectators, and not antagonists. He doesn't just show His glory *to* us; He shows His glory *through* us. Whether we're comfortable with that is not the issue. It's His desire. He can do what He wants with the people He has created. He is fully free to lavish His goodness, grace, and glory on us however He wills.

IN DEED

How do we respond to such extravagance? We let Him. We realize our part in the redemption story and live as restored creatures fully alive and thoroughly saturated with the presence of God. We have no need to be pushy, pretentious, or contentious in our relationships with others; we live as those who are deeply, forever loved. Yes, we may pray bold prayers for truth to be known and miracles to be displayed, but we leave the results up to Him. We no longer live in futility or fear; we live as those who are highly favored. And we do it in the midst of deep darkness, where glory shines the brightest.

ADDITIONAL READING: Romans 8:17-18

Numerous passages of Scripture assert that the manifestation of the glory of God is the great end of creation.
ROBERT HALDANE

Drawn to Glory

All nations will come to your light; mighty kings will come to see your radiance. Isaiah 60:3

IN WORD

Even from the beginning, it was clear that God was interested in more nations than just Israel. By calling this chosen people His "firstborn" (Exodus 4:22), He implied there would be others. After all, firstborn does not mean only-born; there have to be others for something to be the first. And as often as God gave directions regarding the "aliens among you," instructed His people to be a light for other nations, and declared that many would be drawn to the Temple in Jerusalem or to the Jewish people as a whole, it's clear that His mission was global from the beginning. His presence becomes a magnet for those with ears to hear and hearts to know Him.

Though Isaiah 60 seems at first glance to be speaking of the end—of the Kingdom of God in all its fullness in the new heaven and new earth—it clearly speaks of a time when earth is still shrouded in darkness. It speaks of our age. And it tells us that in this age, God's people can rise and shine and reflect His glory. Even in an age of darkness, there is a time when nations come to the light, not just of His glory, but of His glory *in you*.

We've seen that to a degree; faith has made inroads in virtually all of the nations and large ethnic groups of the world, though many remote people groups remain unreached. While we pray for more to come into God's light, He prophesies that they will come into ours. As we step fully into our calling as redeemed and restored human beings, both created *and* restored into His image, nations will be drawn to His/our glory.

IN DEED

It's possible to live well beneath the glory of God even while He is holding it out to offer it to you. We do that when we work *for* Him rather than *with* Him, pray *to* Him rather than *in* Him, and reason *about* Him rather than receiving *from* Him. But the nations are depending on our capacity to reflect the nature of God, whether they realize it or not. They are waiting to see who is truly not of this age. They are looking for the difference. And as we open ourselves to His glory, they will see it.

ADDITIONAL READING: 1 Peter 5:10-11

> If Christ lives in us, controlling our personalities, we will leave glorious marks on the lives we touch.
> EUGENIA PRICE

Relentless Hope

Even when there was no reason for hope, Abraham kept hoping. Romans 4:18

IN WORD

We have few problems with hope when all is going well and the future looks bright. But God doesn't normally cultivate our hope in that context, does He? No, He lets our hope run into obstacles and challenges and contradictions far more often than we're comfortable with, stretching us to near-breaking point until our hope either fades or stands in unrealistic defiance against visible circumstances. At times, He even seems to oppose our hope Himself, seeing if we'll hang on to what we know to be true about Him, though all reason suggests we're wrong. These are the fires in which real hope—the kind rooted in eternity—is forged.

We don't like that process. We aren't comfortable with hoping "against all hope" (Romans 4:18, NIV) or when there is "no reason" visibly supporting us. We don't enjoy critics who think we're irrational or delusional or naive. Like all human beings, we love respect and affirmation. But when all the underpinnings for our hope seem to have been removed, we don't get much understanding from those around us. We can only wait for vindication at the end of the promise.

That's what Kingdom hope looks like. It's rooted in love, the kind that allows us to look at our King with complete trust that He will not let us down. Without that foundation, hanging on to our hope is a hopeless endeavor. But knowing who He is—relentlessly clinging to His character and goodness and love—puts us on solid footing in His Kingdom. We see things that other people can't see. We look for evidence of His Kingdom coming into dark places. We pray persistently for the signs of the Kingdom and the will of the King. We hope no matter what.

IN DEED

Whatever it takes, cultivate hope in your heart. God is never pessimistic about your life; neither should you be. See through hope-colored lenses. Refuse to listen to any thought that doesn't come from the mind of God. Be as stubborn as Abraham in waiting for God's promises. Eventually, true God-given hope is fulfilled.

ADDITIONAL READING: Hebrews 11:8-10

Hope can see heaven through the thickest clouds.
THOMAS BENTON BROOKS

Fully Persuaded

He was fully convinced that God is able to do whatever he promises.
Romans 4:21

IN WORD

God spoke, and worlds were created—a vast universe, a planet springing with life, image-bearers crafted from dust and filled with the divine breath. No wonder Paul appeals to the God who calls things that are not as though they are, who utters a word and creates new things out of nothing (Romans 4:17, KJV and NLT). If we are going to place relentless faith and hope in any being, it needs to be this kind of God who makes something out of nothing.

Can our faith do that? When we see nothing yet hope in what will be, are we accomplishing anything substantial? Perhaps. As those made in God's image, it stands to reason that we might be able to utter words by faith and see things that don't exist come into existence. Any such capacity is derived from Him, of course, but so is anything else we do in His Spirit. Jesus made it clear that we can do nothing without Him (John 15:5). But with Him? Well, we can do a lot. Praying, hoping, speaking, and believing regardless of what we see has powerful implications for what we *will* see in the future.

That's why Kingdom people are to live fully persuaded. We are to have complete trust and confidence in the King who has a tremendous track record in birthing new things, ushering in new seasons, blazing new trails, and creating new creatures. Impossibilities are not impossible with Him. Setbacks can be turned into promotions with Him. Even death can be turned into resurrection. We serve a powerful God as beings who bear His powerful image and are inhabited by His powerful Spirit.

IN DEED

Live with confidence, regardless of what you see. A human being with a Kingdom mind-set will hope, dream, pursue, create, believe, speak, expect, and press forward relentlessly. An image of the Creator and the Son could do no less; the image is always made in the likeness of the original. Anchor yourself in the faithfulness of the one who promised you the Kingdom. He has the power to accomplish it.

ADDITIONAL READING: John 15:5-8

> What is more elevating and transporting than the generosity
> of heart which risks everything on God's word?
> JOHN HENRY NEWMAN

Prosperity and Purpose

When the righteous prosper, the city rejoices. Proverbs 11:10, *NIV*

IN WORD

Most people don't rejoice when other people prosper. Some get jealous; others just ignore the prosperity of others as irrelevant to their own lives. So why does Scripture tell us that the city rejoices when the righteous prosper? Because the righteous—not simply those who have been justified by God but those who live in a way that reflects the Kingdom of God—use their prosperity for the good of all.

Think about it: If we're living with a Kingdom orientation, how likely are we to use our positions selfishly? To have influence without using it for the good of those who need advocates? To build networks without those relationships becoming an influence for good? To build mansions without building lives? To do a job without serving others in it? No, the Kingdom mind-set looks for ways to exemplify the Kingdom everywhere. And when the righteous prosper, the opportunities to exemplify the Kingdom multiply. That's good for everyone.

Look at it this way: The Kingdom is a realm of no injustice, no lack, no abuses, no brokenness. And Kingdom citizens long to be pictures of the Kingdom culture, so we offer foretastes of it. We find ways to embody it and bring people into it. We see our jobs, our platforms, and our networks as Kingdom collateral that advances Kingdom ways. So when Kingdom citizens prosper, everyone benefits.

IN DEED

For far too long, whether intentionally or not, the church has preached a message of going to church on Sundays, worshiping and tithing, and sharing our faith during the week. All of that is good, but it's woefully short of a Kingdom lifestyle. Kingdom citizens repair and restore cities. Being a lawyer, teacher, real estate agent, or anyone else who lives righteously to serve and influence the system is a sacred calling. When we serve society with a Kingdom perspective, we serve the Kingdom. And the city rejoices.

ADDITIONAL READING: Proverbs 29:2

The Bible must be considered the great source of truth by which men are to be guided in government as well as social transactions.
NOAH WEBSTER

Born to Bless

Through the blessing of the upright a city is exalted. Proverbs 11:11, *NIV*

IN WORD

We sit in traffic and complain about all the cars blocking our way. Or we stand in line wondering how long we will have to wait and lamenting the waste of time. The conversations that go on in our minds at such moments are often filled with criticism or frustration. But there's one voice that we should listen to above all others. It's the voice that says, "Look at all the people I've put in your line of sight to bless! Look at all the problems in front of you that you could be praying about! Look into the hearts of the people around you and ask Me to meet their needs!" In other words, we have numerous opportunities to bless people. And we miss them.

Those opportunities aren't limited to prayers, of course. Virtually everyone lives, works, or studies among other people who, in some way or another, could be influenced by a godly attitude and a desire to bless. The Christian community has a plethora of platforms among us, and we could use them to improve lives, encourage hearts, and show glimpses of the Kingdom way. Instead, many of us use our time in arguments and critiques on social media, or by focusing on our immediate needs and not the needs of others, or by looking for a chance just to get away from it all. But God has given us a multitude of open doors to get into it all in a way that blesses the neighborhood, the community, and the city. He has called His people to be blessers as a demonstration of what the Kingdom looks like.

IN DEED

The Kingdom doesn't benefit when we withhold our influence, resources, and relationships from those outside of it. The Kingdom's reputation isn't enhanced when we miss opportunities to demonstrate the Kingdom in the world. And no lives are touched when we forget to say a blessing, even a silent one, over the needy lives and families around us. When the upright serve the welfare of the community, the community responds with joy. That's what the Kingdom looks like. It certainly will later; but it can even now.

ADDITIONAL READING: Romans 12:14-17

There is always time to look up to Him for His smile.
F. B. MEYER

Righteousness Within

Unless your righteousness is better than the righteousness of the teachers of religious law and the Pharisees, you will never enter the Kingdom of Heaven!
Matthew 5:20

IN WORD

The Pharisees were upstanding members of society. Some of them were judgmental and legalistic—we read about their confrontations with Jesus frequently—but most were genuinely interested in doing God's will and respected by society for their devotion. They were in many ways the first-century equivalent of today's dedicated churchgoer. And they were very intent on following God's law to the letter.

In their focus on the details of God's law, Pharisees sometimes missed the heart of it. We can relate; we've all focused on rules, principles, and formulas while neglecting the Spirit's intent. But no one would have accused the Pharisees—or us today—of being unrighteous for that reason alone. Except Jesus. Jesus saw the Pharisees' works and knew what they were missing. Their attempts at total obedience were not enough. Their hearts had not been fundamentally changed.

That's a sobering message for us. No matter how fully we obey God in our actions, we aren't righteous unless our hearts have been transformed. We know from the rest of Jesus' teaching and especially later New Testament writings that we have the righteousness of Christ by faith in Him. So our righteousness exceeds that of the Pharisees and legal experts because it's His righteousness in us, not ours. Still, this righteousness is never simply theoretical. It's meant to be practical. Deep down inside, the heart fit for the Kingdom is one whose nature is changed at the core.

IN DEED

Jesus' goal is to prepare His people for life in His Kingdom, so He produces a heart that is clean on the inside, not just a lifestyle that looks good on the outside. That doesn't mean we become sinless, but it does mean we are growing out of sinful tendencies. His work in us is never superficial; He goes to the root. He produces the Kingdom inwardly before we can live in it outwardly.

ADDITIONAL READING: Romans 10:2-4

There cannot be perfect transformation without perfect pureness.
JOHN OF THE CROSS

Where to Invest

Wherever your treasure is, there the desires of your heart will also be.
Matthew 6:21

IN WORD

Jesus told His followers to store up their treasures in heaven, not on earth. Clearly He meant that the material goods of this age are temporary and not ultimately satisfying. Money and possessions get stolen, wear out, or are simply used up. But His statement raises questions for us: What exactly does it mean to store up treasures in heaven? How can we do that? What kind of treasures is He talking about?

Any answers we come up with will inevitably direct us back to earth. Why? Because that's where we live. Right here, in this physical world, in this present age. We store up treasures in heaven by what we do on earth—how we give, sacrifice, pray, treat other people, and invest ourselves in the Kingdom. Our treasures in heaven depend on our relationship with God, our relationships with people, and our activities in the here and now. They aren't the same activities as a person solely in pursuit of wealth or status might have, but they are still here-and-now activities. We live life in this realm with an eye on another. But we can't escape the fact that the two realms intermingle.

IN DEED

Jesus is certainly not telling us to invest our hearts so far away from here and now that we have no impact in this world. He isn't telling us to shake the dust from our feet and wait for our escape. No, He is telling us to invest our hearts in the interests of heaven, both in the here and now and the there and then. We are agents of heaven in this world, not agents of this world waiting for heaven. Before we ever "go up," we are to bring heaven down—in us and through us for the sake of a captive world.

If this is what we treasure—if we truly long to see the Kingdom come in every corner of the universe, including ours—our hearts will continually point us to opportunities to represent the King. And we will store up treasures that last forever.

ADDITIONAL READING: 1 Timothy 6:17-19

> Lives based on having are less free than lives
> based either on doing or on being.
> WILLIAM JAMES

Choose Your Master

No one can serve two masters. Matthew 6:24

IN WORD

Living in a Kingdom has plenty of implications for our lives, none bigger than this one: We live under a King. That has enormous benefits for us, but we don't really get to experience all of them unless we understand both sides of the relationship. Not only is He our King, we are His subjects. That means we have chosen Him to be our master and have decided to consider His words of far greater import than anyone else's. We have chosen His agenda, His purposes, His ways.

Every choice has its opportunity costs. When we choose to invest our time in one thing, we are choosing not to invest it in something else. When we spend money on something, we have chosen not to spend it on something different. So when we choose to follow God as our King, we have chosen not to follow other masters. That explains why Jesus doesn't simply say, "Don't follow two masters." He says we can't. It isn't possible to hold two differing agendas in highest esteem. One will inevitably become subordinate to the other.

In the Kingdom we have chosen, we necessarily rule out all conflicting claims on our lives. We can pursue money, but only for what it can do as Kingdom collateral in supporting our lives, furthering God's purposes, and blessing others. We can pursue status, but only for the influence it gives us as Kingdom ambassadors in this world. We can seek relationships, but only in the context of the King's character and integrity and for His purposes of reaching human beings with His love. In all, it's a pretty simple lifestyle. Having only one master tends to clarify a lot of things.

IN DEED

Money is a complicated master. So are status, pleasure, and fame. All of these are usually substitutes we use for finding our identity or getting people to affirm us. But choosing God as master makes life much less complicated—not easier, but more streamlined. We receive everything we need from Him; we give everything we have to Him. And we serve without the pressure of satisfying a difficult master.

ADDITIONAL READING: 1 Timothy 6:9-10

I will place no value on anything I have or may possess,
except in relation to the Kingdom of Christ.
DAVID LIVINGSTONE

A Dangerous Environment

Can all your worries add a single moment to your life? Matthew 6:27

IN WORD

In many ways, the Kingdom culture is countercultural—a revolution against the ways of the world. But it's also a revolution against the ways of our own inner nature, our fallenness and habits and misperceptions. One of the greatest misperceptions we have is that we have to look out for ourselves. That deep, almost imperceptible belief breeds worries and fears, multiplying them with each new threat we perceive, whether real or not. In fact, many of us lie awake at night wondering what can go wrong and planning for adversity we will never actually have to deal with. We live in an inner environment of danger and fear.

If that seems overstated, consider the things that make you anxious and ask yourself how many of them actually come true. Some do, to be sure, but most don't. We are masters at planning for contingencies, hoping to keep ourselves safe from every possible threat. But most of those threats are empty, and even if they weren't, we have to come to terms with one inarguable fact: The King we have chosen to serve has promised that He is looking out for our best interests. He is willing and able to deal with every threat that comes against us. When we worry, we are making a profound statement that we don't trust Him to do that. We know He lets people experience hardship, and we don't want that. So we reject the story line He has offered and embrace the story lines in our own minds. And those story lines are filled with all kinds of worries.

IN DEED

Rise up against that inner environment of fear. Overthrow it. Do whatever you can to expose its lies and undermine its power. It is not giving you a picture of truth but rather a picture of life outside the King's protection. It is filling you with images beyond the realm of the Kingdom. Instead, envision the King's promise. See it play out in your life. Step into it daily. Whatever story He is writing for your life—even if it is difficult—is very, very good.

ADDITIONAL READING: Philippians 4:6-7

> The beginning of anxiety is the end of faith, and the beginning of true faith is the end of anxiety.
> GEORGE MÜLLER

Comprehensive Mercy

The standard you use in judging is the standard by which you will be judged.
Matthew 7:2

IN WORD

We human beings have a nasty tendency to apply one standard of mercy to ourselves and a different standard to others. Most people think they judge themselves as harshly as others, but hardly anyone really does. We sin, but not like *that* person. We have flaws, but not nearly so damaging as *those* people. We gossip about how much we hate so-and-so's tendency to gossip, get really impatient with so-and-so's tendency to get impatient, and get really angry at arrogant people because their pride has somehow wounded our own pride. And the "tolerant" are remarkably intolerant toward some viewpoints that express intolerance. Yes, multiple standards abound in the human heart.

Jesus had a few things to say about that. One of His best-known statements—which in a variation of Matthew 7:1 from the King James Version is often rendered, "Judge not, lest ye be judged"—has become part of the vernacular of our contemporary culture. In fact, the phrase is often quoted with a very judgmental attitude by people who don't want to be judged themselves, which further demonstrates the hypocrisy of our inner thoughts. Of course, Jesus would never tell His disciples to drop all standards of right and wrong and have no discerning opinions about other people. But He apparently did rebuke His followers and everyone else for having double standards and being unmerciful toward others. His solution? Deal with your own issues, and be as merciful with others as you would be toward yourself. In other words, have some humility.

IN DEED

Kingdom people simply cannot be known as self-appointed judges. We can be discerning, and we can declare what God has said is right and wrong. But we can't do it with any attitude that is less than radically, profoundly merciful. The truth is that God has rescued us from disastrously futile lives, not because we deserved it but because He loves us. And He insists that His royal children be exactly like Him. If we want comprehensive mercy, we have to offer it to everyone else. The Kingdom's standard is always the nature of the King Himself.

ADDITIONAL READING: James 2:12-13

Mercy imitates God and disappoints Satan.
JOHN CHRYSOSTOM

Persist

Keep on asking, and you will receive what you ask for. Keep on seeking, and you will find. Keep on knocking, and the door will be opened to you.
Matthew 7:7

IN WORD

God is a welcoming God. He extends His invitation and spreads His mercy far and wide. Entrance into the Kingdom is never earned, always given. So why do Kingdom benefits come so slowly sometimes? Why do we rarely get immediate answers to prayer? Why do we have to wait to hear God's voice, receive His promises, and fulfill our calling?

Because (1) we don't live on uncontested territory, and (2) the Ancient of Days who has patiently worked out His purposes and endured eons of resistance wants His people to know the value of persistence. Kingdom citizens aren't "drive-thru window" kind of people. We understand the nature of the battle and are willing to endure to the end. The King is not cultivating impatient, entitled petitioners in His Kingdom. He's growing mature, patient people with an eternal mind-set. He has to; that's the kind of Kingdom He has created.

The world is full of people who have given the "Christianity thing" a shot and walked away after a little trouble or some unanswered questions. It's also full of people who still consider themselves Christians but have given up on ever experiencing its fullness. But the real Kingdom treasures are given to those who see far across the landscape and long into the future. He rewards those who have overcome.

IN DEED

Learn to overcome. No books or movies focus on people who hit a couple of minor speed bumps and kept going, or on those who encountered major setbacks and gave up. Good stories involve enormous obstacles, intimidating odds, and the will to endure in faith, and God is always writing a good story. Yours will require tenacity because His Kingdom is contested and often obscured. But those who endure will receive. Doors will open to the persistent. Prayers are answered for the tireless. And those who keep on going will get what He promised.

ADDITIONAL READING: Hebrews 6:11-15

> The ability to wait, and stay, and press belongs
> essentially to our intercourse with God.
> E. M. BOUNDS

Real Fruit

Just as you can identify a tree by its fruit, so you can identify people by their actions. Matthew 7:20

IN WORD

Orange trees produce oranges, and apple trees produce apples. It's a simple enough correlation, and we've experienced it often. But it isn't always so easy to discern. Jesus Himself remarked on how the inner condition of the religious leaders didn't match their outward appearance. They looked righteous but weren't. And the disciples? They looked inexperienced, unqualified, and incapable—but would bear the fruit of the Kingdom that changed an empire and the course of world history. So how exactly do we identify people by their actions?

Carefully. We have to be able to discern real qualities of the Kingdom rather than judging people outwardly. After all, fruit can be faked. Houses and offices around the world are well stocked with artificial plants. And churches are often stocked with artificial leaders—people who have the outward appearance of spiritual maturity but are only playing a role. Meanwhile, others appear to be fruitless but are really in a season of preparation. No tree bears fruit constantly, does it? Only spiritual discernment can distinguish between real and false fruit, and between latent seasons and dead ones. We have to know the ways of the Kingdom in order to determine its fruit.

IN DEED

Citizens of the Kingdom can't afford to be people of snap judgments. If we were, we might have marginalized Abraham, Jacob, Moses, Deborah, Gideon, Samson, Ruth, David, most of the prophets, all the disciples, and plenty of other people who didn't seem to be good trees on the surface. And we would have embraced people like Esau, Saul, and the impressive prophets, kings, and scribes who led Israel astray. We can discern fruit only over time, at deep levels, and by God's standards. In other words, we can see people's actions in light of the Spirit working within them. Only He can bring forth the Kingdom in His people. And only He creates real change that lasts.

ADDITIONAL READING: 1 John 4:1-6

If you judge people, you have no time to love them.
MOTHER TERESA

The Works of Heaven

[Jesus said,] "Not everyone who calls out to me, 'Lord! Lord!' will enter the Kingdom of Heaven. Only those who actually do the will of my Father in heaven will enter." Matthew 7:21

IN WORD

We know we can't earn salvation by our works. That would be receiving the Kingdom through self-righteousness and not as a gift of grace, which isn't possible. Even so, Jesus makes it clear that being a Kingdom citizen necessarily involves doing something. Calling Him "Lord" isn't enough, even though Paul and John later say that whoever professes that Jesus is Lord and that He is the Son of God is giving evidence of salvation (Romans 10:9; 1 John 4:15). Prophesying in His name and doing miracles in His power are not evidence of salvation either, even though such things can be done only in His strength. Only those who do the will of the Father can enter the Kingdom of Heaven.

Does this mean obedience earns the Kingdom for us? Of course not. It does, however, mean that those who are truly in a relationship with God through the work of Jesus and the presence of the Spirit will hear His voice and follow Him. We will have hearts inclined toward Him. It isn't the works that save; a heart rightly motivated to do the works is one that has been truly transformed by grace and the power of the Spirit. In other words, someone can say "Lord" without a changed heart. But no one can live as though the Lord is everything without one. That is the evidence that salvation is genuine.

IN DEED

Do the will of the Father, the works of heaven, but not out of obligation or even to prove that you belong to Him. Do them because the love in your heart for Him motivates you to seek the Kingdom above all else and see it coming to whatever degree possible in your generation. The point isn't to call Him Lord; it's to see Him reign—inside of you, outside of you, everywhere. It's great to pray, "Your Kingdom come." It's even better to be part of the answer.

ADDITIONAL READING: Matthew 12:50

> Love for God and obedience to God are so completely involved
> in each other that any one of them implies the other too.
> F. F. BRUCE

The Kingdom Constitution

[Jesus said,] "Anyone who listens to my teaching and follows it is wise, like a person who builds a house on solid rock." Matthew 7:24

IN WORD

We live in the most idea-prolific generation in human history. A multitude of thought streams, all with innumerable variations, surround us daily. The ease and reach of communication today would have been almost unthinkable just a generation ago, and there are more voices on the planet today than ever before. Communicators build "tribes" of listeners and readers who follow their words. And all of it is constantly shifting.

Well, almost all of it. The core message of Jesus stands forever. It's the constitution of our Kingdom. Even that message may confuse us, as it has exploded into countless iterations and interpretations. Christianity has divided into more than thirty thousand denominations, and Christian communicators are extraordinarily diverse in expressing the essence of our faith. A dizzying array of opinions—all claiming to be Christian truth—keeps us ever tweaking what we really believe. But at the foundation are the teachings of Jesus and His first followers. In our desperate attempt to grab hold of a message that isn't moving, that's the one that matters most.

Discussing ideas is healthy, of course. We could spend eons probing the depths of the gospel. But we need to make sure the core truth of the gospel remains the core truth for us. We need to build our lives on what really matters in the only Kingdom that will last.

IN DEED

It's natural, even necessary, for Christians to keep seeking good interpretations of what Jesus said. And it's also natural and necessary for His words to be applied in different ways across different cultures and eras. But there's a difference between diverse application of the message and diverse reinventions of it. And we have to know the difference. When in doubt, read Jesus' own words in conversation with Him. Ask Him to speak clearly through His Spirit, without whom you can't understand the truth. As much as possible, seek His true meaning without bringing long-held assumptions (yours or anyone else's) into the conversation. Anchor yourself on the rock that lasts forever.

ADDITIONAL READING: Isaiah 40:8

> There is no discovery of the truth of Christ's teaching
> . . . without committing oneself to His way of life.
> J. B. PHILLIPS

Where God Lives

The LORD says: "I am returning to Mount Zion, and I will live in Jerusalem."
Zechariah 8:3

IN WORD

The most glorious predictions of the prophets are for a future time. The world hasn't seen their fulfillment yet. They are sweeping and majestic, so much so that many people take them to be exaggerated symbolism. But they are not. God is building His Kingdom, and it won't be small or incomplete. It will be worthy of His majesty and glory. It will be even better than the prophets describe.

Zechariah prophesied during a time of rebuilding, when captives had returned to Jerusalem and begun the work of restoration. In case the laborers forgot the magnitude of their sacred task and began to see it as simply a building project, Zechariah's prophecy gave them a powerful motivation: God Himself was returning to Zion. The restoration of Jerusalem was not a manual labor nightmare. It was a privilege of the highest order.

There's a parallel for those of us who have been grafted into God's Kingdom. The things we do in His name, even the most mundane of tasks, are eternally significant. To the extent that we are given over to His purposes, we are laborers in a sacred endeavor. And our task is focused on something far greater than a temple of stone in which our Lord will dwell. We're craftsmen of a temple of flesh in which each one of us is a building block—and in which the King of Glory lives. There is no higher service in the universe.

IN DEED

You may have gotten up this morning dreading the work you have to do, or perhaps being completely bored with the prospects of your day. If so, consider the magnitude of your position. You are a key element in the eternal Kingdom, and your labor is never mundane. Whatever you have to do today, you can do it in the Spirit of Jesus, with grace and reverence, knowing that God uses even small stones to build His Kingdom. Your potential today is huge—and it's absolutely sacred.

ADDITIONAL READING: Ephesians 2:21-22

> There is nothing so secular that it cannot be sacred, and that is one of the deepest messages of the Incarnation.
> MADELEINE L'ENGLE

How God Feels

This is what the LORD Almighty says: "I am very jealous for Zion; I am burning with jealousy for her." Zechariah 8:2, *NIV*

IN WORD

Many people believe God to be calm, objective, unemotional, and completely dignified. It's an idea that comes from humanity's highly cultivated religious imagination. It's a noble spiritual thought that comes from our understanding that God has foreknowledge and is never surprised, and that He is omnipotent and able to accomplish whatever He wants. Theoretically, He has no reason to get excited about much. And He has no inclination to feel emotional pain.

That very religious perception, however, is completely wrong. It isn't the way God portrays Himself in Scripture. No, when God paints His self-portrait in the words of the prophets, He's deeply passionate—a Husband wounded by His bride's adultery, a Father grieving over His prodigal children, a Potter frustrated with the clay He is shaping. And it isn't all negative: God rejoices and sings with delight over His beloved. There's nothing bland about Him. He experiences the highest highs and the deepest lows.

That may be hard to express theologically—theology always has a hard time with the emotions of God—but it's a thoroughly biblical picture. God is burning with jealousy over His people. He zealously accomplishes His purposes. The intensity of His feelings would be overwhelming to us if we experienced them. We would short-circuit if we got a real glimpse of them. Our infinite God has infinite emotions, and He often has them in regard to us.

IN DEED

Spend some time thinking about that today. God's love isn't just sentimental pleasantry; it's an intense burning of passion that is never quenched and refuses to be thwarted. His delight over His children is more than an encouraging word for the day; it's an ecstatic celebration in heavenly places. And His grief over our sin?— Just a taste of it would be enough to destroy us. The point is that God feels deeply. When we realize the depth of His feeling for us, it's enough to change our lives forever.

ADDITIONAL READING: Ephesians 3:16-19

> Human love is capable of great things. What then must
> be the depth and height and intensity of divine love?
> LORD SHAFTESBURY

When God Appears

In those days ten men from different nations and languages of the world will clutch at the sleeve of one Jew. And they will say, "Please let us walk with you, for we have heard that God is with you." Zechariah 8:23

IN WORD

The Bible makes it clear that God does not show favoritism (Acts 10:34). He is "no respecter of persons" (KJV). Peter spoke those words when God called him to go to the house of Cornelius, a Gentile who, according to traditional Jewish opinion, was outside of the Kingdom of God. But God's message to Peter was that the doors of the Kingdom were wide open to anyone who would believe and who would seek God on His terms. The blessings of God are global, not national.

God's impartiality notwithstanding, He has demonstrated throughout Scripture that He is a God who chooses to reveal Himself in context. He chose an individual (Abraham) and then a people (Abraham's descendants through grandson Jacob). Then He birthed the Messiah through that nation. The Messiah is the one who blew the doors of the Kingdom open. He's the one who offers life to anyone and everyone who will receive it. Selectivity expands to inclusiveness during the course of salvation history. The seed of Abraham grew into a tree of life, and the fruit is there for all.

So what does Zechariah mean when he prophesies a day when the world will seek the God of the Jews? He means that we cannot enter His Kingdom without knowing a very Jewish Messiah who came in the context of one nation's revelation of law, worship, and religious culture. It's impossible to know God without knowing how God revealed Himself in Judaism and its Messiah. When He appears again, it will be clear: Everything in Hebrew history points to Him.

IN DEED

We who believe in Jesus have been grafted into this vehicle of revelation, this religious/ethnic culture that became the soil for our Messiah. Like Israel, we are priests to our world. As Israel was ordained to do, know how to point to Him. As one chosen by God, offer His blessings to everyone.

ADDITIONAL READING: Ephesians 2:11-18

God did entrust the descendants of Abraham
with the first revelation of Himself.
C. S. LEWIS

For Those Who Love Him

Hasn't God chosen the poor in this world to be rich in faith? Aren't they the ones who will inherit the Kingdom he promised to those who love him?
James 2:5

IN WORD

When several truths are packed into one biblical statement, which is almost always the case, at least one of them is likely to be overlooked. That's certainly true of James 2:5, which seems to focus on the poor and their attraction to the Kingdom message. But James adds a phrase that reminds us of the true nature of this Kingdom. It isn't just about the poor or those who believe or our inheritance. Which Kingdom is he talking about? *The one God promised to those who love Him.*

So this isn't just a Kingdom for the poor—clearly, since the New Testament refers often to believers who have wealth. Neither is this a Kingdom that requires only faith and no other attitudes or affections to go with it. No, this is a Kingdom for those who love—specifically those whose hearts are intimately connected with the King Himself. It isn't enough for this King to surround Himself with beings who obey His Word or believe in Him without also loving Him. His desire is for people to respond to Him from the heart.

Kingdom citizens often don't understand that. We turn the gospel into an impossible standard of obedience or a mental agreement with its truths. We forget that God created us for love, sent His Son to die for us in love, and describes Himself as love incarnate. In other words, we forget to live with passion, letting our hearts be shaped by our love more than by our disciplines. And we miss the heart of the gospel.

IN DEED

Get it back. Whatever it takes, embrace passion for God as the driving force of your life. If you love Him well, you will follow Him naturally and instinctively. You will pour your life out for Him because it seems like the only reasonable response. And like everyone else who loves Him deeply, you will inherit the Kingdom, just as He promised.

ADDITIONAL READING: Matthew 22:36-38

We are shaped and fashioned by what we love.
JOHANN WOLFGANG VON GOETHE

Wholeness

I will give them an undivided heart and put a new spirit in them.
Ezekiel 11:19, *NIV*

IN WORD

Ezekiel's prophecies are harsh, stern indictments against Judah and her sins. But sandwiched between the many rebukes are several passages of marvelous hope. This is one of them, and its message is repeated later in chapter 36. It's a promise not just to bring God's people back into the land He had promised them long ago; it's a promise to correct the fundamental problem that led them into judgment to begin with. He promises to fix their hearts.

That's an amazing promise if you think about it. Many propose for our world political, economic, military, social, and religious remedies. We've heard that the answer is education or adequate health care or pursuing world peace. But God promises something more fundamental, more at the heart of the problems of the human race. He promises to change what's in our core. It's the only plausible solution for a world that has tried all of the above answers and failed. You won't get perfect solutions from flawed people. God foretells a day when He will address the fundamental flaw.

And what is that flaw? We have divided hearts and dead spirits. That happened at the Fall in Eden, when for some reason we decided to believe the serpent's suggestion that God must be holding out on us. It was a lie of epic proportions, and the consequences have been devastating. East of Eden, where God seemed so much more invisible and distant than before, we learned to depend on ourselves. It was the only way we could cope, we thought. But in so doing, we developed other allegiances—attachments to what we thought would fulfill us, give us power, or save us. We became idolaters.

IN DEED

God has a solution. He foretold it in Ezekiel and elsewhere, and He fulfilled it in His Son. The radical truth of the Kingdom is that the human heart really can, contrary to popular opinion, change from the inside out. It can be reborn, reconstructed, rewired for the Spirit of God Himself. It can be made whole.

ADDITIONAL READING: 2 Corinthians 5:17

It is impossible for us to be the children of God
naturally . . . we must be born again.
OSWALD CHAMBERS

Kingdom Birth

Jesus replied, "I tell you the truth, unless you are born again, you cannot see the Kingdom of God." John 3:3

IN WORD

If the Kingdom of God was simply a better government or a societal shift, anyone could enter it. All they would need is the right perspective or an adjusted lifestyle. And while the Kingdom of God certainly includes good government and other social systems—at least the part of the Kingdom that manifests through God's people on earth does—it's much more than that. It's a quality of life that can't be experienced by sin-saturated humanity. It requires more than a natural mind-set and human ingenuity. It requires a radically transformed heart and eyes that see eternal spiritual realities.

No one can have that kind of heart or see with that kind of eyes unless he or she is born of God's Spirit. In order to think like Him, see like Him, and live like Him, we have to have His Spirit living and moving within us. We must function as citizens of another realm even while we are living in this one. We can't do that by changing ourselves. We have to be born again with a new nature.

Many old-nature observers don't see a different nature in Christians than they find in themselves. That's unfortunate, but it doesn't mean that new nature doesn't exist. It simply means many Christians haven't fed the new nature very well, that we are drawing our strength and energy from our own reserves rather than from the Spirit of God. Life in the Kingdom comes from beyond ourselves.

IN DEED

Never assume the Kingdom of God is simply "heaven" or a there-and-then reality rather than a here-and-now experience. On the other hand, never treat it only as an alternate approach to life on earth that can be fully realized with better human institutions. We can't solve humanity's problems by imposing God's laws or morality on everyone else. We can, however, fill this world with heaven's resources according to the power that works within us (Ephesians 3:20). And that power works within us only when we've been birthed by the source of power Himself.

ADDITIONAL READING: Ephesians 3:20-21

> I remember this, that everything looked new to me . . . the fields, the cattle, the trees. I was like a new man in a new world.
> BILLY BRAY

Blown by the Wind

The wind blows wherever it pleases. You hear its sound, but you cannot tell where it comes from or where it is going. So it is with everyone born of the Spirit. John 3:8 NIV

IN WORD

Things blown by the wind—leaves, tumbleweeds, plastic bags—move in a general direction but take unexpected twists and turns. We don't really analyze their movements; we just recognize that the wind is behind them. That's how Kingdom citizens are meant to appear to the rest of the world. Why? Because we're in tune with God's voice. The Spirit speaks. And He directs us in ways that don't make sense to natural eyes.

That means we might give away resources while others are hoarding them. We might buy when others are selling or sell when others are buying. We might move to dangerous places rather than take refuge in safe places because our sense of mission demands it. We may befriend people who don't enhance our standing, live beneath our means rather than above them, or reason in ways that don't make sense from a human-centered point of view. We are blown by a source of wisdom, power, and love that sees everything from an eternal perspective. We are designed to move contrary to natural logic but perfectly in sync with the Spirit within us.

That's the Kingdom lifestyle. It looks odd to others, and that's okay. Nowhere in Scripture are we told to blend in to our surroundings and look "normal." No, if we're fueled by a supernatural Spirit, we will live a supernatural lifestyle.

IN DEED

Living naturally may seem easier than living supernaturally, but it's far less rewarding. Choose to be blown by the breath of God, not guided by your own wisdom or fueled by your own strength. All the resources of another realm are available to you if you ask and tune in to what God is doing in your life. You are not bound by every human limitation; you are given resources to transcend many of them. Ask for God's wisdom, His strength, His open doors, and receive everything He offers.

ADDITIONAL READING: John 16:12-15

> The Spirit-filled life is no mystery revealed to a select few. . . .
> To trust and obey is the substance of the whole matter.
> V. RAYMOND EDMAN

Seeds of Glory

It is sown a natural body, it is raised a spiritual body. 1 Corinthians 15:44, NIV

IN WORD

An acorn embedded in the ground somehow becomes a mighty oak tree. An apple seed somehow produces a plenitude of apples. A sperm and an egg eventually result in a mature human being. Why? Because God has written a profound principle into His creation. Small elements with genetic coding can, with the right nurture and conditions, develop into something altogether greater and more meaningful.

That's how it is with our natural bodies. In their fallen state, they are like seeds that fall on concrete and never become more than seeds. But filled with the DNA of God Himself—the divine nature He has shared with those who believe in and love Him—our flesh-and-blood bodies become something altogether different. Like seeds in the ground, we are raised up as flourishing spiritual beings with a glory we can hardly comprehend.

Think of the opportunities this spiritual dynamic points to. We can sow material wealth into God's Kingdom and leverage it for eternal fruit. We can redeem fleeting time by investing it in everlasting pursuits. We can use our human, physical existence as a foreshadowing of an eternal Kingdom. The material becomes spiritual when we see the end of the story.

IN DEED

Learn to see your life as an investment. Refuse the common temptation to divide life into sacred and secular or material and spiritual. God is not so limited in His vision that He would create entire segments of His world to be meaningless. No, it's all purposeful, all good, and all redeemable for greater purposes and lasting legacies. When we live as His children, everything we touch has the potential to be meaningful in His Kingdom. If you're a Kingdom citizen, nothing in your life is truly mundane. Even your body itself—that passing vessel of clay—was given life by the breath of God and will spring up into a glorious resurrection. Let that picture fill your mind and heart with hope, anticipation, and joy. Invest everything in the now and forever Kingdom.

ADDITIONAL READING: Matthew 13:43

The only way to get our values right is to see . . . not in the light of time but in the light of eternity.
WILLIAM BARCLAY

The Imperishable Life

*I declare to you, brothers and sisters, that flesh and blood cannot inherit
the Kingdom of God, nor does the perishable inherit the imperishable.*
1 Corinthians 15:50, *NIV*

IN WORD

Flesh and blood lives in God's Kingdom. That's indisputable in light of the New
Testament's references to the Kingdom in present tense and Jesus' instruction to pray
that the Kingdom would come on a very material earth. But flesh and blood—natural,
fallen humanity without the Spirit of God dwelling within—can never inherit the
Kingdom. We may observe the Kingdom, and we may even live among it and enjoy
its benefits. But we can't inherit it as the family estate unless we're actually part of the
family. And we can't be part of the family unless we are spiritually raised to new life.

That's why God's restoration project ends with new heavens, a new earth, and
people with new, resurrected bodies. The perishable cannot inherit the imperishable.
Just as we can't put new wine in old wineskins without bursting them, separate new
paint colors that have been mixed from old ones, or put popcorn back in the kernel, we
can't entrust the eternal Kingdom to perishable, unredeemed flesh. We can't integrate
the Kingdom into existing governments (though the Kingdom can have an impact);
we can't live out heavenly visions with human wisdom; and we can't fill our relationships with divine love if we don't have it flowing within us. The Kingdom comes from
the throne room of God. The substance of this world cannot fully contain it.

IN DEED

Seek to live beyond your means—not financially, but spiritually. If you're like those
around you, your dreams are too small, your plans are too limited, and your desires
and resources are too fleeting. The Kingdom is bigger than you, and that's good. Your
flesh-and-blood humanness is not enough to receive it or express it. Only the divine
nature within you can do that. That's the nature you must live from to see the Kingdom
realized in your life now and forever. Bring your future into your present. Cling to
things that last.

ADDITIONAL READING: Matthew 9:16-17

> I thank you, Lord, that you have so set eternity within my
> heart that no earthly thing can ever satisfy me wholly.
> JOHN BAILLIE

Always Worthwhile

So, my dear brothers and sisters, be strong and immovable. Always work enthusiastically for the Lord, for you know that nothing you do for the Lord is ever useless. 1 Corinthians 15:58

IN WORD

High in the Andes Mountains, a plant known as the *puya raimondii*—or the Queen of the Andes—grows to more than 30 feet and can live well over 100 years. But the plant flowers only once, and even then only at the end of its life. At some point between 80 to 150 years of age in the wild, its massive spikes flower into a glorious display, and then the plant dies. In other words, it takes a really long time for anyone to see its stunning beauty.

Some investments are like that. They show little or no growth for years, only to offer unexpected returns at an opportune time. That isn't always the case in the Kingdom of God; sometimes our investments of time, talent, and resources bear visible fruit quickly. But often they don't. As with slow-flowering plants or slow-growth investments, only patient endurance allows us to see the end and reap the reward.

Because this is a common dynamic in the Kingdom, we need to be extremely patient and persistent in our eternal investments. Our prayers may not show many results for a while, but they are still accomplishing much. Our work may not seem productive at the moment, but it will nevertheless produce much. Our attitudes may not seem to rub off on those around us, but they eventually will. Our love may not appear to make a difference, but as an expression of God's heart, it certainly will. In itself, time is not a significant variable in determining the value of a Kingdom investment.

IN DEED

Kingdom citizens must be tenacious. We must be willing to hang on to a promise for decades, pray over a problem with persistence, and keep sowing seeds of God's purposes and resources whether we see results or not, knowing they will eventually bear fruit. After all, they are His seeds, and He is the source of life. How could they not? Everything He touches will eventually flourish, including us.

ADDITIONAL READING: Galatians 6:7-10

There must be a beginning of any great matter, but the continuing to the end until it be thoroughly finished yields the true glory.
FRANCIS DRAKE

Wherever

Wherever you set foot, you will be on land I have given you. Joshua 1:3

IN WORD

When God gives a promise, He gives us everything we need to have it fulfilled in our lives. He rarely fulfills it unilaterally; there's usually something for us to do, even if that's only a simple response of faith. In the case of Israel's entry into the Promised Land, God designated a territory and told them to take it. "Wherever you set foot," He explained to Joshua, "you will be on land I have given you." He would give it; they would have to walk in it. That was the deal.

That's a great picture of our Kingdom. In fact, much of the book of Joshua is a field manual in how to take territory for God's Kingdom according to His promises. He sets the adventure in front of us, and then we respond in faith by actually going into it. There are conditions and parameters—Joshua will receive instructions about how to conquer and whom to avoid. And though every bit of it probably felt like work to Israel, it was really God's doing. Just like we live our lives in Him.

Many people don't understand that. They believe that God's grace implies that we do absolutely nothing but sit down and wait for God to accomplish His purposes through us. We receive salvation by grace through faith, and then assume the rest of life is entirely independent of our actions. It isn't. God is calling us into works that He has prepared for us. He has promised territory that is there for the taking. He is waiting for us to enter an arena of fruitfulness that we can't enter simply by waiting for Him to act. We step in; He gives. That's how it works.

IN DEED

Never let faith be an excuse for inactivity. Joshua and the nation of Israel actually had to walk fearlessly, follow God's strategies, and fight battles in order to receive what He had promised to freely give. We do too. That doesn't mean we receive salvation by works. It means we experience His Kingdom by participating in it. He has promised to reward every step of faith.

ADDITIONAL READING: Ephesians 2:8-10

> I sometimes think that the whole secret of the Christian
> life is to know how to use the word "therefore."
> MARTYN LLOYD-JONES

Focused

Meditate on it day and night so you will be sure to obey everything written in it. Only then will you prosper and succeed in all you do. Joshua 1:8

IN WORD

"Only then." Sure, there are plenty of ways to prosper in this or that area of life, but God's instruction to Joshua is more comprehensive than that. Prosperity as He defines it goes deeper and lasts longer, applying to everything His people do. So what is the condition for this great guarantee of certain prosperity? How was Joshua—and how are we—supposed to receive successes from the God of victory? Step one: Be strong and courageous. Step two: Meditate on His Word day and night for the purpose of implementing it in life. That's it. An attitude and an action. That's how real success comes.

We are designed to live in a Kingdom of victories. We know life isn't that simple; we've all experienced failure, and we've all known of instances when the right approach didn't yield the right results. God is not a formula, after all, and we can't treat Him like one. But we can position ourselves to receive whatever He has promised us. We may not prosper every way we expect to if we are faithful to His Word, but we certainly won't prosper meaningfully without it. We have to be people whose lives are consumed with hearing and following His voice.

That's a key approach into any promised land, a foundational truth for experiencing the best of God's Kingdom. We can't afford to waste time trying to love God without also loving His Word. The relationship doesn't work that way. If we love Him, His words will matter to us. If they don't, we're deceiving ourselves.

IN DEED

There's a difference between meditating on God's words a few minutes each day and being so consumed with them that we apply them to every area of life. One helps to keep us aware of Him. The other keeps us anchored in Him and moving in His will. The all-of-life approach to His voice rivets our attention on what He is doing and captivates us with His purposes. And it comes with a life-changing promise.

ADDITIONAL READING: John 14:15-21

The Word of God is the food of the soul.
GREGORY I

Bold

Be strong and courageous! Do not be afraid or discouraged. For the LORD your God is with you wherever you go. Joshua 1:9

IN WORD

There must be a reason God repeats this instruction to Joshua three times in the space of four verses and surrounds it with assurance after assurance. Joshua must be afraid or tentative or reluctant. But God insists that this is not a time for fear. His promises are not to be entered into tentatively.

Most of us would claim not to understand God's promises as clearly as Joshua did. After all, God had spoken quite clearly over the course of a generation. Joshua even understood the promise forty years earlier, when he and Caleb reported about the land with hope. And now that the people were about to enter, God had clearly not changed His mind. These were remarkably precise directions. Obviously Joshua was to step forward in strength and courage.

We are too. As reluctant as we can be to claim we've heard God's voice, He has nevertheless clearly spoken about some things. He has sent us into the world with a strong message and the power to reflect His nature. He has given us promises about prayer and strength and courage. He has assured us that love, joy, and peace are possible in this age. He has invited us to exercise the authority of the Kingdom with the wisdom of the King, available simply by asking. He has pledged that we will overcome obstacles with faith and evil with good. In other words, He has laid out in front of us vast territories that we have not yet taken.

IN DEED

That's the mission of the Kingdom—to possess territories that are not currently under God's reign. We don't do that with the same attitudes and strategies familiar to other Kingdoms; this is not a hostile takeover. No, it's an uprising that wins the world with the goodness of God, which He has promised to display to all who receive Him. The battle may be different from Joshua's, but the certainty of victory is not. We have nothing to be afraid of. We can live with unbounded trust that He is with us wherever we go.

ADDITIONAL READING: Psalm 18:30-36

To know the will of God, we need an open Bible and an open map.
WILLIAM CAREY

Prepared

*Purify yourselves, for tomorrow the L*ORD *will do great wonders among you.*
Joshua 3:5

IN WORD

The people were about to cross the Jordan River, led by priests carrying the Ark of God. God had been in their midst before—the stories from the Exodus generation make that clear. Entry into the land would be one of those occasions when His presence was especially needed. But they needed to purify themselves for the encounter.

That was before the crossing, and the process would continue at the camp on the other side. Before the approach to Jericho, God instructed this generation of men to be circumcised as the previous generation had been (Joshua 5:2ff). He was setting them apart for His purposes, identifying them as a distinct group of people to be devoted exclusively to Him. They were about to enter a season of wonders.

Is purity necessary for victory? On the one hand, anything we receive from Him comes by grace through faith and not of our own doing. On the other hand, God is taking territory for His Kingdom, and He wants to fill it with those who will reflect Him well and who will not squander the victory selfishly. He doesn't want His people to win territory and then turn it back over to the enemy through their own disobedience. So no, purity is not necessary to qualify for victory. But yes, purity is necessary to handle it. We are, after all, living with a God of wonders in our midst.

IN DEED

The message of grace is a beautiful and encouraging truth, but we can never let it become an excuse not to conform to the image of our God. And we can never expect grace to win our battles without our cooperation. Grace gives us not only the position of being accepted but also the power to be transformed. Only those who understand that will be able to experience Kingdom wonders consistently. God puts in places of victory those people who can handle it. And only those who are fully committed to Him—not perfect, but wholehearted—are ready.

ADDITIONAL READING: 1 Peter 1:13-16

> Are we prepared for what sanctification will do? It will cost an intense narrowing of all our interests on earth and an immense broadening of our interest in God.
> OSWALD CHAMBERS

Divine Initiative

Joshua went up to him and demanded, "Are you friend or foe?" "Neither one," he replied. "I am the commander of the Lord's army." Joshua 5:13-14

IN WORD

On the eve of the conquest of Jericho, Joshua encountered a divine being. Whether an angel, the preincarnate Messiah, or the Father Himself—these things are fuzzy in our perceptions of Hebrew Scripture—this was clearly a message from God. Joshua wanted to know whether this mysterious figure was friend or foe. "Neither," came the reply. This was not a battle between human armies in search of divine favor. It was a divine battle in which human armies would take sides.

That's really the perspective of the Kingdom. It's okay to talk about God being on our side. Scripture certainly does (Psalm 56:9; 118:6; Romans 8:31; Hebrews 13:6). But in truth, He is not fighting our battles simply because we asked Him to. He fights our battles because they are actually His battles. He hasn't chosen sides; we have. We entered into His Kingdom, and the Kingdom agenda is now ours. He is not our mascot; He's our commander. There's a difference.

It's important to know that because many people have followed their own purposes while assuming God was going to help them. In His mercy, He often supports us anyway. But sometimes we have failed because we haven't sought His direction first. We expected Him to be on our side while He was waiting for us to be on His.

IN DEED

Come to God regularly to ask Him what's on His heart. Seek His agenda in this world and step into His purposes. Rather than making plans and asking Him to support you, find the plans He has already made and choose to support them. Look for territory He has promised rather than designating the territory you want to take. Battles go much better when He leads. We find Him fully on our side when we have already chosen to be on His.

ADDITIONAL READING: 2 Chronicles 20:15-17

Thy way, not mine, O Lord, however dark it be. Lead me
by Thine own hand, choose out the path for me.
HORATIUS BONAR

Listen, Follow, Believe

Shout! For the LORD has given you the town! Joshua 6:16

IN WORD

Our desire is to see heaven on earth. That's the Kingdom hope. We haven't abandoned this world to the enemy; we fully expect Jesus to come again, and in the meantime to answer our prayers for God's will to be done on earth as it is in heaven. So when we read about God's strategies for Israel to take possession of the Promised Land, we have to wonder what the implications are for the territory He has promised us. If He has told us to pray His Kingdom into this world and live as Kingdom citizens, and if His nature hasn't changed over the centuries, how do we realize His victories?

If God had a uniform methodology, the answer would be simple. We would keep repeating the first strategy in the Promised Land. We would march around cities, literally or figuratively, and then shout loudly in faith, waiting for walls to fall. Then we would go in and plunder the enemy, taking back territory that rightfully belongs to God. There are deep lessons in that approach, including the necessity of listening to God, opening our minds to absurd strategies, following Him in faith, and letting Him do the heavy lifting in this endeavor. Those are always good plans.

But God's strategy is more diverse than the one employed at Jericho. Nowhere else in the Promised Land did He instruct His people to march around a city, blast trumpets, and wait for walls to fall. There were times when they used vast numbers for an obvious attack and others when they approached in stealth. There were times when they waited and times when they pursued. The keys were listening and following and believing. Other than that, Kingdom strategy is wildly diverse.

IN DEED

Remember the basics in taking territory in this world. Invite God in and look to Him to establish His Kingdom. Listen, follow, believe. Boldly go where He says to go, and patiently wait when He says to wait. Expect breakthroughs. He has sent us on a mission of reconciliation and restoration, and He has promised to give great victories.

ADDITIONAL READING: Deuteronomy 31:8

Rest assured: Do what God tells you to do now, and,
depend upon it, you will be shown what to do next.
ELISABETH ELLIOT

Comprehensive

[The Lord said,] "I will not remain with you any longer unless you destroy the things among you that were set apart for destruction." Joshua 7:12

IN WORD

God had promised to remain with Joshua and the people of Israel—to personally go ahead of them, without fail (Deuteronomy 31:6, 8). And in a universe in which He is omnipresent, how could He not? He is everywhere at all times, and particularly present for His people. But God's promise was shaded with an ominous "unless" when His people suffered an unexpected defeat. One man had taken what was forbidden at Jericho, and God threatened to withdraw His presence from the whole nation. The forbidden had to be purged.

We rarely approach our relationship with God that way. We know He loves us and will never withdraw His love. We depend on His grace and trust that our status with Him doesn't depend on our works. We have been born of His Spirit and don't expect His Spirit to leave. So a little impurity, a little indiscretion here and there, a few tolerated flaws . . . why go overboard in purging them? What do we have to lose?

However we understand our salvation and our growth in God's Spirit, we can't read of Achan's sin without realizing how zealous God is for our hearts. He isn't content with a little sin in one part of the camp or in our lives; He is intent on bringing us into His fullness. He knows that our best, most rewarding experience with Him will be a comprehensive one. Anything less is disappointing.

IN DEED

We get to experience the Kingdom by grace through faith. God has dealt with the judgment of our sins. But our fellowship with Him grows deeper and stronger the more we grow to be like Him. We experience the Kingdom more fully when we let the Kingdom sink more fully into us. If His presence is the key to our battles, we need to be zealous about His presence—and about cultivating everything He loves and ridding ourselves of everything He doesn't.

ADDITIONAL READING: Hebrews 12:1

No sin is small. No grain of sand is small in the mechanism of a watch.
JEREMY TAYLOR

Ask and Listen

They did not consult the LORD. Joshua 9:14

IN WORD

No one had yet defeated the Israelites in direct confrontation except the men of Ai, and that result was soon overturned when Israel purged itself of forbidden plunder. So the Gibeonites came at them with deception, playing the part of distant travelers and finagling a binding treaty out of their rivals. It's a common strategy for the enemies of God's people; if frontal assault doesn't work, undermine them with deception, corruption, and compromise. And it certainly worked in this case, as Joshua and Israel's leaders fell for the ploy and yoked themselves to the inhabitants of the land. They were stuck with a burden for years to come.

What was their mistake? They did not consult the Lord. They relied on their understanding, their concept of "best practices" for entering a land of promise. They assumed that they could apply uniform principles to the diverse situations they would encounter in the land. Though they had heard from God uniquely about Jericho, and then uniquely about Ai, they now neglected to ask Him about the travelers and the treaty. They assumed.

That's why life with God is not a matter of principle. There may be principles involved, but as soon as we begin to rely on them, we have stopped following Him and replaced His leading with ideas and practices. Instead of a personal relationship, we have an impersonal set of behaviors. That might make us very religious people, but it won't suffice in our interaction with Him or the diverse circumstances of our lives.

IN DEED

We need specific guidance from God in every situation. Sure, there are times when we can count on wisdom He has already given, but we can't learn precepts and call that a relationship. The strategy He gave us yesterday may not apply today because the battles of life keep changing. We have to learn how to hear His voice and follow His lead. The Kingdom is given to those who listen carefully to the King.

ADDITIONAL READING: Isaiah 30:21

When we fail to wait prayerfully for God's guidance and strength, we are saying . . . that we do not need Him.
CHARLES HUMMEL

Whatever It Takes

The sun stood still and the moon stayed in place until the nation of Israel had defeated its enemies. Joshua 10:13

IN WORD

The ill-advised treaty with Gibeon soon pressed Israel into an unexpected battle. In fear, a neighboring king attacked Gibeon, and as new allies, Joshua and his forces had to step in. But as is often the case with God and His people, the setback turned into an opportunity to advance. With the force of a catapult, what had previously pulled Israel back from its destiny then launched them further into it. God rose to their aid, defeated an enemy, and further established their position in the land.

God could have said, "You made a treaty without asking me, and now you'll need to suffer the consequences." Or He could have said, "I'll help you scratch your way out of trouble if I must." But He came through at an astonishing level of intervention, answering the bold, public prayer of Joshua that the sun would shine until the enemy had been defeated. He showed Himself willing to move heaven and earth—or hold them still—in order to defend His people.

We long for such answers to prayer. Sometimes God answers quickly and dramatically, but we may have more experience with delays and subtleties. Even so, we know what He can do, and therefore we trust Him with whatever He decides to do. There are no limits to His power; therefore, all other answers are driven by His wisdom and love. When the time and situation are right, He steps in with everything we need and does whatever it takes to give us victories.

IN DEED

Knowing who God is and what He is capable of doing, we can fight Kingdom battles and go on Kingdom adventures in full confidence that He is available in times of need. Even when we have made missteps, as Joshua did with the Gibeonite treaty, we can trust that He has not left us. As long as we are not in willful rebellion against Him, He fights on our behalf. Our progress in His Kingdom is backed by the King Himself.

ADDITIONAL READING: Psalm 18:6-17

What is impossible to God? Not that which is difficult to His power, but that which is contrary to His nature.
AMBROSE OF MILAN

Why Wait?

How long are you going to wait before taking possession of the remaining land the LORD, the God of your ancestors, has given to you? Joshua 18:3

IN WORD

The land was under Israel's control, and some of the tribes had begun settling their territories. But some had not, and they seemed to be waiting on Joshua for the next move. But Joshua's words put the onus back on them. "How long are you going to wait?" It wasn't up to him or the army to take the land for them. The land lay open before them, and their mission was to go and fill it.

Virtually every believer is familiar with being ready to move forward before God is—and having to wait for His timing. But fewer realize the many occasions when He is ready and we are waiting. We ask Him to open doors, and then we stare at them—rather than trying the knob—wondering why He doesn't do something. He looks at the same doors and wonders why we don't approach them, knowing they will swing open when we go forward in faith. He may remove some obstacles before we begin to move, but many will remain until we take a step of faith. Not every answer from Him is "wait."

Still, one of the most significant variables in much of our relationship with God— prayers and petitions, growth, mission, taking territory for His Kingdom—is timing. We obsess about the "when" of our requests and our work, but God is more focused on the "what" of it all. That difference can be frustrating, particularly when we think He has denied a request but He has simply set the timing for later. We often find ourselves pressing our longings on Him or stepping ahead in action while He waits for a better time.

IN DEED

God gives, but He doesn't always lay His gifts in your lap. You often have to get up and take possession of what has already been offered. When asking Him, "How long?" listen for the same question from Him. If you hear it, go forward and receive His promise by faith.

ADDITIONAL READING: Deuteronomy 1:8

> God isn't going to ask, "What did you dream? What did you think? What did you plan? What did you preach?" He's going to ask, "What did you do?"
> MICHEL QUOIST

Living the Promise

Each one of you will put to flight a thousand of the enemy, for the LORD your God fights for you, just as he has promised. Joshua 23:10

IN WORD

God gave Israel some extraordinary promises about possessing their inheritance and overcoming their enemies. It's hard to imagine such favor playing out in the lives of fallen human beings, yet God still offered enormous opportunities for success. But these promises, from the earliest days of the Exodus to the last days of the conquest, were almost always surrounded with exhortations to love Him, serve Him, and remain zealously faithful to the terms of the covenant. Next to their potential glory was a very big "if," sometimes stated but always at least implied. Israel would experience extravagant blessings *if* they were diligent about keeping His words.

As we know, they didn't—at least not consistently or for long. But the blessings showed up at times in the nation's history, and they presumably still apply to all who receive them. We know we don't live up to the law well enough to earn them, but we know Someone who did on our behalf. And we know that accepting Him as our proxy in life, death, and resurrection implies the need to grow into His likeness. In every respect, we qualify for God's promises in Jesus, the "amen" to every promise given (2 Corinthians 1:20). The nature of God offered to Israel is offered to all who believe in Him and receive His nature. And that includes extraordinary opportunities for success and victory.

IN DEED

In your quest for Kingdom territory, you can put to flight a thousand of the enemy. Why? Not because you're strong, clever, or resourceful, but because the Lord fights for you—*if* you are in the covenant that fulfills His Word. The big question, then, is whether you are believing it, living it, breathing it, applying it, growing in it, and acting on it. If you are, you might be surprised by what you can accomplish in the Lord's strength, and the enemy is alarmed by it. The Lord is ready to fight on your behalf.

ADDITIONAL READING: Luke 10:19

When a man has no strength, if he leans on God, he becomes powerful.
D. L. MOODY

Choose

Choose today whom you will serve. . . . As for me and my family, we will serve the LORD. Joshua 24:15

IN WORD

It seems like a choice that should have been made long ago. In fact, it was, at least at times and in certain degrees. Israelites who had made it to the Promised Land had already pledged loyalty to God and His chosen leaders at key moments. They had expressed their intentions. Yet idols remained among them (Joshua 24:23). Like many of us, they had been following God while hanging on to a supporting cast of deities. But the supporting cast wasn't very supporting, and in fact undermined their best intentions. We see that clearly as Scripture and history played out over the next few centuries; no one can truly serve multiple masters. One has to reign supreme.

That's why Joshua called the people to an emphatic, decisive commitment. "Choose today whom you will serve." God had called for this choice repeatedly, reminding His people that He was the one who had delivered them from captivity, defended them, protected them, provided for them, and made a covenant full of extravagant promises for them. But even at the end of the conquest, they needed to be called again to a choice. They needed to make a commitment that would stick.

IN DEED

So do we. We can't criticize ancient Israelites very harshly because we are guilty of the same pattern. We make once-and-for-all commitments to God again and again and again, only to find ourselves clinging to worthless idols years later. We have to remember that we were born into this life to love and to serve. Period. We belong to another, and everything He has designed for us is good. Every choice we make in our own self-interest that contradicts His choices for us is really a self-inflicted wound. We have to plant a stake in the ground as a marker forever and choose—not just once, but every single day—whom we will serve. And whatever it takes, we have to ensure that this commitment never fades into the background of our lives.

ADDITIONAL READING: 1 Kings 18:20-39

Don't touch Christianity unless you mean business.
I promise you a miserable existence if you do.
HENRY DRUMMOND

Sheep

[Jesus said,] "I am the good shepherd; I know my own sheep, and they know me." John 10:14

IN WORD

The Bible offers us plenty of images of our relationship with God. He is the Potter, we are the clay. He is the Vinedresser, we are the vineyard. He is a shield, a refuge, a fortress, and we are the protected. Some of these descriptions are rather impersonal, but this one begins to reflect the relational tenderness of God: He is the Shepherd, and we are the sheep.

Several writers in Hebrew Scripture used this image—Isaiah described us as sheep who have gone astray (53:6)—but David, the shepherd-king of Israel, stated it most poetically and profoundly. In his most famous psalm, he describes how our Shepherd provides all we need; guides us into safe and refreshing places; watches over us even in the deepest, darkest valleys; gives us victory in the presence of our enemies; and fills our lives with goodness and love. The Shepherd is leader, provider, protector, rescuer, and more. The sheep are helpless apart from their Shepherd, but He is everything they need.

We can be grateful for the richness of that image. Jesus used it to describe how the true Shepherd leaves His flock of ninety-nine to find the one that strayed, and to illustrate how His own followers hear His voice and are saved from the thief who comes to steal, kill, and destroy. Our pride may not like the fact that sheep aren't known for intelligence or resourcefulness, but we know the image fits. We really do get lost, don't know the right way to go, find ourselves in predicaments, and follow the crowd even when we shouldn't. And our Shepherd knows exactly what to do in each of those situations.

IN DEED

As a Kingdom citizen, you are a sheep at heart. That isn't the highest image of you, as we will see in the coming days, but it's a true one. This is a relationship of absolute dependence; you depend entirely on His resources and not on your own. You can't embrace that image without a lot of humility, but when you do, it's quite a relief. He isn't waiting for you to figure things out. He's waiting for you to follow Him through them.

ADDITIONAL READING: Psalm 23

The more we depend on God, the more dependable we find He is.
ANONYMOUS

Servants

[Jesus said,] "I have given you an example to follow. Do as I have done to you. I tell you the truth, slaves are not greater than their master." John 13:15-16

IN WORD

We value our freedom. Nations have been founded on its virtues, and we instinctively recognize basic liberties that every human being should have. So when Scripture refers to us as servants, slaves, or any other term of subservience, it puts us on edge. We don't want to feel trapped. We trust God, but we love our freedom. And slavery doesn't sound very appealing.

At times, Paul called himself a servant, slave, or bond servant of Christ (Romans 1:1). He was not only referring to his circumstances as a captive in prison for Jesus' sake, he was also expressing his deep commitment to serve his Master. A person can do that only when (1) he trusts God implicitly, without reservation, to look out for his best interests; and (2) he understands the voluntary nature of the term. The biblical ideal for servanthood is to willingly offer oneself to meet the needs of others. It's tragic when freedoms are taken from us, but beautiful when we give them up for a cause. Paul gave them up out of his love for Jesus, and he urged his readers to do the same.

Astonishingly, even Jesus came to us in this role. He declared Himself a servant on our behalf and washed the feet of His followers. While Roman culture then and Western culture today look down on servanthood, Jesus lifted it up as the key to greatness. You want to go up in God's Kingdom? Go down. Embrace humility. Serve God, and in serving Him, serve others. "Low" is an extremely high Kingdom value.

IN DEED

Enjoy your freedom. Even fight for it, not only for yourself but for others. But in your freedom, choose to be bound to Christ in His service. Trust Him so thoroughly that you can relinquish all your concerns and decisions to Him, defaulting to His guidance above all other inclinations. Know that the Master will use you not only for the good of the Kingdom, but also for your own good. There is absolutely nothing to fear in His service. When you abandon all to Him, you receive all from Him.

ADDITIONAL READING: Matthew 20:25-28

A servant of God has but one Master.
GEORGE MÜLLER

Friends

[Jesus said,] "You are my friends if you do what I command. I no longer call you slaves." John 15:14-15

IN WORD

God wants more than servants. It's true He is worthy of our unequivocal service; we owe Him our entire lives. But He didn't create human beings in His image simply so we could carry out orders. Angels and any number of unknown creatures could do that (Psalm 103:20-21). No, He wants a relationship founded in love and reciprocated by hearts like His. We may serve Him, but we aren't simply servants. Jesus calls us friends.

That's one of the many features that makes the Kingdom of God an extraordinary environment. All Kingdom citizens are friends with the King. It isn't an equal friendship, of course, but there are times in Scripture when God treats it as though it is. He gave Abraham the right to negotiate with Him and called him "friend," wrestled with Jacob, spoke face to face with Moses as with a friend, and let David speak to Him in intimate terms and even argue with Him at times. The Potter and the clay, the Shepherd and the sheep, the Master and the servant . . . these are true illustrations of our relationship with God, but they aren't sufficient. By themselves, they are too impersonal. Clearly God wants the kind of relationship where hearts connect and converse and exchange ideas and desires and dreams.

IN DEED

Don't squander that relationship. We all need to learn to serve well, but God doesn't leave you strictly in the role of servant. He is calling you higher. It's entirely possible that when you are most focused on obedience, He is trying to draw you into a deeper conversation on more intimate terms. Express your heart to Him and listen to His. Ask Him what His deepest desires are—for your life and for those around you. Like John at the Last Supper, lean against Jesus and listen to His whispers. He shares confidential information with those who have learned to love Him well. In so doing, you begin to fulfill your original design as one made in His image. You step into the relationship you were designed for.

ADDITIONAL READING: James 2:23

> What brings joy to the heart is not so much
> the friend's gift as the friend's love.
> AELRED OF RIEVAULX

Children

Jesus told him, "I am the way, the truth, and the life. No one can come to the Father except through me. If you had really known me, you would know who my Father is." John 14:6-7

IN WORD

God called Israel His "son" at times in the Old Testament (Exodus 4:22-23, for example), an image that has connotations of familial love, permanence, and inheritance. He even inspired prophets to portray His maternal love (Isaiah 49:15; 66:13; Hosea 11:3-4). The New Testament picks up the theme of His parenthood but applies it more directly to us as individuals. Jesus told us to pray to our Father in heaven. Paul wrote about how we have been adopted as children and how the Spirit has put into our hearts the instinct to call God "Father." We are even given full freedom to consider God as our "abba," our papa, our intimately connected parent with all the care and comfort that relationship provides. We aren't just sheep or servants or even friends. We are part of the family.

As members of the royal family, we have privileges. Unlike dignitaries seeking audience with a president or prime minister, we have access to the King at any time. We have the knowledge that He is looking out for our best interests in every area of life. We can live life freely and securely in His love, without fear of being forgotten or forsaken. And we have an inheritance that is bigger than we can imagine and that lasts forever.

Yes, those are the family perks, or at least a few of them. But greater than the privileges and inheritance is simply the fact that God chooses to relate to us on family terms, without considering whether we deserve that relationship or not. Like a strong father who gets on the floor to relate to his toddler, He comes down to our level to discuss, encourage, make decisions, and envision plans together. He lets us be at home with Him.

IN DEED

It's good to remember the majesty of God and bow before Him in awe, but never let that side of the relationship overshadow the intimate warmth of His love. Kingdom citizens are simultaneously servants, friends, and family members. Live each role to the fullest.

ADDITIONAL READING: Matthew 6:9

> Whoever God adopts for His child . . . not only bears his heavenly Father's name, but His image.
> THOMAS WATSON

The Bride

[Jesus said,] "When everything is ready, I will come and get you, so that you will always be with me where I am." John 14:3

IN WORD

Jesus told His followers that He was leaving them to prepare a place for them in His Father's house. These are the same words a groom might speak to his intended bride, fitting the custom of the time, when a bride would leave her family and join her husband's to live in a newly prepared add-on to the family's home. This intimate image was a signal to the disciples that something greater than friendship would eventually be desired of them. In the divine plan, God wants His people as close to His heart as possible.

Earlier in John's Gospel, John the Baptist referred to Jesus as the bridegroom (3:29). It's an image Jesus frequently used of Himself, both in parables and in pointed comments to those who fasted and mourned in His presence rather than rejoicing as if at a wedding. And it's a stronger image of relationship than any other in Scripture. We aren't just clay pots, sheep, or servants. Neither are we merely friends or children. We are all of these things and more. We are the beloved bride.

Let that soak in. God could have used plenty of other human relationships as an illustration of His love for us—and He often did—but He took it as far as we can imagine with this one. There is no greater level of intimacy and affection than this. When it comes to relating to those who love Him, God is a romantic at heart.

IN DEED

That thought unnerves a lot of people who want only the majesty and dignity of God and not the passion of knowing Him deeply. The truth is that both sides are true, and one without the other leads either to a cold and distant relationship or a sentimental, casual one. God wants both awe and intimacy, but the ultimate expression of His love is to relate to us as a bridegroom to a bride. We know that because Scripture ends with a wedding. The betrothal at Sinai (Jeremiah 2:2) is fulfilled at the coming of the Son in splendor. And the story really does end with "happily ever after."

ADDITIONAL READING: Revelation 19:6-9

The church is in Christ as Eve was in Adam.
RICHARD HOOKER

His Own Body

All of you together are Christ's body, and each of you is a part of it.
1 Corinthians 12:27

IN WORD

According to Scripture, a married couple becomes one flesh; the two are united into one. So when Jesus calls Himself the Bridegroom and His people the bride, what does that say about our union with Him? We have become one flesh, thoroughly united with Him. Just as He and the Father are one, we and He are one.

The New Testament repeats this theme often, declaring us to be the body of Christ—literally His flesh on earth. First and foremost, this is a corporate calling; a body has many members, each functioning together as part of the whole. But as believers filled with the Spirit of Christ, each one of us individually is an expression of His physical body on earth, functioning as His mouth and hands and feet. This union is a great mystery, but it's indisputably biblical. We are one with Jesus, He in us and we in Him. He is the head, and as members of His body, we are the living, breathing expression of Christ on earth.

We may grieve at how far short of this identity we fall, but it's still our true identity. According to His promise, we should be able to exercise His authority (Matthew 16:19; 28:18-19), speak His words (Matthew 28:20; 1 Peter 4:11), and do His works (John 14:12). Whether this has been our experience yet is not the point; it can be. As His body, we express His heart to each other and to the world.

IN DEED

In most earthly kingdoms, kings have certain representatives and emissaries who represent them to others. In the Kingdom of God, the King has chosen every citizen for that role. And our representation isn't simply honorary, ceremonial, or theoretical. It's real. He is actually living within us. He guides our wills, desires, words, actions, relationships, circumstances, and steps according to the power of His Spirit at work within us. Our relationship with Him is beyond one-to-one; it's simply one—He and us in union with each other. And the more we believe that, the more we will experience it each day.

ADDITIONAL READING: Ephesians 5:29-32

> One person works upon another person from the outside inward, but God alone comes to us from within outward.
> JAN VAN RUYSBROECK

Redeeming Time

This vision is for a future time. It describes the end, and it will be fulfilled.
Habakkuk 2:3

IN WORD

Habakkuk was confused by God's delay. He had to look at the injustice and brutality, the sin and suffering around him, and he wondered why God didn't do something about it. This God who said He hated sin, would punish disobedience, and would deliver from the enemy was strangely silent. Was He suddenly tolerant of evil? Did He enjoy letting people suffer the consequences of their own mistakes? Did He take any pleasure at all in the conflict of His people? Surely the answer to all these questions was no. But if the answer was no, where was He?

We have the same questions. We see sin and suffering around us, conflicts that end in violence, immorality that devastates lives, and abuses of all kinds. We all know people who are depressed and lonely or angry and bitter. We see societies that are lost and drifting, aimlessly going in directions no one understands. And we have our own complaints, either overtly or subtle and internal, about the situation. We wonder why God doesn't do something. God has done something, of course. He has already won the victory and redeemed the world. He sends us into it with the promise of victory. While we wonder why God doesn't do something, He wonders why we don't do something. He has given us the power of the Resurrection. We aren't helpless if we have faith in Him.

Still, there's a promised deliverance coming when Jesus will fulfill His Kingdom work. The end of all suffering is coming. The pain of the world has an expiration date. Creation is being made new.

IN DEED

Don't forget that we are participants in the prophecies of the end. We don't sit silently and wait for Jesus' return. Deliverance comes on the heels of people with faith and a promise. And faith, as we are told, is always active. Work with an eye on the end. Habakkuk saw the fulfillment from a distance and rejoiced. You can too.

ADDITIONAL READING: Habakkuk 3:18-19

I've read the last page of the Bible. It's all going to turn out all right.
BILLY GRAHAM

Waiting to Soar

If it seems slow in coming, wait patiently, for it will surely take place. It will not be delayed. Habakkuk 2:3

IN WORD

God's Word fills us with hope. He has given us a multitude of promises assuring us of His fullness, abundance, and peace. His Spirit highlights those promises for us when we come to Him in need. When we believe Him, we're filled with expectancy about the specific provisions He has sworn to us. We set all our hopes on Him.

The problem we often face is the gap between promise and fulfillment. God's predictions always come about, but they aren't always immediate. His Word is always fulfilled, but usually we have to wait. Whether the promise we believe concerns the deliverance of a nation (as with Habakkuk), the coming of Christ and the end of the age, or the supply for this month's needs, God usually has a schedule for it. And His schedule usually takes longer than ours.

We don't always understand why God's processes are so lengthy. We know He's very thorough, but we often don't see Him working on the hidden details while we wait. But the Word is full of instructions to "wait on the Lord," and it gives us promises even for the waiting. Those who ask Him for direction and then wait for His answer before moving forward will be led into victory. Those who can be patient and rest in their faith will have renewed strength and begin to soar.

IN DEED

Most of us would love to soar, if given the offer. And in fact, that's exactly the offer God gives us. Hope in God's promised guidance, deliverance, and provision is meant to drive us to faith. Faith is meant to mature into "rest"—the kind of trust that stops fluctuating with each moment and worrying with each sleepless night. What begins with "I hope God can" ends with "I know He will."

Waiting is excruciating when the end is in doubt. It can be exhilarating when the end is certain. Let the integrity of God's promises assure you of the end. Let faith bring you into a place of rest. While you wait, learn to soar.

ADDITIONAL READING: Isaiah 40:31

> There is no place for faith if we expect God to fulfill immediately what He promises.
> JOHN CALVIN

Until Fulfillment

Then he said to me, "Speak a prophetic message to the winds, son of man.
Speak a prophetic message and say, 'This is what the Sovereign LORD says.'"
Ezekiel 37:9

IN WORD

Why does God tell Ezekiel to "speak a prophetic message to the winds"? God is sovereign, as the passage emphasizes repeatedly. Sovereignty isn't dependent on the words of human beings to accomplish its purposes, is it? Or is there something in the spoken word that affects God's plan as nothing else can?

The reason is mysterious, but the answer is clear: God intervenes in the affairs of humanity at the spoken invitation of humanity. Perhaps that's why we are taught to pray to a sovereign God who could do anything He wanted to do regardless of our prayers. Maybe the human voice matters more than we think it does. Maybe the words we speak directly correlate to the intervention we eventually see.

Regardless of the reason, God has told us to speak. There's a pattern in this passage that is repeated elsewhere in Scripture: God informs a person of His plans, implicitly or explicitly urges the person either to intercede for or proclaim those plans, and then accomplishes them. God initiates, we express, then He fulfills.

IN DEED

Does that sound like your prayer life? If you're like most Christians, probably not. We usually think our prayers arise from our own initiative—our pleas based on our needs and desires. But the biblical pattern is often for God to initiate our prayers and petitions. He puts His will within us, or spells it out for us to see, and then we pray it into reality. The unseen becomes seen by the process of faith, prayer, and proclamation.

If that isn't the pattern of your prayer life, try to make it so. Ask God what He wants you to pray. Ask Him to shape your dreams and desires, to guide you through His Word and His people, to let the Spirit within you reign. Then pray your heart out. Trust that your petitions line up with His revealed will, and believe that He will fulfill them. Speak the breath of God as He breathes through you.

ADDITIONAL READING: Matthew 21:21

God shapes the world by prayer.
E. M. BOUNDS

A New Economy

Come, all you who are thirsty, come to the waters; and you who have no money, come, buy and eat! Isaiah 55:1, *NIV*

IN WORD

Imagine living in a world where no money is needed. Everyone is industrious, not from a sense of obligation, but from a sense of honor and service. No salary scales are needed because every job is equally important and everyone works equally hard. When you need something, you get it without cost because products and services are offered to you generously, just as you offer your products and services freely to others. It's a utopian economy where trust and loyalty rule and where competition is nonexistent. No one ever lacks.

That's a picture of the Kingdom of God given in Isaiah 55. The Kingdom will be that kind of system—spiritually and materially—because it's based on the character of God Himself. It's the kind of Kingdom earthly political philosophers have long dreamed of and even tried to attain, not realizing that it can only work when every participant is redeemed and fully sanctified. It cannot happen until God reigns in every heart.

Our salvation is a foretaste of that Kingdom. It is freely given and freely received; in fact, it can't be obtained any other way. God is generous with His grace, but only those who are willing to come to Him on those terms can have it. And salvation is only our entry into the Kingdom. It's a gateway into this new way of thinking, this radically different economy where God has paid every price and freely shares all He has with those He loves.

IN DEED

It's hard for us to think in such terms because we're so used to a world of competition and costs. We even have a saying about it: "There's no such thing as a free lunch." But in God's Kingdom, "free" is the only kind of lunch there is. Every blessing He gives is given by grace, and grace is always free. Get used to it. Those will always and forever be His terms.

ADDITIONAL READING: Revelation 21:6-7

The entrance fee into the Kingdom of God is nothing.
HENRY DRUMMOND

The Kingdoms of the World

Then the devil took him up and revealed to him all the Kingdoms of the world in a moment of time. "I will give you the glory of these Kingdoms and authority over them," the devil said, "because they are mine to give to anyone I please."
Luke 4:5-6

IN WORD

Apparently the kingdoms of this world belong to the devil. During the Temptation, that claim came straight from the evil one's mouth, and the true King didn't contradict him. Other places in Scripture affirm this claim, calling Satan "the god of this world" (2 Corinthians 4:4) and declaring that friendship with the world equals enmity toward God (James 4:4). Even Jesus called him the prince or ruler of this world (John 14:30). Clearly the kingdoms of this world are not part of the Kingdom of Christ.

But they will be. The kingdoms of this world will become the Kingdom of our Lord, and He will reign forever and ever (Revelation 11:15). The question isn't whether the kingdoms of earth ultimately belong to Jesus. The questions are how and when. And the more relevant question for us in this age is whether the status quo is acceptable. When Scripture declares Satan's current influence, should we simply accept it? Or is God's Word urging us to do something about it?

Millions of Christians, having seen the influence of evil in places like Wall Street, Hollywood, and the capital cities of the world, have declared them "of the devil" and walked away from them. But perhaps they are "of the devil" because we've abandoned them to him. Maybe we are called to have influence in those places that supersedes the influences already there. Perhaps the salt, the leaven, the mustard seed of the Kingdom is meant to season, expand, and grow up in the places that will eventually become the Kingdom of Christ anyway. Perhaps we're neglecting our calling.

IN DEED

Jesus told His followers to go into *all* the world. That doesn't mean just remote jungles; it means any territory held captive by evil. Take up your mission to plunder evil, wherever you are. You are guaranteed ultimate victory.

ADDITIONAL READING: Revelation 11:15

> Some like to live within the sound of church or chapel bell.
> I'd rather run a rescue shop within a yard of hell.
> WILLIAM BOOTH

Inaugural Address

The Scripture you've just heard has been fulfilled this very day! Luke 4:21

IN WORD

Isaiah's words at the beginning of chapter 61 of his writings were seen as a messianic prophecy, a picture of the coming Kingdom. This is where God was eventually headed with His people, even though they were under the oppression of injustices, illnesses, poverty, and every other manifestation of the frustrating condition of fallen humanity. So when Jesus opened the scroll at the synagogue and read from this passage—how this Kingdom figure would have God's Spirit to bring good news to the poor, the captives, the blind, and the oppressed—and said it was now fulfilled, He was making a landmark statement about His identity. He was declaring the coming of the Kingdom and, more specifically, the King Himself.

We have a tendency to do exactly what the Jews of Jesus' day were prone to do: expect Scripture to be fulfilled, but not in our presence. We certainly believe the Kingdom is coming; but we typically don't expect to see it manifesting in us, through us, around us, and for us. We expect the King to come one day, but not today. We expect the Spirit to do amazing things to heal, deliver, and transform the world, but for now we expect spiritual-only evidence that He's at work. We don't really expect Christian politicians to radically transform government, Christian businesspeople to exhibit the Kingdom in their work, or Christian artists and performers to express the sounds and scenes of heaven. Most of all, we don't expect to see miraculous healing or supernatural signs, even though we pray for them. We look to the future through lenses of great hope, but we look at the present through lenses of disappointment.

IN DEED

Not all of God's promises are for "one day." Jesus is at work even now, still fulfilling Isaiah's prophecies. We are, after all, living in the Kingdom age, or at least the age in which the hidden Kingdom is being revealed. How do we know? Because the King came. He inaugurated His mission. He equipped and commissioned His followers to carry it forward. Even today, Scriptures are being fulfilled in our hearing. Expect more. Believe in the power of the King for today.

ADDITIONAL READING: Mark 16:15-18

Jesus is the yes to every promise of God.
WILLIAM BARCLAY

A Simple Manifesto

He has anointed me to bring Good News to the poor. He has sent me to proclaim that captives will be released, that the blind will see, that the oppressed will be set free. Luke 4:18

IN WORD

The messianic prophecies could have focused on routing the kingdom of darkness or on building a utopian society. They could have emphasized the big picture to the exclusion of individual lives. After all, Jesus would touch on all of these aspects, speaking strong words about the gates of hell and offering parables about the celebration of the final Kingdom age. But the prophecy quoted by Jesus on this day was focused on the weak and hurting, and it was simply an announcement of the Good News. Like His advent as a baby in a manger, He launched His ministry discreetly—like reading a humble prophecy at an up-country synagogue, quietly turning water into wine at a wedding, and being baptized alongside desperate sinners in a river. Though the Kingdom would grow to be flourishing and widespread, it would truly begin with small, mustard-seed characteristics.

That's why the Good News really is good news. It isn't an announcement for the elite, the most devoted and spiritually impressive among us. It isn't a grand plan that may or may not include commoners like us. In God's Kingdom, there are no commoners. All of us, even the desperate, poor, and blind, are elite. We don't have to qualify for His blessings, fill out an application to see if we're accepted, or take a number to wait. We just come. That's really, really good news.

IN DEED

Never forget that. Many Christians turn the gospel (Good News) into a burdensome lifestyle, trying to achieve what we can only receive. We grab for what is already given, work for what is already accomplished, and ask for what is already offered. Like a poor, captive, blind, oppressed soul, receive the Kingdom from the King—in every area of your life. Declare the Kingdom as good news to those around you, and live in a way that shows that it truly is good. Embrace the blessings offered by the King and share them with everyone. Be fully alive, fully free, and fully at home in what the King has already done.

ADDITIONAL READING: Mark 1:14-15

There are two things to do about the gospel—believe it and behave it.
SUSANNA WESLEY

Favor

. . . and that the time of the LORD's favor has come. Luke 4:19

IN WORD

Isaiah's prophecy declared the year of the Lord's favor and the day of vengeance of our God. To his readers, those two points were likely the same: God's favor on His people implies vengeance on their enemies. But Jesus stopped immediately after His proclamation of the Lord's favor, right in the middle of Isaiah's sentence. Why? Because the day of vengeance has not yet come; it was never a feature of His earthly ministry. There will be a time, a Second Coming, when God's anger toward enemies is expressed, but not now. This is the age of favor. And that's why the Good News is good.

Christians who are pessimistic about the course of history or about their own lives have forgotten that this is an era of favor. So have Christians who point fingers of judgment at others, as though the primary focus of this age is to condemn those outside the Kingdom rather than invite them into it. In an age of favor, we can expect goodness from Him in every area of life at all times, and we can offer it to everyone we meet, whether we agree with them or not. We may experience hardships, but we don't incur His wrath. If we're in Christ, we never will. For those who aren't, the time of judgment has not yet come. Favor is still the climate of the Kingdom.

IN DEED

Pessimism and criticism are not part of the Kingdom culture. This is not an age for hopelessness or defeatism. We are called to be like our God, who has never had a moment of hopelessness or ever felt defeated. That means that if we fully embrace the Kingdom message, we expect goodness from His hand.

Surround yourself with hope. Fill yourself with high expectations for God's goodness, regardless of what you see in your immediate surroundings. Receive the perfect love that casts out fear (1 John 4:18). Refuse the critical, negative thinking that fills so many hearts, even Christian ones. Resolutely insist that right now is the time of the Lord's favor—for you and for everyone around you. And offer His favor generously, just like He does. It's the only message that can change lives.

ADDITIONAL READING: Psalm 5:11-12

The future is as bright as the promises of God.
ADONIRAM JUDSON

Mission Impossible

Jonah got up and went in the opposite direction to get away from the LORD.
Jonah 1:3

IN WORD

Three prophets, one era. Jonah, Hosea, and Amos were contemporaries, each ministering the word of the Lord in the northern kingdom of Israel. Hosea had sacrificed a pure marriage for the sake of his message. Amos had left his shepherding and gotten in trouble with the king. And Jonah . . . well, Jonah bailed out. To him, the prophetic sacrifice would be too great. The last thing he wanted to do was to preach judgment in a very hostile city.

To get an idea of Jonah's task, imagine being told by God during the height of the Cold War to stand in Moscow's Red Square and shout judgment on communism. Or imagine an assignment to march through the streets of Mecca denouncing Islam. In either case, it would be understood as a suicide mission. Jonah wasn't in the mood to die just yet, so he fled.

Nearly three thousand years later, we may find it easy to criticize Jonah's disobedience—after all, plenty of other prophets willingly sacrificed their lives—but we should be able to appreciate his dilemma. Nineveh was the center of Assyria, the dreaded enemy of Israel. Just a few decades later, it would be used by God to destroy the northern kingdom according to the words of the prophets. Just because God wanted to give Assyrians a chance to repent didn't imply that an Israelite prophet would see their repentance as even a remote possibility.

IN DEED

But God doesn't call us to do the possible, does He? He searches the hearts of people who are willing to embrace the impossible for the sake of His name. Such heroic risks are defined in His Kingdom as "great faith," and they inspire His people for generations to come. Hebrews 11 lists people of faith who accomplished great things for God and who often died in the process. But in the eternal Kingdom, they are honored above all.

When God asks the impossible of you, how do you respond? Let faith—great, risky faith—guide your life.

ADDITIONAL READING: Hebrews 11:13-16

I am one who would rather sink with faith than swim without it.
STANLEY BALDWIN

Understanding Redemption

Nineveh has more than 120,000 people living in spiritual darkness, not to mention all the animals. Jonah 4:11

IN WORD

God has filled His creation with order and wisdom. He has spoken His Word, and the Word has clothed Himself in human flesh and dwelt among us. We've been taught right from wrong and truth from error. The intricacies of creation speak of God's design, and the vastness of the heavens speak of His grandeur. And the majority of people in this world don't understand any of it.

Apparently, the ignorance of the godless masses didn't grieve Jonah. Surprisingly, it doesn't grieve many of God's people today either. Our world is reeling, oblivious to the character and ways of its Creator, and few people shed tears over its ignorance. We're bothered by the attitudes of the world against us more than its unawareness of God Himself. We have to wake up to the contradiction: On the one hand, billions of people have no idea which way is up; on the other hand, Jesus clearly told His followers to go and teach them.

The book of Jonah is about God's heart for the world. It's a missionary book, a preview of the Great Commission. In God's poignant explanation to an angry prophet, the salient fact about the Ninevites was not their brutal attacks on Israel or their enormous, self-exalting pride. God preoccupied Himself with another problem: They didn't know right from wrong, and they needed to. They needed to come face to face with Him—in His mercy.

IN DEED

It's easy to get mad about all the injustices in the world. It's natural to be outraged at those who abuse and terrorize innocent people. But does God tell us in Scripture always to do what's easy and natural? No, He puts His Spirit within us so we'll know His character and have His heart. He wants us to focus on redemption, not vengeance; on mercy, not judgment. Those aren't easy goals, and they certainly aren't natural. But they're from God. He sees the devastation of the world as an opportunity to save. Seize that opportunity with Him.

ADDITIONAL READING: Matthew 28:18-20

The nearer we get to Christ, the more intensely missionary we become.
HENRY MARTYN

Understanding Compassion

The LORD said, . . ."Shouldn't I feel sorry for such a great city?" Jonah 4:10-11

IN WORD

Jonah didn't understand God's ways. More than that, he didn't understand God's heart. He thought God was zealous about punishing His enemies, when in reality He was zealous about being gracious to those who humble themselves in His sight. Jonah didn't realize that God is more interested in mercy than in punishment. He wanted a God who would wipe out the ungodly, not change them.

Centuries later in salvation history, we witnessed the character of God in the person of Jesus. In Him, we saw God's heart toward sinners, how He didn't condemn those who deserved condemnation, but with mercy and kindness turned their hearts back toward God. We learned that although Jonah wasn't willing to spend three days in a darkened, deathly belly for the redemption of evildoers, God incarnate was. We came to understand that God will judge when He has to, but He much prefers to save.

The religious impulse of human beings doesn't understand that. We're a lot like Jonah; right and wrong have to be established, and justice must be weighed. God, of course, is the Author of the principle in the first place, but His enforcement of it looks more merciful than we ever imagined possible. He took justice upon Himself so He could function out of His love for lost cities and souls. He did what His prophet couldn't grasp: He preached judgment because He loved the lost enough to tell the truth.

IN DEED

Do we really understand God's heart for those who don't know Him? We comprehend it at an intellectual level, but do we feel His compassion for the vile and offensive rebels of this world? Not unless His Spirit breathes such compassion into us. It doesn't come naturally. Our natural selves want to get even with those who hurt us, not get friendly with them.

Ask God for His heart. Pray to be overwhelmed with concern for a city ignorant of His love. Grasp what Jonah couldn't. Ask God to breathe His love for others into you.

ADDITIONAL READING: Isaiah 30:18-20

The Christian's compassion must be like God's—unceasing.
WILLIAM BARCLAY

In the World

[Jesus prayed,] "I'm not asking you to take them out of the world, but to keep them safe from the evil one. They do not belong to this world any more than I do." John 17:15-16

IN WORD

"In the world but not of the world." It's a common description of our position as residents of this realm but citizens of another. We know we are born from above, citizens of heaven, but the world around us is very tangible, very present, and very persistent in reminding us of where we serve. Sometimes we're enthusiastic about life in this world, and sometimes we aren't. Sometimes it's just oppressive.

Many Christians have resigned themselves to the perception that life in this age is all hardship and that the only joy for the believer is in looking forward to another realm. It's an understandable point of view, but it renders the believer ineffective in this world. When we decide we must simply endure life now in order to experience true life later, we accept spiritual paralysis for the present time. This sense of escapism is tempting, but it isn't a Kingdom attribute. We can't give in to it.

It's good to look forward to the fullness of the Kingdom, but we can't afford to live with an escapist mentality. While many of us are looking forward to leaving this world to enter the Kingdom, God wants to fill us with the Kingdom and send us into the world. While we let ourselves be influenced by the world, God wants us to influence it. While we give up the battle and look for another realm, God urges us to bring another realm into the battle. We are in the world for a reason.

IN DEED

Don't give up the battle. Don't give in to escapist thinking. See yourself as a Kingdom outpost in hostile territory, if necessary, but certainly not in a hopeless or futile position. God hasn't placed you where you are simply so you can look forward to going somewhere else. Yes, cling to hope in the coming Kingdom; but let the Kingdom come in you now. You are from another world, but you are living in this one. Make the most of your privileged position.

ADDITIONAL READING: John 18:36-37

> The church's mission in the world is absolutely dependent on its being different from the world.
> JIM WALLIS.

The Greater Works

[Jesus said,] "I tell you the truth, anyone who believes in me will do the same works I have done, and even greater works, because I am going to be with the Father." John 14:12

IN WORD

On the night before He left this realm, Jesus gave His followers an extraordinary promise—they would do the works He had been doing, just as He had trained them to do. In fact, they would do even greater works. They surely had difficulty trying to imagine anything greater than what Jesus had done, but His promise was clear. They would carry on His ministry in this world. They would demonstrate the Kingdom in this realm.

Throughout church history, Christians have tried to explain this verse. Perhaps Jesus meant that His immediate followers—people like Peter, John, Paul, and other apostles—would be able to do miracles, but then those miracles would fade away. Or maybe He meant that collectively, the body of Christ throughout the ages would do more works and minister directly to more people than Jesus did in only three years of ministry. But Jesus didn't limit His promise to the apostles; He included "anyone who believes in me" and gave no expiration date. And He didn't imply quantity of works over quality of works; "more works" are not the same as "greater works," and Jesus chose the latter. No, this extravagant promise is for all who believe. We can expect faith to accomplish miracles.

IN DEED

Has this promise proven true? Consider the multitudes of people who have been born again—the spiritually dead raised to spiritual life. Consider also physical resurrections, healings, deliverances, multiplied resources, and many other unexplainable manifestations of God's power, all of which have happened in church history, as testified by people of faith. Yes, there have been false miracles, but Jesus promised true ones too. He invited His followers to seek them—and to keep seeking them, asking for them, and persevering in pursuing them. In other words, He promised a supernatural life. Expect it. Believe Him for it. Relentlessly seek it as long as you are in this world.

ADDITIONAL READING: Matthew 21:21-22

All the resources of the Godhead are at our disposal!
JONATHAN GOFORTH

Exile

The time for judging this world has come, when Satan, the ruler of this world, will be cast out. John 12:31

IN WORD

History is full of dictators who have been exiled yet still exert influence in their home countries. So when Jesus said the prince of this world would be driven out of it, it's entirely realistic for us to envision that he has been removed and is still exerting his influence. But the rest of the New Testament doesn't speak of him as distant; he's very present. Paul called him "the god of this world" (2 Corinthians 4:4), John said the whole world is "under the control of the evil one" (1 John 5:19), and Peter said this evil creature "prowls around like a roaring lion, looking for someone to devour" (1 Peter 5:8). Even though Jesus declared Satan's end, he hasn't gone away.

How is this possible? For one thing, though Jesus unseated the enemy from his place of power, multitudes are still unwittingly loyal to his corrupt and deceptive ways. Scripture is clear on two things: There are still spiritual forces of evil in heavenly realms (Ephesians 6:12), and these powers of darkness have been stripped of power and publicly exposed (Colossians 2:15). The battle rages on, but the outcome has already been decided.

At the Cross, Jesus pulled the plug on Satan's authority. Like an impostor cop, the evil one still poses as powerful, dresses the part, and inflicts his vengeance on many. But the authority he stole long ago has been stripped away. And when Jesus said he would be driven out, He was inaugurating a new era. From the Cross forward, Jesus would begin imposing His will on the enemy's plans. He would drive the enemy out of God's good creation. And He would do it through His people.

IN DEED

That's right. When Jesus said the prince of this world would be driven out, He wasn't describing a transaction behind the scenes. He was commissioning His followers to begin the process. The life, death, and resurrection of Jesus gives us the authority; the Spirit gives us the power; and the assignment gives us marching orders. We have to know who we are. And we must take the territory once held by evil.

ADDITIONAL READING: 1 John 5:19

The devil fears a soul united to God as he does God Himself.
JOHN OF THE CROSS

The Language of Victory

You are my King and my God. You command victories for Israel. Psalm 44:4

IN WORD

We know the end of the story. Jesus comes back, and we win. Evil will be destroyed, creation will be restored, and those who have been redeemed from their fallen condition will live joyfully with Him forever. It's the biggest, most decisive victory we can imagine, and we get to be a part of it.

Even so, many believers feel defeated. Our lives may look mundane and even powerless, and we may go through our days without great expectations that anything worthwhile might happen for us. We've disengaged from battles because we don't really expect to win any. We know God is King, but we've forgotten to declare His kingship and represent His authority in our specific circumstances.

One way out of that quagmire is to begin worshiping God as King. Like the psalmist, tell Him: "You are my King and my God. You command victories for Israel." Whether you are a descendant of Israel or not, you are one of its heirs by faith. You are one of God's people. He declares victory for you—especially when you worship Him for His victories. When you need Him, worship the facet of His nature that you need. When you need victories, appeal to the God who commands victories.

IN DEED

Choose to live with a victory mentality, regardless of what you see. Assume success, even if you encounter temporary setbacks. Kingdom citizens can't afford to be defeatist in our outlook. God speaks the language of victories, not defeats. We know that our faith will be challenged, and sometimes we will seem to suffer loss. But nothing is lost in the Kingdom; all things work together for the good of those who love God and are called according to His purposes (see Romans 8:28). That's more than a consolation prize; it's ultimate success. Assume victory in every battle, refuse to let your faith falter, and wait for God to come through. He commands victories for His people.

ADDITIONAL READING: 2 Chronicles 20:21-28

One drop of God's strength is worth more than all the world.
D. L. MOODY

The Source of Strength

I do not count on my sword to save me. You are the one who gives us victory over our enemies. Psalm 44:6-7

IN WORD

A boxer can spend months, even years, preparing for a fight. He trains physically, strengthens himself mentally, works himself up emotionally, and thinks strategically. When the time comes, he draws on all his resources, knowing that it's all up to him. His trainers and his fans won't be in the ring with him. He's the only one he can depend on.

We prepare for fights too—physically, mentally, emotionally, and strategically. We know our Kingdom is at war against false kingdoms, and we are on the front lines in this world. It makes sense to equip ourselves and ready ourselves for the conflict. But unlike the boxer, we can't simply draw on all our own resources. They aren't enough. We need help. We need a power from beyond ourselves.

One of our key strategies in preparing for spiritual battles is to learn how to rest. When we rest, we declare our own strength insufficient and lean into God's. We fight His battles in His wisdom and His power. Yes, we're on the front lines, but we aren't the central characters. We represent someone altogether more powerful.

God will give us power in battles according to the source we're depending on. If we're depending on ourselves, He will let us fight in our own strength. If we're depending on Him, He fights for us. It's up to us. What we experience depends on who and what we're relying on. And though it goes against our instincts, our greatest successes come when we declare our weakness, worship Him for His strength, and trust Him to fight.

IN DEED

Be fully present in your battles, and do whatever God says to do in them. Make your moves as He leads, but never trust your own power. Kingdom citizens win victories not only in the name of the King but also in His strength. Joshua, Gideon, David, and many more have found His battle plans to defy human logic, but they won extraordinary triumphs. Your sword may be necessary, but it isn't enough. Emphatically declare your own dependence on Him, and trust Him to fight on your behalf.

ADDITIONAL READING: Psalm 20:7-9

When God is our strength, it is strength indeed. When our strength is our own, it is only weakness.
AUGUSTINE OF HIPPO

Following to Hear

After he has gathered his own flock, he walks ahead of them, and they follow him because they know his voice. John 10:4

IN WORD

Sheep are followers. They aren't smart followers; they will go straight down a dangerous path if the one in front of them is leading them there. That means the welfare of the sheep is up to the shepherd. They can't look after themselves, so someone has to do it for them. They have no problem going somewhere, but they have little discernment about which way is best. Sheep need to be led.

That's why Jesus compared us to sheep. We need to be led. We like to think we're intelligent—and according to our God-given design, we are—but we have little discernment about which way is best. What seems most logical and most sensible to us is often what is most dangerous. We can't see the entire landscape, but our Shepherd can. He knows what lies ahead. And He knows how to get us to a place of safety and peace. He knows where all the green pastures are.

Followers need to be able to hear the one who is giving direction. Jesus assures us that He goes before us, fully aware of what is on the path ahead. We may not see very far, but we can trust the Shepherd who does. We need to learn His distinctive sound so well that we instinctively follow where He's leading. We need, like Jesus said, to follow not just because we are followers but because we know His voice.

How do we do that? A good first step is to follow what we've already heard. Just as the sheep follow the Shepherd because we know His voice, we also learn His voice by following Him. The two go hand in hand. The more we embrace current insights, the more He gives us new ones. He speaks to those who have proven they have ears to hear.

IN DEED

Follow what you know to be true. Kingdom citizens have to be good hearers, but listening alone is not enough. We have to act on what we've heard. If the Shepherd is leading and we're standing still, His voice will become fainter and fainter. But if we follow, we'll hear more. That's the way of the Kingdom and a key to learning its ways. Sheep follow because they hear, and they hear because they follow.

ADDITIONAL READING: Luke 6:46-49

It is essential that we acquire the habit of hearkening to His voice.
FRANÇOIS FÉNELON

A Kingdom of Joy

The thief's purpose is to steal and kill and destroy. My purpose is to give them a rich and satisfying life. John 10:10

IN WORD

Perhaps you've heard a rumor that Jesus didn't come to make you happy. It's a statement pointed at those who pray selfish prayers, live with a sense of entitlement, and act as if God exists for their own pleasure. But it isn't entirely true. As Jesus would say later in this Gospel, His will for His followers is that they would have joy (John 15:11). Fullness of joy, in fact. And at some level, that involves a good bit of happiness.

Jesus was rather blunt about another agenda: The thief doesn't come to make us happy. Instead, he comes to steal, kill, and destroy. If we're pointing fingers at those who don't see our happiness as important, this is where we need to point first. The enemy of God is also the enemy of His Kingdom and of our souls, and he wants to make people miserable. He even convinces many that to be good Christians they must rid their lives of everything that gives them pleasure. Meanwhile, Jesus presents an alternate agenda: He came so we could have life. Abundant life, full life, complete life—the *shalom* that includes wholeness and overflowing goodness in every area. Yes, we may encounter hardships, but we can maintain our joy in the midst of them, knowing that our joy is important to God. It's one of the primary reasons He sent Jesus into the world. Jesus said so Himself.

IN DEED

Never fall for the lie that the Kingdom is anything other than a realm overflowing with joy. God takes pleasure in Himself, His domain, and His people—and He expects us to experience His pleasure too. Whatever steals, kills, and destroys in your life is not from Him, even if it comes dressed in religious clothing. There may be some discomfort as we transition from the old nature to the new, but that transition never does violence to our true identity in Him. We are people of the extravagantly happy Kingdom, now and forever. We are meant to rejoice in everything.

ADDITIONAL READING: Philippians 4:4

Joy is the serious business of heaven.
C. S. LEWIS

A Singular Voice

[Jesus said,] "My sheep listen to my voice; I know them, and they follow me."
John 10:27

IN WORD

The world has almost always been a noisy place, but now more so than ever. We have access to a multitude of voices every minute of every day—through radio and TV, Internet and social media, and more. The public discussion has grown drastically larger and louder in our time. We're virtually bombarded with opinions and noise.

Some of these voices are easily recognizable, and we instantly know whether to listen to them or not. Some are more subtle; they blend into the background, come from a distance, or bubble up from questions and confusion in our own minds. Some are nice to us, and others are downright rude. But all of them compete for our attention.

Jesus gave us a profound illustration about shepherds and their sheep. Sheep may hear other shepherds calling out, but they have learned to recognize the voice of the one who guides them. They don't follow just any shepherd; they follow *theirs*. They may hear other voices, but they don't really *hear* them. They are tuned in to the distinctives of their master's call. When they hear it, they follow wherever he is leading.

Our goal is to be uniquely tuned in to a singular voice. We can do that because the Shepherd said He knows us—individually. He has taken time to communicate with us, learn our inclinations and characteristics, and appreciate us individually. We are drawn to Him because of that, and His voice resonates more deeply with us than any other. Because He cares for us, we care what He says. We know He's watching out for us. Our interests are best served by His will.

IN DEED

Ask God to fine-tune your hearing to His voice alone. You'll hear a multitude of other sounds, but they won't resonate with you the way His voice will. They are just noise. Let Him draw you into a learning process that will connect you with His heart and open your ears to hear. Know even before you ask that this is possible. In fact, it's promised. The Shepherd could not possibly leave you in silence. His voice is waiting to be heard.

ADDITIONAL READING: Habakkuk 2:1

There is hardly ever a complete silence in our soul.
God is whispering to us well nigh incessantly.
FREDERICK WILLIAM FABER

The Simple Agenda

The LORD has told you what is good, and this is what he requires of you: to do what is right, to love mercy, and to walk humbly with your God. Micah 6:8

IN WORD

The prophets of Scripture gave us plenty of glimpses behind the scenes of our lives. What did they show us? God's nature, His purposes, and His assessments of His people, among other things. Or in other words, pictures of His Kingdom and how it should apply to our lives. Though page after page of prophetic messages may confuse us with ancient imagery and the politics of an obscure age, the themes are remarkably simple. They boil down to the rightness and goodness of God Himself. His will for His people is to be like Him. And He is just, merciful, and good.

Micah presents a courtroom scene between God and His people. God has a case against those He has called to be like Him. In the midst of this legal drama, the prophet offers a summary statement that begins with a simple fact: The Lord has told you what is good.

Really? Yes. In spite of our human tendency to complicate things, or to apply situational ethics to our dilemmas, we really can know what is good—and it isn't complicated. God is good, and everything against His will is bad. That's all there is to it. Light and darkness. Truth and lies. Good and evil. In confusing times, it helps to get back to the basics.

IN DEED

It's true that human life in a fallen world is textured and layered with nuances and even a few exceptions, but when we get caught up in complexities, we need to remember to anchor ourselves in the basics. God is good, even when circumstances seem to be giving us a raw deal. Truth, justice, and mercy—all of which flow out of His love—are foundational aspects of His goodness. The Kingdom culture really isn't complicated as long as we hold to what we know to be true. And that has already been revealed. We can trust the revelation. To stand for goodness is to stand with God.

ADDITIONAL READING: James 1:16-18

> If you love the justice of Jesus Christ more than you fear human judgment, you will seek to do compassion.
> MECHTILDE OF MAGDEBURG

Be Ethical

And this is what he requires of you: to do what is right, to love mercy, and to walk humbly with your God. Micah 6:8

IN WORD

"Good" isn't relative with God. Human beings may have different ways of defining it, but God's character doesn't shift with circumstances or suffer from comparison with other ideals. No, He is the source of all goodness; it all flows from Him. So when He tells us what is good, we need to embrace His description tightly.

What is good in the eyes of God? To do justice, to love mercy, and to walk in humility with Him. The first two may seem contradictory to modern ears; how do we balance justice and mercy, after all? But when we understand that the prophetic call to justice is not about punishing wrongdoers but about defending those to whom wrong has been done, we understand. Justice and mercy go together. Defenders of the oppressed and hurting are merciful. If that means wrongdoers must be stopped, so be it. But they should be stopped by those who, like God, prefer mercy over judgment. They must do what is necessary to end the injustice or its recurrence without becoming oppressors themselves. They must love mercy and be meticulously ethical.

This is foundational to Kingdom culture. Many people have come to God for salvation but have not given Him their offenses, their bitterness, or their desire for revenge. They have asked for His mercy without extending it to others. They have humbled themselves in His sight while taking pride in how they compare with those around them. It's a huge contradiction that doesn't fit the Kingdom. They love mercy for themselves and judgment against others. And that offends the heart of God.

IN DEED

Never seek spiritual gifts, spiritual growth, or spiritual fruit without also anchoring yourself in justice and mercy for those who have been beaten up by the world. Embrace the kind of humility that always seeks good, even at the expense of your own goals. Recognize the character of the Kingdom and seek ways to express it. Especially to those who need to experience it.

ADDITIONAL READING: Matthew 18:21-35

The pearl of justice is found in the heart of mercy.
CATHERINE OF SIENA

Hearts Shaped for Eternity

When this earthly tent we live in is taken down (that is, when we die and leave this earthly body), we will have a house in heaven, an eternal body made for us by God himself and not by human hands. 2 Corinthians 5:1

IN WORD

Earthly versus heavenly. It's a distinction that isn't always made in the Gospels, particularly when Jesus implies that the Kingdom of Heaven is coming to earth. Nevertheless, it's clear that there is a very spiritual realm in which God's Kingdom is the only one, and a very material realm in which competing kingdoms clash. This difference between visible earth and the highest heaven explains many of our longings—how we know deep down inside that we were made for something larger and greater than what we are experiencing, how we feel stuck in futility in a fallen world, how our natural capabilities seem like a momentary prequel to a supernatural life. All creation groans in expectation, waiting for a revelation of the children of God (Romans 8:19). We do too, knowing the seeds of this new creation have already been planted within us. It's an aching expectation, but one that is certain to be fulfilled. We don't mind earth; we just don't want to be so earthly.

With echoes of Romans 8, Paul gives us a picture in 2 Corinthians 5 of the new creation emerging from a cocoon-like preparation—a struggle for reality that is painful but inevitably rewarded. Our earthly tent is not going to last, even as the Kingdom is coming on earth and a new heaven and earth are created. We become something altogether different, even while retaining our true, God-given selves. We live in the finite but get glimpses of the infinite. And we groan with anticipation.

IN DEED

Many Christians have lost that tension, either because the present is too painful or the promise seems unrealistic. If you have, come back to the place of longing, the aching anticipation where Kingdom dreams are formed and nurtured. There is purpose in these longings; God accomplishes great things through those who can hang on to them. His Kingdom is being built by the faith forged in hearts shaped for eternity.

ADDITIONAL READING: Romans 8:18-25

Heaven will be the endless portion of every man who has heaven in his soul.
HENRY WARD BEECHER

The Pledge

God himself has prepared us for this, and as a guarantee he has given us his Holy Spirit. 2 Corinthians 5:5

IN WORD

We look to the Holy Spirit for power. We ask God for the fruit of the Spirit. We want to be filled by Him and to receive His gifts. We ask for His guidance and comfort, just as Jesus promised. And He fulfills all of these roles. But one role the New Testament solidly points to is the Holy Spirit as a deposit, a guarantee—earnest money on a pending investment. He is evidence that the Kingdom is ours.

That may not be comforting for those who see the Spirit as a theoretical force, but if we look to Him for actual experience and empowerment, His presence is evidence of things to come. His gifts, fruit, power, comfort, and counsel are only a foreshadowing, small tastes of something much greater. Paul's profound statement here, reiterated in Ephesians 1:14 and elsewhere, is that those who have experienced the Spirit can rest in the fact that His work now is only just the beginning. We don't have to wonder if He is temporarily in our lives, if He comes and goes, or if He is already working in us at full capacity. No, the fact that we have encountered Him, that His presence is within us, is as promising as a down payment on a car or a house. It's surety for the full measure. He doesn't just *make* promises or fulfill them; He is one.

IN DEED

Look to the Spirit as a promise from God that you belong to Him and that He has destined you for much greater experiences with Him. Foretastes of power are an indication of future increase. Budding fruit now is a herald of a significant harvest. Whispers now are hints of full-voice conversations later. Most of what God gives us in this age is a starting point that will only increase in the age to come.

The Spirit is God's manifestation on earth in this age—and His promise for another realm. He is also the beginning of your inheritance. Count on it. Greater things—vastly greater things—are coming.

ADDITIONAL READING: Ephesians 1:13-14

> We might almost say that the whole advantage of having the kingdom within is that we look for it somewhere else.
> G. K. CHESTERTON

AUG
30

Seeing the Unseen

*We are always confident, even though we know that as [ ]
bodies we are not at home with the Lord. For we live b[ ]
seeing.* 2 Corinthians 5:6-7

IN WORD

The same apostle who wrote so often of being in Christ and of Christ being in him—
who was convinced that God's power was at work in him, and who even saw Jesus
personally on a road to Damascus—also wrote that when we are in the body, we are
not at home with Jesus. We may envision Paul having a constantly close, almost face-
to-face relationship with Jesus, but even he acknowledged the gap that can only be
filled by faith. The presence of Jesus is real, but so is the distance. In a very physical,
fallen world, God is not as tangible as we want Him to be.

That doesn't mean He won't show Himself in various tangible ways; we see evi-
dence of His work and sense His presence often. But we don't generally *see* Him.
Like seeing the effects of the wind without ever seeing the wind itself, we must know
Jesus by being very observant and piecing together the evidence of His movements.
Whether we like it or not, faith is the norm in the Kingdom. Sight comes later.

Kingdom citizens must become proficient in the art of believing—of seeing with
spiritual eyes, acting on what we see, and insisting on truths that others might consider
far-fetched. We can't afford to be pessimistic or cynical, and we can't lose heart. Others
may rise and fall on the waves of circumstances, but we are anchored on the promises
and purposes of the Kingdom. Regardless of what we see with our eyes, we know at a
deeper level. We become accustomed to living in an unseen world.

IN DEED

That's why Paul can say we are always confident. We know things other people don't
know because we have ways of seeing what can't be seen. We live in the presence of a
Lord who seems to be far, far away but is closer than we can imagine. Whatever it takes,
cultivate Kingdom eyes. Instead of seeing in order to believe, believe in order to see.

ADDITIONAL READING: Mark 11:22-24

Faith is like radar that sees through the fog.
CORRIE TEN BOOM

Treasure Hunt

We have stopped evaluating others from a human point of view. . . . Anyone who belongs to Christ has become a new person. The old life is gone; a new life has begun! 2 Corinthians 5:16-17

IN WORD

Many people saw Jesus as a man. He was certainly an unusual man, but in their eyes, still just a man. They didn't understand the cosmic conflict behind the scenes, the spiritual significance of His work, or the divine source of His words. They regarded Him from a worldly point of view.

That was a mistake. Spiritual eyes see differently, and some people saw clearly enough to recognize Jesus for who He is. Jesus demonstrated this kind of vision by calling Peter a rock long before Peter acted like one, by recognizing Nathanael's sincerity before they even met, and by seeing the potential of a woman with a bad reputation. He saw with spiritual eyes, which rarely agree with the superficial vision we so often apply to each other. He looked into hearts and recognized true identity.

We have to learn to do that too. In the Kingdom, we have to ignore natural perceptions and see the truth of each other's identity. We no longer define people by their past or even by their present. We anticipate their potential in Christ. We no longer consider only the exercise of their natural gifts but also the quality of their faith, through which God can do wonders. We see children as mighty people of faith, the poor as privileged experts in depending on God, the quirky and eccentric as those who are free to follow the Spirit rather than being enslaved by the opinions of human beings, the servant-hearted as great in the Kingdom of God. We don't measure with worldly measurements; we measure with the heart of God.

IN DEED

Cultivate true vision. Hunt for treasures in people rather than looking for flaws. Instead of seeing what someone has done, see instead what God can do in them. Before you were a new creation, you were potentially a new creation. Everyone in the world falls into one of those two categories. Learn to look past the old and see the new.

ADDITIONAL READING: Colossians 3:1-4

Faith is the sight of the inward eye.
ALEXANDER MACLAREN

Royal Ambassadors

He gave us this wonderful message of reconciliation. So we are Christ's
ambassadors; God is making his appeal through us. 2 Corinthians 5:19-20

IN WORD

Our King is on a mission. He isn't content with the current population of His realm.
There are people who were designed to relate to Him who nevertheless are at odds
with Him and standing outside His domain. Many kings would let them go, but not
ours. He's a rescuer at heart. He will pursue the ones who can still respond to Him. He
will gather all He intends to gather.

How does He do that? Through us. The sovereign God could reach them entirely
on His own, but He has decreed another way. He has commissioned His own citizens
to build bridges—even to *be* the bridges—of reconciliation between Him and those
who don't know Him. Why? Perhaps because long ago in a garden, He designed those
in His image to steward His creation. A tempter exploited that privileged position,
but the mandate hasn't changed. Human beings are still the stewards of this planet's
welfare. Whether or not that's the reason, the mission is clear. God's people are His
ambassadors, and He has never offered a plan B. Those who have been reconciled
become the carriers of reconciliation. We make appeals as though God Himself were
working through us. Because He is.

IN DEED

The reconciled are meant to be an everexpanding community because we are called
to be representatives of the rescuing God. Not all of us take on that mission, but the
mission still stands. Paul emphasized that Christ's love compelled him to pursue the
yet-to-be-reconciled in our world, implying that if we've experienced that love for
ourselves and sensed it for others, we'll be compelled to do the same. And he's right;
the more we bask in the love of the Lord, the less we're able to keep it to ourselves.
Kingdom ambassadors are driven by the heart of the King.

ADDITIONAL READING: Ephesians 6:19-20

God is not saving the world; it is done. Our business
is to get men and women to realize it.
OSWALD CHAMBERS

Praying Prophecy

I, Daniel, learned from reading the word of the LORD, as revealed to Jeremiah the prophet, that Jerusalem must lie desolate for seventy years. Daniel 9:2

IN WORD

Daniel, among the exiles in Babylon, read the words of Jeremiah given some seventy years earlier. He could have responded with confidence that God was going to fulfill His promise and just waited. He could have told everyone to pack their bags because the time to return to Jerusalem had come. What did Daniel do instead? He prayed. He didn't assume a unilateral fulfillment of the promise. He understood that God's promises almost always require faith on the part of the recipient before they are accomplished. Daniel knew God wasn't going to deliver until repentance was complete.

So Daniel began to pray intensely, pouring his heart out to God that the promise might be fulfilled. He took the Word literally and begged its completion. Though God's integrity is never in doubt, His promises to human beings are often conditional. The chosen people began with the faith of Abraham, and faith had always determined the difference between blessing and curse. If the promise was to be fulfilled, someone was going to have to believe it.

Daniel stepped up. It weighed on his heart to think of God watching over His Word while the people of God ignored it. He was moved to pray with passion and zeal.

IN DEED

Is that your normal response to God's promises? When God has said He is going to do something, He's prompting His people to look for it, giving them a treasure map and waiting to see who will believe it. Prophecy is more than information to have; it's information to act on.

It is never inappropriate to ask God to do what He has promised to do. It's no coincidence that Simeon and Anna were praying at the Temple for the Messiah when the infant Jesus was brought to that same Temple. And it's no coincidence whenever God pours His Spirit out on the earth according to His Word. What promise do you want to see Him fulfill?

ADDITIONAL READING: 2 Corinthians 1:20

> The purposes of God are His concealed promises;
> the promises, His revealed purposes.
> PHILIP HENRY

Believing Love

O Lord, you are a great and awesome God! You always fulfill your covenant and keep your promises of unfailing love to those who love you and obey your commands. Daniel 9:4

IN WORD

Daniel knew the basis of prayer. Our relationship with God is not based on performance. Obedience is part of it, of course, but this is first and foremost a "covenant of love." God's promises for blessing and His answers to prayer come from the goodness of His heart, the outpouring of love He offers to all who love Him. Obedience is the result of the relationship of love, not its source.

Many people don't understand that. In fact, most theistic religions believe that the favor of God is based primarily on the performance of the people who worship Him. That's human nature, and it can affect the mind-set of Christians as much as anyone. Our tendency is to base relationships on works, not to base works on relationships. But God defies our tendencies. He keeps His covenant of love.

IN DEED

Remember this truth when you are pleading God's promises. It isn't a matter of twisting His arm or finding all the right hoops to jump through. God's will for our lives isn't a jigsaw puzzle that will ultimately frustrate us because we couldn't see the picture clearly enough. His will is a covenant of love, and He is more than willing to fulfill it. He responds to our humble faith, not our impressive spiritual qualifications.

When you realize what God has prophesied and promised for a particular situation in your life, avoid the two extremes. On the one hand, don't sit passively by as though God's promise is fate, sure to happen whether you participate in it or not. On the other hand, don't shift into performance mode in a subtle attempt to bribe God with good behavior or convince Him with persuasive arguments. Simply come to Him in faith, asking Him to do as He has said. The great and awesome God, who keeps His covenant of love, will answer you on that basis alone.

ADDITIONAL READING: Numbers 23:19

The permanence of God's character guarantees
the fulfillment of His promises.
A. W. PINK

Confessing All

We have sinned and are full of wickedness. Daniel 9:15

IN WORD

Daniel was one of the most righteous people of his generation. He had refused to be defiled by Babylonian food, and he had chosen near-certain death in a lions' den over compromise in his worship. If anyone could claim to have had none of the guilt that brought Judah to Babylon, it was Daniel. The nation was by no means in exile because of him.

Even so, Daniel prayed for forgiveness. He knew the corporate nature of sin, that no one is only an individual. The righteousness (or lack thereof) of any person has consequences in the community as a whole, and repentance on the part of a few can speak for the many. Daniel understood that God looks for representatives of a nation or a people. Just as God would later let His Son die on behalf of the world, Daniel let his own repentance plead for the exiles. He mourned the nation's sin because he was part of the nation.

We have a hard time understanding that, as individualistic as Western culture can be. We emphasize individual rights to the point that we hardly see the effects of a few on society as a whole. We have a mind-your-own-business philosophy that inhibits corporate confession and repentance. So when God looks for someone to represent a people, we point to those most responsible.

IN DEED

According to God, we are the ones responsible. We are like society's leaven or the salt of the earth, having both the opportunity and the obligation to live as priests before God. Both our sins and our faith can stand on behalf of others. So when God is looking for repentance, we qualify. Even if we're as righteous as Daniel.

In fact, those who are righteous are more likely to repent for the nation than those who are not. That means that when a church needs to heal, you can repent for those who have injured it. When social sins rip the culture apart, you can confess them and ask for forgiveness. When God looks to a group, represent the group. Pray "we" more often than "I."

ADDITIONAL READING: Joshua 7:1

Plenteous grace with Thee is found . . . let the healing streams abound.
CHARLES WESLEY

Be Merciful

O Sovereign LORD, please stop or we will not survive, for Israel is so small.
Amos 7:5

IN WORD

God looked at the awful condition of sinful humanity and marveled that there was no one to intercede (Isaiah 59:16). That's the Word of the sovereign God, the God who can do anything He wants to do at any time He wants to do it. So why is He looking for someone to intercede? Because He gave humanity dominion over things on earth. For things on earth to be rectified, humanity has to exercise dominion.

That's why God ultimately sent His Son to intercede for us; no human being was righteous enough to represent us to a holy God. But chosen servants before and after the intercession of the Son have been granted the opportunity to perform the same function. The redeemed are a nation of priests performing a service of sacrifice. When God pronounces judgment, we intervene.

That's how He designed it. As people conformed to His image, we can reflect His judgment or His grace. His eye searches out those who embody the same priorities that He does: mercy over justice. The revelation of His righteousness is given for those who will plead the words of Amos. God invites us to invite Him to relent.

IN DEED

How much of your prayer life is directed toward interceding? God has placed us squarely in the gap between His righteousness and the world's unrighteousness. What will we do with our position? Is our heart in conformity with God's?

Make sure that it is. The heart of the Christian is designed to understand God's judgment and give Him a human voice of intercession. His mercy is meant to flow through the priests He has ordained on behalf of the world. In other words, He saved us by grace for a reason.

Let that be your reason for being. Develop a heart of mercy, and plead with God for Him to withhold His judgment. Never forget that He delights in such pleas. They reflect His heart exactly.

ADDITIONAL READING: Isaiah 59:16

> Do not let us fail one another in interest, care, and practical help; but supremely we must not fail one another in prayer.
> MICHAEL BAUGHEN

Be Truthful

Amos is raising a conspiracy against you in the very heart of Israel. The land cannot bear all his words. Amos 7:10, *NIV*

IN WORD

"It's a conspiracy." That's the assessment of a paranoid priest warning a corrupt king of a prophet's declaration of God's plans for Israel. When Amos told the truth, he was considered a troublemaker, a disturber of the national peace, a mudslinger void of constructive criticism. Never mind that his message came directly from the God of Israel; the leaders of Israel didn't like it. They saw it as an attempt to undermine the public order.

That's almost always the criticism when God's people express God's righteousness. "God is a God of love; He wouldn't be so judgmental." "Why can't you be more tolerant? God wants people to get along, to live and let live." "You must be a miserable person to be so critical. The God I know has more compassion than that." Such rebuttals have a lot of truth in them, but it's truth out of balance. And truth out of balance is error.

The truth is that God is loving and compassionate and a promoter of peace. But the truth is also that God is holy and righteous and cannot let sin reign in His Kingdom. Like any loving father, God sometimes rebukes His children, and sometimes the rebuke is stern. The God of love is a God of true love—love based on true foundations and uncompromising in its integrity. True love doesn't let evil flourish.

IN DEED

Every believer who expresses the will of God in a balanced way will draw criticism from those who have an unbalanced concept of God. The idea that God is intolerant of evil is seen as a threat to the public order. We who know God's righteousness are seen as problematic. Citizens of God's Kingdom are troublemakers to this world, while citizens of this world are troublemakers in God's Kingdom. There is nothing wrong with pointing out the difference. Stand firm for truth and be salt and light in your world. The land can—and must—bear the words of warning.

ADDITIONAL READING: Ezekiel 3:17-19

> Men boast of their tolerance who should be ashamed of their indifference.
> WILLIAM HOUGHTON

Be Available

The LORD called me away from my flock and told me, "Go and prophesy to my people in Israel." Amos 7:15

IN WORD

Amos was there in the pasture, minding his own business, when God disrupted his life. "Go and prophesy," God told him. So a man who had spent his career tending sheep and picking figs was now the mouthpiece of the Almighty. Lives can't get disrupted much more drastically than that.

It fits God's pattern, though. A shepherd with a multicolored coat became an Egyptian ruler and sustained God's people during a famine. A shepherd on the back side of the wilderness was called to give Pharaoh a harsh message and set God's people free. A shepherd with six older brothers slew a Philistine giant and was anointed as king. And shepherds minding their own business outside of Bethlehem one night were disrupted with an announcement of the world's most momentous occasion. Why wouldn't the shepherd of Tekoa become a prophet? The divine Shepherd chose one of His own.

God's choosing a shepherd isn't remarkable, given His track record. What is remarkable is a shepherd so available to let his life be disrupted by an overwhelming task. Shepherds don't normally rally a nation around an ominous message. Kings and priests know how to quash such rebels. Only someone who knows God is with him can leave his sheep to call an apostate leadership to task.

IN DEED

God is in the habit of disrupting lives. Those of us who insist on fulfilling our plans are apt to miss Him when He calls. Our Father enjoys directing His children in unexpected ways, hoping they will choose His adventures over their status quo. The call of a Christian is often no less drastic than the call of a fig-picking shepherd-turned-prophet. Listen carefully to God, be available to His call, and don't be surprised when He surprises you.

ADDITIONAL READING: Matthew 4:18-20

> God doesn't call people who are qualified. He calls people who are willing, and then He qualifies them.
> RICHARD PARKER

Be Ambitious

I'm not a professional prophet, and I was never trained to be one. I'm just a shepherd, and I take care of sycamore-fig trees. Amos 7:14

IN WORD

Amos was a shepherd and a farmer. He didn't have a prophet's skill, a rabbi's education, or a politician's influence. He knew the ins and outs of tending sheep and pruning trees, and there's every indication that these comprised the family business. He was not a likely candidate for rebuking a nation.

So why did God choose him? The same reason He chooses anyone. He picks the simple to confound the wise, He selects the weak to display His strength, and He is drawn to the willing to rebuke the stubborn. When God looks for servants, He looks for hearts. Everything else can be supplied later.

That should define your life more than anything else. If God met you at a dinner party, He wouldn't ask what you do for a living or how many people are in your family. He would ask you what moves your heart, what dreams you have, and how committed you are to them. He doesn't define us by the things we do. He defines us by our loves.

We can't know completely all the reasons God chose Amos—how much of His choice was based on the personality and integrity of the shepherd. What we do know is that God is always focused on the things that count. He considers skills and qualifications usable, not indispensable. He isn't limited by our limitations.

IN DEED

Have you let a sense of position or probability limit your labor in God's Kingdom? Don't. If your heart is right, He considers you much more qualified than you think. Don't measure your life by externals. If the visions and dreams He has given you are inspired by Him, you have no reason not to go for them. A heart that is right with Him will always result in a life that is fruitful for Him.

ADDITIONAL READING: Psalm 37:4

The vision must be followed by the venture. It is not enough
to stare up the steps. We must step up the stairs.
VANCE HAVNER

The Heart of a Child

[Jesus] said to them, "Let the children come to me. Don't stop them! For the Kingdom of God belongs to those who are like these children. I tell you the truth, anyone who doesn't receive the Kingdom of God like a child will never enter it." Mark 10:14-15

IN WORD

We know how to complicate things. The human brain is built for analysis, and our emotional wounds and unmet longings exploit that tendency endlessly. We lie awake at night reviewing conversations and circumstances in our minds and imagining as many outcomes as we can think of. We want to understand every aspect of a decision before we make it. We want to plan for every contingency before it happens. We entertain far more scenarios than we could ever possibly experience.

Sometimes we need to just accept the truth that is given to us. We shouldn't abandon all discernment, but when it comes to our relationship with our Father, we have to accept Him with the trust of a child. If we wait to fully understand the Kingdom before we enter it, we will never enter it. We will have to embrace things our minds can't grasp, hold the hand of the One who is leading us without knowing exactly where we are going, and look at His world and His work with a sense of wonder and adventure. That's what children do, isn't it? The Kingdom was made for people who can appreciate it simply.

IN DEED

God isn't opposed to understanding; He urges us to seek it. Wisdom is good. But when Jesus tagged the children as ideal Kingdom citizens, He wasn't downplaying wisdom and understanding. He was downplaying cynicism, skepticism, complacency, and the pride of judging things we know little about. And if we're honest, we have to admit we know little about the Kingdom. It isn't a theological truth to analyze nearly as much as it is a realm to embrace and enter into with gratitude. In other words, our Kingdom life doesn't need to be complicated.

Let go of the need to overanalyze. Live simply. Embrace awe and wonder. Be free to enjoy the Father. That's what the Kingdom is all about.

ADDITIONAL READING: Psalm 8:2

Purity of heart and simplicity are of great force with almighty God.
GREGORY THE GREAT

The Heart of a Servant

Jesus said again, "Dear children, it is very hard to enter the Kingdom of God. In fact, it is easier for a camel to go through the eye of a needle than for a rich person to enter the Kingdom of God!" Mark 10:24-25

IN WORD

If God were opposed to wealth, He would never have given it to Abraham, Isaac, Jacob, Joseph, David, Solomon, and many others He loved. Neither would He have called it a blessing at several points in His Word. It's true that many passages of Scripture decry riches, but they always do so in the context of people who have been seduced by them. In itself, wealth can be an enormous blessing.

So why does Jesus emphasize how difficult it is for a rich person to enter the Kingdom? Because the Kingdom is easily obscured by other agendas, and the agenda of earning money is one of the strongest pulls known to man. The King is our master, and Jesus made it clear that no one can serve two masters. The King isn't opposed to money, but we can't seek Him wholeheartedly if our eyes are full of dollar signs—or status, position, achievements, possessions, or a certain lifestyle. We can work hard and accept the opportunities and provisions given to us. We can even have ambitious financial goals. But we can never place our trust in them, prioritize them above eternal treasures, let them undermine our relationships, or be crushed if they don't work out. We have to seek the Kingdom above all else.

The point is this: Entering the Kingdom is a matter of trust and priorities, and people with money skew these far more easily than others do. The idea that wealth satisfies our souls is a deadly lie. It doesn't. Only the King can do that.

IN DEED

If you build wealth, do it for the Kingdom. Never let it be an end in itself, or even a means to your own happiness. Let it be a tool for funding the Kingdom, enjoying the Kingdom, and bringing others into the Kingdom. Remember that money serves you, you don't serve money. You serve God alone.

ADDITIONAL READING: Matthew 6:24

> The real measure of our wealth is how much we'd be worth if we lost all our money.
> JOHN HENRY JOWETT

The Victory of Hope

Listen to the village musicians gathered at the watering holes. They recount the righteous victories of the LORD and the victories of his villagers in Israel.
Judges 5:11

IN WORD

God's people had been ruthlessly oppressed for twenty years by a Canaanite general with a big army and nine hundred chariots. It was their own fault; they had turned from God and worshiped idols, so they lived in defeat. Year after year, they saw the power of the enemy and were intimidated. They resigned themselves to futility and discouragement.

Deborah didn't. She saw the situation through different eyes. She knew God not only as the Judge who punishes but also as the Warrior who delivers from punishment. She had risen to prominence as a judge of Israel over all other potential candidates because she regularly sat under a tree and listened to God. From His perspective, the odds against Israel weren't overwhelming, and Deborah recognized His timing. So she called the armies of God to exercise faith and boldly declared His plans without regard for how unlikely they seemed. She saw hope when others saw hopelessness. And that hope resulted in victory.

How we see God makes an enormous difference in how we live and what victories we will enjoy. Citizens of the world know how to nurture guilt, shame, futility, condemnation, frustration, and apathy. Kingdom citizens are fueled by hope. We nurture our sense of identity, privilege, and power—not in ourselves but in the King who gave us our citizenship. We know who we are and what He intends for us.

IN DEED

Learn to see life through lenses of hope. Be confident in the King who gave you your identity. Like Deborah, learn to discern His seasons, stir up faith among His people, and declare His victories. He looks at no situation with despair, and we need to learn to see through His eyes. Be willing to lead the way when everyone else is afraid. The Kingdom is a place of relentless optimism because the King always knows victory is coming. We do too.

ADDITIONAL READING: Psalm 33:20-22

> In hope we count on the possibilities of the future and we do not remain imprisoned in the institutions of the past.
> JÜRGEN MOLTMANN

The Strength You Have

The LORD turned to him and said, "Go with the strength you have, and rescue Israel from the Midianites. I am sending you!" Judges 6:14

IN WORD

The angel of God found Gideon hiding from Midianite raiders in a winepress. Needless to say, this was not a position of strength. Gideon even voiced his insecurities, not only about his own strength but about God's: "If the LORD is with us, why has all this happened? . . . Where are all the miracles?" (Judges 6:13). This cowering clansman considered himself, his family, and his tribe the least likely to succeed. And he saw the oppressors as virtually unstoppable.

It's in that context that God called him a mighty hero. God saw the warrior within, a Kingdom nature before Gideon's own people ever even became a kingdom. The clan would try to make him a king, but Gideon wasn't interested in ruling. He was, however, qualified to lead, even when he saw no strength in himself. With God on his side, he had strength enough.

God proved that later, reducing Gideon's army from thirty-two thousand men to three hundred and accomplishing a great victory against an intimidating foe. He takes delight in choosing the weak, foolish, poor people of this world and making them great. He confounds enemies not by overwhelming their strengths but by exposing them as mere facades. He is great at reminding the proud how unfounded their pride is. He displays His strength through those who humbly let Him.

IN DEED

That's why we are to be fearless people—not because we are so strong but because He is. We can embrace weakness because the King we serve uses our lack of power as an opportunity to display His. In the process, we find that while we were cowering in fear, we were simply hiding from the opportunity He wanted to use for His purposes and our good. We didn't know that the strength we already had was enough for us to get up and move in faith. All along, God's perspective was true. A mighty hero really was inside us, waiting to come out and win victories for the Kingdom.

ADDITIONAL READING: 1 Corinthians 1:27-28

The way to grow strong in Christ is to become weak in yourself.
CHARLES SPURGEON

Irrevocable

You will become pregnant and give birth to a son, and his hair must never be cut. For he will be dedicated to God as a Nazirite from birth. He will begin to rescue Israel from the Philistines. Judges 13:5

IN WORD

The holy visitor announced specific plans for the coming child, which included his being set apart under a vow and his role as a deliverer of Israel. So when Samson grew up to violate the vow often and squander the strength he had been given, we could assume that the plan had been forfeited. If he didn't live up to his conditions, God surely wouldn't follow through with the promise, right? God had big plans, and Samson had blown them.

To a degree, that's true. Samson fell tragically short of his potential because of his recklessness. Yet God still made him a deliverer of Israel. The prophecy was fulfilled. Samson began to throw off the yoke of Philistine oppressors. And in his cavalier approach to life, he illustrated a great mystery in the divine-human relationship that we still have not unraveled: how a holy God can work through extremely flawed people to accomplish His good purposes, even when those people violate His words.

Yet this is exactly what God does. When we think we've messed up His plan, He accomplishes it anyway. Looking back, we can see how He accounted for our mistakes even before we made them. He knew the future, including its tragic and regrettable turns. When He makes a promise, He already knows every obstacle that will come against it. And He knows the promise will stand.

IN DEED

We may wonder why God chose Samson as a deliverer in the first place. There had to have been people with better character to choose from. Perhaps He intended for Samson to be an example as well as a deliverer, evidence to future generations that He does not revoke His gifts even when His people fail. He loves faithfulness, but He can work through those who stumble every step of the way. In spite of our flaws, God always finds a way to fulfill His promises.

ADDITIONAL READING: Romans 11:29

God is not defeated by human failure.
WILLIAM J. C. WHITE

The Rescue Mission

He has enabled you to share in the inheritance that belongs to his people, who live in the light. For he has rescued us from the kingdom of darkness and transferred us into the Kingdom of his dear Son. Colossians 1:12-13

IN WORD

Scripture is the story of a rescue mission. Not long after the beginning of the story, a rebellion marred a beautiful creation, enslaved the rebels, and put the world into the hands of an evil impostor ruler. God's rescue mission involved piercing the darkness that shrouded the world and freeing the slaves who had formerly rebelled against Him. The Son of the King invaded the depths of darkness and emerged to the height of glory. It was a brilliant plan that not only stripped the enemy of his victories but re-created the human race into something greater than it was at first.

That's why this was more than a rescue mission. Jesus didn't just deliver us from danger and put us into a place of safety. He opened the doorway into the family so we could share in the inheritance. We have been put in a position of honor and privilege, free from our self-imposed captivity, healed of our self-inflicted wounds, and cleansed of our self-promoting sins. Colossians 1 tells that story, urging us to believe it and enter into its promise. If we do, we are transferred from death and darkness to life and light. And that makes a world of difference.

IN DEED

It's possible to read this story with such familiarity that it no longer excites us, and many people do. But whatever it takes, try to read it with fresh eyes as though you've never known it before. Notice the trajectory of the Rescuer—from extreme height to extreme depth to extreme height again—and how your own trajectory is folded into His by faith. When that really sinks in, nothing in life is ever the same again. Your inheritance includes the fullness of God's presence and all the blessings of His Kingdom. And that is worth celebrating forever.

ADDITIONAL READING: Ephesians 1:3-11

O for a thousand tongues to sing my great Redeemer's praise,
the glories of my God and King, the triumphs of His grace!
CHARLES WESLEY

The Disarming

In this way, he disarmed the spiritual rulers and authorities. Colossians 2:15

IN WORD

You were dead. Now you're alive. That's the simplified version of your role in the story of God's rescue mission to recover the lost captives of His world, but on His end it was a lot more complicated than that. We see the suffering Jesus endured; that's plainly explained to us in the Gospels. But behind the scenes was a raging spiritual battle that pitted the enemy against the Son, one trying to exterminate or corrupt the other until the end, when it looked like the rescue had failed. As we know, it didn't fail at all; the end wasn't the end. And somewhere mixed in with the Cross and Resurrection was a humiliating defeat for the enemy and his forces.

We're told that Jesus disarmed the spiritual rulers and authorities. We didn't see that battle; we had to be informed of it by the revelation of the Spirit. We sometimes even wonder if we're experiencing it because it isn't always visible in our lives. But here's what we do know: If Jesus disarmed the rulers by canceling all our offenses and debts against God, then they must have been armed with those same offenses and debts. That was their ammunition against us. We were being held under the legal penalty for rebellion against God, a curse of separation from Him—and from life. And spiritual forces opposed to Him were making sure the penalty was enforced.

In removing the penalty by paying for our offenses and debts, Jesus didn't just provide for our forgiveness. He provided for our release from the eternal debtor's prison. Rather than spending forever in the soul's darkest dungeons, we've been placed in a garden of life and a city of God, fully enjoying the experience.

IN DEED

Don't squander that release by paying any more visits to the soul's darkest dungeons. Refuse to live under the pressure that has legally been removed. Repudiate all guilt and shame and choose to thrive in the light. Those who have been set free are free indeed.

ADDITIONAL READING: John 8:34-36

Jesus Christ is the key which unlocks the door of the
prison cell of our own making and sets us free to live
in the wide world of God's love and purpose.
KENNETH PILLAR

The Heart of a King

Don't judge by his appearance or height, for I have rejected him. The
Lord doesn't see things the way you see them. People judge by outward
appearance, but the Lord looks at the heart. 1 Samuel 16:7

IN WORD

Israel's first king started well but ended up completely self-absorbed. He apparently thought God was building his kingdom rather than calling him to build God's Kingdom. So after a string of revealing episodes in which Saul acted rashly, selfishly, and stubbornly, God spoke through Samuel to inform Saul that his reign would be stripped from him and given to someone with a different heart.

That speaks volumes about the nature of God's Kingdom. As the nation of Israel morphed from a collection of tribes to a unified monarchy, God gave them an illustration of what a king shouldn't be before giving them a picture of what a king should be. Saul was head and shoulders above the rest, and he was even influenced by the Spirit to prophesy and lead on more than one occasion. But the overall direction of his life served his own purposes, and he became paranoid, obsessive, and manic in trying to hang on to them. In Saul's place, God gave His people a shepherd with a heart like His own—fiercely protective, passionate for worship, zealous for justice, drawn to the troubled and hurting, creative and artistic, and inspired with divine insights. And when he failed, he was able to repent without his ego getting in the way. He wore the heart of a king on his sleeve.

IN DEED

We see an even better picture of kingship in Jesus, the exact image of the Father. But before the ultimate King was revealed, God wanted His people to know what kind of Kingdom He would establish and more importantly, what kind of king should sit on its throne. Why? Because the heart of the king will be increasingly reflected in the hearts of the people who serve him. God is looking for hearts that overflow with passion, purpose, creativity, inspiration, compassion, justice, and zeal. Just like His.

ADDITIONAL READING: Psalm 78:70-72

To be like Christ. That is our goal, plain and simple.
CHARLES SWINDOLL

The Kingdom Within

God is working in you, giving you the desire and the power to do what pleases him. Philippians 2:13

IN WORD

You have desires. We all do. In an effort to follow Jesus well, you may have laid them down, perhaps even crucified them. Many Christians do. But what if those desires were placed in you by God? What if your will overlaps with His will more than you thought? What if the plans and purposes you thought were yours were actually those of the Spirit at work within you? Then crucifying everything inside is not only paralyzing to your Kingdom mission, it's contrary to God's plans for your life.

It's right and good to submit everything to God; He is Lord, after all, and to follow Him means we submit to His leadership. But having done that, we need to be willing to let Him cultivate desires within us and satisfy them. It's unreasonable to expect that whatever His will is, it will inevitably be contrary to ours and a hardship to accomplish. Believe it or not, He might actually want us to have a sense of fulfillment. At some point, we have to trust the Spirit within us.

One of the marvels of God's Kingdom is that it isn't imposed from the outside; it's cultivated from the inside. Most kingdoms begin outwardly and try to work their way into people's hearts. God's Kingdom takes root in the inner core of our being and moves outward, eventually into every relationship and every corner of our world. Kingdom goals, dreams, desires, and plans will therefore begin in the hearts of God's people. Seeds planted there, if not smothered, will grow and bear fruit in the lives of others.

IN DEED

Trust the Spirit within you. Begin to cultivate the dreams and desires that God has put in your heart. Vet them with Him, of course, and give Him full access to rearrange them, redirect them, or whatever else He wants to do. But don't crucify the Spirit who is at work in you, both to will and to work for God's good pleasure. Give Him freedom to thrive, and enjoy the process. The good purposes of the Kingdom—and your own desires—may manifest in ways you never expected.

ADDITIONAL READING: John 15:7

> When the dream in our heart is one that God has planted there . . .
> all of the spiritual resources of the universe are released to help us.
> CATHERINE MARSHALL

Already Qualified

By his divine power, God has given us everything we need for living a godly life. We have received all of this by coming to know him, the one who called us to himself by means of his marvelous glory and excellence. 2 Peter 1:3

IN WORD

Jesus promised His followers that they would be able to do His works. He gave them extravagant promises of answered prayers and the manifest presence of God. He gave them Kingdom power and sent them out to demonstrate it. He called them higher, deeper, and further into the Kingdom mission.

So why aren't many of us experiencing the fullness of these promises? Because we think we aren't qualified for them. Perhaps we haven't fully grown in the spiritual disciplines we think we need. We aren't prayer "masters" or spiritual clones of the apostle Paul. We don't live in the right era, or we don't work in the same culture, or . . . well, the rationalizing could go on forever. But the bottom line is that Jesus promised, and the New Testament writers affirmed His words. And they never indicated, not even once, that we aren't qualified for the full inheritance of the Kingdom.

In fact, Peter plainly tells us in his second letter that we are already qualified. God's divine power has given us everything we need. If we earned spiritual status by our disciplines and efforts, then perhaps we might be justified in having low expectations. But discipleship isn't primarily about us. It's about Him. And He's enough.

IN DEED

Scripture is clear. We aren't partial saints, moderately holy, mostly justified, or somewhat cleansed of our sins. The work of Jesus is complete. Salvation is all or nothing. Those who believe have received all. We certainly have room to grow in our understanding, but in God's eyes we are already as pure and righteous as we will ever be. We are qualified for everything He offers, if we can receive it by faith. That makes any shortcoming a heart-and-mind issue, not a spiritual achievement issue. If we believe—and act on our belief—we can experience the fullness of God's promises. His divine power has already been given. We can begin walking in it whenever we take bold steps of faith.

ADDITIONAL READING: Ephesians 2:6-10

Salvation means the incoming into human nature of
the great characteristics that belong to God.
OSWALD CHAMBERS

Fully Secure

He has given us great and precious promises. These are the promises that enable you to share his divine nature and escape the world's corruption caused by human desires. 2 Peter 1:4

IN WORD

In spite of God's lavish assurances, many of us are desperately insecure in our relationship with Him. Never mind that He has said we can participate in the divine nature. We don't *feel* very divine, and our old nature seems to dominate. So we accept that perspective, try to develop our character, fail often, and lament our shortcomings as if the divine nature were impossibly removed from our grasp.

Check yourself on this. Do you spend more time regretting your mistakes than thinking about opportunities? Is your discipleship more about getting over sin or advancing the Kingdom? Do you approach God asking what you need to stop doing rather than what you need to start doing in order to conform to His nature? If you're constantly dwelling on your faults, you probably haven't fully accepted His forgiveness. More than that, you likely haven't noticed the opportunities He offers. That's insecurity.

God isn't looking at what you've done or haven't done. He's looking at the doors that are open in front of you, waiting for you to walk through them. See His Kingdom, even the part about conforming to His nature, as an adventure rather than a burden, and the obstacles that drag you down will grow smaller and smaller. You won't have time to focus on them. The precious promises of God will keep drawing you forward into ever-increasing glory.

IN DEED

Shift your thinking about God and His Kingdom from "have to" to "get to." Don't think about the sin that weighs you down. Think about the divine nature you get to enter into. Don't think about what you have to live up to. Think about what you get to receive. Perspective makes all the difference when it's anchored in your true identity in God.

ADDITIONAL READING: 2 Corinthians 1:20

> All our salvation consists in the manifestation of the nature, life, and Spirit of Jesus in our inward new man.
> WILLIAM LAW

Right Direction

The more you grow like this, the more productive and useful you will be in your knowledge of our Lord Jesus Christ. 2 Peter 1:8

IN WORD

Many Christians are stuck in spiritual lethargy, unable to focus on anything other than their own progress or, more specifically, lack of it. They know the standard is high and are acutely aware of falling short of it. But Scripture gives us numerous encouragements, many of them sweepingly liberating. For example, there is no condemnation for those who are in Christ (Romans 8:1)—though many of us condemn ourselves easily. We are urged, even commanded, to consider ourselves dead to sin and alive to God (Romans 6:11). All that remains is for us to grow in the nature of God that has been imparted to us.

The question for each of us then becomes not "What am I lacking?" but "Where am I growing?" We no longer focus on needing more patience, compassion, or other such virtue; we rejoice in whatever of that virtue we already have. A profound principle of human nature is that whatever we focus on tends to grow larger in our own minds, as well as in our experience. When we focus on meeting a standard, the standard oppresses us and reminds us of how often we miss it. But when we focus on which direction we're moving in, that direction accelerates.

Therefore, Peter rightly turns our attention to the qualities we possess, not the ones we lack. And he encourages us only to make sure they are increasing, not to be anxious about whether they have fully arrived. As is often said, long journeys begin with a single step. If we keep moving in the right direction, we get to where we're going. And that's something anyone can do.

IN DEED

Focus on your direction. Look at how you've grown, not whether you've measured up. Give yourself plenty of grace to build on what is there rather than trying to make up for what isn't. A wrong perspective can set us up for failure, but God never will. Grow in the nature He has given you.

ADDITIONAL READING: Philippians 1:4-6

> Looking at the wound of sin will never save anyone.
> What you must do is look at the remedy.
> D. L. MOODY

The True You

Work hard to prove that you really are among those God has called and chosen. 2 Peter 1:10

IN WORD

On the surface, Peter's instruction might create a lot of insecurity in us. Isn't our calling already certain? Is God thinking about "unchoosing" us? Doesn't this verse encourage efforts to earn something rather than simply resting in grace? It could easily stir up our anxiety about whether we really belong in the Kingdom.

But Peter's instruction isn't about earning something we don't have yet. It's about demonstrating something we already do have. The original language simply encourages us to be eager to show evidence of who we really are in Christ. Those qualities Peter listed a few verses earlier are not demands imposed upon us. They are an unveiling of our core identity as new creatures in Christ. We don't have to get them; we only need to uncover them. They are already there. This is a description of who we were designed to be.

In that sense, this verse doesn't create insecurity. It does the opposite. It assures us that our calling is validated simply by our response to it—not by our perfection or inherent goodness, but by our acceptance of it. It unveils the Jesus who is already within us, the Spirit from which we were born when we believed. The fact that we can have the qualities Peter has listed is great confirmation that we are God's children. His nature is within us. We are free to display it whenever and wherever we please.

IN DEED

Any time Scripture instructs you to do or be something, don't look at it as a command to be something you're not. Look at it as an invitation to be who you really are. The Spirit within you has already equipped you with everything you need—today's passage has assured us of that—and it only needs to be revealed. When it is, you confirm your true calling and chosenness. You step forward as a Kingdom citizen and a child of God, the very evidence the world has been looking for (Romans 8:19). You become a reflection of the King who chose you as His own—just as He has always intended.

ADDITIONAL READING: 1 Thessalonians 1:2-7

> Spiritual growth consists most in the growth of the root, which is out of sight.
> MATTHEW HENRY

Great Exploits

The people who know their God shall be strong, and carry out great exploits.
Daniel 11:32, *NKJV*

IN WORD

Daniel's prophecy tells of the shifting of nations and rulers, and of one particular ruler who would oppress and abuse God's people and violate their sacred places. Many would fall victim to this oppressor, but those who know their God will rise above him. The statement is translated various ways, but its implications are clear. In the clash between kingdoms, the people who know the heart of their King stand against their enemies, are strong, take action, and carry out great exploits. They will do damage to the kingdom of darkness.

That's our calling, and it's a daunting one. Are we really able to plunder the lords of darkness? Are humble creatures like us really destined to venture into ominous kingdoms and win great victories? Apparently so, and it isn't because we have superior strategies, overwhelming strength, or devastating weapons—at least not in ourselves. Our great exploits come because we know our God. That's it. That's where our strategies, strength, and weapons come from. He gives us everything we need to stand firm, take action, and plunder the enemy that everyone else flees from.

The problem is that so few believers know this that we tend to remain in a state of defeat or frustration. We resign ourselves to the status quo, not realizing that God has called and equipped us to overturn the status quo. As ambassadors, representatives, and mobile outposts of His Kingdom, we are meant to be resisters against evil and influencers for good. And to the degree we know Him, we can.

IN DEED

That's the key: knowing God. Not knowing about Him, not merely understanding His truths, not simply practicing His principles, but *knowing Him.* The closer we draw in intimate communion, the more He imparts His solutions, strategies, character, and purposes to us. We may not even be conscious of it, but it happens. When opposing circumstances arise, we rise up. And our great exploits are celebrated in heaven.

ADDITIONAL READING: Ephesians 6:10-18

Never yield to force; never yield to the apparently overwhelming might of the enemy.
WINSTON CHURCHILL

Waking Up

I keep asking that the God of our Lord Jesus Christ, the glorious Father, may give you the Spirit of wisdom and revelation, so that you may know him better.
Ephesians 1:17, *NIV*

IN WORD

In the beginning, as God breathed life into dust, and the form of dust opened his eyes and saw his Creator, humanity had an unbroken connection with the Kingdom realm. We can reasonably speculate that Adam saw God, heard Him clearly, even walked with Him tangibly in the cool of the day. There was presumably no veil of separation between the Creator and those made in His image. Adam didn't need to pray for the Kingdom to come on earth because earth was fully part of the Kingdom. The spiritual realm was just as real to him as the natural realm.

But ever since sin entered in, we have been born blind and deaf. We don't see God unless He chooses to show Himself in unusual and unexpected ways. We don't normally see angels, though some have at times. We don't hear God's voice nearly as clearly as we want to—usually only with deliberate focus and prayer. Our blindness and deafness keeps the realm of heaven "behind the veil" to natural eyes and ears.

The gospel changes that. Not radically or suddenly, necessarily, though for Paul it certainly did. The Kingdom promise is that we will see and hear again in this age, whether immediately or as we grow. Jesus assured His followers we would hear His voice. We can learn to see with new eyes. The Spirit of wisdom and revelation is available to us so we may know Him better. We are awakening to another realm.

IN DEED

Learn to see beyond your natural vision and listen with ears to hear. Pray with Paul—daily, even hourly—that the Father would give you the Spirit of wisdom and revelation, that the eyes of your heart would be enlightened. Let yourself be stirred by the echoes of heaven. You'll have to let go of some assumptions to do so, but the rewards are worth it. Don't try to figure out how; just ask. Persistently. And let "real" be redefined for you however He chooses.

ADDITIONAL READING: Colossians 1:9-10

This truly is the vision of God . . . one must always, by looking
at what he can see, rekindle his desire to see more.
GREGORY OF NYSSA

Hope

I pray that the eyes of your heart may be enlightened in order that you may know the hope to which he has called you. Ephesians 1:18, *NIV*

IN WORD

Out of faith, hope, and love—Paul's three significant virtues in his famous chapter on love—we generally give a lot of emphasis to faith and love, but much less to hope. Why? Perhaps because of what the English language has done to hope. It can imply a casual wish, an unrealistic fantasy, or a desperate longing. But the biblical word is much more certain; it's confident expectation of what hasn't happened yet but will. And it's always looking for God's goodness.

Many Christians wish for God's goodness but don't really expect to see it in this age. They interpret difficult circumstances as evidence that God is holding out on them, letting them down, or punishing them. They see the world through disappointment, bitterness, or cynicism. They know God is good; they just don't experience Him that way. At least not yet.

Kingdom citizens are called to be relentless hopers. We are to expect goodness in every aspect of our lives, even when life seems on the surface to be taking a negative turn. We don't look on the surface; we look deeper and acknowledge that even when we don't understand, God is good. We see Him and others through lenses of hope, fully confident that the end of the story will thrill us and fulfill us. Instead of seeing the junk in other people, we see the treasures, no matter how hidden they are. Instead of reading the headlines with fear and anxiety, we read them as opportunities for God to intervene in this world. In other words, we read between the lines of life to discern the God we know to be faithful and true.

IN DEED

Insist on hope. You may have to retrain your brain to think in different patterns, and you may need to tell your heart to handle disappointment differently than you ever have. Even so, choose hope. Expect the goodness of God in the land of the living. Know the certainty of your calling and His delight in you. And live as one whose hope can never be shaken.

ADDITIONAL READING: Psalm 27:13-14

Everything that is done in the world is done by hope.
MARTIN LUTHER

Inheritance

I pray that the eyes of your heart may be enlightened in order that you may know . . . the riches of his glorious inheritance in his holy people.
Ephesians 1:18, *NIV*

IN WORD

Paul has prayed that the eyes of our hearts would be enlightened, that we would be flooded with light in order to see all that God has freely given us in Christ. Only with the eyes of the Spirit can we see the hope of our calling, and only with those eyes can we see the riches of our inheritance. That's a marvelous, extravagant promise, and we rejoice that it's true. But if you ask Christians what their inheritance is, most would not have a very clear answer. We know we want it. We just don't know what it entails.

The bottom line is that Kingdom citizens inherit the Kingdom. Jesus used this phrase often, as did Paul. Peter referred to our inheritance too. It's imperishable, immortal, and available only to those who have been born of the King. It's characterized by a wealth of grace and freedom of knowing God as Father. It's eternal life, but it's more than that; it's the *glory* of that life. As Paul says clearly in Romans 8:17, we are coheirs with Christ. In other words, whatever Jesus inherits (which is everything), we inherit with Him.

Why do we need to know that? Because too many of us live with a sense of defeat. Because a common perception of heaven is that it involves clouds, harps, wings, and a good bit of boredom. Because we need to understand inheritance now in order to live with the outlook and authority heirs are allowed to have. If we understand our inheritance, everything changes. We live as those who know who they are.

IN DEED

Spend some time meditating on what it means to inherit the Kingdom. Think about its present implications as well as its future fulfillment. Learn to live as a child of the King and a reflection of His glory. How you envision your riches in Christ has everything to do with the attitudes, actions, and vision you live with now. Ask that the eyes of your heart, the floodlights of your inner being, would enable you to see the truth of who you really are in Him.

ADDITIONAL READING: Romans 8:17

An inheritance is not only kept for us, but we are kept for it.
RICHARD SIBBES

Power

I pray that the eyes of your heart may be enlightened in order that you may know . . . his incomparably great power for us who believe.
Ephesians 1:18-19, NIV

IN WORD

Ephesus was a city steeped in the magical arts. People from all over the region came to worship at shrines and buy tokens of power such as amulets and spells. So when Paul referred to supernatural wisdom and power, he was speaking their language. But what he prayed was not for an increase in the power they wanted; it was for another kind of power altogether. They were worshiping inferior gods and goddesses. He directed them to the true source.

We have access to that true source too. Many people feel powerless; they resign themselves to fate, or to some Christian version of fate. It isn't that they don't believe God can act on their behalf; they just don't believe He will. But Scripture assures us again and again that God's power is at work in us, through us, and for us. Later in Ephesians, Paul tells us that God can do beyond our imagination by the power that is already working within us (Ephesians 3:20). But here he narrows the scope: God's incomparably great power is for those of us *who believe.*

Does that mean everyone who believes the gospel or those who actively have faith in God's practical promises for everyday life? Regardless, the condition is clear. Those who believe are the ones who receive. Those who don't . . . well, God may act on their behalf because after all, He's full of mercy. But there are some things He does only in response to faith. As Jesus told some blind men, God will do for us according to our faith (Matthew 9:29). God's power is strongest among those who believe it.

IN DEED

That's why our hearts need to be flooded with light and vision into another realm. The more we see God's goodness and power, the more we believe He will act on our behalf. Our vision and our faith are integrally linked. We hardly believe what we can't envision Him doing. But He responds in power to those who believe. Open your eyes to His good intentions, and watch Him powerfully accomplish them all.

ADDITIONAL READING: Matthew 9:27-29

Belief is a truth held in the mind. Faith is a fire in the heart.
JOSEPH FORT NEWTON

Lavish Love

See how very much our Father loves us, for he calls us his children, and that is what we are! 1 John 3:1

IN WORD

God loves us. We know that, don't we? We sing about it, tell each other about it, and even quote well-known verses about how He is love and how He so loved the world that He gave His only Son. The love of God is foundational to our faith because it explains why Jesus died for us and motivates us to demonstrate His love to those around us. The two greatest commandments are about loving God and loving others. Clearly, we are saturated in the love of God—aren't we?

Truth is, we're more convinced of God's love for others than for ourselves. We can say "God loves you" to any hurting, broken person, but when we're hurting and broken, we wonder why we feel so abandoned by Him. Many hear an internal voice that says, "Yes, but . . ." after every declaration of God's love. "Yes, but He has to. That's His job description. God loves everyone." Or "Yes, He may love me, but I don't think He likes me very much." As much as we declare God's love, most of us are insecure in it anyway.

Insecurity with God shows up in a lot of ways. Perhaps we don't want to bother Him with "the small things." Or maybe we think our desires don't matter to Him. Maybe we ask for a hundred confirmations when we think we might possibly have heard His voice—because we just can't believe He might be speaking to us. Whatever the manifestation, the insecurity is real. And we have to learn to get over it.

IN DEED

Sensing God's love—fully accepting it, breathing it, swimming in it—is foundational to God's Kingdom. Why? Because it's the truest expression of His nature. He lavishes love on those who come to Him. His children are precious to Him. If we live as Kingdom citizens, royal heirs, children of the Most High, we have to live not from a place of fear or insecurity but from full confidence of His delight in us. You aren't worthy of it, you say? Of course you aren't. No one is. That's the gospel. He loves anyway. Accept that, and your faith will swell. And that changes everything.

ADDITIONAL READING: 1 John 4:18

> We are never nearer to Christ than when we find ourselves
> lost in a holy amazement at His unspeakable love.
> JOHN OWEN

The Watchman

"I am watching to see that my word is fulfilled." Jeremiah 1:12, *NIV*

IN WORD

God's Word is full of promises and predictions. Many of them, like the words of judgment found in Jeremiah, are painful to think about. The others, though—the promises we cling to in desperate hours, the assurances and comforts of the character of God—sometimes seem like our only source of life.

That's the pose of every Christian who hasn't given up in the trials of life. We have our disappointments—broken relationships, illness and pain, shattered dreams, and far-too-distant hopes—but we trust in our God as a Restorer, Redeemer, and Healer. We sometimes waver between a crushed spirit and a victorious life, and we look for evidence of the latter. We watch eagerly, zealously, achingly, and longingly for God to fulfill His Word to us.

We aren't the only ones. God, too, watches to see that His Word is fulfilled. Did you think you were the only one with a stake in His promises? No, He's even more zealous about them than you are. He's a Father of love and integrity who is absolutely determined not to lose face with His children. He may not meet us according to our expectations or timing, but He will always meet us according to His Word. The God who set us apart, who called us to do specific tasks and exploits in His Kingdom, backs us with His promise. And nothing in all of creation can put Him in a position of having to break it.

IN DEED

Much of the Christian life involves pleading God's promises. Yes, we have to embrace the discipline and judgments found in His Word as well, but those seem to come to us quite naturally anyway. Those who know their sin need no convincing about the righteousness of God. But human nature finds it hard to trust Him for the extraordinarily extravagant blessings He's offered, and we have to remind ourselves of them often. Sometimes we feel as if we need to remind Him, too. Remember, in those times, that He remembers His promises better than we do. And He is watching—zealously watching—to make sure they are fulfilled.

ADDITIONAL READING: Psalm 130:5-6

The promises of God are just as good as ready money any day.
BILLY BRAY

Live the Message

Get up and prepare for action. Go out and tell them everything I tell you to say.
Jeremiah 1:17

IN WORD

You have a message, and you are constantly delivering it. You may not even know what it is. It may be a message of redemption or of guilt, of confidence or of insecurity, of faith or of doubt. But one way or another, your life is an embodied message of whatever you believe to be true.

That's frightening, isn't it? We can handle the thought of delivering a message when God tells us to, but the thought that we are always implicitly living a message means we may have preached the anti-gospel many times. Every time we sowed seeds of discord, every time we got comfortable with sin, every time we said something that minimized God's goodness or exaggerated our own, we gave a false message. We might think we've never presumed to speak for God, but as creatures made in His image, we have. We may have spoken truth, or we may have spoken lies, but we have spoken. Wearing the name of "Christian," we have made some kind of impression—positive or negative, sometimes both—on this world.

God's words to Jeremiah are words to all of us. "Get up and prepare for action. Go out and tell them everything I tell you to say." It isn't that we can be quiet until God tells us to say something. We're already saying something. And God wants us to live the message He gives, not the messages we hear from ourselves or others. He wants us to be incarnations of truth.

IN DEED

Sounds intimidating, doesn't it? It really isn't. That thought may give us lots of regrets about the past, but when we realize the opportunity before us—not one day, when God picks us out of a crowd and gives us a special assignment, but right now on this very day—we can live with purpose. We already have a message to deliver. We can stand up wherever we are in our world and be authentic human beings—not perfect, of course, but Kingdom citizens who are redeemed, restored, and remade in the image of God.

ADDITIONAL READING: Ephesians 5:1-2

> Our task as laymen is to live our personal communion with
> Christ with such intensity as to make it contagious.
> PAUL TOURNIER

Open Your Ears

Stand up, son of man," said the voice. "I want to speak with you." Ezekiel 2:1

IN WORD

Ezekiel fell facedown when he saw the glory of the Lord by the river Kebar. That's an appropriate and seemingly unavoidable reaction to the holy Presence. But whenever someone encounters God, it seems he is told to get up and listen (Daniel 10:11; Revelation 1:17). Apparently, God prepares His servants with humility and then speaks to them with clarity. He requires their attention before He communicates.

Many Christians don't realize that. We often assume that if God wants to speak to us, He knows our number. So we live life "normally," thinking that hearing the voice of God is an uncommon phenomenon and only a few people with special assignments are likely to hear it. We consider clear direction as the exception rather than the rule.

Perhaps God's words to Ezekiel are a clue to the contrary. Perhaps we don't hear God's voice as often as we'd like because we aren't ready to hear it. It's possible, in fact, to read our Bible, pray, and even ask God to guide us without ever really expecting Him to—or trusting that we've actually heard Him. Or maybe we listen for His voice as one opinion among many, open to obeying it if we like how it sounds and ignoring it if we don't. The result is that we probably hear God often without actually hearing Him, second-guessing every divine communication as a figment of our imagination or the product of psychological processes. Maybe we don't know we hear Him because we haven't gotten up from humble reverence and stood with open ears.

IN DEED

Develop a lifestyle of hearing. Spend time worshiping in His presence and then stand with expectancy. God always communicates with those who listen on His terms with a mind toward obedience. The person who thinks God might speak will probably not hear Him. Those who know that He will speak can trust what they hear.

ADDITIONAL READING: Jeremiah 33:3

> In one short hour, you can learn more from Him than you could learn from a man in a thousand years.
> JOHANN TAULER

Be His Voice

At least they will know they have had a prophet among them. Ezekiel 2:5

IN WORD

God is grieved when His people refuse His voice. He says often that He takes rebellion personally, as a husband would be offended by the adultery of his wife. When people choose to part ways with their Creator, God laments the loss of relationship and the blessings He would have given to anyone close to His heart.

But even more than grieving those who refuse His voice, God grieves those who are so far out of touch with Him that they can't even acknowledge that He has spoken. That was the case of rebellious Israel, and it is the case with secular culture today. While God speaks through His creation, His Word, His people, His miracles, and more, people remain oblivious to His voice, many wondering if He even exists. So when God intervenes to judge or redeem a lost people, He wants to make one thing clear: He has spoken.

Whether they listen or not, God says, they at least need to know that a prophet has been among them. The world needs to know that He has spoken so they can make a choice whether to run into His embrace or coldly slap His face. But they can't make the choice unless they hear. Hearing is paramount.

IN DEED

If the need to be heard was heavy on God's heart in exiled Judah, it is certainly heavy on His heart now. That's why Jesus told His disciples to go into all the world under His authority and preach the gospel. In a society that wonders if God even exists (or if He's relevant), there needs to be some kind of evidence among the people who are called by His name. In words, in deeds, and in lifestyle, the church is to be the prophet of God. We are to embody mercy and grace, and we are to be supernaturally endowed with His holy character. We are to live in a way that is unexplainable to a watching world, so that before final judgment comes, they will know that a prophet—the voice of a seeking, redeeming God—has been among them.

ADDITIONAL READING: Romans 10:14-15

According to the New Testament, God wills that the church be a people who show what God is like.
STANLEY GRENZ

Eat Your Words

Son of man, let all my words sink deep into your own heart first. Listen to them carefully for yourself. Ezekiel 3:10

IN WORD

A biblical prophet is more than an oracle giver. Many religions have "seers," people who can discern a message from a supernatural source and tell it to someone else. But when God calls a person, He usually gives that person more than an oracle. He makes him wear the message, intertwining the prophetic word and the prophet himself.

Such was the case with Ezekiel. Throughout his prophecy, we read of Ezekiel performing bizarre, visual illustrations of God's word to the captives. In the story of his call, he is told to eat the scroll of God as a visual demonstration that the Almighty's words would dwell within him. Ezekiel's name means "God strengthens." Truly the message and the messenger were one and the same.

That has always been God's way. Abraham didn't have a message about faith, he was a man of faith. David didn't just write about worship, he was a worshiper. Elijah didn't just say "the Lord is God," he lived that message and even bore the message as his name. And Jesus, as we know, isn't just a message about salvation; He is salvation. With God's people, message and messenger are fully united.

IN DEED

Can you say that about your life? Is your message consistent with who you are as a messenger? Does the deep work that God has done in your heart show up in who you are outwardly?

God told Ezekiel to "listen carefully and take to heart" the words given to him to speak to the exiles (NIV). They weren't simply to be repeated, they were to be lived. And perhaps more than any other prophet, Ezekiel lived his message. We have no hint that he was lukewarm about anything he said; in fact, just the opposite. He suffered enormous ridicule and objection as a representative of God. Why? Because a representative of God is more than a speaker. He embodies the Word itself.

ADDITIONAL READING: Revelation 10:8-11

We are the Bibles the world is reading.
BILLY GRAHAM

Nothing, but Everything

Jesus explained, "I tell you the truth, the Son can do nothing by himself."
John 5:19

IN WORD

Jesus had to know His assertion would be controversial. Many of the Jewish leaders believed that this is an age of God's rest, and they had solid scriptural evidence for their belief. In the Ten Commandments themselves, God said the Sabbath was patterned after His own work. First He created, then He rested (Exodus 20:11). So when Jesus said in John 5:17 that the Father is always at His work, and therefore so is the Son, they became agitated. Not only was He contradicting their belief about God's rest, He was calling God His Father and thereby elevating Himself to divinity.

But Jesus made it clear—to them and to us—that He was among us not as a man with divine advantages, but simply as a man. He is the example of what a human being can be and do when rightly related to God and in tune with His purposes and power. Whatever works Jesus could do, so could His followers. When He said the Son could do nothing by Himself, He was right. A human being can only do the works of God if empowered by God.

We don't normally think that way. We assume that Jesus was exercising divine attributes as an exception to the human race, not as its example. He could resist temptation, heal people, and speak with God's wisdom because He was the Son of God. Obviously we can't be like Him, right? But Jesus assured His followers they would be able to continue in His work by the Spirit's power (Matthew 10:8; John 14:12; Acts 1:8). The citizens of the Kingdom are stewards of the authority of the King.

IN DEED

Don't fall for the "I'm only human" lie. There's no "only" about it. If Jesus was "only human," that should be our highest goal. Like Him, we can listen for the Father's voice, watch what He is doing, and step into it with confidence that His power will accompany us there. Yes, we have a lot of learning to do, but He nevertheless calls us into a supernatural lifestyle. We can do nothing by ourselves. But with Him, nothing is impossible.

ADDITIONAL READING: Philippians 2:5-8

> The miracles of Jesus were the ordinary works of His Father,
> wrought small and swift that we might take them in.
> GEORGE MACDONALD

Mutual Honor

Anyone who does not honor the Son is certainly not honoring the Father who sent him. John 5:23

IN WORD

The Father and Son are so united that to honor one is to honor the other, and to dishonor one is to dishonor the other. But there's a corollary to this truth: Believers in the Son are so united with Him that to honor them is to honor the Son, and to dishonor them is to dishonor the Son. That means that even those believers who rub us the wrong way, even those who offend us and perhaps sin against us, are still heirs of glory and must be honored as children of God. If we are like our Master, the way others treat us may be an indication of their attitude toward Jesus. Likewise, the way we treat others among His followers may be an indication of ours.

Jesus said as much in saying that whoever hates us or persecutes us is really demonstrating their beliefs about the Son. Because a servant is not greater than his master, those who hate the Master will hate His followers, too. That should encourage us when we face persecution, but it should be a profoundly sobering warning about our attitudes toward others. Kingdom citizens are, in one way or another, a reflection of the King—and sometimes a reflection we don't particularly approve of. Perhaps their familiarity with Him offends our sense of awe, or vice versa. Or maybe we look down on their high standards as legalism, while they look on our freedom as license—or vice versa. Whatever the case, some people reflect some aspects of God that are foreign to us, and we reflect some aspects that are foreign to others. And Jesus would urge us to honor anyone who bears His name.

IN DEED

Does that mean dispensing with all discernment and accepting everything? Of course not. It does, however, mean remembering that discernment can't be a cover for a spirit of criticism and judgment. And it means that if Jesus treasures someone, so must we. Why? Because just as He and the Father are one, so are He and His people. And all of them are worthy of honor.

ADDITIONAL READING: Romans 12:10

The union of men with God is the union of men with one another.
THOMAS AQUINAS

Works of Faith

[Jesus said,] "I tell you the truth, those who listen to my message and believe in God who sent me have eternal life. They will never be condemned for their sins, but they have already passed from death into life." John 5:24

IN WORD

Those who listen and believe. That's the message Jesus and the New Testament writers preached: salvation by grace through faith. Yet only a few verses later, Jesus muddies the water by declaring that those who have done good will have eternal life and those who have done evil will be judged. His first statement is all about faith. His second is all about works. And we're left wondering exactly how we can enter the Kingdom.

Of course, our simplest explanation is that salvation comes by hearing and believing, but faith always results in works. Therefore, works don't secure our Kingdom citizenship; they simply reflect the fact that we have become Kingdom citizens. We don't earn salvation; we demonstrate it. But in smoothing out our theology on this point, we often miss an important emphasis—that Jesus really does expect His people to do the works of the Kingdom. We can't be passive citizens. Our salvation is the beginning of a mission, not the end of one. In this world, we are vital representatives of the King.

What are the works of the Kingdom? Miracles of healing and deliverance certainly qualify, but the core of the Kingdom culture is the King's heart. He is drawn to the hurting, the oppressed, the captive. He defends the defenseless and befriends the lonely. He doesn't just wait for people to come to Him with their needs; He seeks them out.

IN DEED

Works of the Kingdom are evidence that the King is at work in us. They authenticate the faith we say we have. They aren't a standard to live up to; they are a lifestyle to fit into. That's a process, and God is infinitely patient as we grow. But this is the direction to grow. Justice, mercy, compassion, grace, empathy, and whatever fits His nature—these are to be the attitudes behind our actions. Jesus doesn't just call for faith and words. He insists on faith and works.

ADDITIONAL READING: Matthew 21:28-32

We do the works, but God works in us the doing of the works.
AUGUSTINE OF HIPPO

Salvation Story

When the group of prophets from Jericho saw from a distance what happened, they exclaimed, "Elijah's spirit rests upon Elisha!" 2 Kings 2:15

IN WORD

Elijah's name means "Yahweh is God," which was exactly the message he preached. He was zealous for pure worship of the one true Lord, both in his own life and in the national culture of God's people. He was outraged that the God of Israel, who had carefully chosen and powerfully delivered His people, was being brazenly rejected in favor of idols of wood and stone. He had a jealous spirit for God.

Elisha received the Spirit that was working in Elijah, but the message came out different. After Elijah preached uncompromising truth, Elisha demonstrated the mercy of God in the midst of a cursed land. Elijah declared the sins of the nation; Elisha remedied them. Elisha did things like heal lepers, bless cursed cities, promote reconciliation, feed a multitude, and raise the dead. (That should all sound familiar to anyone who has read the Gospels.) And Elisha's name reflects the message of his life: "God saves."

We see that dynamic often in Scripture. Moses, the prophet of the Law, took God's people to the edge of the Promised Land; Joshua (whose name also means "God saves") took them in. The captivity disciplined the nation; Joshua the high priest (same name, same meaning) led the worship of God's people afterward. John the Baptist pointed out the sins of the nation; Jesus (whose name also means "God saves") came to heal them. The Old Testament emphasizes why we need a Savior; the New Testament gives us one. In every case, uncompromising righteousness is followed by fulfillment.

IN DEED

Elijah and Elisha illustrate the heart of God. God never compromises His righteousness, but He is always willing to redeem and satisfy our lack of it. In fact, Elisha—the mercy emphasis in the prophetic duo—received a double portion of the Spirit. God's mercy is always a higher priority to Him than judgment (James 2:13). God's heart will always draw Him to those who need His grace.

ADDITIONAL READING: James 2:12-13

> Among the attributes of God, although they are all equal, mercy shines with even more brilliance than justice.
> MIGUEL DE CERVANTES

Attention

Elisha saw it and cried out, "My father! My father! I see the chariots and charioteers of Israel!" 2 Kings 2:12

IN WORD

Elisha had made a request of his mentor: to receive a double share of Elijah's spirit. Elijah gave him a very specific answer: "If you see me when I am taken from you, then you will get your request. But if not, then you won't" (2 Kings 2:10). Then as the two men were walking together, a chariot of fire appeared between them, and a whirlwind took Elijah up. This was no casual event.

Perhaps this was Elisha's test of whether he really wanted a double portion of Elijah's spirit. After all, if chariots and horses of fire suddenly appear, it would be pretty easy to take one's eyes off of the person standing next to him. Only someone hanging on to a specific instruction to stay focused could keep watching the master. As Elijah and the chariot ascended with the whirlwind, Elisha made it clear where his focus was: "My father! My father!" He knew his answer; the difficult thing for which he'd asked would be given to him.

Elisha picked up Elijah's cloak and struck the waters of the Jordan with it, asking, "Where is the LORD, the God of Elijah?" (2 Kings 2:14). But this was simply a confirmation of what he already knew. In an extremely chaotic and fantastic experience, Elisha had kept his eyes on his master. He demonstrated how badly he wanted the spirit of Elijah.

IN DEED

How badly do you want God's Spirit to rest on you? Yes, you're already born of His Spirit, but do you hunger for the evidence of His touch in your life? Are you focused enough that daily life, unexpected distractions, and even wild horses of fire will not take your gaze off of your master? If so, your sense of expectation will be rewarded in full. God always pours Himself out on those who hunger exclusively for Him. He never disappoints those who keep their eyes on Him despite the dramatic—and completely undramatic—distractions of life.

ADDITIONAL READING: Hebrews 12:2

A man's heart has only enough life in it to pursue one object fully.
CHARLES SPURGEON

Faith

So fifty men searched for three days but did not find Elijah. Elisha was
still at Jericho when they returned. "Didn't I tell you not to go?" he asked.
2 Kings 2:17-18

IN WORD

The company of prophets wanted to check it out, just to make sure. Maybe the whirl-wind had dropped Elijah unceremoniously somewhere in the desert sand. Maybe the visible evidence of Elijah's spirit resting on Elisha didn't necessarily imply that Elijah had departed. Maybe they would have among them two prophets fully endowed with God's Spirit, even though they had already prophesied Elijah's translation into heaven. Maybe they just couldn't believe what had allegedly taken place. So, consistent with human nature, they had to go see for themselves.

Elisha knew what they'd find: nothing. He knew what he'd seen. For the younger prophet, there was no need to verify what had already been foretold and then clearly witnessed with his own eyes. Searching for evidence to make sure God really did what He said He would do is a futile endeavor. Miracles can't be discounted by search parties.

IN DEED

Faith knows what it has seen. It's fine to speculate about what God has done or what He might do in the future, but faith is not swayed by speculation. It has eyes to see truth, never needing to try to explain away a miracle or look for evidence to contradict it. Faith isn't gullible, of course; but when God has clearly done something, supporting evidence is superfluous.

In what areas of your faith are you still looking for evidence? Nothing is wrong with discernment; we are all required to be wise in what we embrace as coming from God. But once God has answered a prayer, are you skeptical about whether it was really Him? Do you secretly search for alternate explanations? Do you play the role of the seeker until God answers, then play the role of the skeptic afterward?

Many believers do. Elisha didn't. The eyes of faith see God clearly enough to be satisfied. When you have seen God work, be confident in what you have seen.

ADDITIONAL READING: John 9:17-25

> A man with an experience is never at the
> mercy of a man with an argument.
> LEONARD RAVENHILL

Persistence

Elisha replied, "As surely as the LORD lives and you yourself live, I will never leave you." 2 Kings 2:6

IN WORD

Many Christians approach discipleship casually. It's a self-improvement endeavor—great to do, but not particularly urgent or intense. In fact, many believers are quite content with their relationship with God. It sufficiently sustains them.

That's one of the influences of our culture. The world supports those who are driven by financial and political success, but it hardly encourages those who are serious about faith. It even uses disparaging terms like *radical* or *guilt-ridden* for people who are devout beyond expectations. The world loves social conformity.

Elisha was not a socially acceptable disciple. He followed a radical prophet who had successfully challenged the idolatry of the age, and he insisted on following Elijah from city to city on the day the elder prophet was taken up. In other words, Elisha was a spiritual pest. And God honored him for it.

God always honors spiritual pests, people who are not content with a casual relationship with Him. Jesus responded to a blind man who would not quit yelling for Him, and He lauded a woman who wouldn't take no for an answer. He illustrated prayer with parables about a man banging on a neighbor's door and a woman pestering an unrighteous judge. He blessed those who hunger and thirst for righteousness.

IN DEED

What is your level of spiritual persistence? Are you content with how clearly you see God? With the fruit He's bearing in your life? With the warmth and intimacy with which you relate to Him each day? The biblical message affirms that God is pleased with those who press in to Him and keep pressing in. It encourages people to keep on asking, keep on seeking, and keep on knocking. You will find God's presence to the degree that you seek His presence. And no one who seeks ever gets to a point of saying, "Okay, that's enough. That's all of Him I need." Don't let yourself rest at that point. God will honor your hungry persistence.

ADDITIONAL READING: Luke 18:1-7

> If there is anything in your life more demanding than your longing after God, then you will never be a Spirit-filled Christian.
> A. W. TOZER

Ears to Hear

Anyone with ears to hear should listen and understand. Mark 4:9

IN WORD

Paul and his companions visited Berea during his second missionary journey, right after he fled Thessalonica because of a riot. His reception in Berea was much better, at least at first. The Jews of Berea were more open-minded and noble than their counterparts in Thessalonica, and they searched Scripture to see if Paul's words were true. Many of them, as well as many Greeks in the city, believed the message of Jesus.

Many people today call themselves "Bereans" and claim the gift of discernment, but generally they aren't looking to see if various teachings are true; they are looking to see if they are false. There's a world of difference. The original Berean approach was one of open-mindedness. Today the more common approach is practically determined at the outset to sniff out falsehood and expose it, and anything that doesn't look familiar must be judged and proven wrong. We see the same difference in approaches during the ministry of Jesus, as some people had a voracious appetite for His words, while the religious leaders were out to prove Him false. One group of people found life; the other went down in history for rejecting a visitation from God Himself.

Jesus had an expression for those who listened for the unconventional voice of God: He said they had "ears to hear." This listening attitude doesn't approach every teaching with an agenda to rule it out because it doesn't fit current assumptions. It enables us to accept what we don't yet understand, or at least consider it, since clearly we may not understand everything God teaches at first. Those with ears to hear do not dismiss claims rashly. They consider, ask God, and let Him lead. They even admit when they are wrong. And they grow in God's wisdom.

IN DEED

Having ears to hear is a vital Kingdom attribute. We can't thrive in the Kingdom culture without it. We have to become accustomed to a God who blows our minds and ignores our categories. We must ask Him often, "Lord, are these things true?" Only then can we step into all the places He has called us.

ADDITIONAL READING: Acts 17:10-12

Vision encompasses vast vistas outside the realm
of the predictable, the safe, the expected.
CHARLES SWINDOLL

On the Outside

[Jesus] replied, "You are permitted to understand the secret of the Kingdom of God. But I use parables for everything I say to outsiders." Mark 4:11

IN WORD

Like Isaiah before Him, Jesus spoke to people, knowing up front that many would not even listen to His words. If we were in that position, we would want to make things as clear as possible and answer questions before they were even asked. Not Jesus. He spoke in parables, obscuring the truth for those who weren't really listening for it in the first place, and opening it up for those who were hungry to hear and understand. Even His disciples—those who were already following Him and fully on board—needed explanations, and Jesus gave them when necessary. The secret of the Kingdom had already been given to them. But He said it would remain obscure to those outside of it.

Why is the Kingdom secret? Because the key to Kingdom life, the currency of the Kingdom itself, is faith. God almost always reveals Himself in ways that distinguish between faith and unbelief. There's always enough evidence to believe, rarely enough to prove empirically. That's because He isn't looking for the best minds; He is looking for the right hearts. Parables have a fantastic ability to distinguish between those who are truly hungry and those who are not.

IN DEED

Be careful how quickly you dismiss things you don't understand. The Kingdom will come to you in secrets, and those who are unobservant or preoccupied or driven by their own agenda will miss them. Like a gold prospector looking for treasure, you may have to do some digging. But if you're truly hungry, you will. This is God's design, the way He distinguishes between active listeners and passive hearers, hearts that love Him and hearts that are only mildly interested, those who hunger and thirst and those who don't. The Kingdom is given to those with the faith of a child and the spirit of an adventurer. When you are truly seeking His heart, He opens up its treasures. And its secrets become plain.

ADDITIONAL READING: Matthew 11:25

He who will believe only what he can fully comprehend
must have a very long head or a very short creed.
CHARLES CALEB COLTON

Before the Harvest

May all the nations praise you. . . . Then the earth will yield its harvests.
Psalm 67:5-6

IN WORD

Let's face it: The Kingdom culture is counterintuitive. We couldn't figure it out with our own logic if we tried. It isn't *illogical*. It's *extralogical*, above our ability to explain it. So when psalmists, prophets, and Jesus Himself put forth paradoxes and unexpected principles, we can choose to accept them or reject them. But we can't opt to fully understand them before we decide to believe them. They are first and foremost matters of faith.

One of those unexpected principles is that praise comes before increase. This is an absolutely vital key to Kingdom living. It's evident at various times throughout Scripture, and Psalm 67 is a subtle statement of it. The sense of the praise is present tense, and the sense of the harvest is future. When the people praise, the harvest will come. While the rest of the world plans to be grateful and joyful after the harvest comes, God's people learn that the gratitude and joy come first. It's a profound and powerful principle in our lives that we will miss if we get the order wrong. When we can learn to worship beforehand, we will see harvests increase—in any area of life. Our praises are the truest, deepest seeds we sow, and our lives reap the fruit of them.

IN DEED

Don't wait for harvests, victories, or any other form of success to worship, praise, and thank God. In His Kingdom, circumstances don't set the tone of our relationship with Him; the tone of our relationship sets the circumstances. Historically, followers of a deity give thanks and fulfill vows after the results have been secured, but that's a business-deal approach to the divine. We are involved in a relationship, not a transaction. Our hearts belong to Him, even if He doesn't come through for us. But He does. In one way or another, He responds to the praises of His people. That doesn't mean we never face adversity or go through dry seasons, but it does mean our love doesn't hinge on His favors. He simply delights in blessing those whose hearts are His. Our worship reveals that they are.

ADDITIONAL READING: 2 Chronicles 20:21-24

God can never receive too much praise.
ANONYMOUS

Before Sight

Jesus responded, "Didn't I tell you that you would see God's glory if you believe?" John 11:40

IN WORD

Jesus had said it and demonstrated it often. "If you believe." "Because of your faith." "All things are possible." "Your faith has made you well." Now, standing at Lazarus's tomb facing an impossible situation, Jesus reminds Martha that faith leads to sight. To her, the stone at the entrance was the final word. To Him, it was a minor obstacle. The glory of God comes to those who believe.

Clearly, there's a connection between what we believe and what happens as a result. It may not be as direct a correlation as we expect at times, but there's still a correlation. This is another vital key to Kingdom living, one of those unexpected truths that forces us to reverse the order of our normal thinking. We usually approach life with the attitude that sight leads to faith. "I'll believe it when I see it," or something along that line. But the Kingdom way is different. We will see it when we believe it. Faith comes before sight. We have to stand on what God said before we experience the fulfillment of His words.

It isn't easy going against our instincts. When we see a final decision, accept disappointment, look at the size of our circumstances, or embrace any other such evidence that a situation is impossible, the sense of futility can be overwhelming. We don't want to be unrealistic, escapist, delusional, or anything else others will conclude about us if they think we are clinging to faith in a fantasy. But there's a difference between a fantasy and a promise of God. When He has spoken, when His plans have been revealed, when He is leading us down a path toward a worthy goal, the stones against the entrance are never the final say. Faith overcomes impossibilities. That's the Kingdom way.

IN DEED

Don't give up. Listen to God's voice—and be discerning to recognize it, of course—but don't forfeit anything He has promised. Much of your experience depends on "if you believe." When you do, in one way or another, you will see the glory of God.

ADDITIONAL READING: Hebrews 11:6

Faith, mighty faith, the promise sees, and looks to that alone;
laughs at impossibilities and cries: it shall be done.
CHARLES WESLEY

Before Understanding

The disciple who had reached the tomb first also went in, and he saw and believed—for until then they still hadn't understood the Scriptures that said Jesus must rise from the dead. John 20:8-9

IN WORD

Like many approaches to knowledge throughout history, the modern mind-set is rooted in empirical observation. We look at the evidence, and then we draw conclusions. There's nothing wrong with that; it's how great scientific advances have occurred, and Paul even applies it in Romans 1:20 to the knowledge of God. We know truth from what we see and experience.

That's also how it was when John entered the tomb. Jesus wasn't there, so John believed in the Resurrection. But he nevertheless had to embrace a Kingdom principle that most of us have difficulty grasping. Acceptance of divine truth usually comes before we fully understand it. John didn't see, wait for a thorough explanation, agree with the coherence of the explanation, and then decide to believe. He saw and believed, even though he did not yet understand how it could be possible. Like many in Scripture—Joshua at Jericho, Mary at the Annunciation, Peter on the waves—he had to accept before he could fully comprehend. He had to get the order right.

We do too. Infinite truth isn't irrational, but it's far greater than finite minds can grasp. Those who will not accept any evidence of the divine until they can understand it—even if they have already seen it—will miss out on quite a few Kingdom blessings. In the Kingdom life, we have to be able to embrace things that are greater than our ability to comprehend. Why? Because the Kingdom is bigger than we are.

IN DEED

That doesn't mean understanding never comes. Remarkably, when we believe truths that are greater than our minds can grasp, we begin to grow in our understanding of them. That's because the Spirit enlightens believing minds. Wisdom comes to those who accept it up front. Those who accept God's ways are those who will eventually understand them best.

ADDITIONAL READING: Hebrews 11:3

> Understanding is the reward of faith. Seek not to understand that you may believe, but to believe that you may understand.
> AUGUSTINE OF HIPPO

Before Greatness

Whoever wants to be a leader among you must be your servant. Matthew 20:26

IN WORD

Everyone wants to be great. That doesn't mean everyone wants to be rich, famous, or recognized for greatness, but deep down, beneath whatever wounds and resignation may obscure their true desires, everyone wants to accomplish something significant and do life well. And there's absolutely nothing wrong with that longing. When James, John, and their mother asked for a privileged position, Jesus didn't rebuke them for the desire to be great. He simply corrected their perception of how to make it happen.

One of the paradoxes of the Kingdom is that the way up is down. If you want to become great, you need to get low and become a servant. That's what Jesus did, leaving His privileged position in glory and living among us as a human being destined to die. And as Jesus indicated on more than one occasion, His followers are to be like Him. If we're trying to work our way up the ladder to greatness while claiming to follow the one who descended from heaven to wash our feet, we're contradicting ourselves. Following Jesus means adopting the same attitudes and heeding His words. We take on the character of one who is exalted over all because He emptied Himself of glory and died.

IN DEED

That's the path to greatness, and it's a shocking paradox. Not many in this world can accept that the way up is down, although some might concede the point if you redefine greatness as a matter of principle. But Jesus, both by words and example, made it clear that His way to greatness leads not only to the admiration of others; it leads to actual, meaningful exaltation and glory in God's Kingdom. This isn't something we *have* to do but rather something we *get* to do. It's a stunning opportunity. We aren't simply acquiring a great character trait; we're acquiring a greater position in the Kingdom governance. The more we serve, the more God elevates us in the social structure of His realm. And no form of upward mobility is greater than that.

ADDITIONAL READING: John 13:1-17

> The most radical social teaching of Jesus was His total reversal of the contemporary notion of greatness.
> RICHARD FOSTER

Before Authority

Just say the word from where you are, and my servant will be healed. I know this because I am under the authority of my superior officers, and I have authority over my soldiers. I only need to say, "Go," and they go, or "Come," and they come. Matthew 8:8-9

IN WORD

He could have said, "Like you, I'm a man of authority" and left it at that. But this Gentile commander who approached Jesus found a connection with the Son of God first and foremost as a man "under authority." He understood structures of governance. He knew that his right to issue commands came not because someone had endowed him with power but because he had learned to submit to the authorities above him. He had proven to be responsible. He could issue orders because he had been faithful in carrying his orders out.

This is a subtle paradox of the Kingdom, yet a powerful one. We rejoice when Jesus promises His followers the keys of the Kingdom and answers to prayer, but we need to understand that our experience of those realities directly relates not to our ability to lord it over others but our willingness to submit to a higher lordship. That's why many Christians flounder in frustration at the impotence of their alleged Kingdom authority. It makes no sense to declare the will of the King if we've been careless about following it. If we want to live in this authority, we have to accept every aspect of it.

IN DEED

Recognize the power of the Kingdom paradoxes. They are keys to getting where we want to go. Never mind that they defy our reason; they work. If we want to wield the authority of the Kingdom, as we've been promised, we must take great care to submit to the authority of the Kingdom in our own lives. That means embracing its values, doing its works, seeking its fruitfulness, and above all, paying attention to the heart of the King. When He expresses a desire, we need to become preoccupied with it. His will becomes ours because our hearts are connected. Then the truths of the Kingdom can come out of our mouths with power. Our prayers and commands have effect. Living under authority puts us in position to exercise it.

ADDITIONAL READING: Matthew 18:18

Prayer is the secret of power.
EVAN ROBERTS

Before Strength

When I am weak, then I am strong. 2 Corinthians 12:10

IN WORD

Every society values certain virtues. Wisdom, loyalty, perseverance, humility, and others are almost universal—though in some times and places, pride and the ability to deceive have been lauded as well. But weakness shows up in hardly any culture's definition of praiseworthy characteristics. It may be understandable and even pitied, but it isn't sought after, with the exception of one culture: the Kingdom of God.

In the Kingdom, weakness isn't honored for the sake of weakness, of course. It's honored because of how it enables God to enter into our lives and show Himself strong. The goal isn't to remain weak; it's to rely on the power of another. As Paul claimed, our powerlessness opens the way for His power on our behalf.

That's easy for us to picture but difficult to implement. Our instincts tell us to make ourselves strong, to seek to be well-positioned and as invincible as we can make ourselves. Throughout history, the powerful have preyed on the vulnerable with great success. But when the vulnerable depend on the God of the universe for their protection . . . well, that changes the narrative. We may experience hardship, and we may even suffer. But we don't lose. Not when God is on our side.

IN DEED

The counterintuitive command of the Kingdom culture is for us to rest in God's strength. He fights our battles. He may have specific instructions for us, just as He did with Moses, Joshua, Gideon, David, Jehoshaphat, and many others. But we don't trust in chariots and horses or any modern equivalent. If we did, we would only be getting in the way. God often lets us experience such futility. But we are called rather to trust in the name of our God. We stand still and see His salvation, cry out for His help and expect Him to come, be still and know that He is God. We aren't passive, but neither do we take charge. Our active trust gives Him room to work. And our acknowledged weakness makes it clear that we are empowered by the might of someone far greater than ourselves.

ADDITIONAL READING: Psalm 33:16-22

> The martyrs shook the powers of darkness with
> the irresistible power of weakness.
> JOHN MILTON

Before Breakthrough

When troubles of any kind come your way, consider it an opportunity for great joy. James 1:2

IN WORD

Related to Paul's "strength in weakness" claim is James's "rejoice in trials" message. In fact, Paul essentially tied the two together in 2 Corinthians 12:10, writing about how he delighted in persecutions and hardships. We can hardly understand such an attitude; our natural responses are fear, anger, frustration, or a desire either to escape or go to battle. But rejoice? In a trial? No, that doesn't make sense.

Since when do the ways of the Kingdom make sense to us? Or since when should we even expect them to? We grow accustomed to reactions that defy our own instincts, knowing that having God in the equation changes everything. If we were left to face our trials on our own, not knowing whether they would turn out for our good, insecure in every twist and turn they take us on, then we might have reason to panic. But we've been given ample promises to assure us that we are overcomers and that all things work together for our good. We know the victory at the end of each of our stories even when we don't know how the victories are going to come. Whatever happens in adversity, it's going to work out to our advantage if we keep trusting in the One who promised. We really can rejoice.

IN DEED

This is more than an offer to relax. It's a powerful key to overcoming anything we face in life. God doesn't just tell us it's okay to rejoice; He insists that it will be better for us if we do. The benefits are numerous—character, endurance, stronger faith, and the like. But they include more than just assistance in making it through our trials. Rejoicing in advance—the intentional, razor-sharp, strategic practice of joy—is a powerful weapon that undoes everything the enemy intended to accomplish by opposing us. When we rejoice, not only do we win, which was going to happen eventually anyway, he loses whatever short-term gains he hoped to achieve. Bringing the celebration of heaven into the trials of earth has a profound ability to undo them. Joy comes before breakthrough.

ADDITIONAL READING: Romans 8:31-39

> Joy is very cheap, and if you can help the poor on with a garment of praise it will be better for them than blankets.
> HENRY DRUMMOND

Before Honor

Humble yourselves under the mighty power of God, and at the right time he will lift you up in honor. 1 Peter 5:6

IN WORD

Paul wrote profoundly about the trajectory of the Incarnation in Philippians, where he describes Jesus emptying Himself of all the privileges of deity and becoming a man, humbling Himself to the point of death, after which God raised Him up and exalted Him above all. Eventually, every knee will bow to give Him honor. Jesus demonstrated that larger trajectory Himself when He laid aside His robe, donned the garments of a servant, knelt down to wash His disciples' feet, and then got back up and put His rightful garments on. With His life, His words, and His acts of service, He demonstrated a deep humility that the Son of God would never have to reflect if He didn't want to. But it's His nature; He's humble at heart. And in His Kingdom, the humble are lifted up to places of honor.

Humility comes before glory. Human nature forgets that. Many people think glory is something to achieve, but in the Kingdom, it's something to receive. We don't boast, make a name for ourselves, or make it a point to draw attention to ourselves. Some people do so out of insecurity, but we can be thoroughly secure in the Father's love. And some do out of sheer pride, but we would never have been able to admit our sin and come to Christ if we were proud. So we have no need to seek glory by normal means. We can humbly rest in what God has done and receive whatever glory He offers.

IN DEED

Don't be uncomfortable when He lifts you up. Many believers think they aren't worthy of any glory at all, but we were created for it—in His own image, to be exact. Just as it's impossible to bear His image without reflecting His glory, it's impossible to expect the God of glory to leave His humble friends in lowly places forever. It's another befuddling paradox, but the way to honor in His Kingdom is not to seek it. It's to be preoccupied instead with serving, loving, offering, sacrificing, and meeting needs. When we are humble enough to do that, He is more than willing enough to lift us up at the right time.

ADDITIONAL READING: Philippians 2:5-11

By the lowliness and humility of our Lord Jesus Christ, we climb up as on a true ladder to heaven into the heart of God.
JOHANN ARNDT

Before Receiving

Give, and you will receive. . . . The amount you give will determine the amount you get back. Luke 6:38

IN WORD

Most people, even those without a solid faith foundation, have little trouble asking God for things. Human beings are wired to receive. But giving doesn't come quite as easily, even though we were originally wired for that, too. Our fears and insecurities instill in us a desperation to get what we can whenever we can get it. And we spend much of our lives trying to grab as much as we can.

Jesus doesn't condemn our need to receive, but He offers us a better way. When we live in a me-centered environment, we may get some things but we lose a lot more. But if we can shift to a we-centered environment in which providing for others' needs is as important to us as providing for our own, we end up getting more than we give. It takes an intentional and radical change in perspective, but the rewards are worth it. Generosity—materially, spiritually, emotionally, and more—is like sowing seed into fertile ground. Eventually, there's a rich harvest.

That doesn't mean we give simply in order to receive. We give because we genuinely want to help other people out and are concerned for their well-being. But if we can invest in other people's abundance, God demonstrates how interested He is in investing in ours. He loves a magnanimous spirit because it's a reflection of who He is. When we enter into a generous attitude, we have entered into heaven's environment. And we experience heaven's fruit.

IN DEED

Learn to give—not because you are focused on getting something out of your generosity, but because it reflects the heart of God and the culture of His Kingdom. Invest yourself in others. When you do, you will find that others invest in you at a greater level. God Himself will honor your generosity by giving you greater experiences of His own.

ADDITIONAL READING: 2 Corinthians 9:6-9

> A man there was, though some did count him mad;
> the more he cast away, the more he had.
> JOHN BUNYAN

Before Life

If you try to hang on to your life, you will lose it. But if you give up your life for my sake and for the sake of the Good News, you will save it. Mark 8:35

IN WORD

It's perhaps the greatest Kingdom paradox. If we want life, we shouldn't seek it. We should give it up. Lay it down. Cast ourselves into the soil like seed destined to become something other than seed. We invest ourselves in God and others. We want life, of course, and there's nothing wrong with that longing. But getting it involves surrendering our desperate search for glory and giving it instead.

That isn't easy to do. No one instinctively pursues a desperate desire by forsaking it. That just isn't natural. No, if we want life, our instincts tell us to do everything we can to grab it wherever we can. For many, that results in the relentless pursuit of whatever makes them feel alive—power, sex, romance, entertainment, money, travel, or any other package that promises excitement.

Eyes of faith see through all that. God is looking for those who recognize the difference between what leads to life and what doesn't. Nothing is wrong with pleasure, excitement, and adventure; those cravings were built into us. But to see the pleasure, excitement, and adventure in Him rather than in superficial gifts . . . that's faith. And in a very real sense it requires some kind of death before we experience the life He promises.

IN DEED

Knowing the future of His disciples, Jesus is actually hinting at martyrdom in this passage. But the truth applies to much more than physical death. The way to Kingdom life involves forsaking all the self's strategies and investing in others' lives. Then, almost apart from our own awareness, we find ourselves receiving the life we once craved. We don't attain fulfillment, we receive it. When we pour out ourselves, He pours Himself into us. And the death we thought we embraced becomes our means to life.

ADDITIONAL READING: Galatians 2:20

It is in dying that we are born to eternal life.
FRANCIS OF ASSISI

A Willing God

[God said,] "I have promised to rescue you from your oppression in Egypt. I will lead you to a land flowing with milk and honey." Exodus 3:17

IN WORD

The first time Moses left Egypt, he fled into a wilderness and settled there for forty years. Midian wasn't a terrible place to live, but it wasn't flowing with milk and honey either. The second time he left Egypt, he and his people wandered through that wilderness for forty more years. At the end of the wandering lay a land of promise, the fulfillment of God's will. The end of misery was in sight.

The interesting thing about Moses' journey is that he began in a palace, then lived for years on the far side of a wilderness, raided the center of his people's captivity, and led them to the Promised Land. That sounds a lot like a Savior we know, who left the throne room of heaven to identify with His people in a world of wilderness and captivity. But this Savior doesn't just lead us to the edge of the Promised Land; He brings us into it. The first prophet-deliverer took his people as far as the law could take them; the last prophet-deliverer takes them by grace into their destiny. The picture of Moses is a picture that prepares the way for the Messiah and tells us what Messiah is going to do.

Moses illustrates God's desire for us: to bring us into our destiny. God has a land prepared for us, and we can begin walking in it even now. The land is full of goodness and fruitfulness, prosperity and blessing. It will one day be more visible than we ever thought it could be, but we can certainly see signs of it until then. The prophet who delivers shows us the God who is a Deliverer—and the God whom we can experience now.

IN DEED

In what areas of your life do you need deliverance? According to the prophetic pictures of the Word, the history that speaks to us from ages past, God is able to deliver you. Not only is He able, He is more than willing. He demonstrated that by sending Moses to a hostile Pharaoh and Jesus to a hostile Satan. Ask Him for your promised land.

ADDITIONAL READING: Psalm 81:10

> Thou art coming to a king; large petitions with thee bring. For his grace and power are such, none can ever ask too much.
> JOHN NEWTON

A False Identity

Moses pleaded with the LORD, "O Lord, I'm not very good with words. I never have been, and I'm not now, even though you have spoken to me. I get tongue-tied, and my words get tangled." Exodus 4:10

IN WORD

Telling an omniscient God that He doesn't have all the information is usually a bad idea. So it was with Moses, who was pretty sure God had forgotten about his lack of eloquence or his difficulty as an adopted Egyptian-speaking Hebrew. God, of course, had to rearrange Moses' perception of his Lord and also of himself. Moses didn't understand his own identity.

We don't either. Our identity is not made up of the ideas we have formed over the years; it's made up of whatever God says about us. If He says we are His children, then we are, whether we feel like it or not. When He says we are precious to Him, then we are, even if we don't consider ourselves very precious. And when He calls us to a task, the task is suited for us perfectly, whether we imagine that it fits our gifts or not. Whatever God says of us, that's who we are.

When you came to Christ, you gave yourself back to God, acknowledging His right to your life. Have you ever considered that with all the rights you defer to Him, you also are pleasantly obligated to give up your own self-perception? In other words, you don't really have the right to tell God how ill-fitted you are for your calling, as Moses did, or even how short you will fall of His glory. If God says you are His beloved child, seated with Him in heavenly places, treasured as a specimen of His redemption and glory, cleansed of all sin, and gifted for divine works, you have no business contradicting Him.

IN DEED

Think of how many times your assessment of yourself contradicts God. Read through Scripture with an eye for His description of the redeemed, and then embrace that description. Don't do what Moses did, telling God that your self-perception is more accurate. What God says about you is always true. Believe it.

ADDITIONAL READING: Philippians 4:13

God is Truth. Who in his right mind would contradict Him?
ANONYMOUS

A Testimony of Evidence

What if they won't believe me or listen to me? What if they say, "The LORD never appeared to you"? Exodus 4:1

IN WORD

This isn't a question that only prophets ask. Every believer wonders what will happen when his or her faith shows up in the real world. We struggle with putting our faith on the line because we aren't sure how to respond when it is confronted with opposition. Worse yet, we're afraid we might undermine our own witness by our faults and mistakes.

Moses certainly struggled with such issues, but God called him anyway. God didn't say, "Oh, you're right, I forgot that you might not be a charismatic leader with an innate power of influence." He simply promised to back Moses up. He promised that when His will was on the line, there would be evidence to prove it.

God may not back us up with exactly the same kind of evidence He gave Moses. Few of us can count on even finding a shepherd's staff, much less making it turn into a snake to impress the skeptics. Even so, don't underestimate the power of God to prove Himself in your witness for Him. Anyone who is called by Him, filled with His Spirit, obedient to His will, and open about the truth of the Kingdom will find God in the midst of his or her life. He may show up in visible and obvious signs, or He may show up in more subtle moves of His Spirit. But He will be there. He doesn't leave His prophets—or any of His people—dangling without a net to catch them.

IN DEED

Have you ever asked God this "what if" question? Many of us have. What if people hear our testimony and tell us it's just what we learned as children, or a psychological crutch, or give us some other skeptical rebuttal? That may happen, but God never called us to let the reaction of others guide our relationship with Him. He promised that signs, wonders, and changed lives would surround His people, and everyone will have to choose whether to see the evidence or not. We can live our lives with confidence that God will always back us up.

ADDITIONAL READING: Acts 5:12-16

> Miracles are the great bell of the universe,
> which draws men to God's sermons.
> JOHN FOSTER

A Holy Commission

God replied to Moses, . . . "Say this to the people of Israel: I AM has sent me to you." Exodus 3:14

IN WORD

Moses was no ordinary deliverer. He never sparked an uprising, he never led a group of insurgents, and he never wielded a weapon. This first prophet, sent by God to a captive people, could put only one legitimate claim on his résumé: God had sent him.

That's really all the résumé anyone needs. If God has sent someone to do His work, no other qualifications will suffice, and no others are needed. God had plenty of reasons for choosing Moses: his symbolic deliverance as a baby, his unique background as a Jew who had grown up in Pharaoh's household, and probably many more. But those attributes alone aren't nearly enough to equip someone to deliver a nation of captives. That job requires the presence of the God who is, who was, and who always will be. It requires supernatural intervention.

The church forgets that. We focus on having the right background and the right plan to serve our world and meet its needs. But our experience and our plans are nothing without an intimate sense of relationship—in power, presence, and purpose—with God.

IN DEED

The church needs to be a Moses in this world. There's nothing wrong with the training we receive or the strategies we implement, at least not in themselves. But if the first item on our résumé isn't "God has sent us," we can't possibly deliver a captive world. Why? Because being sent by God implies that His presence and His power are fueling the ministry.

We may think of prophets and priests as individuals, but Kingdom people themselves are prophets and priests (1 Peter 2:9-10; Revelation 5:10). God speaks to the captives of this world through us, and He mediates His covenant through His Son and those who follow Him. Whatever house of fellowship you attend, never lose sight of this. You and the believers around you are to march into the throne room of the world's enslaver with one primary conviction within you: "I Am has sent us."

ADDITIONAL READING: Revelation 5:10

> Nearness to Christ, intimacy with Him, assimilation to His character—these are the elements of a ministry of power.
> HORATIUS BONAR

Worthy of Your Calling

I, a prisoner for serving the Lord, beg you to lead a life worthy of your calling, for you have been called by God. Ephesians 4:1

IN WORD

We love the fact that we are forgiven, reborn, blessed, gifted, and called. We celebrate the status God has given us as His children and the mission He has given us as citizens of His Kingdom. We talk about how we could never live up to the standards of His holiness and don't deserve His mercy (which, by definition, is why it's mercy). And all that is true. But there are implications to the blessings, status, calling, mission, and mercy we've been given. We need to live them out. And in order to do that, we as Kingdom citizens need to live in a way that reflects the nature of the King.

Impossible? Not really. If it were a matter of human achievement, nothing we do would ever be enough. But as Paul describes his plea to live lives worthy of the calling, he mentions qualities like humility, gentleness, and patience. These aren't things to achieve; they are things to allow. We don't get them by striving for them; we get them when we cease striving for our own agendas and our expectations for other people. When we learn to rest in Christ, surrender to His purposes, and gaze at His nature, we begin to take on His character. We become like Him. The Kingdom qualities grow in us as we release everything contrary to them. We don't grab hold of them; we let go of their opposites.

IN DEED

That's why it's possible to live a life worthy of our calling. Most sin comes from our own desperate attempts to satisfy ourselves, make a name for ourselves, or pursue our own plans. The best, truest, most godly qualities grow organically within us when we stop feeding ourselves and start feeding others. Ironically, that's also the path to the satisfaction and fulfillment we once sought by self-directed means. When we let go, we gain. That's the way of the Kingdom. And that's how we live up to the calling we've been given.

ADDITIONAL READING: Philippians 2:1-4

> The responsible person seeks to make his or her whole life a response to the question and call of God.
> DIETRICH BONHOEFFER

Spoils of War

When he ascended to the heights, he led a crowd of captives and gave gifts to his people. Ephesians 4:8

IN WORD

After winning a key battle and conquering his enemy, an ancient king would lead a procession of captives—often shaved or stripped for humiliation—back to his home city and distribute to his own citizens the plunder he had taken. That's the picture given in Paul's writings of the victory of Jesus, who stripped the principalities and powers of darkness and humiliated them at the cross (Colossians 2:15). Here Paul refers to the same victory procession in order to convince his readers that they have been given supernatural gifts, distributed by the victorious King.

What are these gifts? They include everything necessary for building up the Kingdom—apostleship (or being sent as leaders and equippers), prophecies about Kingdom insights, the spreading of the Good News, the shepherding of people, and the teaching of Kingdom truths. In other words, Jesus has given whatever the people of God need for their Kingdom mission, not only for their own use but in the further equipping of many others. They are more powerful than talents and skills, more valuable than we might think, and more adaptable to unique personalities than we often treat them. They are precious commodities in the Kingdom economy.

IN DEED

Scripture gives us a picture of Kingdom citizens in this world that portrays us as one organic whole with multifaceted functions and assignments. We are all gifted with some supernatural capability—a fact we often miss when dealing with the simple humanity of people around us. And we are all destined for some key role in reflecting the heart of the King and equipping or mobilizing His people in this world. We can't afford to overlook or downplay these truths; they are vital to our purpose in this age. The enemy has already been plundered, the citizens have already been lavished with spoils of war, and untaken territory lies gaping all around us. What's left? To step into it armed with faith, gifts, and the backing of the King Himself.

ADDITIONAL READING: Colossians 2:13-15

> [Spiritual gifts] are not trophies, but tools—
> tools for touching and blessing others.
> JOHN WIMBER

Set Your Heart

Since you have been raised to new life with Christ, set your sights on the realities of heaven, where Christ sits in the place of honor at God's right hand.
Colossians 3:1

IN WORD

Perspective is a funny thing. Everyone has one, but few of us are conscious of the specifics and limitations of our own. We notice how easily the perspectives of others are skewed, but we live from ours quite naturally. It shapes everything we think, say, and do.

If a perspective can be that influential in our lives, we certainly want the best one. We want right instead of wrong, broad instead of narrow, helpful instead of harmful. In other words, we want something beyond our finite, faulty point of view. We want to see from a much higher vantage point and aim for much higher goals. We want to live from a better, truer, higher, deeper realm.

We can. As citizens of the realm of God, we are called to invest our hearts fully in His Kingdom. Everything in us—emotions, thoughts, attitudes, perspectives, everything—is meant to thrive in the environment of heaven rather than falter in the environment of a broken world. We are to see all of life as though we are living above, with Jesus on the throne. Instead of seeing the worst in people, we see who they are (or can be) in Christ. Instead of seeing problems, we see solutions. Instead of lamenting losses, we leverage them for gain. We are seated with Christ on the throne (Ephesians 2:6). We might as well live as if it's true.

IN DEED

Like all human beings, you have been well trained to live from a thoroughly human point of view. The fact that Christ is in you by faith gives you the opportunity to rise to a new perspective. You don't have to live from a place of futility, defeat, and lamentation; you can have God's perspective. But only if you invest your heart in whatever is above, where Jesus is, in the realm of God. You can no longer afford to set your heart on pain and brokenness, or even on any goals less than eternal, beautiful, and good. An entirely new realm is offered to you. Live in it fully.

ADDITIONAL READING: Ephesians 2:6

Vision is the art of seeing things invisible.
JONATHAN SWIFT

The Opposite Spirit

You used to do these things when your life was still part of this world.
Colossians 3:7

IN WORD

Being a new creation in Christ implies a lot of change—not subtle adjustments but radical overhauls. We no longer think the same way, talk the same way, or walk the same way. Our attitude shifts because our identity has shifted. We are no longer "only human." We are fully human, with the archetype of true humanity living inside of us. And that means we are no longer under the thumb of this world's oppressive spirit.

Yet something strange happens to us new creatures when we walk back into old situations. We have a tendency to conform to old ways. In order to influence business, we may get sucked into a spirit of corporate greed, or in an attempt to influence the political arena, we might be drawn into "politics as usual." Old relationships trigger us into old relational patterns. Past environments stir up past habits. Soon we are swimming in competitiveness, manipulation, criticism, and all the dynamics of the former nature—even when we were trying to make a difference and influence our world with God's ways.

IN DEED

How can we break out of that magnetic pull of the world? We have to walk in the opposite spirit of the arenas we live and work in. If we enter an ego-filled entertainment industry, we have to go in humility. If we enter a profit-obsessed corporation, we have to go in without a hint of greed. If we're in education, we need an attitude of learning rather than a spirit of indoctrinating. In politics, we need truth and respect rather than deception and manipulation. In media, we need hope rather than negativity. Whatever spirit holds any area of life captive, we can only begin to undo it in the God-given opposite spirit. When we walk in His perspective and His ways, evil may oppose us for a while. But it eventually must bow.

Relentlessly insist on higher ways. Never embrace the spirit of the world in place of the Spirit of Christ. In every area of life, live in the new. The old has no power over you anymore.

ADDITIONAL READING: Ephesians 2:1-5

Christian experience is not so much a matter of imitating
a leader as accepting and receiving a new quality of life.
H. A. WILLIAMS

New Clothes

Since God chose you to be the holy people he loves, you must clothe yourselves with tenderhearted mercy, kindness, humility, gentleness, and patience. Colossians 3:12

IN WORD

The Kingdom of God does not require uniforms. We'll be dressed in robes of righteousness, of course; white is always "in" in the Kingdom. But we remain individuals with unique personalities, preferences, and styles. We have different gifts, different callings, and different demonstrations of the nature of Christ within us. We conform to one Person, but He expresses Himself through us in a dazzling variety of ways.

But that doesn't mean our wardrobe is unlimited. Jesus doesn't offer us the same old clothes we used to have. Where we once dressed ourselves in insecurity, a need to impress, competitiveness, shame, manipulation and control, and so much more, we are given a beautiful new wardrobe full of compassion, kindness, humility, gentleness, and patience. And honestly, we look better in the new clothes. Some people may not think so; the fashions of the Kingdom are a little off-trend for the world's tastes. But their subdued elegance has the effect of tastefully standing out.

We are called to stand out—not just to admire the clothes of the Kingdom or to have them hanging in our closet, but to actually put them on and wear them in public. Regardless of the world's dress code, these clothes are appropriate for any occasion because they were given to us by the King to wear in His Kingdom. As citizens of that realm, we are to have a certain style. It's okay not to blend in. We have the amazing opportunity to dress ourselves in clothes that fit our new nature perfectly.

IN DEED

As you get dressed every morning, see yourself also putting on the new clothes of the Kingdom. Wear the royal attitudes daily. Let them adorn you beautifully, for all to see. And when you walk the red carpet of the Kingdom, no one will have to ask who made that dress or designed that tux. They'll know. It all comes from the wardrobe of the King.

ADDITIONAL READING: Ephesians 4:20-24

> [We] are not merely to mark time, waiting for God to step in and set right all that is wrong . . . but to model the new heaven and new earth.
> PHILIP YANCEY

Peace Rules

Let the peace that comes from Christ rule in your hearts. Colossians 3:15

IN WORD

When you walk in the new nature and wear the new clothes of the Kingdom, you find an inner *shalom* that you were designed to carry. That *shalom*—the peace, wholeness, fullness, and rightness of life as it was meant to be—is a satisfying place. It's more than the absence of conflict and tension. It's restoration of the true human nature given in Eden and re-created through Jesus. It's a gift of life from the Prince of *Shalom* Himself.

Many Christians lose that peace and fullness when they begin applying the Kingdom ways to everyone around them and make righteous demands on people who have only the old nature to draw from or are in a different place in their discipleship journey. Scripture tells us to walk in the new nature and wear the new Kingdom clothes, but it never tells us to decide the path for others and dress them the way we see fit. Yes, there are common expressions of Christ that all should embrace, and we are free to teach them. But the Kingdom is not a place of finger-pointing. It is always calling us to look on our old nature with judgment but never to be judgmental toward others. When we take verses meant for us and apply them to others—often out of season for their lives—we lose whatever peace we had gained. We become like the righteous scribes and Pharisees who, deep inside, weren't very righteous at all.

IN DEED

Apply the Word to yourself. Even teach it to others. Explore it with those around you, and exhort and encourage one another with its hope and calling. But as one who has received an extraordinary amount of mercy, never look unmercifully at another. And certainly never judge those in the old nature by the standards of the new. These are not attitudes that make for peace.

No, peace comes from your inner communion with Christ and will manifest with the same mercy and love that He expressed to people who were really immature and may have made very bad decisions. Let love and mercy rule in your heart, and peace—*shalom* in its fullness—will flourish.

ADDITIONAL READING: Ephesians 4:1-4

Nothing graces the Christian soul as much as mercy.
AMBROSE OF MILAN

Whatever You Do

Whatever you do, whether in word or deed, do it all in the name of the Lord Jesus, giving thanks to God the Father through him. Colossians 3:17, *NIV*

IN WORD

"In the name." It's an extremely common phrase, both in Scripture and at the end of our prayers. But what exactly does it mean? You'll encounter quite a few answers to that question, but most of them will include something like this: "In the name" of Jesus implies living, working, and praying as if we were Jesus—or at least His representative. Just as a diplomat becomes the voice of his or her country in a foreign land, qualified to sign documents and act as a proxy for the home government, every believer is given the right to become the voice, signatory, and proxy of the King. We may not realize that responsibility or exercise it well, but it's there. We are to "become Jesus" in this world.

That's why Jesus gave such extravagant promises to His followers, telling them that whatever they asked in His name or whatever they decided with the keys of His Kingdom would be established in heaven. We may footnote those promises with ample caveats about what they don't mean, but Scripture doesn't. It just lays them out there, even with the possibility of people abusing them. The only appropriate response is not to explain them away; it's to be thoroughly sobered by the weight of them and make every effort by faith and action to live up to them.

IN DEED

That's why Paul says "whatever you do." This is a comprehensive calling. There are no segments in our lives that can be separated from living "in His name." No secret places hidden from His eyes, no underground agenda, nothing but His purposes. Are you a Kingdom citizen? Then you are a representative of the King. Period.

Think, speak, and act like one. Upon hearing a Christian appeal to "live like royalty," envision the most generous, good-hearted king or queen you can imagine, not those who have lavished all luxury on themselves. This is a noble calling for a noble creature. In Christ, you are living as Him.

ADDITIONAL READING: Ephesians 1:15-23

> We are here to represent Christ—to present Him again, to re-present Him.
> MALTBIE BABCOCK

The Gaze

We all, who with unveiled faces contemplate the Lord's glory, are being transformed into his image with ever-increasing glory, which comes from the Lord, who is the Spirit. 2 Corinthians 3:18, *NIV*

IN WORD

Some human beings are problem-avoiders, but the more responsible among us are problem-solvers by nature. When we see a problem, we focus on it. Sometimes we even obsess over it, turn it inside out, and analyze it to death. That rarely helps, but we do it anyway, even to the point of losing sleep. Our attention is drawn to the negative because we feel compelled to fix it.

That approach doesn't work very often in many areas of life, but it's particularly deadly when we're dealing with the old nature. Nowhere does Scripture tell us to focus on sin in order to get rid of it. Anyone who has tried—whether through self-discipline, wallowing in guilt, or any other tactic that draws attention to the sin—has certainly found themselves stuck in a horrible condition. Why? Because we grow in the direction of our gaze. Always. And gazing at our problems only intensifies their effects.

The biblical approach to conforming to Jesus is to look at Him. That's right; we stare. With unveiled faces, we gaze at His glory. We stop paying attention to sin and start paying attention to a vision of our future. We may not know how it happens, but that gaze will transform us. We'll look back and realize that we were once stuck in the old nature and now we've grown to be much more like Christ. Our focus will always shape us, so Scripture tells us to focus exclusively on Him.

IN DEED

That isn't hard to understand. Little Leaguers focus on professional athletes and begin to walk, talk, and spit like them. Rock enthusiasts start to dress, pierce, and strut like their idols. We conform to what we love. So if we love Jesus—if we are constantly fixing our eyes on Him and ignoring our old nature—a new nature begins to reshape us. We become like Him. And we are perfectly formed for His Kingdom.

ADDITIONAL READING: 1 John 3:2

To become like Christ is the only thing in the world worth caring for.
JOHN DRUMMOND

The Run

Let us run with endurance the race God has set before us. We do this by keeping our eyes on Jesus. Hebrews 12:1-2

IN WORD

If a marathon runner focuses on the distance he has already come, he may be satisfied with progress but unaware of his next steps. If he focuses on the people lining the path, he will get distracted. If he tries to focus on a finish line so far in the distance that it can't be seen, he will get discouraged. But if he focuses on the runner in front of him, he keeps going. His mind is on the race, and his goals are clear. He keeps pressing ahead.

We have a runner in front of us, and He isn't part of the competition. He is our friend, our pacesetter, our leader. Though many other Christians focus on the past, the sidelines, or the finish line—or any number of other distractions—we know to focus on a Person. That's because we don't win the race by accomplishing great things, impressing other people, or either clinging to or avoiding the past. We put everything behind us and press on toward the goal. And what is that goal? Being like Jesus. Not medals, not accolades, not money or power or status. Our one assignment in this world is to be conformed to His image. And the best way to do it is to fix our eyes on Him.

IN DEED

That's why the writer of Hebrews tells us to fix our eyes on Jesus as we run the race. We lay aside every encumbrance—sin, other agendas, personal issues, past mistakes—and refuse to pick them up again. That means letting go of guilt, shame, and dreams that conflict with the Kingdom. No one overcomes the power of the old nature by looking at the old nature. We cannot overcome anything unless we resolutely turn our attention toward the One who leads the way. Only then can we follow in His steps and take on His nature.

Much discipleship instruction involves a set of principles and precepts that may or may not be helpful, but the core of our calling is extraordinarily simple. We look at Jesus. We become captivated by Him, knowing that captivation will powerfully shape us. He *is* the race marked out for us. Run with an eye for nothing less.

ADDITIONAL READING: Philippians 3:12-14

The disciple is one who, intent on becoming Christlike,
. . . rearranges his affairs to that end.
DALLAS WILLARD

Invade

Upon this rock I will build my church, and all the powers of hell will not conquer it. Matthew 16:18

IN WORD

According to the attitudes of many believers, if not their actual words, we are under the enemy's attacks day and night, and losing the battle. The Antichrist will arrive shortly, and from all appearances, he will win this world over. Jesus will come to rescue His people at the last minute because the church could not demonstrate His victory in this world. But that's okay, because it was never about this world in the first place. We write it off as a total loss and look forward to heaven's glory.

Is that the gospel? Not exactly. Yes, there are trials and tribulations in this world, but Jesus did not present us with a defeatist gospel. Just the opposite in fact. One of the reasons the "Good News" is actually good is that the gates of hell cannot prevail against God's people. We will not be overcome, either with a far-off "one day in heaven" perspective or a down-to-earth, in-this-life perspective. We will suffer losses, but we will win the war.

In Scripture, gates serve several purposes. One is as a physical barrier for the protection of a city or domain. Another is as an expression of the center of power, the place in the city where leaders in Bible times met and made decisions. Either way, hell's defenses and decisions are subject to the invasion of Kingdom citizens. Hell's forces don't plunder us; we plunder them. Life may not look like that at times, but it's true. God's glory will cover the earth because His people will cover the earth. Ultimately, we win.

IN DEED

We are not meant to live on the defensive, no matter how oppressed we feel. We encounter evil often, but it doesn't get the best of it. Kingdom citizens are called to be on the offensive—gates can't attack us, after all; we attack them. We don't have a reactive lifestyle; we adopt a proactive one. Like Jesus, we take the initiative to invade enemy territory. And the gates of hell can do nothing to overcome us.

ADDITIONAL READING: Habakkuk 2:14

The purpose of the church in the world is to be the worshiping and witnessing spearhead of all that is in accordance with the will of God.
DONALD COGGAN

Govern

I will give you the keys of the Kingdom of Heaven. Matthew 16:19

IN WORD

Everyone thought the religious leaders had the keys of the Kingdom. They were the ones with authority, the ones who opened and shut doors, but mostly shut them. They were the ones who defined what was legal and what wasn't, and their definitions were narrow. Their authority offered no life.

Jesus held the keys to the true Kingdom, and His followers must have been astonished when He shared them. Clearly Jesus had spiritual authority—His miracles and messages were evidence, and He confirmed Peter's declaration a verse earlier. But a band of fishermen, a tax collector, and others at society's margins? Who would entrust them with the authority of the messianic Kingdom of the living God?

Jesus did, and the people of God have carried the keys of the Kingdom ever since. The church has argued about whether the words were addressed to Peter or to all followers of Jesus, but they were echoed two chapters later for the body at large. We're left with an unambiguous statement that some degree of divine authority has been given to human beings in relationship with Jesus—not to wield apart from Him but to exercise with Him. In other words, we are once again His appointed governors of this world, just as our first parents were first appointed to be. Whatever of our stewardship was lost in Eden has now been returned.

The difference between Eden and now is that our first parents did not govern a broken world full of evil. We do, and we have our hands full—so much so that we often assume helplessness and defer to God. But He calls us back into partnership with Him to make decisions that impact earth. We have a huge responsibility.

IN DEED

Whatever the keys of the Kingdom are, they imply a sacred stewardship and an invitation into more authority than we might be comfortable with. Step into it. Be a human agent of the divine will. And pray, speak, and act with awareness of His full backing.

ADDITIONAL READING: John 20:21-23

> Power in complete subordination to love—that is
> something like a definition of the Kingdom of God.
> WILLIAM TEMPLE

Bind and Loose

Whatever you bind on earth will be bound in heaven, and whatever you loose on earth will be loosed in heaven. Matthew 16:19, NIV

IN WORD

In a Hebrew context, "binding and loosing" implies authority to dictate what is permissible and what isn't. Peter did it in Acts 15, when he insisted that Gentiles were genuinely filled with the Spirit apart from the law. Paul did it when he declared all things lawful but not necessarily beneficial (1 Corinthians 6:12). Jesus Himself reiterated this binding-and-loosing authority when He gave His followers the authority to forgive sins (John 20:23). Though Christians interpret and apply this verse in a variety of ways, it's clear that we have some level of authority, at least as a body, to declare the divine will on this planet.

That doesn't mean we can dictate to non-Christians what they should or shouldn't do. They aren't yet in the Kingdom. Nor does it mean that every declaration will perfectly line up with God's will. But it does mean that God wants our thoughts, our words, and our policies to reflect those of heaven and to bring heaven's environment to earth. This isn't a matter of making demands nearly so much as it is paving a highway for heaven's gifts and blessings to flow into our world. We bind hell's agenda and loose God's through our words and activity in this realm. That's an enormous privilege.

Few Christians take advantage of this privilege or even understand it. And it's true that we may spend a lifetime exploring all it means. But rather than giving up on the opportunity because we don't understand, we have every incentive to ask God for wisdom, experiment with this authority, and wield it in our prayers and confrontations with religious legalism or the dark realm.

IN DEED

Refuse to see yourself as "just an ordinary believer," unless you understand that "ordinary" comes with extravagant gifts and opportunities to walk in Kingdom authority. Bless this world with the presence of the King in you. Bind evil. Set people free from false constraints. And know that heaven is with you.

ADDITIONAL READING: Matthew 18:15-20

> You are not a citizen of this world trying to get to heaven; you are a citizen of heaven making your way through this world.
> VANCE HAVNER

Where Back Is Forward

Everything that has happened to me here has helped to spread the Good News.
Philippians 1:12

IN WORD

Paul is under house arrest, having already spent more than two years in prison and taken a long, shipwreck-marred journey to Rome. While there, he learns that some people are preaching Christ competitively and contentiously. On top of that, he doesn't even know if he's going to live or die, and in many ways, death would be better. And all of this, Paul says, is good.

That's because Paul knows that there are no setbacks in the lives of Kingdom citizens with faith. Everything that appears to be a setback is really an advance—some opportunity to further the Kingdom, some event or relationship that enhances its message, something that works for the good of God's people rather than against them. We don't know how that works, just that it does. We see it early in the pages of Scripture as Joseph suffers setback after setback, each one putting him closer to the fulfillment of his destiny. We see it in the Cross of Christ, where the worst setback proved to be the greatest victory that has forever changed the world. Paul understands this Kingdom dynamic and embraces it. We can too.

It isn't easy. When we suffer a setback, our first instinct is usually to lament it, analyze it, wonder what we did wrong, and try our hardest to get out of it. A better instinct is to ask God what He is doing in it and open our eyes to the opportunities it creates. Does it give us a platform to show His mercy? His power? His compassion or patience or love? Whatever situation we find ourselves in, there is some way to reflect God's face, and there may be overt opportunities to demonstrate His Kingdom. Our crises are usually His stage.

IN DEED

Train yourself to think differently about your hardships. See them as opportunities for God to manifest His character and His Kingdom. Pray toward that end and step through the open doors. Everything that happens to you is under His hand—and somehow useful in yours.

ADDITIONAL READING: Romans 8:28

You will never need more than God can supply.
J. I. PACKER

Infinite Value

Everything else is worthless when compared with the infinite value of knowing Christ Jesus my Lord. Philippians 3:8

IN WORD

Perhaps we've thought too much about the Kingdom as a place. Or maybe we've considered it a state of being. Perhaps we see it in terms of a conquest or an adventure or a future promise. And though it is multifaceted and surely a bit of all these things, we need to remember what is ultimately valuable in the Kingdom realm. Above all, it isn't an activity or a place or condition. It's a Person. Experiencing the Kingdom is all about knowing the King.

That is what Paul considered infinitely valuable, far above his background, his training, his ambitions, his activities—everything. Anything we can possibly possess or experience in life is worthless in comparison to knowing the King Himself. That's why Christian faith isn't a religion or a set of principles or a plan for behavior modification. It's a deeply mystical, relational, intimate connection with the Godhead that transforms us, fulfills us, and satisfies the One who made us for Himself. This is where our purpose in life intersects His purpose in creation. We become one with Him.

IN DEED

Make that your priority every single day of your life. Nothing else matters if this relationship isn't right. You won't experience all the fruit you were meant to bear, enjoy all the relationships you were meant to thrive in, or take as much territory for the Kingdom as you were designed to take. Like a boat on dry land or a car without gas, you'll be missing your primary function. You will fill your life with peripherals and be hollowed out at the center if the infinite value of knowing Jesus isn't infinitely valuable to you. Whatever it takes, dive into the depths of the relationship that matters most.

How? Spend time with Him. Have conversations with Him, leaving long silences for Him to speak and inspire and impress. Ask Him what's on His heart and listen for His answers. Treasure every word that He has spoken. Fill your life with knowledge of Him, and watch Him fill you with His presence. There is literally nothing more important.

ADDITIONAL READING: John 17:3; Ephesians 1:17

We are called to an everlasting preoccupation with God.
A. W. TOZER

Undoing Evil

The Son of God came to destroy the works of the devil. 1 John 3:8

IN WORD

Most Christians try to circumvent the devil's work. Or when we can't get around it, we endure it. We appeal to God for help, pray for strength, and ask questions about why bad things happen to God's faithful people. What we often don't realize is that we are called to do more than tolerate evil. We are called to undo it.

That's one of the reasons Jesus came into this world, according to John. He came to destroy the works of the evil one, to render him powerless, to fix whatever was broken. We realize that we live in a still-broken world, but we also have to believe that Jesus' solution isn't simply escaping to a better place. The devil's works simply cannot continue to rage on in the presence of people filled with God. If Jesus came to destroy the enemy's works, and the Spirit of Jesus is alive in us, then we will be somehow compelled to destroy the enemy's works too.

What does that look like? At the very least, it means being engaged in works of healing, restoration, reconstruction, deliverance, compassion, reconciliation, and love. It means showing comfort wherever comfort is needed, praying boldly for miracles, shining with the glory of God from within, standing aggressively against darkness, and seeing everyone and everything around you with Kingdom eyes. It means radiating love—not the kind of sentimentality that brings a tear but changes no lives, but the kind that fiercely seeks the good of everyone, even human antagonists. Whatever attitudes and actions we see in Jesus, we are to embody in ourselves.

IN DEED

Whatever goals you have in life, make this one of them. Don't just avoid evil or tolerate it. Find ways to destroy it. Ask God for opportunities to reconcile, heal, and restore. Break the enemy's works by carrying the Spirit that undoes them. Wherever there is discord, sow peace. Wherever shame, sow grace and acceptance. On and on, opportunities will present themselves. Turn them into occasions for Kingdom building.

ADDITIONAL READING: Luke 10:19

The kingdom of Satan retreats only as the Kingdom of God advances.
JOHN STOTT

Come Back

Repent, for the Kingdom of heaven has come near. Matthew 3:2, *NIV*

IN WORD

"Repent" has been thrown around a lot, and usually in a way that feels more condemning than hopeful. If, upon hearing the call to repent, we were to ask why, we might get a response about avoiding sin and hell. While that response is certainly arguable from Scripture, it isn't the rationale Jesus gave His listeners. No, after telling them to repent, He followed up with a reason: because the Kingdom of Heaven has come near.

That's a fuller, much more positive purpose than we might have heard before. Repentance—in Hebrew thought, to change one's direction; in Greek thought, to change one's thinking—is not primarily about avoiding something; it's about entering something. It's a plea to those who are walking away from God's beautiful realm to turn around and walk into it. It's not an oppressive command; it's a welcoming invitation. It is God's way of saying to those who are about to miss Him, "Come back! Come inside! Enjoy the wonders of My realm."

If that's what biblical repentance is all about, who would pass it up? Who forgoes the adventure of a lifetime? Who gives up a front-row seat to history's most thrilling events? Who wouldn't want to enter into the throne room of ultimate power and sit at His feet? Who doesn't want a new start, new eyes, new wisdom? Why would anyone disregard access to the supernatural Kingdom? Only those who don't recognize what's at stake. Only those who think their way is the right one and no turning around is needed.

IN DEED

History is full of such tragic mistakes, but we have a daily opportunity to align ourselves with truth, beauty, love, and goodness. We are zealous about repenting—changing thoughts, feelings, words, and actions—in order to see more, do more, and live more fully. The word "repent" may be laden with extra baggage, but the decision is remarkably free of it. Stepping further into the Kingdom experience is always a good thing.

ADDITIONAL READING: Matthew 10:7-8

> To move across from one sort of person to
> another is the essence of repentance.
> A. W. TOZER

Highways from Heaven

Prepare the way for the Lord's coming! Clear the road for him! Matthew 3:3

IN WORD

John the baptizer played a unique role in God's Kingdom. He was a prophetic carry-over from the Hebrew Scriptures to the time of the Messiah, the trailblazer who prepared a path for God-in-the-flesh. People flocked to him because many had long wondered if a true prophet would come to Israel in their lifetime. John fit the description, looking a lot like the common perceptions of Elijah. He was the one who piqued hearts and prepared them for an encounter with Jesus.

In one sense, John's role is unique, never to be repeated. In another sense, it's to be repeated every day by us. We're followers of Jesus, of course, not of John. And we have the Spirit of the Holy One within us so we can walk in the works of Jesus Himself. But we also perform a prophetic, John-like function in preparing other hearts to encounter Jesus for themselves. We make paths straighter, removing obstacles and twists that might hinder His work in their lives. In reflecting His image and walking in His purposes, we pave a highway for Him into the lives of people who need Him.

How can we do that? For one thing, we can represent Him well. We welcome those on the margins, meet the needs of the suffering and brokenhearted, offer healing and hope to the hurting and hopeless, and speak inviting words that give vision to those who hear them. When we express His attitudes and actions, we prepare for Him. And when we don't . . . well, we don't.

IN DEED

Christendom is full of people who speak harsh words when kindness is more appropriate, lecture about their own beliefs rather than being patient with those of others, create noise when they should be listening, act holy when they really aren't. The Kingdom doesn't need any more of those. It needs highway pavers who know how the King rides in, people who express His heart appropriately and trust Him with the results. Like John, we may shake some things up and ruffle the status quo. But Jesus will come in on paths designed for Him.

ADDITIONAL READING: 2 Corinthians 6:1-2

> The real mark of a saint is that he makes it
> easier for others to believe in God.
> ANONYMOUS

Kingdom Fruit

I tell you the truth, corrupt tax collectors and prostitutes will get into the Kingdom of God before you do. . . . I tell you, the Kingdom of God will be taken away from you and given to a nation that will produce the proper fruit.
Matthew 21:31, 43

IN WORD

It was one of several heated encounters with the religious leaders. At the end of this one, the authorities began plotting ways to arrest Jesus without incurring the wrath of the crowds. Essentially He told them that these gatekeepers of the Kingdom would have it taken from them and given to, of all people, the sinners who surely had forfeited any right to the Kingdom long ago. Jesus made this startling claim to their faces, not to encourage them to be more kindhearted and godly, not to remind them of their role as gatekeepers of the Kingdom, but to declare that a decision in heaven had been rendered. They would no longer be allowed to exercise authority in their prominent clerical roles. Their prestige and power, at least in God's eyes, would be given to the spiritual rabble. The lowlifes of society could, by faith, step into the high life of the Kingdom—ahead of those considered most qualified.

That's because God defines "qualified" far differently than we do. Truth be told, there isn't much difference between a religious leader and a prostitute or tax collector. One sins outwardly, the other inwardly. Both are trapped in the human condition—not the original one we were given in Eden, but the fallen one we inherited afterward. That condition cannot produce Kingdom fruit, either in the life of an upstanding citizen or a marginalized undesirable. The Kingdom can be manifest only in someone born of the King.

IN DEED

That's why some of the least likely candidates end up as prominent Kingdom citizens, and why the Kingdom is ripped from the hands of false leaders and given to those who bear Kingdom fruit. Jesus' warning to one generation of Jewish leaders applies to all Kingdom people throughout the ages. Know the source of your fruit and flourish from His strength. It's the only way the Kingdom grows.

ADDITIONAL READING: Luke 14:15-24

> We have no power from God unless we live in the persuasion that we have none of our own.
> JOHN OWEN

The Future Kingdom

We have a priceless inheritance—an inheritance that is kept in heaven for you, pure and undefiled, beyond the reach of change and decay. And through your faith, God is protecting you by his power until you receive this salvation, which is ready to be revealed on the last day for all to see. 1 Peter 1:4-5

IN WORD

To those who think the Kingdom is only a future event, we point to the promises and prayers Jesus lavished on His followers, as well as the Kingdom assignments He gave to them and us. But to those who suggest that the Kingdom is *only* in the here-and-now, we point to verses like these. We have an inheritance, but we don't yet experience it fully. We are saved, but there is a salvation that is coming and is not yet revealed. We live in a Kingdom era, but the Kingdom shifts into a different era when the King comes again. We partner with Him to build the Kingdom until He comes, but it will never be fully established until that day. Those who are future-oriented need to know that the Kingdom is now; the now-oriented need to know something much greater is coming.

Wherever you stand on that spectrum, you can always seek more of the Kingdom in the present as well as stir your hope for the Kingdom in the future. Both are fully appropriate. And it's worth noting that however fully you are participating in the Kingdom now, Peter says you and your inheritance are being shielded through faith by God's power until you see the Kingdom coming in all its fullness. Your faith today is like a seed that will manifest its potential glory when Jesus comes.

IN DEED

Seek the manifestation of the Kingdom now in every way possible, but know that whatever you experience of it is merely a foretaste of future glory. It isn't always easy to live in the now and not-yet, but to emphasize either one to the exclusion of the other is to have an unbalanced perspective on the King's purposes. Never let your future hope distract you from present opportunities, and never let present experiences undermine your future hope. You are not only a citizen of two realms; you live in two ages. Make the most of both.

ADDITIONAL READING: Mark 4:26-32

The great thing is to be found . . . living each day as though it were our last, but planning as though our world might last a hundred years.
C. S. LEWIS

Be Holy

Now you must be holy in everything you do, just as God who chose you is holy.
For the Scriptures say, "You must be holy because I am holy." 1 Peter 1:15-16

IN WORD

"Holy" is such a religious-sounding word, with connotations of an unattainable level of divine connection and perfection. To many, it sounds oppressive. But is that really what Scripture means? Is holiness the same as sinlessness? No, holiness simply means being set apart for a specific purpose. Because we're set apart for God, it certainly means becoming like Him and reflecting His goodness. It involves transformation. But it doesn't mean becoming a separatist who can no longer stoop to interact with the world, work in the marketplace, or spend time with spiritual riffraff. To be holy is to realize that what may be acceptable for some people is not acceptable for you because you are called to a specific mission and can afford no distractions. It's to live in the set-apartness.

In a sense, we're already there. We're set apart because God has called us, adopted us into His family, made us citizens of His Kingdom, and placed us in Christ. He already sees us as clean, forgiven, and free from sin and judgment; there's nothing to add to the holiness He gives. But Peter's words aren't so much about our position in Christ as they are about how we live it out. You're holy? Then live like it in every area of life. Don't compartmentalize, as though the Kingdom life might be only your day job or a hobby on the side. Holiness has already been accomplished for us. Living it hasn't.

So live as one who is designated for something extraordinary. This isn't a demand to stop being yourself. It's an invitation to be like God, to be an expression of His nature as you were originally designed to be. Like anyone open to love, He is looking for someone who will share His heartbeat. That's holiness.

IN DEED

In everything you do, seek God's heartbeat. That will make you different from the world around you, whether you intend to be or not. That's holiness, and it fits you for His Kingdom perfectly.

ADDITIONAL READING: 2 Corinthians 6:14–7:1

> Holiness is not the laborious acquisition of virtue from
> without, but the expression of the Christ-life from within.
> WILLIAM WAND

As Foreigners

Remember that the heavenly Father to whom you pray has no favorites. He will judge or reward you according to what you do. So you must live in reverent fear of him during your time here as "temporary residents." 1 Peter 1:17

IN WORD

Living with an eye on the future Kingdom doesn't mean taking our eyes off the present Kingdom. It does, however, involve an acute awareness of a day of judgment, a reckoning, an assessment of all we've done. We needn't fear punishment; perfect love casts out fear (1 John 4:18), and we've been amply assured that there is no condemnation for those who are in Christ (Romans 8:1) because our sins have been paid for. Still, we will see the true impact of our lives; rewards will be decided for faithfulness and fruitfulness, for investing the gifts God has given for the advancement of His Kingdom.

That's a sobering thought. If we let it sink in, it guides our use of time and resources, our major life decisions as well as our daily activities, our relationships with others and our prayers for them. If we are truly Kingdom-minded, we will find ourselves being drawn to Kingdom-impacting endeavors. We will sacrifice the substance of this world for the sake of eternal gains. We will find that day of assessment to be a powerful force in our lives. The promise of the future will shape everything in the present.

IN DEED

The world under its current systems is not our home, and we can't afford to act as if it is. When we live as citizens of this age, we lose sight of our true purpose and mission. We lack clarity. We won't be prepared for that day of unveiling, when the King comes and the fullness of His Kingdom is revealed. No, we live as foreigners, fully aware that the day is coming when everyone will give an account. Are we afraid? Perhaps a little. A bumpy airplane, a roller coaster, or looking straight down from a skyscraper can be frightening, even though we know we'll be fine. An encounter with Jesus at His judgment seat will drive us to our knees, but we'll come through with mercy and salvation intact. Even so, our Kingdom investments will be shown for what they are, even down to the motives behind them. Live with that day in mind.

ADDITIONAL READING: Matthew 25:14-30

> Our duty as Christians is always to keep heaven in our eye and earth under our feet.
> MATTHEW HENRY

From the Heart

You were cleansed from your sins when you obeyed the truth, so now you must show sincere love to each other as brothers and sisters. Love each other deeply with all your heart. 1 Peter 1:22

IN WORD

Jesus told parables about what loving one's neighbor should look like. He declared a commandment from Leviticus about loving others to be one of the two greatest commandments God had given. He urged His followers to love even their enemies. So when Peter writes that we should have a sincere, deep, heartfelt love for one another, he certainly isn't coming up with a new concept. It's as old as Scripture itself.

So why does Peter reiterate an oft-iterated command? Because the question isn't whether we know it; the question is whether we do it. And both in Peter's time and today, most Christians don't. At least not to the extent that Scripture urges.

That's where an eye on the future Kingdom helps. If we base our love on the present condition of those around us, we won't be very motivated to love. But if we see the Kingdom condition—or at least the *potential* Kingdom condition—of those around us, we should be highly motivated. Every person is either a child of the King or a potential child of the King. Everyone is created to experience and to reflect His glory. Seeing a person in his or her pettiness or problems today may not be very inspiring. But if you got a glimpse of that person's future glory? Love would be the only appropriate response.

That's why the biblical command to love is not anchored in the here-and-now, visible realm. This can't be the kind of love that flows naturally as a spontaneous affection. No instruction would be needed for that. It has to be the kind of love that is chosen, a decision to act in the best interests of each other whether we feel like it or not. It makes sense that our love would be prompted by our vision of the coming Kingdom. That's the only context in which this kind of love makes perfect sense.

IN DEED

If you want to love well, learn to see well. See the redemptive stories that surround you. See people as everlasting lives. Then love radically. From the heart.

ADDITIONAL READING: Romans 12:9

> Accustom yourself continually to make many acts of love, for they enkindle and melt the soul.
> TERESA OF AVILA

For the World

You are a chosen people. You are royal priests, a holy nation, God's very own possession. As a result, you can show others the goodness of God, for he called you out of the darkness into his wonderful light. 1 Peter 2:9

IN WORD

Chosen by God Himself to belong to Him. Royal by virtue of adoption and delegated authority in this world. Priestly in standing between heaven and earth to represent God to humanity and humanity to God. A special possession, set apart for a distinct purpose. All of this and more as citizens of this Kingdom. Why? In order to declare His praises for taking us out of the realm of darkness and putting us in the realm of light.

That's what happens when we live with a future perspective in a present world. We see things. Where skeptics and cynics see decay, corruption, and meaninglessness, we see life, truth, and purpose. Where darkness clouds the understanding of yet-to-be-redeemed humanity, we serve as chosen kings and priests who reflect His loving face and offer His answers to human problems. We've stepped out of the darkness, even while standing among it. We have a light source that others don't have. And because of that, we praise God.

It's no coincidence that Peter places this statement between a passage on human rejection of Jesus and one on life in a pagan society. Like the chief cornerstone, we are living stones in a living temple, hosts to the presence of God in a world that doesn't see Him. Our job? To give them a view of who He is. To be light in dark places. To stand in the darkness as something decidedly different from it. That's the goal of our privileged position. We are here for people to see God.

IN DEED

Be visible. That isn't the same as being ostentatious, noisy, or self-promoting. As Jesus said, we are to let our light shine as a people and as individuals. We are to give the world a clear alternative. The only way to do that is to step into Scripture's lavish description of who we are, to live up to the calling. And to declare the praises of the one who has forever transferred us from darkness to light.

ADDITIONAL READING: Matthew 5:14-16

> Lighthouses do not ring bells and fire cannons to call
> attention to their shining. They just shine.
> D. L. MOODY

Staying Power

The seed that fell on the footpath represents those who hear the message about the Kingdom and don't understand it. Then the evil one comes and snatches away the seed that was planted in their hearts. Matthew 13:19

IN WORD

Jesus didn't always explain the meaning of His parables, but this one comes with defining details. After all, the "secrets of the Kingdom" had been given to these followers (Matthew 13:11); they needed to know what the secrets meant. In this case, Jesus gave them a powerful picture of our responses to Kingdom truth. Some people don't understand it; some accept it eagerly but can't hold on to it through pain and persecution; some receive it and get distracted by this-world concerns, rendering their lives unfruitful; and some receive it, understand it, and flourish in it. Four responses: rejecting it, dropping it, choking it, or growing in it. And four outcomes: missing out; having but losing; having but without power; and having and thriving. Everyone who hears the Kingdom message falls into at least one of these categories—sometimes several over the course of his or her life.

We have to recognize the adversaries and obstacles in the Kingdom life. There's an enemy that snatches truth out of people's hearts. There are normal trials and tribulations of life that seem to contradict the Kingdom message. And there are anxieties and concerns related to money, work, relationships, health, and more, which deceive us about what's important and draw our attention away from Kingdom purposes. Everyone faces these adversaries and obstacles, but not everyone responds to them the same way. Only those who cling to Kingdom truth above all else will flourish in the Kingdom.

IN DEED

That's why it's vital to pay attention to God's voice, persevere in following what He says, and refuse to be distracted from it. Only people with vision and resolve can do that. Others may taste the Kingdom without ever flourishing in it, but we want the full experience. Our goal is not just to survive; it's to thrive. Cling to words of life, and you'll receive whatever they promise.

ADDITIONAL READING: Luke 12:22-31

It is unbelief that prevents our minds from soaring into the celestial city and walking by faith with God across the golden streets.
A. W. TOZER

Fruit in the Field

The Kingdom of Heaven is like a farmer who planted good seed in his field.
Matthew 13:24

IN WORD

Some instinct within us wants to define Kingdom citizenship. We want to know who's in and who's out. We notice evidence of Kingdom fruit and works, but we realize that outward evidence isn't always a reflection of inward reality. We also realize that true Kingdom citizens bearing good fruit are flawed and as human as we are. So how do we discern who the true Kingdom citizens are? How can we separate the genuine believers from the false?

We can't. We can have a general idea, but the separating isn't up to us. We aren't called to sort everything out, to settle our boundaries and form an exclusive club. Even though the enemy will sow the seeds of weeds into our midst, we still have to embrace all who come. A harvest will come, and Jesus will sort everything out. But we don't have to. We can be free from that burden.

That means we will experience a lot of discomfort within the body of Christ, dealing not only with the human frailties of believers but also the issues of those who aren't. It also means outsiders will lump us all together and criticize the whole field for the things the weeds have done. That's okay; we have an advocate, a defender who will guard us and keep us even in the mess of human speculation. Our goal is simply to be Kingdom citizens, not define those who aren't or explain why the Kingdom on earth looks so weedy. We can trust the harvester to make everything clear whenever He chooses to do so. In the meantime, we are called to live with Christ, the hope of glory, within us. That's it.

IN DEED

Don't get distracted by the imperfections within the church. Some of them come from the fact that we are all human beings in the process of becoming like Jesus, even after we've been with Him for years. And some come from the painful fact that not all among us are truly His. Regardless, our only responsibility is to follow Him and let Him be formed within. True fruitfulness is never limited by the weeds.

ADDITIONAL READING: Matthew 7:21-23

We get no deeper into Christ than we allow Him to get into us.
JOHN HENRY JOWETT

Kingdom Quantity

The Kingdom of Heaven is like a mustard seed planted in a field.
Matthew 13:31

IN WORD

After the exiled Jews returned from captivity in Babylon and Persia, they began to rebuild the Temple. It had none of its former glory—at least at the beginning. Neither did the city, the land, or the culture, all fragmented and weakened during the years of exile. The restoration project seemed disappointing. But Zechariah prophesied that no one should despise the day of small beginnings (Zechariah 4:10). Why? Because great things often arise from small, almost imperceptible beginnings.

That's almost always how it is with God. The story of a chosen people began with one childless couple. The greatest king of the chosen nation began as a shepherd marginalized by his own family. The most significant event in world history began with an out-of-the-way birth in an out-of-the-way town because there was no room at the inn. The mission of the Messiah was handed to twelve followers who had no idea how to begin a movement. Yet a third of the world's billions today claim to be followers of this faith and are increasing in number daily. The prophecy of Isaiah has proven true: The King's Kingdom has never stopped increasing (Isaiah 9:7).

That should be a profound encouragement to every small business, church, or endeavor. If God is beginning something, it doesn't matter how small and insignificant it looks. It will grow into whatever He intends it to be. Like a mustard seed, His Kingdom work usually begins beneath the radar of opposition and can attract much contempt, even from believers without eyes to see. But it grows. The smallest seed becomes the biggest plant in the garden.

IN DEED

Don't get discouraged. It's not a Kingdom attribute. Know the ways of the King, and expect Him to do a lot with a little. That's how He works, and it's perfectly normal. His work in this world is spreading to fulfill all His purposes. And people with mustard-seed faith will certainly see them fulfilled.

ADDITIONAL READING: Zechariah 4:8-10

Renewals and revolutions begin quietly, like faith itself. They start growing from one staggering thought: *Things don't have to be like this*.
JOHN V. TAYLOR

Kingdom Quality

The Kingdom of Heaven is like the yeast a woman used in making bread. Even though she put only a little yeast in three measures of flour, it permeated every part of the dough. Matthew 13:33

IN WORD

Research on Christianity's positive impact on society isn't yet extensive, but it's beginning to show how profoundly cultures have been shaped by the Christian message and the missionaries who have spread it around the world. Democracies and prospering societies have been forged on the values embedded in Christian truth, though a skeptical world hardly recognizes the fact. Where Christ is preached and taught, things like freedom, education, meaning, compassion, and growth follow. As with imperceptible yeast mixed into an enormous mass of dough, the whole loaf is affected.

That's how God designed the world to work. Not only has the Kingdom been increasing in number; it has been increasing in influence. We may not be able to determine exactly how—the mechanisms of influence are hard to discern—but His Spirit has a way of infiltrating the earth through His people. We are told that God's glory will cover the earth, and one way of accomplishing that will surely be through His people. As we go into the world carrying truth, hope, and the presence of God, society is renewed and restored. We may not know the timing of the process, and we may not see the evidence at first. We may even see wholesale rejection of our message. But that won't stop the spread of truth. The influence of the Kingdom can't be quenched.

Most kingdoms influence from the top down, forcing matters by government decree. God's Kingdom is meant to come from underneath, from the humble, often-unnoticed servants of others who instill values rather than enforce them. The simple truth is enough to bless the world and glorify God.

IN DEED

You have more influence than you think. It may be hidden from your eyes, but it's there. If you carry the truth within you and live it out in this world, you are a force for restoration. Live the culture of the Kingdom, and the culture will influence all others around it.

ADDITIONAL READING: Matthew 5:13-16

Blessed is the influence of one true, loving human soul on another.
GEORGE ELIOT

Treasure Hunt

The Kingdom of Heaven is like a treasure that a man discovered hidden in a field . . . like a merchant on the lookout for choice pearls. Matthew 13:44-45

IN WORD

The Kingdom message is out there. We cross paths with it every day. The problem is that most people don't have eyes to see or ears to hear; on the surface, the message doesn't appear to have enough value to make a difference. But it does, radically changing lives and societies. It's like a treasure, a priceless pearl, an immeasurable wealth of truth that opens doors to life and eternity. If only it is seen.

That's the issue, isn't it? Kingdom truth doesn't fall into our laps. We have to look for it with the same kind of zeal that a treasure hunter would. The field looks like nothing more than dirt; an oyster like nothing more than a mollusk. Yet in each lies a precious fortune that only those with insight and determination would find. God has designed His Kingdom the same way. Those without hunger, faith, and perseverance will dismiss it because it doesn't seem to be worthwhile. They won't discover what it really means. Those who can see past the visible, who long for something more and aren't afraid of truth, will persist long enough to find the treasure no matter how hidden it is. And they will give up *anything* to get it.

IN DEED

Even Christians have to wrestle with this truth. The gospel of salvation is at the core of the Kingdom message, but it isn't the entire message. Even when we have come into the Kingdom, we still have to cultivate eyes to see what God is doing in our lives and the world around us. We have to learn how to recognize His voice, how to discover His plans, and how to align ourselves with them. We have to develop insights that superficial minds can't discern.

Always look deeper. Ask God questions and expect Him to answer. Notice what He is doing in the hidden, mundane, undistinguished twists and turns of life, and make yourself available to Him. Align yourself with His work. Life is meant to be a treasure hunt. Discover what God has hidden and bring it into the open. It's worth everything.

ADDITIONAL READING: Proverbs 25:2

> I place no value on anything I have unless it is in relationship to the Kingdom of God.
> DAVID LIVINGSTONE

Good Fish, Bad Fish

The Kingdom of Heaven is like a fishing net that was thrown into the water and caught fish of every kind. Matthew 13:47

IN WORD

A dragnet pulls up everything. It can be a great way to get what the fisherman is looking for, but it gets a lot more too. When the catch is pulled in, the process isn't over. Everything has to be sorted out. The good fish are kept, the bad are thrown out.

It's hard to imagine Jesus calling human beings "good" or "bad," but not everyone becomes fit for the Kingdom. He draws us toward Him and enables us to accept His truth. When we do, He transforms us, shaping us for the Kingdom life. But there are others in the net who don't accept Him and don't allow Him to shape them for His realm. He has told us He will make distinctions when He returns. In the meantime, He charges us with making the nets full.

What does that mean? Spreading the Kingdom message far and wide, for one thing. We aren't to make the distinctions He will one day make. But the message is more than an invitation to salvation; it's an expression of Kingdom ways. We are never to withhold the goodness of the King.

IN DEED

Offer Kingdom blessings to everyone, even if they aren't in the Kingdom, even if they are hostile to it, even if they will benefit without giving anything in return. God sends rain on the just and the unjust; He gives common graces that every human being can enjoy, even those who reject Him. He does not show favoritism with His generosity. He offers it to everyone.

In spite of His universal generosity, not everyone is drawn to Him. That's not our responsibility. While many Christians tend to offer God's goodness to believers and hold nonbelievers at a distance, we are sent into this world with exceedingly good news and, more significantly, a heart that shows God's goodness to everyone. We aren't supposed to keep people out of the net. We draw everyone in and trust Jesus to sort it later. It's how He has chosen to grow His Kingdom on earth. And it's how we join Him in His work.

ADDITIONAL READING: Romans 12:14-21

Christ sent me to preach the gospel, and He will look after the results.
MARY SLESSOR

Old and New

Every teacher of religious law who becomes a disciple in the Kingdom of Heaven is like a homeowner who brings from his storeroom new gems of truth as well as old. Matthew 13:52

IN WORD

There are treasures in the law of God. While the law doesn't bring life, it does reflect His nature. Perhaps surprisingly to the modern Christian, Jesus doesn't reject the teachers of the law as out of touch with God's will. There are Torah teachers who become Kingdom disciples, and they are highly valued. Why? Because they recognize how God has been working from ages past and is fulfilling His purposes today. They see the connection between covenants. They see Jesus in the Hebrew Scriptures and rejoice at His coming. Their storeroom is full of treasures that everyone should experience.

Israel was given guardianship of the Kingdom until Christ came; Paul says the law was like a tutor who guided us until that time (Galatians 3:24-25). Though the majority of scribes and teachers of the law in the time of Jesus didn't recognize Him—they missed the time of their visitation that had been prophesied for centuries—some did. Nicodemus came to Him by night. Others were sympathetic to His teaching. Paul encountered Him on a road to Damascus and was forever changed. In the centuries since, messianic believers have seen the richness of God's work throughout the ages and shown us the deep symbolism and layers of the Word. Teachers of the law have had marvelous insights into what God has done.

IN DEED

Why does this matter? For one thing, the Gentile church has often divorced itself from its Jewish roots, losing context and depth of meaning in our interpretation of Scripture. For another, prophecy and the movements of this generation tend to point toward a time of reconciliation when Jews and Christians see each other as friends. God honors that friendship, and the Kingdom grows through it. Many are drawn to Him as He moves among His people, reconciling people of all backgrounds to Himself. And the treasures of the storeroom become more visible for all to see.

ADDITIONAL READING: Zechariah 8:20-23

It is the sharp needle of the law that makes way
for the scarlet thread of the gospel.
SAMUEL BOLTON

A Culture of Mercy

The Kingdom of Heaven can be compared to a king who decided to bring his accounts up to date with servants who had borrowed money from him.
Matthew 18:23

IN WORD

Peter asked Jesus a question about forgiveness and how far it should be extended to an offender. Jesus answered with a Kingdom parable about a servant who was called in to pay an enormous debt. Unable to pay, he pleaded for mercy. After the master forgave the debt, the man went out and demanded the payment of minor debts owed to him. Having received extravagant mercy, he refused to offer even a hint of it to others. When the master heard about it, he became furious and handed the man over to debtor's prison and its torturing jailers. He withdrew the mercy he had previously given.

The beginning of the parable is thoroughly comforting. We can be forgiven of enormous debts, offenses we could never repay on our own. God's mercy is big enough to cover *everything*. But the parable takes a convicting turn, and Jesus' closing line is chilling. Our King will withhold mercy from those who do not forgive each other *from the heart*. Superficial forgiveness isn't enough. It has to be heartfelt.

That's an extremely sobering thought. Most of us have been deeply wounded or offended by someone, and the thought of forgiveness is hard to grasp. We can *say* we forgive, but bitterness sometimes remains deep in our hearts. How can we overcome it? Only by knowing how deeply we've strayed from God and by embracing His all-encompassing forgiveness. We can't extend radical mercy unless we've experienced it ourselves.

IN DEED

We have two choices: We can live in a culture of mercy, or we can live in a culture of judgment. We can't apply one standard to ourselves and another to others. If we try, we reveal our true agenda: that we want to receive the benefits of God without giving them. But when we fail to recognize the Kingdom of mercy in all situations, have we really ever experienced it? If not, we need to dwell on the enormity of God's forgiveness. He offers us freedom from judgment. We need to offer it too. That's what His Kingdom is like.

ADDITIONAL READING: James 2:12-13

> He that demands mercy and shows none ruins the
> bridge over which he himself is to pass.
> THOMAS ADAMS

The Generosity of the King

The Kingdom of Heaven is like the landowner who went out early one morning to hire workers for his vineyard. Matthew 20:1

IN WORD

A landowner hired day laborers for his vineyard and agreed with them on their wages. But late in the day, he needed more workers and hired whoever was available near the end of the shift. When it came time to pay, every worker received the same wages, whether he had come early or late in the day. And those who had come early were outraged. The owner had to remind them that he paid them exactly what he had promised.

The Kingdom is like that. The owner of the universe can make everyone equal if He wants. It isn't unfair to promise us something and fulfill it. It may look unfair if we compare ourselves to others, but only if we're operating with a sense of entitlement and working as though we're earning something. But if we truly serve Him out of gratitude, then we will be grateful with the rewards of our service, regardless of what anyone else receives. "That's not fair" is a very unbecoming claim for a citizen of the Kingdom.

Not everyone enters the Kingdom at the same time or in the same way. Some people are born of the Spirit when they are young, others just moments before they die. Though more time in the Kingdom during this age allows us to bear more fruit, it doesn't give us a greater degree of salvation. God is generous to all, even when we feel that we deserve more of His generosity. He loves to lavish His blessings on those who aren't worthy of them. And it helps to remember that we fit that description.

IN DEED

Remember that in God's eyes, we are all varying shades of "unworthy," yet He graciously makes us worthy by placing us in Christ. Any comparison with other human beings is, from a heavenly perspective, petty quibbling. Why bother? He has already promised us a comprehensive inheritance and every spiritual blessing from His realm. What more could we want? The wealth of the Kingdom belongs to the children of the King. All of us.

ADDITIONAL READING: James 1:17

> The Christian life starts with grace, it must continue with grace, it ends with grace.
> MARTYN LLOYD-JONES

What to Wear

The Kingdom of Heaven can be illustrated by the story of a king who prepared a great wedding feast for his son. Matthew 22:2

IN WORD

History is heading in a specific direction. Many people don't believe that, but it's true. Scripture has told us so from the beginning, and God's prophecies to this point have proven true. There is a consummation coming, a fulfillment for the human race and for God's original design for us. When Jesus returns and evil is fully overcome, there's going to be a wedding. And everyone is invited to the feast.

This parable of Jesus tells us that not everyone will accept that invitation. Those who seem most likely to attend—the context is pointed sharply at the religious leaders of the time—don't think it's worth their time and find something else to do. Even so, the banquet hall will be full. God sends out an invitation to all who will accept it, regardless of how esteemed they are by society.

Like many of Jesus' parables, this one has layers of meaning and makes multiple points. Here we see a portrayal of God as someone who is eager to share His abundance with those who are willing to receive it. Like the father of the Prodigal Son, God loves a good feast and wants to celebrate with His people. His only requirement is that they accept the invitation.

But the parable ends with a dark turn. Someone who comes to the feast is not dressed in the right clothes, and he's thrown out of the party. Does he represent those of us who aren't worthy? No, no one who comes to the feast is worthy. Perhaps he accepted the invitation without ever allowing God to "dress" him. Perhaps he has come willing to celebrate but unwilling to repent. Regardless, we know this: The wedding clothes are extremely important.

IN DEED

Later passages in the New Testament talk about being clothed in Christ—wearing His character and taking on His nature. And really, would we want to show up at the wedding in any other attire? No, the Kingdom culture, full of grace, nevertheless has a dress code. Let Jesus clothe you in Himself daily.

ADDITIONAL READING: Romans 13:11-14

To be like Christ is to be a Christian.
WILLIAM PENN

How Much?

When the apostles were with Jesus, they kept asking him, "Lord, has the time come for you to free Israel and restore our kingdom?" Acts 1:6

IN WORD

We've seen that in a very real sense, the Kingdom has come, is now growing, and includes blessings and some degree of restoration in this age. We've also seen that the Kingdom is also future, will be fully established at Jesus' return, and will include the creation of a new heaven and a new earth. We pray for God's Kingdom to come on earth, in our lives today. And we look for Jesus to come and usher in His Kingdom completely. It's both now and then.

The disciples didn't know that when they asked Jesus if He was going to restore the kingdom to Israel after the Resurrection. It was a reasonable question; Jesus had been speaking to them about Kingdom issues (Acts 1:3). He didn't reject the question or even redirect it with an explanation about their limited understanding of what the Kingdom is or about Israel's role in the future. No, He simply told them the timing wasn't for them to know. The Kingdom would be restored, but not yet. And then He ascended for an undefined period of time.

Not long afterward, Peter would speak to the crowds about the coming Kingdom: "He must remain in heaven until the time for the final restoration of all things, as God promised long ago through his holy prophets" (Acts 3:21). Two millennia later, we are still asking when this time will come. The early church thought His return might be imminent, but God's plans rarely unfold so quickly—especially when He is doing a deep and lasting work. And the Kingdom is certainly deep and lasting. God is preparing a body of millions of believers who will reflect Him well. This is no small project. It's a reflection of His glory.

IN DEED

The question isn't when the Kingdom is coming. It's how much you can invest yourself in the Kingdom now. The fulfillment is up to Jesus. Your role in the process is up to you. Know that you are spending your life on a dazzling display of His glory. And give it everything you've got.

ADDITIONAL READING: 2 Timothy 4:6-8

The glory of God is man alive, supremely in Christ.
LEON JOSEPH SUENENS

Divine Wisdom

He reveals deep and mysterious things and knows what lies hidden in darkness. Daniel 2:22

IN WORD

Nebuchadnezzar had a dream, and insisted not only that someone interpret it for him, but that someone tell him what the dream was about in the first place. He wanted to make sure no one was guessing. The royal sages were baffled, but Daniel prayed. He appealed to the God who knows all things, who turns frightening crises into Kingdom opportunities, and who is looking for those who will bring His solutions into earthly dilemmas. And God answered.

Many of us can envision God answering this prayer for a Christian ruler who seeks to live by faith. Far fewer would expect Him to bless a pagan king with a divine answer. But the us-and-them mentality is not a Kingdom attribute. God is sovereign over the entire earth and does some of His most impressive work among those who are furthest from Him, showing them His goodness and drawing them to Himself. In Daniel's case, God was more than willing to work through an idolatrous king in order to leverage the situation for His glory. Daniel knew that—and even blessed the king with his words. And a moment of crisis suddenly turned into a dramatic Kingdom event.

IN DEED

Look for ways to bless the secular world with divine solutions. Ask God for revelation in the midst of crises that might bring His wisdom and power into the light. He has a great track record of revealing deep and hidden things, unveiling mysteries through His people and showing the ungodly His goodness. When we ask, He will use us to bless the world and demonstrate the Kingdom culture. When we don't . . . well, we find ourselves just as stuck in dilemmas as our unbelieving counterparts. But that isn't necessary. The world is looking for true children of God (Romans 8:19). Connect with Him on the world's behalf, and look for opportunities to be a vessel of His wisdom.

ADDITIONAL READING: Genesis 41:15-40

It is not just that men speak about God, or for God; God speaks for Himself, and talks to us in person.
J. I. PACKER

Over All

He controls the course of world events; he removes kings and sets up other kings. Daniel 2:21

IN WORD

We like to complain about government. It's the democratic way. If our candidate isn't elected, we'll find reasons to criticize the one who *is* elected throughout his term until someone we like better is finally in office. Then we defend our leader from attacks from the other side. And in the midst of it all—in the context of our passionate sense of "right" and "wrong" and "good" and "bad" leaders—God is sovereign over them all.

Scripture tells us that often. God turned the heart of Pharaoh in Exodus. He put Saul on the throne of Israel and then took him off, replacing him with David. Even in a Roman Empire led by a viciously oppressive dictator, the Spirit inspired Paul and Peter to write about being subject to governing authorities and patiently enduring injustice against believers. As much as we tend to think the world is spiraling out of control and another antichrist is just around the corner, God sits on His throne changing times and seasons, deposing kings and raising up others. Nothing is beyond His control. He knows the abuses of those in power, and He allows them. For a time.

We aren't blind to the world's ways. We know God doesn't approve of everything our leaders do. We realize many of them are not reflecting His character and carrying out His will. Powerful people seem to face quite a few integrity challenges, and all fail at some points, some drastically. We may not understand the difference between God allowing bad decisions and ordaining the ones who made them. We just know that however it shakes down, God is still in control, and He is working through the political maneuvers of human kings to accomplish things for His purposes, quite apart from their own.

IN DEED

The Kingdom perspective is not fatalistic, but we do trust in the sovereignty of God. Regardless of current national and international affairs, we never have reason to be despondent. In fact, we have an open invitation to appeal to a higher authority to build up, tear down, move, restore, and renew. We have the audience of a greater throne room than any other on earth.

ADDITIONAL READING: Psalm 2:1-4

Nothing that is attempted in opposition to God can ever be successful.
JOHN CALVIN

Two Realms

During the reigns of those kings, the God of heaven will set up a kingdom that will never be destroyed or conquered. Daniel 2:44

IN WORD

Centuries before Jesus came, Daniel prophesied that God would set up a Kingdom. After the Babylonian Empire would come the Medes and Persians, then the Greeks, and then the Romans. The new Kingdom, the one unlike any other, would come "during the reigns of those kings"—a reference to the Roman Empire, as well as a key piece of evidence for us today that the Kingdom has already come with Jesus. The God of heaven breaks into human events with something altogether different from anything the kingdoms of this world have ever offered us.

According to Daniel's prophetic interpretation of Nebuchadnezzar's dream, the Kingdom set up by God would break all other kingdoms in pieces and stand forever. It would enter simply as a rock that strikes a statue—a seemingly small beginning, yet with a dramatic result. It then would grow larger than all other Kingdoms and never end. It is indestructible, and it is permanent. Unlike every government the world has ever known, this one will not change hands. It won't be ousted or overtaken. It will endure forever.

IN DEED

If this happened "during the reigns of those kings" two millennia ago, yet the rise and fall of empires has continued ever since, where is that Kingdom now? It's here, fulfilling every word of the prophecy. It is already indestructible, already bigger than all others, already demonstrating every evidence of permanence. And we, therefore, are living in two realms at once, functioning in the kingdoms of earth while holding citizenship in this altogether different Kingdom. It sounds subversive, and in many ways it is. It's a silent revolution. We have a greater allegiance to the King—and to a different agenda—than to any other president or prime minister. One realm lasts, the other doesn't. And only one can change the direction of life and lead to fulfillment.

ADDITIONAL READING: John 18:36

The core of all that Jesus teaches about the Kingdom is the immediate apprehension and acceptance of God as King in his own life.

T. W. MANSON

The One That Wins

It will crush all these kingdoms into nothingness, and it will stand forever.
Daniel 2:44

IN WORD

Couched in Daniel's prophecy is a curious statement. The Kingdom of God will crush all other kingdoms and bring them to an end. From the sequence of the dream, it seemed as if the Roman Empire would give way to the Kingdom of God as soon as the stone hit the statue. But the Roman Empire lasted several centuries longer before giving way to other kingdoms in its place. Since then, governments have risen and fallen, battled and prospered, traded and talked, and shifted their territories like desert dunes in the wind. In other words, Jesus came, and life goes on as usual.

Or does it? Like the mustard seed in the garden or the yeast in the dough, hasn't the Kingdom of small beginnings made a significant difference? Has any other government salted the earth the way the government of Jesus has? Or given people a choice between the fallen human condition and radical renewal? Or offered eternal life to its citizens? No, only the Kingdom of God has made such bold claims, and only the Kingdom of God has compelled people to make a choice between the here and now and the "here and now plus there and then." And only God's Kingdom can promise its citizens the power to overcome even the worst this world can dish out.

IN DEED

Never confuse your loyalties. In this time of overlap, when the kingdoms of earth and the Kingdom of God coexist, we may be able to function well in both. But in some sense, the eternal Kingdom will crush all others. It's an inclusive victory, as the kingdoms of this world become the Kingdom of our God (Revelation 11:15), but it's a decisive one too. Temporary governments and impostor leaders will not continue their reign. Only Jesus will head the Kingdom government, and His reign lasts forever. Every day will offer you opportunities to choose between kingdoms, and sometimes it will be an either-or choice. Influence and support your leaders when you can, but above all, side with the good, the true, the beautiful, and the forever. In the end, it alone will remain.

ADDITIONAL READING: Revelation 11:15

> Ten million buds are forming . . . all next summer is at work in the world, but is unseen by us. And so the Kingdom comes.
> HENRY WARD BEECHER

More than a Moment

*Then the Kingdom of Heaven will be like ten bridesmaids who took their
lamps and went to meet the bridegroom. . . . So you, too, must keep watch!
For you do not know the day or hour of my return.* Matthew 25:1, 13

IN WORD

Jesus has just told a series of parables that warn His followers to watch for His return.
He follows them up with another, this one about ten young women who were to be
part of a wedding procession. They all went out to meet the bridegroom, but only five
of them brought enough oil to keep their lamps burning for a long wait. When the
other five went off to buy oil—an unlikely prospect in the middle of the night—that's
when the bridegroom came. The five who were there went into the wedding banquet.
The five who had left were shut out.

All the young women were sleeping when the bridegroom returned, so that wasn't
the issue. The difference between the two groups of bridesmaids was whether they had
oil for their lamps to burn during the procession; whether they had anticipated a delay
and had prepared themselves. So what are we to make of those who went off to buy
more oil? What do they represent? They can't be true believers; the bridegroom denies
he knows them. Are they people with a claim of Christian belief but no oil of the Spirit?
False believers? People mildly interested but not really dedicated?

Jesus told an alarming number of parables about people who thought they were "in"
when they were really "out." Some of them were overtly directed at the religious leaders
of the day, but others were directed at anyone who wasn't prepared. This one falls in the
second category, and it's somewhat frightening. It reminds us that deferring spiritual
decisions and actions until later is not a wise option. We always need to be "all in."

IN DEED

Kingdom life is not for the impatient. We don't know when Jesus is coming back,
but if we really love Him, we don't have to try to time our repentance, our faith, our
works, or anything else to coincide with His return. We aren't trying to look good for
that moment. True love is always anticipating an encounter. We're ready all the time.

ADDITIONAL READING: 1 Thessalonians 5:4-8

Christ has told us He will come, but not when, that we
might never put off our clothes, or put out the candle.
WILLIAM GURNALL

Freedom to Try

Master, I knew you were a harsh man, harvesting crops you didn't plant and gathering crops you didn't cultivate. I was afraid I would lose your money, so I hid it in the earth. Matthew 25:24-25

IN WORD

A master entrusted his wealth to three of his servants and then went on a journey. The servants didn't receive equal amounts because they didn't have equal abilities. Apparently they didn't have equal attitudes either. Two doubled their portion of the master's wealth by investing it because they were comfortable with a little risk. One went into preservation mode and hid his portion in the ground. And each brought the results to the master upon his return.

The two who doubled their portions received a "well done," a share in the master's joy, and more privilege and responsibility. The one who returned only what had been given to him was rebuked, disappointed, and stripped of future privileges and responsibilities. It's yet another sobering message in a series of them. The master's return will be thrilling for some and devastating for others. Some will rejoice forever, and some will weep forever. The stakes are exceedingly high.

Remarkably, each servant found his perception of the master to be true. Those who saw him as magnanimous and gracious experienced his magnanimity and grace. The one who saw him as hard and foreboding experienced a harsh response. And Jesus portrays this servant not as a sympathetic figure but a wicked one. He represents all whose view of God is harsher than it needs to be.

IN DEED

It's a little ironic to read an intimidating parable about the need to see God as kind, but that's essentially what this is. The only way to thrive in His Kingdom is to feel the freedom to take risks of faith, seek ways to invest and grow His Kingdom, and leverage whatever gifts and resources He has given for His purposes. He cultivates our creative use of what He has given and looks forward to the celebration of increase. We can too.

ADDITIONAL READING: 2 Corinthians 5:6-10

A ship in harbor is safe, but that is not what ships are built for.
JOHN A. SHEDD

Positioned for More

To those who use well what they are given, even more will be given, and they will have an abundance. But from those who do nothing, even what little they have will be taken away. Matthew 25:29

IN WORD

It hardly seems fair. Does Jesus really mean that the rich will get richer and the poor will get poorer? Even though He isn't actually talking about money, isn't the very concept disconcerting to us? Our instinct is to share with everyone involved, even just a little—something to bridge the gap between the haves and the have-nots. But Jesus widens the gap, and seems pleased to do so. Those who knew Him well enough to freely take the consequences upon themselves were rewarded, and the one who blamed the master's attitude for his own fearful response was rebuked and punished. And this, suggests Jesus, is the Kingdom way.

What does that mean for us? First, it means that we need to know the heart of God and feel absolute freedom to invest His gifts wherever we can, even if we risk failure. But beyond that, it means that if we want promotion—to more responsibility, more privilege, more Kingdom fruit—we need to be faithful with what He has already given. That was the master's basis for rewarding His servants with more; they had been faithful with the amounts they had in their hands. They were proven entities. They could be trusted.

Can you imagine the God of the universe declaring His trust in our faithfulness to steward His gifts well? That's what He offers, and if we're honest, it's the assessment we long to hear. Perhaps we've given up on the possibility; we know how fickle we are. But it's still there. If we long for a spiritual promotion and wonder why it lingers, perhaps this is the reason. It's time to trust the heart of the King and invest what we've been given.

IN DEED

In God's Kingdom, the amount of our gifts is not the issue; the amount of our faithfulness is. And we can begin with what we have now. Handling it well prompts greater responsibility and greater and greater reward, on and on as far as we are willing. The heart of the King makes this a safe venture. The heart of His servants makes it a rewarding one.

ADDITIONAL READING: Luke 16:10-12

He who is faithful over a few things is a lord of cities.
GEORGE MACDONALD

No Room for Apathy

All the nations will be gathered in his presence, and he will separate the people as a shepherd separates the sheep from the goats. Matthew 25:32

IN WORD

All of those parables about the day of separation—harvesting weeds out of the field and choosing the good fish from the dragnet—point to this. There will come a time when Jesus calls the nations before Him. All the *ethnoi*, the people groups of the world, those tribes and tongues we see in Revelation, will stand in His presence. This will not be a reckoning hidden away in some obscure corner of civilization; it will be a global event.

And there will be no in-between categories. He will separate His world into sheep and goats, those who belong in the flock and those who don't. No matter how secure we are in Christ, that event will be filled with epic nerve-racking drama. We see the criteria He uses. Who took care of Him when He was sick and hurting? When He was a stranger or a prisoner? When He needed something to wear? Who recognized His fellowship with the hurting and who didn't? Who lived with compassion whether or not they saw Him in the lives of the needy?

Regardless of our current standing with Him—in the faith or outside of it, secure or a little uncertain—this parable issues a clear call to demonstrate the mercy and compassion of God. The Spirit within us will do that, if He is truly within us. If we notice a lack of compassion in ourselves, we should be bothered. We are to some degree out of fellowship with Him. We need Him to influence our hearts, to stir us up, to move us out into desperate places with a visible, tangible message of Good News. Our faith needs hands and feet.

IN DEED

Let this parable have its intended result. Jesus' message leaves no room for apathy. Become passionate about expressing compassion. Don't just pay someone to do ministry; add to your contributions a personal touch. See Jesus in places of deep need. Love others as though you're loving Him.

ADDITIONAL READING: Revelation 20:11-12

Every act of kindness and compassion done by any man for his fellow Christian is done by Christ working within him.
JULIAN OF NORWICH

The Sheep's Reward

The King will reply, "Truly I tell you, whatever you did for one of the least of these brothers and sisters of mine, you did for me." Matthew 25:40, NIV

IN WORD

"Whatever you did." That presents a few challenges for our grace-by-faith theology of salvation, but we can get around it easily enough. Certainly Jesus must mean that those with genuine faith did genuine works of compassion as a result, and those who didn't do genuine works of compassion must not have had genuine faith. That soothes our theological stress, but it leaves a gaping question: What if we aren't doing great works of compassion?

That's one of the big questions hanging from this parable. Another is this: Who are Jesus' brothers and sisters? Does this refer to everyone in need? All who have been adopted into His family by faith? The Jewish people from whom He came? As many of His parables do, this one has prompted a wide range of discussion through the centuries. Some say He separates individuals based on their level of compassion for anyone in need. Others say He separates us based on our mercy not toward the suffering world at large but toward other believers in need. Some even say He separates entire nations based on their response to Israel. Regardless, there's a great divide between those who ministered to Jesus when He—through His people, through suffering humanity, through someone—was hungry, thirsty, and captive.

IN DEED

We have a strong incentive to land on the right side of this divide. How are the sheep rewarded? They are blessed by the Father; they inherit the Kingdom prepared specifically for them since the creation of the world (Matthew 25:34). This Kingdom is the goal of history, the direction the world has been headed, the reason we were made. And it's given not to the movers and shakers, not to the "successful," not to the most outwardly spiritual among us. It's given to the compassionate. That's it—regardless of our Bible knowledge, our worship songs, or our offerings. Compassion is a true, authenticating reflection of the heart of the Father. Let it shine brightly.

ADDITIONAL READING: Hebrews 6:9-12

I would rather make mistakes in kindness and compassion
than work miracles in unkindness and hardness.
MOTHER TERESA

The Highest Mountain

In the last days, the mountain of the LORD's house will be the highest of all—
the most important place on earth. It will be raised above the other hills, and
people from all over the world will stream there to worship. Micah 4:1

IN WORD

In many cultures, and in Scripture, mountains are symbols of power. Worship centers, both true and false, are built on their heights. Like human longings for transcendence, they stretch to the heavens in search of divine connection. On our land, in our culture, in our hearts, mountains speak of the desire of humanity to rule and reign and tap into supernatural influence. They are firmly established swells on the landscape of life.

Here in Micah (and in a parallel passage in Isaiah 2), the Spirit tells us that the worship of God will become the highest mountain on earth. It's hard to imagine Mount Zion in Jerusalem becoming a majestic peak, but it becomes the spiritual equivalent of Everest. By comparison, all other mountains are made low.

That's good to know. Our world is full of seemingly immovable power centers: the dictates of culture, the vagaries of economy, the whims of politics, and the demands of all sorts of structures and principalities in this age. We live and move within these systems, but we often feel confined by them. They are disputed territory, where the Kingdom and its rivals contend for hearts and minds. In North America, we see evil flowing out of Washington, Hollywood, and Wall Street, but we also know they can be influenced by God's people and become influencers of our culture. These mountains will one day be dwarfed by the mountain of God. He will tower over the landscape.

IN DEED

Notice when this is to happen. According to the prophecy, it's not "after the last days." It's in them. That means there is some significant establishment of God's preeminence and glory in the earth before Jesus comes back, and you play a role in it. Your assignment in this life is to live on His mountain and contribute to its influence. The more He is honored in His realm, the more people will come streaming to Him.

ADDITIONAL READING: Psalm 22:27-28

All that is best in the civilization of today is the
fruit of Christ's appearance among men.
DANIEL WEBSTER

A Greater Glory

People from many nations will come and say, "Come, let us go up to the mountain of the LORD, to the house of Jacob's God." Micah 4:2

IN WORD

Many nations will come. Not just people scattered throughout the nations. Actual nations. The *ethnoi* of the earth—the ethnic, linguistic, cultural groups of the human race. Large blocs of people. We rightly celebrate a salvation here and there, and some-times a spiritual movement among a group of people, but history is heading toward a greater climax. Many nations will see the glory of God and come streaming to His throne. Micah 4:3 even says He will settle national disputes. His "mountain" will draw the admiration and honor of the world.

How can this be? As His Spirit moves through His people, demonstrates His heart, and fulfills prophecies uttered long ago, more and more will see Him for who He is. It won't be a peaceful revelation, to be sure; Jesus is always at the center of controversy as people contend for truth. The kingdoms of this world, both behind the scenes and on its surface, don't relinquish control easily. An enemy desperately wants to keep the glory of God veiled, so there will be times of pushback and persecution. But the result will be beautiful. Many will see and come running to Him.

Ancient prophecies tell a different story than some of our narratives today. We often talk about how things will get worse and worse. We magnify the prophecies of tribulation and minimize the prophecies of increase. We unwittingly give honor to a dreaded antichrist, as if his work will be more powerful than the Spirit's movements across our globe. We easily develop an unbalanced vision of the future.

IN DEED

Restore the balance. Envision the increase of the Kingdom. Expect the prophecies of glory to be fulfilled. Some may apply only after the return of Christ, but many clearly come to pass sooner. Put your faith in the Spirit who gives life and restores it, unveiling the beauty of God. Pray for the nations to flock to His mountain to worship Him.

ADDITIONAL READING: Isaiah 11:9-10

> The great end of God's works, which is so variously
> expressed in Scripture, . . . is most properly and
> comprehensively called "the glory of God."
> JONATHAN EDWARDS

Ambassadors of Another Realm

They will hammer their swords into plowshares and their spears into pruning hooks. . . . Everyone will live in peace and prosperity, enjoying their own grapevines and fig trees, for there will be nothing to fear. Micah 4:3-4

IN WORD

Many great thinkers have envisioned utopia, some uncorrupted existence where human beings flourish and evil remains at bay. We long for such a place; it's wired into our nature because we were made for it. We want fulfillment, peace, abundance, joy, and safety—full and satisfying relationships and opportunities to pursue our hearts' desires. This is what we were designed for.

Prophetic voices from long ago give us glimpses of the Kingdom of God, a realm where no one lives in fear of war, loss, or the ravages of nature. They are often simple pictures of people enjoying simple pleasures. They are life on this earth, sometimes with death long delayed but still a reality (Isaiah 65:20). We know these pictures have not yet been fulfilled, but we also know they will be. And in the in-between, we wonder what it means for us today.

What does it look like to represent this Kingdom in this age, when conflict, threats, and losses still overwhelm? After all, we are ambassadors not of the current culture but of another realm. We represent this Kingdom, even though it has not yet come in all its fullness. Jesus demonstrated it in His time on earth and called His followers to do the same. We, like the ancient prophecies, are to offer glimpses of it as often as we can to whomever we can. We are to live the values and the vision of a time to come.

IN DEED

Ask God for opportunities to do that. Don't get bogged down in frustration, assuming that you are as confined to human futility as everyone else is. No, you have access to the King Himself—the flow of His Spirit within you—and can cultivate the discernment for acting and speaking His purposes in this world. Demonstrate the *shalom* of the Kingdom as often as you can.

ADDITIONAL READING: Isaiah 65:17-25

Christians are the trustees of a revelation who go out
into the world calling men to accept and follow it.
WILLIAM TEMPLE

Exhibits on Display

"In that coming day," says the LORD, "I will gather together those who are lame, those who have been exiles, and those whom I have filled with grief." Micah 4:6

IN WORD

God's promises of restoration were prophesied to a punished people, but they extend well beyond the generation they were first given to. We know that because His prophets used larger language to evoke ultimate purposes in a distant future. They reflected His heart to those who were hearing it as well as to those who still today long for a greater fulfillment. They showed them—and us—who He is.

So who does this God want to satisfy? He takes particular delight in elevating the weak and helpless of this world into places of power and authority, of rescuing the desperate and making His name great in those who seemed least likely to demonstrate greatness. He chooses the foolish things of the world to shame the wise (1 Corinthians 1:27), the weak things to overcome the strong, the poor to become richer than the rich, the lowly to rise higher than all, and more. He is the champion of the underdog whenever the underdog's heart is invested in Him. He loves to turn the tables on our expectations.

That should cause us to question our expectations. What are we hoping God will do? How should we position ourselves for the greatest demonstrations of His glory? How do we learn to think like Him? Knowing who He is, what should we expect to see?

IN DEED

Wrestle with these questions. Don't fall into the trap of embracing the world's value systems while expressing allegiance to God. It isn't that He rejects all who are healthy and whole—far from it, as that's His longing for everyone. But He takes great pleasure in showcasing His nature among those who need Him most clearly.

If that's the heart of your Father, let it become your heart too. Those in need are not an obligation; they are an opportunity to demonstrate the King's nature. Those who are weak are not useless; they are wonderful possibilities of His power. Every human being can be an exhibit of His work. Bring the margins of society into the center of His body. The Kingdom is formed through such as these.

ADDITIONAL READING: 1 Corinthians 1:26-31

> We follow a gospel which says that when I am weak, then I am strong. And this gospel is the only thing that brings healing.
> N. T. WRIGHT

The Crowning

Now there is in store for me the crown of righteousness, which the Lord, the righteous Judge, will award to me on that day—and not only to me, but also to all who have longed for his appearing. 2 Timothy 4:8, *NIV*

IN WORD

In some of Paul's final words to Timothy, he turns his focus to "that day," fully aware that there will come a time when God declares the value of each person's work. He won't use many of the standards most of us would use. We would measure impact primarily with things like numbers and time, while God likely measures deeper issues, like how faithful we were and how much we had to overcome in order to do what He called us to do. Regardless, the divine assessment is coming. And Paul, who surely had been faithful in fulfilling his mission, says his life and ministry are being shaped by that awareness.

That's one of the significant differences between the Kingdom now and the Kingdom then. Now, we serve as faithfully as we can without knowing the impact we have or being able to measure the obstacles we've overcome. Then, we enjoy the Kingdom after all those issues have been settled. Both require our loving gaze toward God; but only one requires us to look through a darkened glass, only vaguely aware of the true significance of our lives. In this time, we look back to when He appeared on earth and look forward to His future appearing, sometimes questioning if it was really better for Him to go away, as He said it was. He hasn't left us; in fact, He is thoroughly present in His Spirit within us. But He is less tangible than in the face-to-face times of the past and future. And looking forward to "that day" has profound effects on us now.

IN DEED

Live with an eye on that encounter, that day of assessment when God declares how well you have fought the fight and run the race. Get a vision of His coming, and let it clarify your decisions and prioritize your values. A crown is promised, and you will want to receive it knowing you lived for everything it represents.

ADDITIONAL READING: Revelation 3:11-13

The Kingdom of God has come into the world, and the powers of the age to come are operative even in the age that is now.
PETER LEWIS

Court in Session

I watched as thrones were put in place and the Ancient One sat down to judge.
Daniel 7:9

IN WORD

Daniel has just seen a vision of foreboding beasts, each representing the brutality of empires, merciless in their quest to gain and retain power. They posture in pride and devour their opposition. Among the thrones comes the Ancient of Days, humanlike (in contrast to the animalistic figures of the empires) and full of wisdom and fiery presence. He sits down, surrounded by innumerable subjects, servants, and loyal followers. His court is now in session.

Even now, people around the world are suffering under oppressive regimes. We've emerged from a century of concentration camps, gulags, and genocides, and human nature seems to have made no significant shifts into anything better. Many Christians around the world are martyred every year, and many more are abused and persecuted to lesser degrees. The brutality of the empires in the book of Daniel—Babylonian, Medo-Persian, Greek, Roman—were preceded by other brutal empires and have been succeeded by many more. Power does that to people who, in spite of intimidating representations in prophecy, are still only people. In a bloodthirsty quest for dominion, human beings tend to become something substantially less than human.

So God holds court. The Ancient One renders judgments. Daniel is terrified by his vision, but God is not terrified by anything. He holds infinitely greater power than the powerful ones of earth can grasp. And His throne is the only one that really counts.

IN DEED

We understand evil chronologically. "How long?" we ask Him, waiting for the day of restoration. He sees evil as a transitional part of the story that glorifies Him and works to our advantage. Yes, that story can be painful, but every trial we experience is an opportunity to be catapulted further into our destiny. That's what His courtroom decrees—all things working together for the good of those who love Him. And nothing can overturn His decree.

ADDITIONAL READING: Romans 8:28

God is so powerful that He can direct any evil to a good end.
THOMAS AQUINAS

A Consuming Fire

A river of fire was pouring out, flowing from his presence. Daniel 7:10

IN WORD

Scripture doesn't allow us to see God's throne in isolation. Clouds and thick darkness surround Him (Psalm 97:2). Flashes of lightning and peals of thunder echo over a sea of glass amid an encircling rainbow (Revelation 4:3-6). He has been envisioned among creatures with fantastically bizarre characteristics, mysterious wheels within wheels, and chariots supported by powerfully fast angels. Every writer seems to be stretched for words to describe the environment of God, and their descriptions make one thing clear: He's essentially indescribable.

But the effect of His presence is not. He is both an empowering fire and a consuming fire; He can blaze without damaging a bush (Exodus 3:2) and burn without leaving a trace of sin (Deuteronomy 4:24; Hebrews 12:29). No opposition can stand in His way. A river of fire flows from His throne, purifying His people and rendering His enemies powerless. The terrifying rulers of earth look pitiful in His presence.

Everything is small and powerless compared to God. Whether you are troubled by rogue kingdoms or an oppressive to-do list, you are still allied with a power that dwarfs all others. Sometimes we forget that; our minds know God's greatness while our hearts are filled with fear. In the overwhelming situations of life, we wonder if the gap between His power and our circumstances will be bridged. He's big, but our problems seem bigger. Only when we resolutely focus on His grandeur, His fiery judgments against all that is wrong, and His willingness to act on our behalf do our problems begin to be consumed. The more we magnify Him in our hearts, the smaller our troubles become.

IN DEED

Worship the God whose throne flows with fire. Let Him become bigger than any other issue in your life, not only mentally but at a deep, heartfelt level. Envision His fire consuming the terrorists in your world. And know that the Ancient of Days is on His throne to decree your welfare.

ADDITIONAL READING: Psalm 97:1-6

> The Lord's presence is infinite, His brightness insupportable, His majesty aweful, His dominion boundless, and His sovereignty incontestable.
> MATTHEW HENRY

Power in Numbers

Millions of angels ministered to him; many millions stood to attend him.
Daniel 7:10

IN WORD

Prophecies often speak to us of a remnant of faithful believers. So do biblical stories like Noah's safekeeping on the ark and Israel's return from captivity. Over the course of Scripture, we get the impression that God is filling His Kingdom with the cream of the crop, the few but tenacious hangers-on. Most of the world may be doomed for destruction, but a fraction of humanity can be salvaged. Or so it seems.

Yet Scripture also gives us pictures of throngs surrounding His throne, people of every tribe and nation, multitudes of angels and humans that are so enormous that they can't be counted. When the battle is over, the realm still standing is no small Kingdom. It's massively populated with human beings and angels and creatures we've only scarcely begun to imagine. All of creation, which still extends far beyond what our greatest telescopes and scientific minds can perceive, is filled with creatures glorifying God. He doesn't just win. He wins big.

Think about it. If God is infinite, with manifold attributes and characteristics; and if He is expressed and represented by His creatures, revealed in the stories of their lives; then doesn't it make sense that He would want a near-infinite multitude of beings revealing, representing, and expressing His nature? Doesn't the vastness of His glory require vast numbers of glorifiers to appreciate Him? Doesn't it make sense that the God greater than any of us can conceive would do things in a big way? In fact, He has. His universe is incomprehensibly varied. And so are His people.

IN DEED

If you ever feel outnumbered by evil, take comfort. You aren't. And if you ever feel insignificant, just a number among God's masses, take heart. You are one of who knows how many millions, but you are also a vital piece in the mosaic that describes who He is. Your story is necessary because you reflect something of Him that no one else does. And the numbers—angels, people, and more—are on your side.

ADDITIONAL READING: Revelation 5:9-14

> Angels descending, bring from above, echoes
> of mercy, whispers of love.
> FANNY J. CROSBY

Inexplicable

I saw someone like a son of man coming with the clouds of heaven. He approached the Ancient One and was led into his presence. He was given authority, honor, and sovereignty over all the nations of the world, so that people of every race and nation and language would obey him. Daniel 7:13-14

IN WORD

No wonder Daniel was disturbed. A faithful Jew can accept no other God but God and, as reflected in the *Shema* of ancient Israel, God is one (Deuteronomy 6:4). Hebrew Scripture and the Jewish faith are first and foremost an emphatic statement of monotheism. Yet in Daniel's vision, someone like a son of man—a human figure in the divine court—approached the Ancient One, entered His presence freely, was given authority, glory, sovereignty, and most shocking of all, worship. Just as Isaiah envisioned a child who would be called "Mighty God" and "Everlasting Father" (Isaiah 9:6), Daniel witnessed inexplicable plurality and humanity in the deity. Someone other than God, yet somehow God-like, received the power and glory due only to God.

That's why Jesus kept referring to Himself as the Son of Man. He was clearly invoking Daniel's vision and applying it to Himself. He was like man and like God, Son of both, God in His very nature but not clinging to the privileges of deity (Philippians 2:6). Theologians still have trouble explaining that, but God doesn't have to accommodate Himself to finite minds. The divine King has a Son, who is given the earth as an inheritance. Its power, its authority, its glory, its people, its nations, even its worship—all are handed over to someone other than the Ancient of Days. Yes, this is truly a remarkable scene.

IN DEED

It still is. It will forever be remarkable because a God who celebrates the diversity of His creation chooses to connect with His multitude of creatures at a level we can't comprehend. Between the human landscape and this dazzling vista of heaven stands a figure who can identify with both. And a solution to the troubles of earth begins to be seen.

ADDITIONAL READING: Philippians 2:5-11

The incarnation is the most stupendous event
which ever can take place on earth.
JOHN HENRY NEWMAN

Relentless Opposition

He will defy the Most High and oppress the holy people of the Most High. He will try to change their sacred festivals and laws. Daniel 7:25

IN WORD

Clearly the Son, the royal figure who is given authority and sovereign power, has enemies. Daniel has seen visions of beastly empires and proud rulers who brutally oppress all who stand in their way. They may not realize they are trampling on the very ones God considers precious; they certainly don't think they are rousing Him to vengeance. They don't consider themselves accountable to any higher authority, claiming highest authority for themselves. But the Ancient of Days watches, takes His seat in the courtroom of divine justice, hands all authority over to the Son of God/Son of Man, and waits.

For what? Apparently a ruler from among the empires will arise and oppose the holy ones of God, the people He has chosen. In the waiting, God's people have been promised the Kingdom; they will receive it and possess it forever and ever (Daniel 7:18). But their enemy wages war against them, trying to change the divine decree. Does he aim to alter the prophetic arrangement of their feasts and holy days, or on a broader scale, the sequence of events that leads to their receiving the Kingdom? Either way, he battles against unchangeable edicts from heaven. He fails; no one can alter God's timing. The Ancient One renders judgment and hands the Kingdom over to His own people.

IN DEED

We live during that battle. Daniel's vision applied to his own time, when God's people were in captivity and would face a sequence of oppressive empires up to the time of the incarnation of God. They also applied to end times, when a final battle rages and God ultimately hands the Kingdom to His people. And they apply to every time in between, as empires continue to rise and fall, and battles continue to ravage this world. An enemy is desperately opposed to the Kingdom. Your trials aren't senseless; they are personal, part of a relentless attempt to impede Kingdom citizens from their destiny. Pray, persevere, and live with purpose. No one can thwart your future as an heir of the Kingdom.

ADDITIONAL READING: Ephesians 6:10-12

The kingdom of God is where we belong. It is home.
FREDERICK BUECHNER

Destined to Rule

Then the sovereignty, power, and greatness of all the kingdoms under heaven will be given to the holy people of the Most High. Daniel 7:27

IN WORD

From almost the beginning, earth has been contested territory. We've seen that often in the Word. The promises of God are almost always opposed by deception, delays, or distraction. The people of God are relentlessly tempted and tested. At the precise time of two prophesied deliverers, ungodly kings were inspired to try to wipe out a generation of boys. Neither Moses nor Jesus was eliminated, but both were subjected to extreme resistance. The latter was offered the kingdoms of the world in exchange for false worship. Why? Because the kingdoms of the world are the contested territory. That's what the battle is about.

Perhaps we thought the battle was only for the souls of men and women, but it's bigger than that. In Daniel's vision, the sovereignty, power, and greatness of all kingdoms under heaven were handed over to the Son of Man. Then in Daniel 7, verses 18, 22, and 27, the Kingdoms are given to the holy ones of God, the people who love Him. This hasn't been just a spiritual battle; it has been a Kingdom battle. The Ancient One has limited His power in order to win with His character—through His people. And His people will reign where brutal emperors and proud dictators once plundered and pillaged and persecuted.

That's certainly the picture we see in Revelation and many other places in Scripture. The people of God, the chosen and faithful ones, aren't just saved. We are raised up to the throne room to reign with the Son of God/Son of Man. We are destined to rule.

IN DEED

You may not have any desire to rule this world. That's good; the Kingdom is not for the power-hungry. But the Son will nevertheless share His authority with you, and the oppressors will finally be under your influence. In fact, some degree of that authority has already been given to faithful followers of the King. Exercise it. Grow in it. Learn what it means. One day, you will walk in it fully.

ADDITIONAL READING: Revelation 3:21-22

> The church is the one institution of which Jesus promised
> the gates of hell will not prevail against it.
> CHARLES COLSON

Vision Matters

His kingdom will last forever, and all rulers will serve and obey him. Daniel 7:27

IN WORD

Earth has never witnessed an everlasting kingdom. Some have lasted centuries, and their citizens may have thought they were everlasting. Caesars of Rome certainly believed their dominion was eternal, and for the better part of a millennium, the republic-then-empire certainly seemed to be so. But it weakened and splintered and died. They all do. They are all a brief moment in the eyes of the Ancient of Days.

When all the brief moments are over and the eternal Kingdom stands alone, all other rulers of earth will come and worship the King. Will they still be rulers? Of something? That isn't clear; the King is generous with His authority toward those who are loyal to Him. But the overlords of this world will be under the dominion of God and His people, with the Son of Man at the center of all worship. As a much later writer tells us, every knee will bow to Jesus and all will confess Him as Lord. That can't be comfortable for those who claimed their own lordship, but it's true. Everything that was wrong in this world will be made right.

Think about that. All the rulers of nations will worship and obey God, fully in line with His purposes. What would such a world be like? No wrangling in congresses and parliaments. No strident public policy debates. No more injustice. No power plays, jockeying for position, or abuses of authority. No wasted resources or selfish gains. A Kingdom we can really believe in.

IN DEED

That's nice, but what does it mean for us? More than we think. These glimpses of destiny are not only for our hope, without which we can't survive. They are also for partnership in the process. God rarely works out His purposes in this world unilaterally. Even His decree to send a Savior was accompanied by prophecies, invitations to envision, and people who prayed the vision. He gives us pictures and proposals so we can partner with Him. We see, we pray, we labor, we believe. The vision is never peripheral. If the Kingdom comes by faith, it comes through us.

ADDITIONAL READING: Isaiah 45:22-23

A man with the vision of God is not devoted simply to a cause or a particular issue but to God Himself.
OSWALD CHAMBERS

When?

The Good News about the Kingdom will be preached throughout the whole world, so that all nations will hear it; and then the end will come. Matthew 24:14

IN WORD

Jesus told of a time when the Temple would be torn down, and the disciples asked when this would happen. On the surface, it looks like a simple prophecy about the destruction of Jerusalem that we now know came in AD 70. Jesus elaborated with plenty of details, most of which could easily apply literally or figuratively to that terrible time. "All nations" is just as easily translated as "all the tribes of the land," with specific implications for Israel. But at times, the prophecy takes on a more ultimate tone, to the degree that Jesus is clearly referring not only to His coming judgment in the first century but also His second coming for the entire world. Like many prophecies of Scripture, this one has ripple effects that pass through the immediate generation and into the distant future.

So which "end" are we talking about? The end of the age of Israel as the Kingdom? Or the end of the age of human history as we know it? And when does it come? Not even that is clear; Jesus resolutely refuses to designate a day and hour, or even a millennium. But He does give clues. And one of them is that the Good News—not just the gospel of grace as we think of it, but the gospel of the Kingdom—will be preached to all people groups throughout the world before He returns.

IN DEED

In many ways, that has already happened. Every nation (as we define nations) has some Christian witness in it. But some people groups within nations remain isolated without a clear presentation of the gospel or their own translation of Scripture. And though the gospel of salvation has been preached around the world, the gospel of the Kingdom hasn't. We're still learning the fullness of the message. All we know is that there is vast work to be done in reaching this world. And it should never stop until Jesus comes back.

Invest yourself in that work in one way or another. Give, pray, seek, preach, teach, go. Jesus made it a priority; the timing of His Kingdom is tied to it. Make it your priority too.

ADDITIONAL READING: Colossians 1:19-23

The church exists by mission as a fire exists by burning.
EMIL BRUNNER

No Regrets

At last, the sign that the Son of Man is coming will appear in the heavens, and there will be deep mourning among all the peoples of the earth. Matthew 24:30

IN WORD

All the peoples of the earth—or all the tribes of the land—will mourn. Why? Many will grieve because they never recognized Him before He appeared. Even those who rejoice at His coming will be overwhelmed by how much more they could have devoted to Him and will mourn for those who missed their opportunity. In some ways, it will be a day of celebration, but it will also be a traumatic one. The appearance of the Son, crucified unjustly, will be an earth-altering crisis.

Some look forward to that day and others dread it, but another response is better than those. We need to imagine all the thoughts, motives, regrets, dreams, and goals that will be stirred up then and apply them to our lives today. Might we have regrets on that day? Then we need to take care to live without regret now, doing the things we would later regret not doing. Might His appearance rearrange our priorities? Then we should go ahead and rearrange them before He comes. Will any of our dreams prove pointless when we see Him? Then we need to discard those and cultivate dreams in keeping with His Kingdom. Whatever thoughts we can project for that time can be applied and compensated for now. We don't have to be traumatized by His coming.

That's what it means to live in view of that day. Paul, Peter, John, and others lived with the end in sight, and we should too, no matter how far off in the future it happens to be. Whether He returns in our lifetime or not, we know we will encounter Him personally in a matter of mere decades. The fellowship with His Spirit within us will transform into a face-to-face meeting. And we want to have no regrets when it does.

IN DEED

No one should go through life randomly or reactively. We live in the now, but we prepare for the future He has laid out before us. We're intentional and proactive, focused on the purposes He has declared. We can therefore live with clarity. And peace. And a heart that welcomes His coming.

ADDITIONAL READING: 1 Corinthians 13:12

> The primitive church thought more about the second coming of Jesus Christ than about death or about heaven.
> ALEXANDER MACLAREN

Until That Day

I tell you the truth, this generation will not pass from the scene until all these things take place. . . . However, no one knows the day or hour when these things will happen. Matthew 24:34, 36

IN WORD

The statement has baffled readers for centuries. This generation will not pass away? And yet two thousand years later, we're still waiting. How can this be? Was Jesus mistaken about the timing?

Of course not. Those who believe that this prophetic discourse concerns the judgment in AD 70 can easily point to the fact that many of Jesus' hearers were still alive during that time. Clearly, many of His words apply to that event; but with a view to the end of human history as we know it, "this generation" can mean those who witness these signs; or that the end-time signs and fulfillment will all happen within a generation. It can also mean "this people" or "this nation"; that is, the Jewish people will not pass away until all is fulfilled. However we interpret it, Jesus has a clear picture in mind. And His words are highly relevant to every generation.

Even so, many throughout history have ignored His clear declaration that no one knows the timing of the end, not even the angels or the Son of Man Himself. Some think they have discovered the timeline embedded in prophetic Scriptures, some calculate years and months and days as though they are always literal or precisely understood, and some simply think they have gotten special revelation that the poor listeners of Jesus weren't ready to hear. They forget that Jesus always spoke to us about seasons, not about calendars. They claim knowledge that God doesn't give.

IN DEED

That's embarrassing for the church, but Jesus claims us anyway. Far more important than any time frame, however, is the frame of mind of those who follow Him. If He hasn't come, earth isn't ready. That's all we need to know. He is still working His Kingdom into His people and into the world. If that's our focus, we'll be ready.

ADDITIONAL READING: 2 Peter 3:8-9

> We must never speak to simple, excitable people about "the Day" without emphasizing again and again the utter impossibility of prediction.
> C. S. LEWIS

Unlikely Vessels

He will be very great and will be called the Son of the Most High. The Lord God will give him the throne of his ancestor David. And he will reign over Israel forever; his Kingdom will never end! Luke 1:32-33

IN WORD

Mary knew the angel's words pointed to a landmark event, but she couldn't have comprehended how significant that event would be. The eternal Word was planted into human flesh to become everything the first Adam was meant to be—and more. Another genesis was breaking into this world through her own body. This time God wouldn't breathe into dust to create mortal flesh; He would breathe into flesh to create immortal beings who, appearing like all others, were nonetheless unlike anything before. The new creation was planted within her, and the world would never be the same.

Gabriel did at least tell her that she was carrying a King within her. The everlasting throne promised to David long ago would be given to the life growing in her womb. All those questions the scribes and teachers had debated—How was it that the scepter that was never to depart from David had seemed to depart centuries earlier? And how could a promise of God prove untrue?—were now being resolved in the womb of an unknown peasant girl. God had accomplished greatness through a shepherd-turned-king centuries earlier, and now that king's reign was being fulfilled in an even more inconspicuous vessel.

IN DEED

That should be a profound encouragement to all inconspicuous vessels—jars of clay or earthen pots, as Paul would later refer to us. Like Mary, we contain treasure. We are outwardly mortal in a Kingdom that the mortal cannot inherit. But inwardly, we are heirs forever, inextinguishable by mere death. Planted as earthly seeds, we grow into heavenly beings—not just long-lasting but incorruptible—and bring heaven to earth through our lives. Live as Mary, fully aware that a Messiah is within you. The eternal Kingdom is forming in your midst.

ADDITIONAL READING: 1 Corinthians 15:50-56

God became man to turn creatures into sons
. . . to produce a new kind of man.
C. S. LEWIS

Nothing Is Impossible

Nothing will be impossible with God. Luke 1:37, ESV

IN WORD

Unlike Zechariah, who only verses earlier questioned the angel's word, Mary doesn't ask how she can know if it's true. She simply asks how it could possibly happen. That's fair; faith doesn't mean having no curiosity about the mechanism of super-natural events. And Mary has a lot at stake in this process; she has been sexually pure and wants to remain that way for her fiancé. This mysterious pregnancy could have harrowing implications.

Gabriel answers her simply. God's own Spirit will accomplish it; her conception will require no physical activity, no human intervention to make it happen. God only needs to speak in order for something to come to pass. No word of God can fail. Nothing is impossible with Him. When He says something, it's inevitable.

Think about that. It's true not only for Mary and a miraculous conception. It's true for anything God has spoken. All those words about your role in the Kingdom and the inheritance you will receive? Inevitable. All those promises about His presence and His power at work within you? Unshakable. Every comforting and encouraging word about how He will defend, guide, protect, heal, strengthen, deliver, and restore you? Certain. And those assurances that He will answer your prayers and fulfill His purposes for you? Guaranteed. Nothing He has spoken can prove untrue.

Yes, there are conditions to some of those promises, but He has made them clear. They are not onerous. The burden is not on us to live up to our end of the bargain. He takes the fulfillment upon Himself. He offers His faithfulness.

IN DEED

That's good news. We aren't always faithful, but He is. It's His Word on the line, and He will live up to it. When He makes a promise, He will do everything necessary to accomplish it. No matter what we face in life, we can be assured of His faithfulness to His words. Nothing is impossible with God.

ADDITIONAL READING: Numbers 23:19

I believe the promises of God enough to venture an eternity on them.
ISAAC WATTS

Following His Lead

Mary responded, "I am the Lord's servant. May everything you have said about me come true." Luke 1:38

IN WORD

Sometimes we come to God with a plan, our own agenda. We want the dream in our hearts to be fulfilled, so we ask Him if He will endorse it and bring it to pass. We petition Him for something that came from our own thoughts. We might say "not my will but Yours," and we may even mean it; but we still hope He accomplishes our will.

There's nothing wrong with that. David did it with his idea for a temple, and God said yes, though He delayed it until the next generation. And whenever we have a deep need or an urgent situation, it's natural to call out to Him for help. He encourages that. But when He is the one with the plan—when He comes with His agenda and presents it to us—that's when we know for certain He is working through us and on our behalf. We are always on solid ground when we follow His lead.

That's where Mary found herself. This wasn't her idea. How could it be? Only the mind of God could have come up with this plan, and He didn't plant it within her before He announced it to her. But she responded with an attitude that should mark us for life. She declared her loyalty in service to Him and simply asked that His word to her be fulfilled. She put herself completely at His disposal.

IN DEED

To most of the world, that looks like powerlessness. To those who know God, it's where true power comes from. When He initiates and we say yes, He accomplishes great things in supernatural strength. He opens doors and makes the impossible possible. He accomplishes more through one compliant servant than He does through a hundred reluctant ones with a companion agenda. We are never in a greater position of power than when we ask that His will come true through us just as He has said.

Look for opportunities to say that. Ask Him what He wants to do, look for His answer, and join in. The Kingdom comes in power through those who open up to whatever He wants to do.

ADDITIONAL READING: Isaiah 6:8

> If Jesus Christ be God and died for me, then no sacrifice
> can be too great for me to make for Him.
> C. T. STUDD

The Answer

Glory to God in the highest heaven, and on earth peace to those on whom his favor rests. Luke 2:14, *NIV*

IN WORD

The announcement of the Kingdom is good news. The King's advent into this world may be traumatic—it certainly requires a response—but it's the best thing that could possibly happen for the human race. And when heavenly messengers declared it, they gave Him glory and declared peace for His people. It was more than the embellishment of praise; it was a blessing for us to accept, agree with, and live in.

Peace. *Shalom.* That fullness of life we've been longing for. The abundance of overflowing goodness. The wholeness and healing and restoration we need. That sense that everything in my corner of the world is okay, all is well, life is as it should be. We crave that state of being constantly, and even experience it in brief moments. But the angels said it's ours. It's a gift for those on whom His favor rests, for those with whom He is pleased.

That's what the coming of Jesus means to us. Later, a voice from heaven would tell us to listen to Him, but that's a response that comes after we know who He is. First, the heavenly message gives us the simplicity of good news. Jesus did not come with a list of demands. He did not come with grievances or judgments or more hoops to jump through. The King did not come in this world to tell us to do a better job of measuring up. He came to say this: The *shalom* you've been looking for is here.

IN DEED

Do you believe that? Not many people do, even among "believers" who claim to believe it. Christianity has become for many a burden, as if the Spirit puts more on our shoulders rather than setting us free. But the Good News of the Kingdom was heralded among overworked and overlooked shepherds in the fields as an answer for their longings. And if we really understand the heart of God, we'll receive it in exactly the same way.

What do you long for? Somewhere at the root of that desire is a true, deep, God-given question, and the answer is thoroughly given in the One who came. His favor is here. Your truest longings can be fulfilled. His peace is given to you.

ADDITIONAL READING: Isaiah 9:6-7

God is the great reality. . . . His promises are real and glorious, beyond our wildest dreams.
J. B. PHILLIPS

Envision More

I have seen your salvation, which you have prepared for all people. He is a light to reveal God to the nations, and he is the glory of your people Israel!
Luke 2:30-32

IN WORD

Simeon had been eagerly waiting for the Messiah to come. God had even given him a promise that he would see the Messiah before he died. In an age alleged to have no prophets, the Spirit had given to him a very prophetic sign. And when the time came, the Spirit moved him to go to the Temple. We don't know how he recognized Jesus as the one, but clearly the Spirit was guiding him. And when he saw Jesus, he uttered a prophecy and a testimony that caused even Jesus' parents to marvel.

Yes, this infant was not only the heir to David's throne, not only the glory of God's people Israel, as Mary had been told. He was also a light for all nations—even the *goyim* within and beyond Israel's borders. In an age of Roman occupation, this was a remarkable thought. But psalmists had hinted at it, and Isaiah had prophesied it directly. Even the Temple in ancient Israel had drawn Gentile nations to God's presence, and a reluctant prophet named Jonah had shown His mercy to a foreign nation in darkness. Surely this child's mission would extend further than the realm of Israel's people. God must have a bigger agenda than expected.

He does. He always does. Whatever we envision of His work and how He might carry it out, the end result is probably bigger than we thought. He begins with small things, but He doesn't ever end with them. His vision is greater than we can comprehend.

IN DEED

Learn to cultivate greater vision. Wherever your vision is now, it's certainly smaller than what God wants to do through you. His plans may not be flashy or impressive to the world or even the church, but they will have far greater influence than you expected. His mission is comprehensive, and you are part of it. Learn to envision big.

ADDITIONAL READING: Isaiah 49:5-6

Only he who can see the invisible can do the impossible.
FRANK GAINES

Beautifully Dressed

I saw the holy city, the new Jerusalem, coming down from God out of heaven
like a bride beautifully dressed for her husband. Revelation 21:2

IN WORD

The church has flaws. That's not news to anyone. We see it, and the world sees it. We
are quirky and full of issues. We are the spiritual body of Christ, and sometimes just as
wounded as the physical body was. And we make no claims of perfection.

But we are *His*. He has been preparing His people for ages. He has declared us clean,
and in His eyes, we are. He is dressing us for a wedding, and we are already beautiful
to Him. And when we appear—when the Holy City full of all His followers of every
nation is unveiled—we will be beautiful to everyone with eyes to see. We have been
made fully ready for forever. Perfection is in the eye of the beholder, and our beholder
defines who we are.

Sometimes the pain of our present and the flaws we can't seem to escape are more
persuasive than God's picture of us is. That's because we can see the pain and the
flaws much more clearly; they are in our face every day. We don't see that we are being
beautifully dressed for a divine husband as a bride is prepared for her day of glory. We
have His Word that says so, but the visible evidence seems scarce. The solution to that
is to value His assessment more than we value our own. We certainly let the words
of critics stick to us. Why can't His words stick more firmly? They should; He knows
much more than our critics do. Every wound we've suffered from a human being can
be undone by one word from His mouth. He knows who we really are.

IN DEED

We grow into whatever we envision. If we envision ourselves as unworthy, inept spiritual failures, we will remain stuck in that vision. But that is not His opinion of us, and
His is the one that counts. We dare not contradict Him. If we envision ourselves—
corporately as a church and individually as human beings—as a beautiful bride
dressed specifically for Him, we will grow into that vision. We will be transformed.
And the wedding day will be glorious.

ADDITIONAL READING: Isaiah 62:1-5

The church is the only institution supernaturally endowed by God.
CHARLES COLSON

Among Us

I heard a loud shout from the throne, saying, "Look, God's home is now among his people! He will live with them, and they will be his people. God himself will be with them." Revelation 21:3

IN WORD

Prepositions matter. Do we see God high above us? Far away from us? Beside us? With us? In us? These may seem like subtle distinctions, but they dictate how we relate to Him. They determine whether He is near or far, personal or impersonal, connected or detached. They powerfully shape our perceptions.

We know where this ends, though. God has made it clear. He has said He will dwell with His people. Jesus is Immanuel, God with us. He has put His Spirit within us. He lives and walks among us. The last picture He leaves with us in His Word is a wedding. It doesn't get any more personal than that.

This is more than proximity. It's intimacy. Those who perceive God as a hard master don't particularly want Him to dwell among us. That's scary. Those who think judgment triumphs over mercy would prefer that He keep His distance. In fact, that's where much of the world lives; they reject Him to prevent the possibility of His rejecting them first. Isn't that often how relationships work? We avoid wounds. If we think someone doesn't want to be around us, we preempt their rejection by choosing not to be around them. And if that's how we perceive Jesus . . . well, the idea of God with us isn't very comforting.

That's where the wedding comes in. This is no forced union. It's warm and personal, loving and accepting, full of grace and commitment. It's as safe as safe can get.

IN DEED

The final words of Scripture assure us of eternal safety. No more danger, no more tears, no more evil. Nothing but the loving arms of a King who has given us His Kingdom. It's a realm of celebration, joy forevermore. It's a Kingdom of everlasting peace.

ADDITIONAL READING: Psalm 16:9-11

> The relationship between God and a man is more private and intimate than any possible relation between two fellow creatures.
> C. S. LEWIS

Everything New

He will wipe every tear from their eyes, and there will be no more death or sorrow or crying or pain. All these things are gone forever. Revelation 21:4

IN WORD

John saw a new heaven and a new earth. We may have been taught that earth passes away and heaven remains, but that isn't the picture Scripture gives us. God doesn't waste what He created; He restores it. And the new heaven and earth replace an old order of things that will pass away and never return.

Do you realize the implications? The laws of physics as you know them may not function the same way anymore. The biology you learned will have to be relearned, this time with no death and decay involved. Pathogens will cease to exist. Dangers will no longer be a threat. Wolves and lambs will lie down together. We may even swim with sharks.

Most of all, people will not hurt each other. In the new creation, everyone will give and receive grace, and no one will give or receive judgment. We will never have our feelings hurt, never get discouraged, never cry out in frustration, and never make futile attempts at growth and success. Instead, we will overflow with gratitude, enjoy everyone around us, celebrate on a daily basis, sleep in peace if we choose to sleep at all, feast on good food if we want to eat, and see beauty everywhere. How could it be any other way? We know the heart of the King. This is the only kind of Kingdom He could devise.

IN DEED

Even now, don't get stuck in the old order of things. Don't get mired in its thought processes, limited by its perspectives, and trapped in its futility. Yes, you will brush up against those things at times, but they are not your lot in life. You don't live in that climate, not as a citizen of the Kingdom. Even now, you can give people a glimpse of that realm—the unlimited grace and joy, the expectation of fruitfulness, the energy of the celebration of life. It's real. It's lasting. And it's coming.

ADDITIONAL READING: Isaiah 65:17

Take all the pleasures of all the spheres, and multiply each through endless years; one minute of heaven is worth them all.
THOMAS V. MOORE

Wealth

All who are victorious will inherit all these blessings, and I will be their God, and they will be my children. Revelation 21:7

IN WORD

"All these." That's the short description of the inheritance of a child of God. But what exactly are "all these"? Clearly this phrase includes the water of life mentioned in the previous verse, but that's only one thing—an incredible thing, of course, but not plural enough to fit. Can this phrase really refer to everything mentioned up to this point in the chapter?

It can and does, as can be proved by other Scripture references. Included in the inheritance of the children of God are the manifest presence of God, the end of tears and mourning, and best of all, the "everything new" of verse 5. In other words, all of the possessions of the Father are the inheritance of the children. As much as we try to let that sink in, it won't. It can't. It's simply too astounding.

Think about it anyway. Your inheritance—which, by the way, is already being distributed little by little to those who are ready to receive it—consists of everything in the Father's possession. Jesus told His disciples over the course of His ministry that He gave them authority over the enemy, the mystery of the Kingdom, the word of truth, and the Holy Spirit. Most amazing, He told the Father this about His disciples: "I have given them the glory that you gave me, so they may be one as we are one" (John 17:22). God had given Jesus everything; Jesus gives us everything. We are joint-heirs with Him (Romans 8:17). That's incredible.

IN DEED

A good question to ask yourself each morning when you get up is, "How shall I use my inheritance today?" In fact, make that part of your prayers today. Ask God if there's any aspect of His authority, His Kingdom, His purposes, His resources that He wants to entrust you with today. Then watch for your opportunities. They will come. The owner of all that exists—your Father, who has promised everything to His Son and the Son's siblings—has no intention of hoarding "all this."

ADDITIONAL READING: Romans 8:17

> For the saints in the world to come . . . their great possession is unchangeable, but also inexhaustible.
> HENRY BARCLAY SWETE

Radiance

The nations will walk in its light, and the kings of the world will enter the city in all their glory. . . . And all the nations will bring their glory and honor into the city. Revelation 21:24, 26

IN WORD

The glory of God and the lamp of the Lamb (Revelation 21:23) are all the light the world will ever need. When Revelation speaks of the light of the new creation, this is what it's talking about: the radiance of God in Christ. No sun, stars, or moon will be needed. There will be no dark corners in the new Jerusalem, no shadowy alleyways or secret chambers of mischief. There will be no need; corruption will not be allowed into the city. Ever.

What will be brought to the city, however, is the glory and honor of all nations. All of the striving for wealth and power and glory that human governments and kings have sought—at great expense to the human race—will belong to the Savior who humbly forsook the form of deity in this world. While humanity tried to climb its way up, Jesus lowered Himself down. And in the end, the glory and honor of nations will be His. No crown, no treasure, no prestige, no accomplishment will be boasted in by human pride. All that we sought, He'll have. And He'll shine His glory on all who love Him.

That's reason number one for not getting caught up in the world's ambitions—which won't achieve anything worthwhile and won't last. All the radiance of creation shines from a surprising lamp that faithless eyes cannot see: the Lamb of God who humbled Himself to the point of death. Whatever splendor, glory, or treasure you've sought, you won't find it unless you find it in Jesus.

IN DEED

As this year comes to a close, measure your goals and plans. What are your ambitions? Do they fit better with the glory of the world or the glory of the Lamb? In other words, what light do you seek? Make sure every dream you have this year comes under the glow of the glory of the Kingdom of God.

ADDITIONAL READING: Isaiah 60:3-5

> [God] has an inexhaustible enthusiasm for the
> fame of His name among the nations.
> JOHN PIPER

Scripture Index

About the Author

CHRIS TIEGREEN is the author of more than forty books, including *The One Year Hearing His Voice Devotional, The One Year At His Feet Devotional, 365 Pocket Devotions, 90 Days Thru the Bible, Feeling like God,* and *Unburdened.* In addition, he has been a collaborative writer on more than a dozen book projects. He has also written hundreds of magazine and newspaper articles, ranging from cultural commentary to inspirational devotionals to features on ministry and international missions.

Chris is a seasoned photojournalist, a student of languages, a dabbler in art, an occasional pianist, a rabid-yet-reasonable college football fan, and a zealous traveler. He especially loves beaches and third-world adventures. In addition to writing and doing photography for periodicals and books, he has been a pastor, a missionary, and a university instructor on global issues. He currently works at Walk Thru the Bible and serves at Daystar Atlanta church. He and his family live in Atlanta.

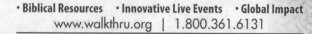

It's both /*and*

{
biblical *and* fun
spiritual *and* innovative
inspiring *and* surprising

Walk Thru *the* Old Testament Live Event

"**Walk Thru the Bible** provided our families with a fantastic journey through the Old Testament . . . filled with laughter, inspiring teaching, and unforgettable lessons about our Creator."
—Dave K. Smith
Executive Pastor, Willow Creek Community Church
Crystal Lake Campus

It's your move. Start here.*

* The **Old Testament Live Event** is designed for any size church.
Learn more: **walkthru.org**

Follow up the **Walk Thru the Old Testament Live Event** with our exclusive 6-week
God's Grand Story churchwide Bible engagement campaign.
Learn more at **thegrandstory.org**

CP0972